Babylonian Talmud

THIS volume is designated the fourth (IV.) because the Tract Erubin (Commixture on Sabbath) is now in press and is the third volume of the Section Moed, which in our edition contains eight volumes: namely, Vols. I. and II., treating of Sabbath; Vol. III., of the Commixture; IV., of Head-duties and New Year; V., of Pesachim (Easter) and Betza (Feast-days); VI., of Yoma and Sukkah (Day of Atonement and Tabernacles); VII., of Megillah and Taanith (the Book of Esther and Fast-days), and VIII., of Hagigah and Moed-Katan (Feast Offerings and Minor Feasts).

The third volume will appear in August next, and the fifth volume in September; and the last three volumes, one every three months thereafter.

As the copper plates of Tract Rosh Hashana (Hebrew and English) were stolen and only a few copies remain for subscribers, we could only furnish for the press Tract Shekalim. The Synopsis of Subjects and the Introduction to Rosh Hashana will nevertheless give an idea of this tract.

In the near future we will give a second edition of Rosh Hashana, which will be revised and enlarged.

The price of each volume to subscribers, from whom advance money will no longer be received, is $2.50.

THE NEW TALMUD PUBLISHING CO.,
54 East 106th Street, New York.

Talmud (Babylonia)

NEW EDITION

OF THE

BABYLONIAN TALMUD

Original Text, Edited, Corrected, Formulated, and Translated into English

BY

MICHAEL L. RODKINSON

SECTION MOED (FESTIVALS)

TRACTS SHEKALIM AND ROSH HASHANA

HEBREW AND ENGLISH

4

Volume IV.

NEW YORK
NEW TALMUD PUBLISHING COMPANY
54 EAST 106TH STREET

1896?

EXPLANATORY REMARKS.

In our translation we adopted these principles:

1. *Tenan* of the original—We have learned in a Mishna; *Tania*—We have learned in a Boraitha; *Itemar*—It was taught.

2. Questions are indicated by the interrogation point, and are immediately followed by the answers, without being so marked.

3. When in the original there occur two statements separated by the phrase, *Lishna achrena* or *Waibayith Aema* (literally, "otherwise interpreted"), we translate only the second.

4. As the pages of the original are indicated in our new Hebrew edition, it is not deemed necessary to mark them in the English edition, this being only a translation from the latter.

TO

ERASMES GEST, ESQ.

OF CINCINNATI, OHIO

MOST RESPECTFULLY DEDICATED BY THE

EDITOR

TRACT SHEKALIM.

CONTENTS OF VOLUME IV.

HEBREW AND ENGLISH

ENGLISH.

TRACT SHEKALIM.

CHAPTER VI.

CHAPTER VII.

CHAPTER VIII.

TRACT ROSH HASHANA.

CHAPTER I.

CHAPTER II.

CHAPTER III.

CHAPTER IV.

THE HEBREW PART.

(*Order of pages, from right to left.*)

TRACT SHEKALIM.

TRACT ROSH HASHANA.

* By these three entrances the editor illustrates his reasons for this enterprise and his method of correcting and translating the original. This has not been translated into English, for the reason that it would be of but little interest to the English reader who does not understand the Hebrew; it is, however, hoped that the reader of Hebrew will find great interest in the matter.

PREFACE TO TRACT SHEKALIM.

AMONG the treatises contained in the Section Moed of the Babylonian Talmud is to be found that of Shekalim, which consists, however, only of Mishnas, the Babylonian Talmud having no Gemara. The Palestinian Talmud contains a Gemara for this tract also, and there is an additional commentary by Maimonides. While we are translating only the Babylonian Talmud, we would not care to omit Shekalim, which is of peculiar historical value and may prove quite interesting to the reader. But the Mishna, without any explanation whatever, would naturally seem obscure, and in some instances would be absolutely incomprehensible; and, the Gemara of the Palestinian Talmud, as well as the commentary of Maimonides, consisting of very complicated and intricate series of arguments, inferences, and explanations, which would be not only difficult of translation but also immaterial to the subject, the insertion of which would be a deviation from our method, and unnecessary, as would explanations of Barthanora, Tosphath-yomtabh, etc., we were forced to provide the text with a commentary of our own, drawn from the most authentic sources. This, we trust, will serve to elucidate any obscure passages not quite comprehensible to the general reader. Accordingly, every sentence or word in the Mishna requiring an explanation is distinguished by a number or an asterisk, and has a corresponding reference in the commentary printed below the text. We may add that, for our personal satisfaction and to guard against any possible errors, we have given this tract for revision to some noted Russian scholars who are competent to judge upon it, and they find it very intelligible.

As stated above, we have taken our commentary from the most authentic sources we could find. We do not, therefore, solicit leniency on the part of worthy critics, but ask them to restrain their criticisms until they shall have carefully studied the commentaries mentioned, as well as *our* commentary, with proper consideration; for ours is derived from the Palestinian Talmud, Maimonides, etc. Conscientious critics will do so without our solicitation; and as for others, who are ready to criticise everything impromptu as soon as it leaves our pen, such a request would be of no avail. We nevertheless will be grateful to any one who will call our attention to things which are not comprehensible in the commentary, this being our first venture of the kind, more especially as we think we shall be compelled to do the same with other Mishnayoths to which the Babylonian Talmud has no Gemara. A separate introduction to Tract Shekalim we think unnecessary, as the contents of this speaks for itself. We nevertheless will return to this when we come to Tract Midoth (Measures).

In compliance with our promise in our prospectus, we add to this volume the Hebrew text of the Tracts Shekalim and Rosh Hashana of our new edition, for the benefit of students and scholars who may desire to compare the translation with it.

M. L. RODKINSON.

NEW YORK, May, 1897.

SYNOPSIS OF SUBJECTS

OF

VOLUME IV.—TRACT SHEKALIM.*

CHAPTER I.

MISHNA *a* treats of: What were the duties of the Beth Din in the month of Adar in the time of the second Temple. When the Megillah (Book of Esther) was to be read in the fortified cities. For what purpose messengers were sent out, and what were the things to be heralded.

MISHNA *b* treats of: What was the punishment for not obeying the commandments of Kelayim in the former times and later.

MISHNA *c* deals with: When the money-changers, with their tables, began their work in the countries of Judea and in Jerusalem. The time for pledges which were taken for not paying the Shekalim. From what persons the pledges were to be taken. If a father might pay the Shekalim for his children.

MISHNA *d* treats of: What ordinance Ben Buchri proclaimed in Jamnia in behalf of the priests, and what R. Johanan b. Zakkai rejoined. The defence of the priests, with their interpretation of biblical passages, which was accepted only for the sake of peace.

MISHNA *e* treats of: The voluntary payment of Shekalim from women, slaves, and minors being accepted, but not from the heathens or Samaritans. Bird-offerings not accepted from persons affected with venereal diseases or from women after confinement. Sin and vow offerings, however, were accepted from the Samaritans. The vow-offerings were also accepted from heathens. The general rule concerning this.

MISHNA *f* deals with: The premium one had to pay in addition to the half-shekel. Who was obliged to do so? The different opinions of the sages and R. Meir. How much one had to pay if given one Selah and taking a shekel in exchange.

---

* See introduction to synopsis in Tract Sabbath, Vol. I., p. xxix. This tract has no Gemara. The synopsis contains the Mishnas, with their commentaries.

MISHNA *g* treats of: The law concerning one who pays for a poor man, for a neighbor, and for a countryman. Law concerning brothers and partners paying together; also, law regarding cattle-tithe. How much was the premium.

CHAPTER II.

MISHNA *a*. One may put together the Shekalim and exchange them for a gold coin called Darkon. Concerning the chests which were given to the collectors in the country and at Jerusalem. What is the law if money were stolen or lost by the messengers of a city, when a portion of the Shekalim was already expended; what is the law if not expended.

MISHNA *b*. Concerning the law when one gives his shekels to another to pay his head-taxes for him; if he pays his shekels from the money of the second tithes or from the money of the fruit of the Sabbatical year. Concerning how he shall replace it and use it for the same purpose.

MISHNA *c*. The law concerning one who gathered single coins little by little and said: "With this money I shall pay my shekels." The different opinions of the schools of Hillel and Shamai in this matter. Concerning the same case when one gathers money for sin-offerings. What shall be done with the eventual remains of such money.

MISHNA *d*. Concerning the explanation of R. Simeon of the teachings of the school of Hillel. The discussion of the former with R. Jehudah. The claims of the latter that the coins of the Shekalim were also changed in times and places. The rejoinder of R. Simeon to this.

MISHNA *e*. The law concerning the remainder of money intended for Shekalim when considered to be ordinary. Regarding the remainder of the tenth part of an ephah, bird-offerings, and guilt-offerings: what shall be done with it. A rule concerning this matter. Also, regulations concerning the remainder of Passover sacrifices, Nazarite offerings, the remainder of moneys for the poor in general and individuals, of money for prisoners, for burial of the dead, and R. Meir and R. Nathan's opinions regarding this matter.

CHAPTER III.

MISHNA *a*. Regarding the appointed periods of the year when the money was drawn from the treasury. The different opinions, concerning this matter, of R. Aqiba b. Asai, R. Eliezer, and R. Simeon. The same time appointed for cattle-tithes.

MISHNA *b*. Concerning the ceremony of drawing the money at all periods of the year. The law regarding measures of the boxes in which the coins of the Shekalim were filled, and the numbers of the chests in which the money was drawn from the boxes for the expenses of the Temple. Which box must be opened first, and which last. What garments the person drawing the money must wear. How a man must stand unblemished before his fellow-man and before his God.

MISHNA *c*. Concerning the custom of the house of Rabban Gamaliel, when the members of the house had paid their Shekalim. The law regarding one who drew money did not commence until he had said to the bystanders, "I will now draw," and they answered, "Draw, draw, draw," three times.

MISHNA *d*. Concerning the covering of the boxes after drawing the money. For which countries the drawings were performed in the first period, the second, and the third.

CHAPTER IV.

MISHNA *a*. What was done with the money drawn? Concerning the watchmen that were sent out to guard the after-growth of the Sabbatical year, of which the Omer and two loaves were taken for sacrifice. The opinion of R. Jose in this matter, and what the rabbis answered.

MISHNA *b*. Concerning the red heifer, the goat that was to be sent away, the strip of scarlet, the bridge for the cow, the bridge for the goat, the canal, the city wall, the towers, and other necessities of the city: all were paid for out of the Shekalim money. What Abba Saul said.

MISHNA *c*. What was done with the balance of the money left over in the treasury. The discussion of R. Ishmael and R. Aqiba in this matter. Some of the many things which are enumerated in the Palestinian Talmud and which were done with this money. Among them was the hiring of teachers for priests to teach them the laws of the sacrifices.

MISHNA *d*. What was done with the remainder of the moneys of the chest. The different opinions of R. Ishmael, R. Aqiba, and R. Hanina, the assistant chief of the priests, concerning profit: if it might be raised from the remaining money or not, and of what money the gold plates for the decorations of the Holy of Holies were made. Also, concerning the benefit of the altar.

MISHNA *e*. What was done with the remainder of the incense (as the incense of the New Year must be bought with the new Shekalim money). The sanctification of the incense on hand then transferred to that money, and then redeemed with the money of the new revenue.

MISHNA *f*. Concerning the law when one devoted his entire possessions in honor of the Lord: what should be done with them. The discussions of R. Aqiba and Ben Asai regarding this matter.

MISHNA *g*. Concerning the law when one devoted his possessions, and among them were cattle, male and female, fit for the altar. The discussions of this matter between R. Eliezer and R. Jehoshua. R. Aqiba is inclined to the opinion of R. Eliezer, which seems to him to be more proper, but adds that he had heard that both opinions were right according to circumstances.

MISHNA *h*. If one devote his possessions, and among them are things fit for the altar, such as wines, oils, and birds, what should be done with them. R. Eliezer decreed it, and no one opposed him.

MISHNA *i*. Contractors, for the delivery of all things for the altar and the improvements of the Temple, were appointed every month; but if the prices changed during the thirty days, the Sanctuary must not suffer any injury. Such was the agreement made between them. The illustration of this.

CHAPTER V.

MISHNA *a*. Concerning some names of the offices and the heads of them in the Sanctuary during the entire period when the second Temple was in existence. What were the officers' duties, and how they officiated.

MISHNA *b*. Concerning the order of the head officers; namely, the king, the high priest, his assistant, two catholicoses, and seven chamberlains, not less than two officers being put in charge of public moneys.

MISHNA *c*. Regarding the seals that were in the Sanctuary, serving for the beverages and meat-offerings which must be brought, according to the Bible, with every sacrifice. Concerning the inscription on the seals and their usage. Ben Azai added one seal for the poor sinner. The names of the officers, of the seal-keeper and the officer who sells the above offerings.

MISHNA *d*. The date must be put on every seal. The law regarding surplus money being found in the treasury of the seal-keeper: to whom it belongs; and if a deficit, who must supply it.

MISHNA *e*. The law concerning one who lost his seal; what must be done.

MISHNA *f*. Concerning the two chambers in the Sanctuary, of which one was called "Chamber of Silence" and the other "Chamber of Utensils." What was done there, during what time they were investigated, and what was done with the presented utensils which were useless for the Temple.

CHAPTER VI.

MISHNA *a*. Concerning the thirteen covered chests and thirteen tables which were in the Sanctuary. How many prostrations took place in the Sanctuary. How R. Gamaliel and R. Hanina, assistant chief of the high priest, added one in the place where the ark was hidden.

MISHNA *b*. Relates how a blemished priest who was engaged in selecting and peeling wood had noticed the place where the ark was hidden, but before he had time to tell it to the others he expired.

MISHNA *c*. Concerning the directions where the prostrations were made. How many gates were in the Temple: their names, and why they were so named; also, different opinions of the sages concerning this. There were two gates which were nameless.

MISHNA *d*. Of what material the thirteen tables were made, where they stood, for what purpose they were used. Concerning the golden table in the Temple itself, upon which the showbreads were constantly lying.

MISHNA *e*. Concerning the inscriptions on the thirteen covered chests in the Sanctuary, and what was done with them. The different opinions of R. Jehudah and the sages as to using certain money put in some chests.

MISHNA *f*. Concerning the amount of articles to be furnished in payment of a vow one made, who did not explain how much he intended to give; for instance, wood, incense, gold coins, etc. A rule that was made concerning this. The hides of all sacrifices belong to the priest.

CHAPTER VII.

MISHNA *a*. If money was found in between the differently marked chests, to which chest the money belonged. Concerning this the rule was: One must be guided by the proximity, even in the case of the less important, etc.

MISHNA *b*. Concerning money found in Jerusalem, in the court of the Temple, in the times of the Festivals and in the ordinary times.

MISHNA *c*. Concerning meat found in the court of the Temple, in the city, and any place where Israelites resided and where Gentiles and Israelites together resided.

MISHNA *d*. Concerning cattle found between Jerusalem and Migdal Eder, and in the vicinity of the city in all directions: what the law prescribes. The different opinions of some sages.

MISHNA *e*. Relates how, in former days, the finder of such cattle was pledged to bring drink-offerings, and how afterwards the high court decreed to furnish them from the public moneys.

MISHNAS *f* and *g*. R. Simeon named seven decrees which were promulgated by the high court, and the above decree was one of them. R. Jehudah, however, does not agree on some points with him. R. Jose has also something to say about this.

CHAPTER VIII.

MISHNA *a*. Concerning streets in which people must walk during the time of the Festival in Jerusalem, for the sake of cleanness. The different opinions, in this matter, of R. Meir and the sages.

MISHNA *b*. Regarding utensils found on the way towards the plunge-baths: if they are clean or not, and the different opinions of R. Meir and R. Jose.

MISHNA *c*. Regarding the butcher-knife, if it was found in the street on the 14th of Nissan; and what is the case if the 14th falls on a Sabbath.

MISHNA *d*. Concerning where the curtain of the Sanctuary must be submerged if it become defiled. The first time it was submerged it was spread out for the people to admire the beauty of the work.

MISHNA *e*. What Rabban Simeon b. Gamaliel had to tell in the name of Simeon, the son of the assistant high priest. How the curtain was made: the great amount of the cost and how many hundred priests were required to submerge it.

MISHNA *f*. If meat of the Holy of Holies became defiled, where it must be burned. The different opinions of the schools of Shamai and Hillel on this point.

MISHNA *g*. The different opinions of R. Eliezer and R. Aqiba concerning anything that had become defiled through a principal uncleanness.

MISHNA *h*. The joints of the daily sacrifices, where they were laid down; the sacrifices of the new moon, where they were placed. The payment of Shekalim, if it was obligatory after the destruction of the Temple. The same law regarding cattle-tithe, tithes of grain, and deliverance of the firstlings. The law if one sanctified Shekalim or firstlings after the destruction of the Temple.

TRACT SHEKALIM.

UNDER this heading the payment of a head-tax is treated of, which amounted to one-half of a shekel (in the Mishna always referred to as a *shekel*) and which had to be paid by every Israelite (see Exodus xxx. 12) upon the completion of his twentieth year. In the times of the existence of the Temple, the proceeds of this tax were applied for communal sacrifices and for the needs of the capital. The manner of collection, investment, and application of this money forms the subject of this treatise. It contains, in addition, many other historical regulations, most of which, however, only held good during the existence of the second Temple.

CHAPTER I.

MISHNA: (*a*) On the first day of the month of Adar, warnings are heralded (from Jerusalem) concerning Shekalim [1] and Kelayim [2] (the prohibition concerning the use, for ploughing to-

---

EDITOR'S COMMENTARY.

CHAPTER I.

MISHNA *a*. [1] Warnings were heralded from Jerusalem concerning Shekalim on and after the first of Adar, in order to prepare for the first of Nissan, before which day the final settlement of Shekalim had to be made. This was inferred by the Palestinian Talmud from the following passage [Exodus xl. 17]: "And it came to pass in the first month in the second year, on the first of the month, that the tabernacle was reared up." This was commented upon by a Boraitha, which stated, that on the day on which the tabernacle was reared up, the entire sum of the Shekalim collected was ready for disbursement.

[2] Warnings were also heralded concerning Kelayim, because that month was the time when ploughing and sowing commenced in Palestine.

gether, of an ox with an ass, and the sowing together of different kinds of seeds). On the fifteenth day of that month the Megillah Esther[3] is read in the fortified cities; and the same day the improvement of country roads,[4] market-places, and legal plunge-baths is proceeded with. Public affairs are again taken up[5]; at the same time, graves are marked with lime,[6] and messengers are sent out on account of possible Kelayim.[7]

---

[3] The Megillah (Book of Esther) was read on the fifteenth day of this month only in such cities as were fortified since the time of Joshua the son of Nun; but in such as were fortified after his day, and in the open cities, it was read on the fourteenth of the month. No mention is made in the Mishna concerning the reading on the fourteenth, because, the majority of the cities being open, or fortified since the time of Joshua ben Nun, it was generally known, and there was no fear of it being forgotten. In the few fortified cities, however, it was necessary to remind the inhabitants that the day on which *they* were to read the Megillah was the fifteenth. The Palestinian Talmud (Chapter I., Halakha 2) states, that we are taught by this Mishna that all commandments which are to be fulfilled on a leap year in the second Adar should not be fulfilled in the first Adar; but we cannot see how that can be inferred from this Mishna, although some commentators have tried to explain it.

[4] The rainy season ended by the first of Adar, and in consequence of the heavy rains the country roads and market-places were in bad condition. In the month of Nissan, travel towards Jerusalem was very heavy; hence the warning to improve the roads, etc., was heralded. The public plunge-baths were also injured by the rains and had to be repaired, for the sake of the public, to whom the law prescribes the taking of a legal bath on or before the holidays.

[5] The Palestinian Talmud states, that at that time the courts of law (Beth-din) would meet in session for the trial of civil suits, criminal cases, and crimes involving the punishment of stripes; for the redemption of such as had devoted all their possessions in honor of the Lord, and such as had given the estimated value of their person, etc.; also for the performance of the rite of the bitter water (see Numbers v. 12–31), and for the performance of the rite of breaking the calf's neck (see Deut. xxi.), and for the rite of the red heifer (see Numbers xix.), and for the ceremony of piercing a serf's ear (see Exodus xxi.). For all this, and any other matters that came up before them, the courts of law assembled in that month.

[6] Such graves as had been injured during the rainy season, and

(*b*) R. Jehudah says: At one time the messengers used to pull out the Kelayim (illegally mixed seeds) and throw them at the feet of the owners! The number of the transgressors, however, being constantly on the increase, the Kelayim were pulled out and thrown into the roads. Finally, it was determined that the entire fields of such law-breakers were to be confiscated.*

(*c*) On the fifteenth of this month (Adar) the money-changers outside of Jerusalem seated themselves at their tables.[1] In the city of Jerusalem, however, they did not do this until the twenty-fifth of the month.[2] As soon as the money-changers seated themselves also in the city, the taking of pledges from

---

were not marked, had to be restored and marked, in order that a man be saved the annoyance of becoming unclean by stepping on a grave. The Palestinian Talmud infers this from the passage [Leviticus xiii. 46]: "Unclean, unclean, shall he call out," and interprets it to signify that the uncleanness itself should call out "unclean" and keep men away from its vicinity. For this reason it was heralded, that the graves were to be marked in order to be a warning to passers-by that such places were unclean.

[7] On account of the severity of the law concerning Kelayim and the frequency with which that law was infracted, it was deemed insufficient merely to herald the prohibition, and messengers were sent out to see the law enforced (Maimonides).

MISHNA *b.* * R. Jehudah's dictum does not intend to dispute the foregoing, but merely supplements it with the statement that the messengers sent out were for the purpose of punishing the infractors of the law of Kelayim. The Palestinian Talmud adduces the right of the Beth-din to confiscate property from the passage [Ezra x. 8]: "And that whosoever should not come within three days, etc., all his substance should be devoted." Whence it may be seen, that a Beth-din has such power.

MISHNA *c.* [1] It was the custom for money-changers in those days to carry their tables with them, and hence they were called "the men of the tables." The Mishna relates, that on the fifteenth of the month the money-changers were ordered to go out into the rural districts with their tables, in order to provide the people with the necessary half-shekels; for the tax had to be paid in half-shekels only.

[2] On the twenty-fifth, when it was high time for payment and the people commenced flocking into the city of Jerusalem, the money-changers returned and sat in the court of the Temple.

the tardy ones commenced.[3] But from whom were pledges taken? From Levites, Israelites, proselytes, and freedmen; but not from women, slaves, and minors. If a father, however, commenced to give a pledge for a minor, he was not allowed to stop. From priests no pledges were taken, for the sake of peace (and the dignity of the priests themselves).[4]

(*d*) Said R. Jehudah: Ben Buchri proclaimed the following ordinance in Yavne (Jamnia): "Any priest paying his shekel commits no wrong." R. Johanan ben Zakai, however, rejoined: "Not so! (The ordinance should read:) 'Any priest not paying his shekel, commits a sin.'"[1] But the priests used to interpret the following passage to their advantage: It is written [Leviticus vi. 16]: "And every meat-offering of a priest shall be wholly burnt, it shall not be eaten." (They said therefore:) Were we obliged to contribute (our shekels) how could we eat our[2] Omer

---

[3] The taking of pledges commenced immediately upon the departure of the money-changers from the rural districts, because, if a man had not paid his half-shekel while the money-changers were still within his reach, it was obvious that he either would not or could not pay it, and in consequence a pledge was taken.

[4] According to law, the priests were also in duty bound to pay the half-shekels, the collection of which was mainly intended for the purchase of communal sacrifices, and the priests were naturally included in the community. They, however, found a defect in the law, and held themselves exempt. In consequence of their being in authority during the existence of the second Temple, they were not forced to pay or give pledges, for the sake of harmony.

MISHNA *d.* [1] The difference of opinion between Ben Buchri (who was a priest himself) and R. Johan ben Zakai is, as can be plainly seen, that Ben Buchri holds, that according to law the priests are not in duty bound to pay the half-shekel; but if they do it, they may nevertheless partake of their Omer, two loaves, and showbread, while R. Johan ben Zakai says, that they are in duty bound to pay the half-shekel.

[2] The priests claim, that if they were to pay the half-shekel with which the Omer, etc., is bought, they would naturally have a share in it, and they would eat their share, which, as a priest's offering, must not be eaten by any one. This is, however, an unjust claim; for the majority is considered, and the priests were by far in the minority. As the priests, however, were in charge of the affairs of state, they interpreted the law to suit themselves, and for the sake of peace they were not disturbed.

(first sheaves harvested) and the two loaves and the showbread (which were procured with the shekels of the head-tax)?

(*e*) Although it was ordained that no pledges were to be taken from women, slaves, and minors, if they offered to contribute, their money was accepted. From heathens and Samaritans it was not accepted. Nor were bird-offerings, for men or women afflicted with venereal disease and for women who had recently been confined, accepted; nor sin and guilt offerings.[1] Vowed and voluntary offerings, however, were accepted.[2] The following is the rule: Everything which was vowed as an offering and all voluntary offerings were accepted. Anything not vowed for offering or given voluntarily was not accepted from them (heathens and Samaritans). So it is explicitly declared in Ezra, for it is written [Ezra iv. 3]: "It is not for *you* and us (both) to build a house unto our God."

(*f*) The following are obliged to pay a premium[1] (in addi-

---

MISHNA *e*. [1] This clause of the Mishna refers, according to the Palestinian Talmud and Maimonides, to Samaritans only and not to heathens, while the sin and guilt offerings were accepted from Samaritans but not from heathens, because the latter had not the same laws as the Israelites as regards sin-offerings. The Samaritans, however, claiming to be Israelites, were allowed to bring their sin and guilt offerings. The reason, however, that bird-offerings were not accepted from the Samaritans was because, in the first place, an offering for a person afflicted with venereal disease had to be brought in the form of a sheep; but if the person could not afford a sheep, birds answered the purpose. The Samaritans, however, were not considered trustworthy, and it was feared that they might bring a wrong offering (*i.e.*, an offering of less value than they could afford).

[2] These were accepted from heathens also, because such offerings were for forgiveness of sins in general, and in that respect all men are equal.

MISHNA *f*. [1] The shekel mentioned in the Bible is equivalent to the Sela mentioned in the Mishna, and is worth two shekels of the Mishna. The half-shekel of the Bible was worth (according to Maimonides) the weight of 192 grains of barley in silver, and, for fear that the shekel of the Mishna of that time was perhaps a trifle less than the above weight, a small coin was prescribed to be paid in addition to the above shekel, and which was named from the Greek Colobbus (χόλλυβος). He who gave the half-shekel voluntarily, and not because he was obliged to pay it, was exempt from paying the above "Colobbus." Those of the priests who, regardless of the

tion to the half-shekel): Levites, Israelites, proselytes, and freedmen; but not (priests,) women, slaves, and minors. If one pay (the half-shekel) for a priest, woman, slave, or a minor, he is exempt (from paying the premium); if he pay for himself and another, however, he must pay a premium for one. R. Meir says: "(He must pay) two premiums. One who pays a Sela (whole Bible shekel) and receives in return a half (Bible) shekel must pay two premiums."[a]

(*g*) If one pay for a poor man, for a neighbor, or for a countryman, he is exempt from a premium (because it is charity); if he only advances them the money, he is not exempt. Brothers who (after dividing their inheritance) have their business in common, or partners, when they become obliged to pay a premium, are exempt from cattle-tithe.* As long, however, as they must pay cattle-tithe, they are exempt from a premium. How much does the premium amount to? According to R. Meir, to one silver Meah (one twenty-fourth of a shekel); but the sages say, to one-half of a Meah.

---

claim that they were not obliged to pay the half-shekel, paid it nevertheless, were exempt from the above premium for the sake of peace.

[a] One in addition to the half-shekel and one for the exchange.

MISHNA *g*. * Cattle-tithe must be paid by a man only from such young as his own cattle calve, but not from the calves which he purchases elsewhere. If two brothers inherit cattle or calves from their father, they must pay cattle-tithe, because the cattle are regarded as still their father's. If they have divided their inheritance, even though they shared alike, they are both exempt from payment, because it is regarded as if one brother had bought the cattle from the other. (The same refers to partners. As long as they are in partnership they are liable for cattle-tithe from such young as is calved by their own cattle, but if the partners dissolve even after the cattle had calved, they are exempt, because it is regarded as if one partner had purchased his share from the other.) Now, it is obvious that when the two brothers are still partners and liable for cattle-tithe they are regarded as one, and by paying one Sela for both are exempt from premiums, because the money is still considered as their father's. (This explanation is taken from Rashi in Tract Chulin.) As soon, however, as they are exempt from cattle-tithe, they have nothing more in common, hence must pay a half-shekel each, and thus must also pay the premium.

CHAPTER II.

MISHNA: (*a*) One may put together the Shekalim and exchange them for Darkons[1] (Greek coins of permanent value), in order to be able to carry them more readily. Just as the money-chests were on the order of horns in the city of Jerusalem, so were they also in the country.[2] If the inhabitants of a town sent their Shekalim (to the city of Jerusalem) by messengers, and the money was stolen from them or was lost by accident, if the treasurers had already drawn their share (from the communal Shekalim), the messengers of the city must swear to the fact before the treasurers. If the share had not yet been drawn, they (the messengers) must swear to the facts before the inhabitants of the town, and the latter must make the amount good.[3] If the money was recovered or returned by the

---

CHAPTER II.

MISHNA *a*. [1] The Darkon (Greek Δαρεικός; or *drachm*, biblical term, Ezra viii. 27) was a Persian gold coin worth two Selas, or four half-shekels.

[2] The money-chests were narrow on one side and broad at the bottom, and had a slot through which a Darkon on edge only could be passed, and were given to the messenger locked.

[3] If a portion of the amount of Shekalim collected had already been spent for sacrifices or for the improvement of the Temple, all the Israelites who were bound to pay their Shekalim had a share in such disbursement, and the amount sent by the town, although lost or stolen, was counted as if it had been included in the amount spent, because it was the express understanding that in every shekel spent for sacrifices, etc., all Israelites had a share, in order that they might have a share in the sacrifices. Therefore, the messengers of the city had simply to swear that they had taken the money, and it was considered received by the treasurers. If, however, no portion of the Shekalim had yet been expended, the share of the inhabitants of the town, whose money had been stolen or lost, was not included in the amount on hand, and hence the representatives of the city were obliged to make it good (Maimonides).

thieves, both amounts are considered as Shekalim, and nothing is credited to next year's account.

(*b*) If one give his shekel to another to pay (his head-tax) for him, and the man appropriates it to pay his own tax, he (the latter) commits embezzlement if the share had already been drawn; the same is the case with one who pays his shekel with sanctified money, after his share had been drawn and an animal was sacrificed for it.[1] If he took the money from the second tithes or from the Sabbatical year fruit, he must eat the full value of same in the city of Jerusalem.[2]

(*c*) If one gather together single coins and say: "These shall serve for my Shekalim," the eventual remainder is, according to the school of Shamai, a voluntary gift; according to the school of Hillel, it is not sanctified. If the man say, however: "Out of these I shall pay my Shekalim," the eventual remainder is, according to both schools, not sanctified. If he say: "These shall serve me for a sin-offering," the eventual remainder is, according to both schools, a voluntary offering. If he say: "*Out* of these will I bring a sin-offering," the eventual remainder is, according to both schools, not sanctified.*

MISHNA *b*. [1]The same reason as stated in note 3 of the preceding Mishna applies also to this clause; and, besides, everybody had a share in the sacrifice of the animal, even if the sacrifice were made on the strength of future receipts, for pledges were on hand insuring the payment by the delinquents.

[2]If the money was taken from the second tithes, the value of which had to be consumed in the city of Jerusalem, he must replace it by an equal amount and proclaim that this money is in exchange for the money taken from the second tithe, and then consume it accordingly. If the money was taken from the Sabbatical year fruit, he must replace it and proclaim the same as above and make it public property, as is the law of Sabbatical years.

MISHNA *c*. *The meaning of this Mishna is as follows: If a man gathered money little by little, with the express intention of paying his shekalim tax out of such money, and separated it from other moneys, any remainder which he may have left over after such payment is, according to the school of Shamai, to be devoted for a voluntary offering, because it was separated; and according to the school of Hillel, it is ordinary money, that may be used at will, because it was gathered only for the purpose of paying the amount due, which was already paid. If a man, however, had a sum of

(*d*) R. Simeon says: "What difference is there here between the Shekalim and the sin-offerings? Shekalim have their fixed value, but sin-offerings have not."[1] R. Jehudah says: "Even Shekalim have no fixed value; for when Israel returned from captivity, (half-) Darkons were paid; later (half-) Selas were paid; again, Tabas (half-shekels) were current (but not accepted), and finally people would only pay with Dinars."[2] Rejoined R. Simeon: "Nevertheless, the Shekalim were all of like value at one and the same time, while as for sin-offerings, one brings one Sela's worth, another two, and a third three Selas' worth."[3]

(*e*) The remainder of moneys intended for Shekalim is not

---

money, and declared that he would use *this* sum for the payment of his shekalim tax, the remainder which he may have after such payment is, even according to the school of Hillel, to be devoted for a voluntary offering. With money devoted for a voluntary offering, whole-offerings only were to be bought.

MISHNA *d.* [1] By his teaching in this Mishna, R. Simeon wishes to explain the reason of the decree of the school of Hillel concerning the remainder of money which had been gathered little by little for the purpose of paying the Shekalim, or for the bringing of a sin-offering, and says: "Because it is written [Exodus xxx. 15], 'The rich shall not give more, and the poor shall not give less, than the half of a shekel,' a man when gathering money for the payment of Shekalim knows exactly how much he will need; hence, although he separated the amount gathered, the remainder is ordinary money; but if he gathered money for a sin-offering, which has no fixed value, and for which he did not know exactly how much he would have to pay, his intention in separating the money was evidently to use the entire amount for such purpose, and hence the eventual remainder, which cannot be used for a sin-offering, as it is already sacrificed, should be used for a voluntary offering."

[2] R. Jehudah differs with R. Simeon, and states, that the reason given by the latter for the decree of the school of Hillel cannot be correct, for even Shekalim had not always a fixed value, and when a man commenced to gather money for the payment of his Shekalim he also may not have known how much he would have to pay when the time came, because the value of the coin might be changed in the meantime.

[3] R. Simeon answered R. Jehudah very properly: "Even if the value of the coin was changed, the man knew well that he would pay a certain sum equal to that paid by all others, and the entire amount

sanctified.[1] The remainder of moneys intended for the offering of the tenth part of an ephah [Lev. v. xi.] (sin-offering of the poor), for bird-offerings of men or women afflicted with venereal disease and of women that had been recently confined, and for sin and guilt offerings, are considered voluntary offerings. Following is the rule: The remainder of everything designated for sin and guilt offerings is considered as a voluntary offering.[2] The remainder of whole-offerings is applied to whole-offerings,[3] of food-offerings to food-offerings, of peace-offerings to peace-offerings; that of the Passover-offerings to peace-offerings, and that of Nazarite-offerings to Nazarite-offerings. The remainder of such (offering) as is designated for a certain Nazarite is a voluntary offering. The remainder of moneys for the poor in general, belongs to the poor; of money collected for a certain poor man belongs to that same poor man. The remainder of ransom moneys for prisoners is applied to (the ransom of) other prisoners; of moneys collected for a certain prisoner belongs to that prisoner. The remainder of burial moneys is applied to (the burial of) other dead; of money collected for a particular dead (man) belongs to

---

that he had gathered would not be consumed; as for a sin-offering, however, he never knew exactly just what amount he would need for its purchase, because it had no fixed value; therefore, when he separated the money from other moneys his intention was to use the entire amount."

MISHNA *e*. [1] After explaining the opinions of both schools (Shamai and Hillel) in the preceding Mishna, and the Halakha, as usual, prevailing according to the school of Hillel, this Mishna states the final Halakha anonymously, and then cites the subsequent ordinances, concerning which there is no difference of opinion.

[2] The reason for this rule is: A sin or guilt offering must be brought for each sin separately. If money was designated for one sin-offering, the remainder cannot be applied to another offering for the same sin, nor for another sin which one might commit in the future, hence the remainder must be a voluntary offering.

[3] The remainder of whole-offerings may be used for more whole-offerings, because the quantity of whole-offerings, which are voluntary, is not limited. The same applies to food and peace offerings. The remainder of Passover-offerings, however, which cannot be used for the same purpose again, and should, however, be used for an eatable sacrifice, cannot be used for a voluntary offering, which is a whole-offering, but for a peace-offering, which is eatable.

the legal heirs. R. Meir says: "The remainder remains intact until Elijah comes again" (as the herald of the resurrection).[4] R. Nathan says: "It should be applied to the building of a gravestone for the departed."

---

[4] The reason for R. Meir's dictum is: He holds, that if money is collected for a certain dead man, the remainder belongs virtually to him, *i.e.*, should be applied only for the use of the corpse; hence the heirs have no share in it. R. Nathan, however, says, that the setting up of a gravestone is for the use of the corpse, it being in his honor and not of any benefit to the heirs.

CHAPTER III.

MISHNA: (*a*) At three periods of the year money is drawn from the treasury (of the Shekalim); viz.: Half a month before Passover, half a month before Pentecost, and half a month before the Feast of Booths. The same dates are also the terms for the obligation of cattle-tithing, so says R. Aqiba. Ben Azai says: "The dates for the latter terms are the twenty-ninth of Adar, the first of Sivan, and the twenty-ninth of Abh." R. Eliezer and R. Simeon both say: "The first of Nissan, the first of Sivan, and the twenty-ninth of Elul." But why do they say the twenty-ninth of Elul, why not the first of Tishri? Because that is a feast-day, and it is not allowed to tithe on a feast-day; therefore they ordained it for the preceding day, the twenty-ninth of Elul.*

(*b*) The money drawn from the treasury was brought in three chests, each of three Saahs' capacity. On these chests was written: Aleph, Beth, Gimmel. R. Ishmael says: "They were marked in Greek: Alpha, Beta, Gamma."—The one that drew the money was not allowed to enter (the treasury) with a turned-up garment, nor with shoes nor sandals, nor with Tephillin, nor with an amulet, in order that, in the event of his becoming impoverished, it should not be said that he was thus punished on account of transgression against the treasury; or if he became rich, that he enriched himself by means of money drawn from the treasury. For a man must stand as unblemished before his fellowman as before his God, as it is written [Numbers

---

CHAPTER III.

MISHNA *a*. * The dates of the time for cattle-tithing have nothing to do with the time for drawing the money; for as to that time, all agree upon the dates stated in the Mishna, and the difference of opinion concerning the time of cattle-tithing is explained in the Palestinian Talmud and in Tract Rosh Hashana of the Babylonian Talmud.

xxxii. 22]: "And ye be thus guiltless before the Lord and before Israel"; and [Proverbs iii. 4]: "So shalt thou find grace and good favor in the eyes of God and man." *

(*c*) The members of the family of R. Gamaliel used to enter, each one with his shekel between his fingers, and throw it before the one who drew the money from the treasury, and the latter immediately placed it into the chest (which he took out).—The one who came in to draw the money did not proceed before he had said to the bystanders: "I will now proceed to draw," and they had answered: "Draw, draw, draw," three times. *

MISHNA *b*. * In this Mishna the manner of drawing the money from the treasury is described: how it was accomplished, that the Shekalim for which communal sacrifices were bought should be taken from the treasury in such a manner that all the contributors should have a share in them. The mode of procedure was as follows: About the middle of the month of Nissan, when the money from all Israel had been collected, the treasurers, amid great ceremony, would open the rooms where the boxes in which the money had been deposited by the collectors were situated, and bring out all the boxes contained in the rooms. These boxes were in turn opened, and their contents thrown into three cases, each of which had nine Saahs' capacity, and were covered with a cover. The remainder, after filling the three cases, was called the remainder of the room (and what was done with this will be told later). After the performance of this ceremony one man was selected, while the others withdrew, and he was to transfer the money to be expended, from the cases into three small chests, each having three Saahs' capacity and marked with three letters: Aleph, Beth, Gimmel; or, Alpha, Beta, Gamma.

MISHNA *c*. * After this ceremony, the man, being almost nude—for he had no garments on in which he could conceal a coin, no shoes, no sandals, no hat, no hose; in fact, nothing that would afford a hiding-place for money—would take the chest marked Aleph and bring it up to the first case, and fill it up, after which he would cover the case. Then he would take the chest marked Beth, fill it from the second case, cover the case, and proceed in the same manner with the chest marked Gimmel, from the third box, which contained nine Saahs' capacity; but in the last instance he would leave the case uncovered, as a sign whence to commence filling the chests at the second drawing of money in the same order as before, using the third case first, then the second, and lastly the first. This was done in order that the money should be thoroughly intermingled (*d*) After the man had completed the first drawing, he covered the balance with a cover (of fur); the same was done after the second drawing; after the third drawing the balance remained uncovered; for (the covering in the first two instances) was done only in order not to draw by mistake again what had already been drawn from. The first drawing was performed in the name of the whole land of Israel, the second in the name of the cities near the boundaries, and the third in the name of the inhabitants of Babylon, Media, and all distant lands in general.

---

and everybody have a share in the sacrifices bought with it. The first drawing took place on the fifteenth of Nissan, and sacrifices were purchased for the Passover. The next drawing was held fifteen days before Pentecost; and Pentecost only lasting one day, not so many sacrifices were needed, and the money lasted until fifteen days before the Feast of Booths, when the last lot of money was withdrawn from the cases and placed in the chests. The expenditure of the money was also made in the order of chests, chest Aleph being emptied first, etc.; and the intention was to place Jerusalem first, the surrounding territory next, and all the other places where Israelites dwelt last.

CHAPTER IV.

MISHNA: (*a*) What was done with this money drawn? The daily sacrifices, the additional sacrifices, and the drink-offerings belonging to them were bought therewith; also the Omers[1] (sheaves), the two loaves, the showbreads, and communal sacrifices in general. The watchmen who had to guard the after-growth on the Sabbatical year were paid out of this money. R. Jose says: "One who so desired could undertake the guarding (of the after-growth on Sabbatical years) without pay."[2] The sages answered him: "Thou wilt admit thyself, that the sacrifices (from the after-growth on Sabbatical years) must be brought only from communal property."[3]

CHAPTER IV.

MISHNA *a*. [1] The Omers and the two loaves, which had to be made of Palestinian grain and of the new crop only, were bought out of the Shekalim during the six ordinary years, but in the Sabbatical year, where neither sowing nor reaping was done, where were they obtained? Men were sent out to discover where grain was growing as an after-growth, that had not been sown, and then watchmen were placed there to see that no one disturbed the crop; for it being public property, the possessor of the soil where the grain grew could not prevent its being taken. The men who discovered the grain and the watchmen were paid for their services out of the Shekalim, and such payment was regarded as the price of the grain, so that the grain again became communal property.

[2] R. Jose, in making this statement, holds, that one may present the community with a thing intended for a voluntary offering, and thus the man who guards the after-growth gratuitously, thereby acquiring a right to it, may donate it to the community for a communal sacrifice.

[3] The sages mean to say that the Omer, the two loaves, the showbreads, and the communal sacrifices must be taken from articles that were communal property from the beginning, while other sacrifices may be offered from things donated by a man who does so with a good will. (See Rosh Hashana.)

(*b*) The red heifer, the goat that was to be sent away (on the Day of Atonement), the strip of scarlet, were paid for out of this money. The bridge for the cow, the bridge for the goat that was to be sent away, and the scarlet strip tied between the latter's horns, the canal (at the Temple), the city wall, the towers and other necessities of the city, are paid for out of the remainder of the treasury-money.* Abba Saul says: "The costs of the building of the bridge for the red heifer were defrayed by the high priests themselves."

(*c*) What was done with the balance left over in the treasury (after all the things in the preceding Mishna had been procured)? Wines, oils, and fine meal were bought with it to the profit of the sanctuary (for the purpose of selling it again to those who brought sacrifices).* So said R. Ishmael. R. Aqiba, however, says: "Sanctified moneys or contributions for the poor are not dealt with for profit."

(*d*) What was done with the remainder of the money (taken from the chests)? It is used for gold plate for the decoration of the Holy of Holies. R. Ishmael says: "The mentioned fruit (profit of the wines, oils, and fine meal sold in the Temple) was for the benefit of the altar, and the remainder of the money drawn was for service-utensils." R. Aqiba says: "The remainder of the money drawn was for the benefit of the altar and that of the drink-offerings was for service-utensils." R. Hanina, the assistant chief of priests, says: "The remainder of the drink-

---

MISHNA *b*. * The remainder of the Shekalim, left over after the three cases had been filled, which was called "remainder of the room," was stored in a high place, access to which was very difficult, no ladder being permitted to be used. Out of this money all the accessories for the sacrifices, as enumerated in the Mishna, were procured. The details of these accessories are explained in Tracts Para and Yuma.

MISHNA *c*. * It is known that all those who brought sacrifices were obliged to purchase wine, oil, and fine meal for meal-offerings, and all this was purchased in the court of the Temple. In the Palestinian Talmud many things are enumerated, for which purposes the balance of the money was used; for instance, the hiring of teachers to instruct the priests in the art of slaughtering, in the halakhas pertaining to such matters, etc., also for the payment of those who investigated blemishes in the sacrifices, and a great many other things to be found in that chapter (Halakha 4).

offerings was for the benefit of the altar and that of the money drawn was for service-utensils." The two latter would not admit of the alleged gain from fruit * (profit).

(*e*) What was done with the remainder of the incense?[1] At first the remuneration of the preparers of the incense was set aside from the treasury; the sanctification of the incense on hand was then transferred to that money, and the former was then given to the preparers in lieu of compensation[2]; it is then bought back from them with the money of the new revenue: providing the new revenue was on hand in time, it was bought back with such money; otherwise, the old revenue was used for that purpose.

(*f*) If one devote his entire possessions in honor of the Lord, and among them are things which are fit for communal sacrifices (*e.g.*, incense), the preparers of the incense should be paid therewith. So teaches R. Aqiba. Ben Azai answered him *: "Such is not the right mode of procedure. The compen-

---

MISHNA *d.* * In the preceding Mishna, R. Ishmael declares, that the balance of the money in the treasury is used to purchase wines, oils, and fine meal, to be resold to those bringing sacrifices, and in this Mishna he relates what is done with the profits accruing from such sales. R. Aqiba, however, who would not permit of selling the things mentioned for profit, declares that the money for the altar is taken directly from the balance left over in the treasury; and R. Hanina holds, that the balance of the money drawn is used for the service-utensils.

MISHNA *e.* [1] The remainder of the incense refers to the amount of incense left over at the end of the year. A quantity of incense was prepared for the whole year, and every priest would use a handful at a time; but, as handfuls are not all alike, no fixed amount could be prepared: hence the remainder.

[2] Compensation for labor must not be made with sacrificed articles, for the sanctification cannot be transferred to labor that had already been performed; it can be transferred, however, to actual money, and in consequence the subterfuge for the payment of the preparers of the incense was resorted to as stated in the Mishna.

MISHNA *f.* * R. Aqiba and Ben Azai differ in this Mishna as to whether sanctification can be transferred to labor or not. R. Aqiba holds, that labor can be compensated with sanctified articles; but Ben Azai holds, that it cannot. According to Maimonides the Halakha prevails according to Ben Azai, because in the previous Mishna there is a concurrent opinion.

sation of the preparers must first be separated from such possessions, then the sanctification of those possessions transferred to money; then give the separated things to the preparers for compensation; and, finally, buy them back from them with money of the new revenue."

(*g*) If one devote his possessions, and there are among them cattle fit for the altar, male or female, the male, according to R. Eliezer, shall be sold for whole-offerings and the female for peace-offerings to such as are in need of them; and the proceeds of such sale, together with the other possessions, shall be devoted to the treasury for the maintenance of the Temple. R. Jehoshua says: "The male are sacrificed as whole-offerings, the female are sold to such as are in need of peace-offerings, and the proceeds used for the sacrifice of whole-offerings. The balance of the possessions is devoted to the maintenance of the Temple."[1] Said R. Aqiba: "The opinion of R. Eliezer seems to me to be more proper than that of R. Jehoshua; for R. Eliezer has an even procedure, whereas R. Jehoshua divides it."[2] R. Papeos says: "I have heard that it is done according to both teachers; viz.: According to R. Eliezer if the owner who devotes his possessions explicitly mentions his cattle, and according to R. Jehoshua if he silently includes his cattle in his possessions."[3]

MISHNA *g*. [1]The point of difference between R. Eliezer and R. Jehoshua is this: The former holds, that if a man devoted all his possessions, his intention was to devote them for the maintenance of the Temple only; while the latter holds, that the intention was to devote the possessions according to their adaptability. Hence if, among the possessions, there were objects adapted for the altar, they should be devoted to the altar; if, however, these were female cattle, which could not be brought as a whole-offering, nor, by reason of the absence of the owner, even as a peace-offering, such cattle should be sold and the proceeds applied to the purchase of whole-offerings.

[2]R. Aqiba holds with R. Eliezer, because, in his opinion, a man who devotes all his possessions does so with but a single intention; and this is what he terms an even procedure.

[3]R. Papeos said, that if the man devoted all his possessions to the honor of the Lord, R. Jehoshua would be correct, for his possessions can be used in honor of the Lord in various ways; but if he explicitly stated that he devoted his possessions for the maintenance of the Temple, R. Eliezer's opinion is proper.

(*h*) If one devote his possessions, and there are among them things fit for the altar, such as wines, oils, and birds, says R. Eliezer, the latter things should be sold to such as need offerings of these kinds, and the proceeds used for the sacrificing of whole-offerings; the balance of the possessions goes toward the maintenance of the Temple.*

(*i*) Every thirty days the prices paid by the treasury are determined. If one contract to furnish flour at the rate of four Saah (for one Sela), and the price is raised to three, he must nevertheless furnish the same at four Saah (for one Sela).[1] If he contract at the rate of three and the price fall to four, he must in that case furnish four, for the Sanctuary always has that prerogative. If the flour become wormy, it is the loss of the contractor; and if the wine become sour it is also his loss, and he does not receive the money for his wares until the purchased wares have been favorably accepted as sacrifices at the altar.[2]

MISHNA *h*. * The reason that R. Eliezer decrees that wines, oils, and birds should be sold, and whole-offerings brought in their stead, is because the articles mentioned cannot be redeemed with money.

MISHNA *i*. [1] Every month, bids were received from contractors for the furnishing of the necessaries for the Temple and altar for one month. The lowest bidder received the contract, and it was distinctly understood that, even if prices were raised during the month, his prices were to remain as originally contracted for.

[2] The Palestinian Talmud states, that the money due the contractors was paid them by the priests immediately upon the latter receiving the wares, for the priests were very careful, and never allowed flour to become wormy or wine to spoil.

CHAPTER V.

MISHNA: (*a*) The following were the heads of offices[1] in the Sanctuary: Johanan, son of Pinchas, keeper of the seals[2]; A'hia, (superintendent) of drink-offerings; Mathia, son of Samuel, (superintendent) of the casting of lots[3]; Petha'hia, (superintendent) of bird-offerings.[4] Petha'hia is Mordecai, but why do they call him Petha'hia? Because he used to expound and interpret scriptures, and was master of seventy languages. Ben A'hia was (superintendent) of the cures of priests suffering with abdominal diseases.[5] Ne'huniah was master of the well.[6]

CHAPTER V.

MISHNA *a*. [1] The list of officers enumerated by the Mishna were not all officers at the same time, but served at different periods, and the Mishna merely names the most important and pious among them.

[2] See Mishna *d*, same chapter.

[3] Lots were cast for the determination of the turn of the priests for each particular service. The superintendent would keep a record of such as were eligible for duty, and then cast lots for the priest who was to serve.

[4] Petha'hia was superintendent-in-chief of all those who had charge of the bird-offerings; these bird-offerings were brought by women who had recently been confined; and there were so many of them that a record had to be kept, who came first, whose time was nearly expired, and how much was to be charged for the offerings. Besides this, it often happened that the birds became mixed and required great wisdom to separate them and recognize to whom every bird belonged, as the changing of the birds would make the offering invalid. (See commentary of Israel Lipshuetz.)

[5] Such diseases among priests were of very frequent occurrence and inevitable; for they were dressed during services very lightly, being allowed to wear only four articles of apparel; viz., a linen shirt, linen pantaloons, a linen cap, and a girdle. Besides, they had to walk barefoot on the marble floor, and were constantly eating meat of the sacrifices, which had to be eaten during a specified time. Hence

Gebini was herald.[7] Ben Gabhar was turnkey of the gates.[8] Ben Bebai was master of the temple-guard.[9] Ben Arzah was master of the kettledrums (which were beaten as a signal for the Levites to commence their chant). Higros, son of Levi, was (leader) of the singing. The family of Garmo (superintended) the making of the showbreads.[10] The family of Abtinos (superintended) the preparing of the incense.[11] Elazar (superintended) the making of the curtains.[12] Pinchas superintended the vestments.[13]

---

they needed many attendants, in order that, as soon as one priest took sick, a substitute was brought in his place and he was removed to the sick ward. Ben A'hia was the superintendent-in-chief of these matters.

[6] On account of the immense influx of people into Jerusalem three times a year, the wells for the supply of water, both on the roads and in the city, had to be looked after, and Ne'huniah had charge of this.

[7] The commencement of all services had to be heralded, and many heralds were employed. Gebini was herald-in-chief, and his duty was mainly to call out in the morning: "Priests, to your duties! Levites, to your chants! Israelites, to your places!" He had so powerful a voice that it could be heard eight miles.

[8] He had charge of the keys of the gates and of the men who stood at the gates.

[9] The gates of the Temple had to be guarded day and night, even in times of peace. To properly care for the guard and to punish all negligence in guarding the gates was the duty of Ben Babai.

[10] For showbreads, twelve loaves had to be made every week, and had to be made so that they would keep fresh the entire week. For further details, see Tract Tamid. The family of Garmo had charge of this work for generations.

[11] The incense, which was used twice a day, had to be prepared with especial skill from many different spices, and in proper proportions. Further details are also to be found in Tract Tamid. The family Abtinos had charge of this branch for many generations.

[12] The curtains, which were frequently changed, had to be inspected as to workmanship, cleanliness, etc., and this duty devolved upon Elazar.

[13] The vestments of the priests had to be carefully examined as to cleanliness, and had to be sent out to be laundered regularly. Many rooms in the Temple were devoted to those vestments, and Pinchas had charge of them all.

Much has been said as to the character of the men enumerated in

(*b*) No less than three treasurers and seven chamberlains must be appointed,* and no less than two officers were put in charge of public moneys. Exceptions were made in the cases of Ben A'hia, superintendent of the cures of the sick, and Elazar, superintendent of the preparation of curtains, because they were unanimously elected by the community.

(*c*) There were four seals in the Sanctuary, inscribed with the words Egel (calf), Sachar (ram), Gdi (kid), and 'Houte (sinner, meaning here one covered with sores). Ben Azai says, that there were five (seals), and the inscriptions were in Aramaic, meaning: calf, ram, kid, poor sinner (one afflicted with sores), and rich sinner (one afflicted with sores). The one inscribed with "calf" was used for drink-offerings brought with offerings of the herds, large or small, male or female; the one inscribed with "kid" was used for drink-offerings brought with offerings of the flocks, large or small, male or female, with the exception of rams; the one inscribed with "ram" served for drink-offerings brought only with rams; the seal inscribed with "sinner" served for drink-offerings brought with the three cattle-offerings of those afflicted with sores.*

---

the Mishna, whether they were priests themselves, Levites, or ordinary Israelites. For particularized information regarding this subject, we would refer to "Die Priester und der Cultus," by Dr. Adolf Büchler, Vienna, 1895. It is estimated that the priests in Jerusalem approached the enormous number of twenty thousand. Besides, there were numbers of Levites.

Mishna *b*. * The officers of the Temple ranked as follows: The king, the high priest, the assistant high priest (Sagan), two catholicoses,† seven chamberlains (Amarkolins), three treasurers (Gisbars), and, finally, many smaller officials; *e.g.*, inspectors, officers of the guard, etc. (See "Die Priester und der Cultus," pp. 90–117.) The duties of each officer are described in Tamid and Yuma.

Mishna *c*. * With every sacrifice that was offered, wine and meal

---

† "Catholicos" is here used in the sense of patriarch or head, which term still retains a similar meaning in the "Ecclesiastical History of the Armenian Church," deriving its original meaning from the Greek καθολικός—general or universal. In the latter sense it was adopted at a very early period by the Christian church. In the exclusive sense of denoting the church as the "depository of universally received doctrine in contrast with heretical sects" it is still improperly retained by the Roman Catholic Church. I am surprised to find no mention of the officers of this name and function under the appropriate title anywhere in the "Encyc. Brit."

(*d*) One who desired to bring drink-offerings, for instance, went to Johanan, who was keeper of the seals, paid his money, and received a seal; he then went to A'hia, who had charge of the drink-offerings, gave him the seal, and received the drink-offering. In the evening the two officers came together, when A'hia turned over the seal and received instead the money. If there was too much money, it belonged to the Sanctuary; if too little, Johanan had to supply the deficit: for the sanctuary had that prerogative.

(*e*) One who lost his seal had to wait until evening. If there was a surplus sufficient to cover the seal,* he was given the drink-offering for that amount; otherwise, he did not receive it. The date of the day was on the seal to prevent fraud.

(*f*) There were two chambers in the sanctuary. One was

---

were brought in accordance with the biblical commandment to that effect, and in quantities prescribed by the ordinances. As the drink and meal offerings were bought in the Temple, the person bringing the sacrifice would receive a seal from the priest which he would exchange for the necessary quantity of wine and meal. The drink-offerings with goats and sheep were the same, hence the seal inscribed "kid" served for both. One who brought a ram, however, which required a larger quantity of wine and meal, would receive a separate seal, inscribed "ram." As for offerings of the herds, they were all equal, small or large, male or female; hence the seal inscribed "calf" sufficed for all. Those who were afflicted with sores, and had to bring two rams and one sheep, received a seal inscribed "sin" (which had the hidden purpose of signifying that sores were the consequence of sin). The poor sinners, who had only to bring one sheep, two doves, and one-tenth of an ephah of meal and one lug of oil, without any wine, were, according to the opinion of the sages, not in need of a seal, because the seal inscribed "kid," which they received when bringing the sheep, was sufficient for the other purpose. Ben Azai, however, says, that another seal was necessary, and that an extra seal marked "poor sinner" was given, which was intended as a sign that no wine was necessary. The tradition of Ben Azai, that the seals were inscribed in Aramaic characters, is also true, because, prior to the introduction of the Greek language, all the writing in the Temple was done in Aramaic. (See the mentioned work of Büchler.)

MISHNA *e*. * Providing only the surplus amounted to exactly the amount paid for the seal.

called chamber of the silent, the other chamber of utensils. In the former, devout men secretly gave charitable gifts, and the poor of good family received there secretly their sustenance. In the other chamber, every one who desired to offer a utensil voluntarily, laid it down. Every thirty days the treasurers opened the chamber, and every utensil found to be fit for the maintenance of the Temple was preserved, while the others were sold and the proceeds went to the treasury for the maintenance of the Temple.*

MISHNA *f.* * In the Palestinian Talmud in this chapter (Halakha 15), many legends are related illustrating this Mishna.

CHAPTER VI.

MISHNA: (*a*) There were thirteen curved chests[1] and thirteen tables in the Sanctuary, and thirteen prostrations took place in the Sanctuary. The family of R. Gamaliel and of R. Hananiah, chief of the priests, made fourteen prostrations; this extra prostration was made towards the wood-chamber,[2] because, according to an ancestral tradition, the ark was hidden there.

(*b*) Once a priest[1] was engaged there, and he noticed that one of the paving-stones on one place appeared different from the others. He went out to tell others of it; but he had not yet finished speaking, when he gave up the ghost; thereby it was known to a certainty that the ark of the covenant[2] was hidden there.

(*c*) In what direction were the prostrations made? Four towards the north, four towards the south, three towards the east,

---

CHAPTER VI.

MISHNA *a*. [1] The thirteen chests were used as explained in Mishna *e*, and they were shaped like horns, so that a hand could not be inserted from the top. This Mishna places the number of everything at thirteen (on account of the thirteen kinds of mercy attributed to God). R. Ishmael composed the thirteen rules with which the Law is expounded.

[2] The location of the wood-chamber can be determined in Tract Midoth.

MISHNA *b*. [1] The priest was a man of blemish (deformed), and could not take part in the sacrifices, but was allowed to select and peel the wood used at the altar.

[2] The ark was hidden during the existence of the first Temple in order to save it from the Babylonians, after all hope had been abandoned, and its hiding-place was underground. The priests who subsequently took charge probably noticed some sign made by the former generation when the ark was hidden, and this particular priest died as a consequence of his attempt to reveal the secret.

and two towards the occident; *i.e.*, towards the thirteen gates.[1] The southern gates were near a corner of the western. These were: The upper gate, the fire gate, the firstling gate, and the water gate. Why is it called water gate? Because a glass of water was carried through it for the sprinkling of the altar on the Feast of Booths. R. Eliezer son of Jacob says: At that gate the waters (flowing from the Holy of Holies) commence to flow rapidly downwards, until they again flow out under the threshold of the Temple. Opposite there were the northern gates, near the other corner of the western. These were: The door of Jekhaniah, the gate of sacrifice, the women's gate, and the music-gate; and why is the first one called the gate of Jekhaniah? Because Jekhaniah went through it, when he went into exile. In the east was the gate Nikanur, which also had two small doors,[2] one to the right and the other to the left; lastly, there were two in the west, which were nameless.

(*d*) Thirteen tables were in the Sanctuary: Eight marble ones in the slaughter-house, on which the entrails were washed. Two to the west of the altar-sheep, one marble and one silver: on the marble one the sacrificial pieces were placed, and on the silver table the utensils were placed. Two in the corridor on the inside of the Temple entrance, a marble table and a golden one: on the marble one the showbreads were placed at the time they were brought in, and on the golden one when they were taken out; because the principle is, that the veneration of the

---

MISHNA *c.* [1] That there were thirteen gates in the Temple is vouched for by Abba Jose ben Johanan; but the sages declare, that there were only seven gates and that the thirteen prostrations were made in the direction of the twelve breaches made by the Greeks in the walls of the Temple at the time of the Maccabees, and towards the altar; the twelve breaches had been repaired, and each prostration was a mark of gratitude for the good fortune. From the fact, however, that the Mishna cites nine of the gates by their names and describes their location, it seems that Abba Jose ben Johanan was correct, and had his knowledge of the matter from tradition.

[2] Concerning the gate Nikanur, it is said that the two doors were made in the gate proper, because the gates were very heavy and it required a number of priests and Levites to open them (as explained in Tract Tamid). Hence, in order to facilitate entrance and egress, the two doors were added.

sacred must be heightened and not lessened.* Lastly, there was one golden table in the Temple itself, upon which the show-breads were constantly lying.

(*e*) Thirteen curved chests were in the Sanctuary.[1] On them was written: *Old* shekalim, *new* shekalim, bird-offerings, doves for whole-offerings, wood, incense, gold for the cover of the Holy of Holies. Six were for donations in general.[2] The term *new* shekalim is used for those paid annually. *Old* shekalim were those which were paid by men who had failed to pay them in the year when they were due, and paid them in the following year. "In those marked 'bird-offerings,' the money for turtle-doves was deposited; in those marked 'doves,' money for young doves was deposited: but they were all whole-offerings." So says R. Jehudah. The sages say: "In the former, money for both sin-offerings and whole-offerings was placed, and in the latter only for whole-offerings."[3]

MISHNA *d.* * Because the showbreads were lying on a golden table in the Temple, they were not to be placed on marble tables when taken out.

MISHNA *e.* [1] When a man paid his half-shekel in Jerusalem, he would go to the Temple and throw his half-shekel into the chest marked *new* shekalim. Into the chest marked *old* shekalim, such as had not given pledges for the payment of the Shekalim, and came voluntarily to pay same, would throw their half-shekel. One who wished to donate money for specific purposes, *e.g.*, for bird-offerings, etc., would deposit the money in the respectively marked chests.

[2] Only one of these chests was for donations in general. The other five were marked as follows: One, "For the remainder of a sin-offering," *i.e.*, money left over from a sum originally intended for the purchase of a sin-offering, was thrown into this chest and was used only for sin-offerings; the second, "for the remainder of guilt-offerings"; the third, "for the remainder of bird-offerings of women who had been confined and of persons suffering from venereal diseases"; the fourth, "for the remainder of Nazarite-offerings"; and the fifth, "for the remainder of offerings of those afflicted with sores." If any one had money left over from such offerings, he deposited it in the respectively marked cases. The contents of the chest marked "for donations in general" were used for the maintenance of the Temple. (Maimonides.)

[3] R. Jehudah means to say, that a man who throws money into the chest marked "for bird-offerings" intends that his offerings

(*f*) If one vow, "I will furnish wood for the altar," he must not furnish less than two cords. If one vow (to furnish) incense, he must not furnish less than a handful. If one vow (to furnish) gold coin, he must not furnish less than a Dinar.[1] Six (chests) were for voluntary offerings. What was done with these? Whole-offerings were bought for these, the meat of which was sacrificed to God, but the hides belonged to the priests.[2] The following explanation was made by Jehoiada the high priest, of the expression [Lev. v. 19]: "It is a trespass-offering; he hath, in trespassing, trespassed against the Lord": The rule is: With everything coming in under the name of sin or guilt offering, whole-offerings are bought, the meat of which is offered up to God and the hides of which belong to the priests; hence the two expressions: A guilt-offering for God and a guilt-offering for the priests, as it is written [II Kings xii. 16]: "The money for trespass-offerings and the money for sin-offerings was not brought into the house of the Lord: it belonged to the priests."

---

should be for the altar only, and not for the benefit of those who eat sacrifices, while the sages differ with him, as stated in the Mishna.

MISHNA *f.* [1] In the preceding Mishna the remainder of offerings is treated of, and it made no difference how little the remainder was, it could be thrown into the chest. In this Mishna, the case of a man who vows to bring an offering is spoken of, and a minimum value is placed.

[2] Incidentally we are told that the meat of the sacrifices belonged to the Divinity, while the hides belonged to the priests; and what immense sums were realized from the sale of such hides may be gleaned from the mentioned "Priester und Cultus," by Büchler.

CHAPTER VII.

MISHNA: (*a*) If money is found between the chest marked "Shekalim" and that marked "voluntary offerings," it belongs to the chest marked "Shekalim" if it lies nearer to the same, and to the one marked "voluntary offerings" if it be nearer *that*. So also does it belong to the voluntary offerings if it be found midway between the two chests. Money found lying between the chests marked "wood" and "incense" belongs, if it be nearer the former, to the former; if nearer the latter to the latter, and also to the latter if found midway between the two. Money found lying between the chest marked "bird-offerings" and the one marked "doves" for whole-offerings belongs to the former if it be nearer the former; and if nearer the latter to the latter, and also to the latter if midway between the two. Money found between ordinary moneys and the moneys of the second tithes belongs, if nearer the former to the former; if nearer the latter to the latter, and also to the latter if found midway between the two.* The rule is:. One must be guided by the proximity, even in the case of the less important; but in the event of equidistance, (one must be guided) by the greater importance (of the moneys).

(*b*) Money found (in Jerusalem) on the place of the cattle-dealers is regarded as second tithe.[1] Money found on the Tem-

---

CHAPTER VII.

MISHNA *a*. * There are different degrees of sanctification attached to the several kinds of offerings, some greater and some lesser. In order not to appropriate money belonging to an offering of a greater degree of sanctification to one of a lesser degree, it was decided that proximity of the stray coins should govern the disposition of such money. Where, however, the money was equidistant, it was appropriated to the offerings of a greater degree of sanctification, and the degree may be determined from the Mishna itself.

MISHNA *b*. [1] Because it was rare for priests to visit the cattle-market, but the Israelites who at any time came to buy cattle for

ple-mount is ordinary.[2] Other money found in Jerusalem generally, during the festivals, is regarded as second tithe; at other times of the year as ordinary.[3]

(*c*) Meat found in the outer court (of the Temple) is considered whole-offering if in complete joints; if cut in pieces it is sin-offering.[1] Meat found in the city is considered peace-offering.[2] All such meat must be laid aside for putrefaction, and then be burned in the crematory. Meat found anywhere else in the land is prohibited (to be used) as carrion, if found in whole joints; if found cut in pieces, it may be eaten; and during the festivals, when a great deal of meat is on hand, even whole joints may be eaten.[3]

(*d*) Cattle found all the way from Jerusalem to Migdal Eder, and in the same vicinity in all directions, are considered, if male, as whole-offerings, and if female as peace-offerings. R. Jehudah

---

sacrifices generally bought the same with the money exchanged for their second tithes.

[2] Money found on the Temple-mount was presumably dropped there by priests. It never occurred that a priest should carry money belonging to the treasury about with him; for even if he drew some money for the purpose of purchasing necessaries, he immediately turned it over to the vender. Hence, any money which a priest may have lost was his own, and ordinary.

[3] During the festivals, when all the Israelites congregated in Jerusalem, they brought money only to expend for their second tithes, hence money found in any place is considered as second tithes.

MISHNA *c*. [1] Because whole-offerings were sacrificed in complete joints, but sin-offerings, which were eaten by the priests, were usually cut in pieces. Neither must be eaten, because it might be that the latter had been left over from the preceding day and should be burned; but the distinction is made simply in case one had eaten of the meat that was cut up. If he had eaten of the complete joint, he was certainly guilty, but if he had eaten of the cut meat, it could not be said positively that he was guilty.

[2] This must also not be eaten, because it may have lain more than two days and a night; but if it is eaten, no one is guilty.

[3] Incidentally the rule is laid down as to meat found anywhere in Palestine. If the meat is found in whole joints, it is presumed to be carrion left for dogs, and must not be eaten. During the festivals, when meat is plentiful, it is presumed to be slaughtered meat, and may be eaten.

says: "If they are fit for Passover-offerings they may be used for such purpose, providing Passover is not more than thirty days off." *

(*e*) In former days, the finder of such cattle was pledged until he brought the drink-offerings belonging to such sacrifices; every finder, however, letting such cattle stand and going on his way, the high court decreed, that the costs of the drink-offerings belonging thereto be defrayed out of the public money.

(*f*) R. Simeon says: Seven decrees were promulgated by that court, and the latter was one of them. Further: If a non-Israelite send whole-offerings with the necessary drink-offerings from over the sea, they are offered up; but if sent without the necessary drink-offerings, the costs of the latter are defrayed from public money. If, again, a proselyte died and left offerings, the drink-offerings, if also left by him, are offered up with the others; if not left, the costs of same are defrayed out of public money. It was also a decree of the court, that in the event of a high priest dying, the necessary meat-offering [Leviticus vi. 13] should be paid for out of the public treasury. R. Jehudah, however, declared, that this should be done at the expense of the heirs. In both cases a tenth of an ephah should be offered.

(*g*) Further, that the priests may (at the sacrificial meals) make use of the salt and the wood (from the sanctuary); that the priests do not commit a breach of trust when misusing the ashes of the red heifer[1]; lastly, that the public treasury reimburse

---

MISHNA *d*. * R. Jehudah states, that if the animal found was a yearling and a male, it is considered a Passover-offering, but may be sacrificed only as a peace-offering, because a Passover-offering must be intended for a stipulated number of persons. (See Exod. xii. 4.) The sages, however, say, that on account of the number of whole-offerings which were brought at the time, the animal found must not be eaten, for fear lest it be intended for a whole-offering and a grave offence be committed. Hence it should be sacrificed as a whole-offering only.

MISHNA *g*. [1] It was not allowed to appropriate any part of a sacrifice designated for some special use for any other purpose. If this was done, however, (unintentionally,) it was considered a trespass, and a trespass-offering had to be sacrificed as expiation for the sin. The ashes of the red heifer did not come under the above ruling

for paid bird-offerings that had become unfit.[2] R. Jose, however, says: "He who contracts for the furnishing of the bird-offerings must reimburse for the spoilt."

---

previously (for reason, see Siphri), but on account of the frequent misuse of those ashes a decree was promulgated placing them under the same ruling as other parts of sacrifices, which were not to be misappropriated. Subsequently, this Mishna teaches that, there being no further necessity for the precautionary measure, the decree was reversed and the ashes restored to their former insignificance. This was included among the seven decrees.

[2] A special decree had to be promulgated to cover this case. Had this not been done, contractors would have refused to furnish birds for offerings, because there were very many birds used, and it was burdensome to properly care for them. Still, R. Jose does not agree to this, claiming that the contractor might use it for other purposes and thus save the Sanctuary the loss. According to Maimonides, the Halakha prevails according to R. Jose.

CHAPTER VIII.

MISHNA: (*a*) All spittle[1] to be found in Jerusalem is considered clean, except such as is found at the upper market (for this place was secluded and those afflicted with venereal diseases were in the habit of going there). Such is the teaching of R. Meir. The sages say: In the middle of the street it is at ordinary times unclean, and at the sides of the streets, clean. During the festivals, spittle found in the middle of the street is clean; at the sides it is unclean, because such as are unclean on account of their minority usually walk at the sides of the street.

(*b*) All utensils found on the way towards the plunge-bath, in Jerusalem, are unclean; those found on the way from the plunge-bath are clean: for they were not carried down to the plunge-bath the same way that these were carried up from the plunge-bath. So teaches R. Meir. R. Jose says: "All are clean, with the exception of such baskets, spades, and pickaxes as are used for the bones of the dead." *

CHAPTER VIII.

MISHNA *a*. [1] Concerning this spittle, see Leviticus xv. 8. It being impossible that, of all the people congregated in Jerusalem at the times of the festivals, there should not be some who had running issues and whose spittle was unclean, regulations were made where such men were to walk and where not. These regulations are cited by the Mishna. R. Meir said, that the upper market was the place designated for them, but the sages differ with him, and say, that the regulation was for the healthy men to walk in the middle of the street and the unclean at the sides during the festivals; but the whole year, the order was reversed. It is therefore self-evident, that, wherever the unclean walk, one is liable to contract uncleanness.

MISHNA *b*. * This Mishna is explained by Maimonides and translated by Yost in a different manner than we have rendered it; namely: "All utensils found wrong side up on the way to the plunge-bath are unclean, and those found right side up are clean." This

(*c*) If a butchering-knife be found on the fourteenth day of Nissan, a Passover-offering may be slaughtered with it forthwith. If it be found on the thirteenth, it must be again submerged.* A severing-knife must be submerged both if found on the thirteenth or fourteenth. If the fourteenth, however, fall on a Sabbath, it may be used for slaughtering forthwith; so also if it be found on the fifteenth: if it be found together with a butchering-knife, it is treated just like the latter.

(*d*) If a curtain in the Sanctuary become defiled through some minor uncleanness,[1] it is submerged on the inside of the outer court, and may be put back in its place; if it become defiled through a principal uncleanness, it must be submerged on the outside and then stretched on the rampart, because sunset must be awaited. At the time it is submerged for the first time (when new), it should be spread out on the roof of the gallery, in order that the people may see the beauty of the work.

(*e*) R. Simeon, son of Gamaliel, says in the name of R. Simeon, son of the assistant high priest, that the curtain was one

---

explanation is very complicated, and not in accordance with the literal text and other sources of explanation. Hence we simply translated the literal text and deem it correct. As for the last three articles, they are always unclean, on account of being used for bones of the dead; hence, in our opinion, they were never submerged. (See also commentary of Israel Lipshuetz, who also interprets it according to our explanation.)

MISHNA *c*. * A butchering-knife, being in constant use, is always considered clean, and hence there is no necessity of submerging it. If, however, it be found on the thirteenth, when there is still one day's time, it should be submerged for the sake of precaution. A severing-knife, however, is considered the same as any other vessel, and is treated accordingly.

MISHNA *d*. [1] For the explanation of the term "minor uncleanness," as used in this Mishna, it is necessary to state the different degrees of uncleanness, which are as follows: A corpse is called "the grandparent of uncleanness." One who touches a corpse becomes "a father of uncleanness"; anything touching the latter is, in turn, "a child of (or first of) uncleanness"; anything touched by this latter is a "second of uncleanness"; and so forth, "a third" and "a fourth." (See Tract Taharoth.) In this Mishna a minor uncleanness refers to a first of uncleanness, and a principal uncleanness to a father of uncleanness.

span thick, woven on seventy-two warp-cords, each cord twisted out of twenty threads; it was forty ells long and twenty ells wide, and made (worth) of eighty-two myriads (Dinars).* Two such curtains were made yearly: three hundred priests were required to submerge it.

(*f*) If meat of the Holy of Holies* became defiled, be it through a minor or a principal uncleanness, in the corridor or on the outside, according to the school of Shamai it must all be burnt in the court (in a place appointed for that purpose), except such as had been defiled by a principal uncleanness on the outside (of the court); according to the school of Hillel, everything is burnt on the outside except such as had been defiled by a minor uncleanness on the inside.

(*g*) R. Eliezer says: "Anything that has become defiled through a principal uncleanness, on the outside or on the inside, is burnt on the outside; anything that has become defiled through a minor uncleanness, either on the inside or the outside, must be burnt on the inside." R. Aqiba says: "In the place where a thing became defiled, there must it also be burnt."

(*h*) The joints of the daily sacrifice were laid down underneath the half of the altar-stairs on the westerly (according to others on the easterly) side; those of the additional offerings on the easterly (others say on the westerly) side. The sacrifices of the new moon were placed above the railing (others say beneath) on the altar.[1] The payment of Shekalim was only obligatory during the time that the Temple stood; the tithes from grain, cattle, and the deliverance of the firstlings were in force during the existence of the Temple and even after the Temple.[2]—If

---

MISHNA *e*. *The Palestinian Talmud asserts, that the amount of the cost of and the number of priests required to submerge the curtain is somewhat exaggerated; but, according to Dr. Büchler's "Priester und Cultus," the number of priests is not an exaggeration; and as for the cost, if the smallest existing coin be used for calculation (as in former times the sou in France, so also was the myriad mentioned in the Mishna), not even the sum will be exaggerated.

MISHNA *f*. *For instance, the meat of the sacrifice mentioned in Leviticus vii. 6.

MISHNA *h*. [1] This will be explained in Tract Midoth.

[2] Because the Levites received their sustenance from this source, and having inherited no land from their ancestors, they were sup-

one sanctify Shekalim or firstlings, they are considered sanctified. R. Simeon says: "If one say, firstlings shall be holy, they are not sanctified (because no Temple exists)."

---

ported even after the destruction of the Temple by the same means. The details will be found in Tracts Becharath, Maasroth, etc.

APPENDIX TO CHAPTER VI., MISHNA *a*.

FROM the teaching of this Mishna, we may conclude that the number system of Pythagoras was known and prevailed in the times of the Sages of the Mishna, and accordingly the number 13 was deemed inauspicious even in the earliest days.

Therefore many religious ceremonies were established with the express view of convincing the people of the absurdity of their belief.

It also seems probable that the Sages themselves entertained the superstition, and that they adopted the number 13 in the religious ceremonies as a cure for the mischief believed to have been produced by the inauspicious number.

TRACT ROSH HASHANA

(NEW YEAR).

OPINIONS.

Des Kaiserlichen Rath,
Prof. M. Lazarus, Ph. D., D. D.

Berlin, Koenigsplatz 5.
July 20, 1885.

Dear Mr. Rodkinson:—

In reply to your kind favor of the 14th inst., I wish to say that I read your editorial in No. 298 of הקול with attention and pleasure, but it left me with a regretful feeling. I am delighted to see an idea expressed which affects a great and highly important concern of Judaism, and am saddened by the reflection that in all probability, I shall not live to see its realization.

At some time or other your plan must and will be executed, but only by means of the union and cooperation of a number of competent scholars, who in turn must have the necessary financial support of a large circle of well to do Jewish patrons. Unfortunately, Jews of both circles are possessed of deplorable indifference, while, on the other hand, those that regard the Talmud as a source of knowledge, or use it as such, are dominated by a petty spirit— they lack the broad, liberal conception of historical development which is a prime qualification for success in planning and executing a work of the kind suggested.

However, I shall greet with delight any contribution to its ultimate realization. But I am forced regretfully to decline to take interest or active part in any new undertaking. As it is, I am groaning under a burden of public duties, which I can in no wise lessen. Courage and inclination fail me for new projects, more particularly in cases when the participation of scholars is a highly improbable contingency.

With best wishes for your recovery,

Respectfully,
LAZARUS.

Rev. Dr. M. Jastrow,
Rabbi of "Rodeph Shalom" Cong.
of Philadelphia.

Germantown, October 5, 1894.

Dear Sir!

At your request I take pleasure in stating my opinion that your planned edition of an abridged Talmud will be a great benefit to students who will be spared the wading through the intricate discussions frequently interspersed without direct bearing on the subject treated. An English translation of the book so abridged will then be, though not an easy, yet a possible labor.

Wishing your enterprise the full success it deserves, I am

Very Respectfully Yours,
M. JASTROW.

To Mr. Michael L. Rodkinson.

Prof. Dr. M. Mielziner
of Cincinnati.

Having perused some advance sheets of a part of the abridged Talmud edition which Mr. Michael

L. Rodkinson is about to publish. I find his work to be very recommendable. Such a Talmud edition in which all unnecessary digressions and all disturbing interpolations are judiciously omitted and in which the text is provided with punctuation marks, will greatly facilitate the study of the Talmud especially for beginners.

I trust that the friends of our ancient literature will liberally support this scholar, and enable him to complete this useful work.

Dr. M. MIELZINER,
Prof. H. U. College.
Cincinnati, November, 1894.

Rev. Dr. Isaac M. Wise,
President of the Hebrew Union College of Cincinnati. Editor of "American Istaelite" & "Deborah".

Cincinnati, Ohio, Jan. 14, 1895.
Re. . . . . *)
Dear Sir:—

The bearer of this letter is the well known Mr. M. L. Rodkinson, whom I would recommend toy our special attention.

The work which Mr. Rodkinson is doing, correcting the text of the Talmud and translating it into English is a gigantic enterprise which only such a man would and could undertake. If he succeeds it will give another life to American Judaism both here and abroad.

The question can only be, will he succeed? can he accomplish it? As far as his learning is concerned I am positive he can, and as to his energy I dare say he will; he is an indefatigable worker. We have the duty to afford him the opportunity to publish one volume, as a sample copy, to convince the world whether he is or he is not the man to accomplish this task.

To get him at present the financial support to publish Vol. I. is what I ask of you for him. If this volume is what he promises, he will be the man to accomplish the task. Yours,

ISAAC M. WISE.

*) We heartily thank the venerable writer of this letter for his kind permission to publish same, but the name of the gentleman to whom it was addressed need not be mentioned.

Rev. Dr. B. Szold,
Rabbi of the Cong. "Oheb Shalom" of Baltimore.

Baltimore, Jan. 16, 1895.
To all whom it may concern. *)

Rev. M. L. Rodkinson, a renowned Hebrew scholar of repute and ability happening to be in Baltimore called on me in connection with his project of editing his work to be known as the "Ancient short Talmud". He laid before me a number of Hebrew proof sheets of the Treatise "Berechoth" and the whole of the Treatise "Sabbath" in Manuscript, and asked me to read with an eye of a critic his work, to the end that if it appeared to me valuable I should testify to the its merit and its purpose.

I very carefully read 16 chapters of the M.S. of treatise Sabbath and it affords me the greatest pleasure that I not only conscientiously consider the work of extraordinary

*) Extract from the Original in Hebrew.

merit and value at this time, but that I was exceedingly pleased to find that the editor has carefully arranged the text of the Talmud most consecutively and logically.

He facilitates the reading of the Talmud considerably on account of this excellent orderly arrangement. The commentary of Rashi was also arranged to meet the requirements suiting this edition and the editor has not added any explanations of his own, nor altered the wording of the text.

Although the contents of the Talmud were familiar to me from my youth, yet this new arrangement makes delightful reading and brought new light. The reader can now read the text intelligently, for it seems as if the waters of the Talmud flow directly from their source, and therefore it is with the sincerest pleasure that I hope the work will meet with the greatest success.

Every scholar will readily understand the necessity of such an admirable work at the present time, when the study of the Talmud in its voluminous shape will not without deep and difficult study infuse the student with a knowledge of all its intricacies and fine points. In the Talmud as formulated and abridged by Mr. Rodkinson, however, where all unnecessary repetitions and dispensible debates are discarded, the student will be able to gain a fair knowledge of all desirable and attractive points at the cost of very little time and trouble.

These considerations have constrained me to overstep my well defined limitations, and to beg all friends of our nationality and its estimable old literature to encourage and aid this able author to the end, that success may crown his valuable and much desirable efforts in this direction.

Let this tribute of mine to truth and righteousness be a testimonial for the coming generations of the high esteem felt by our contemporaries of the 19th century, toward the Talmud and our National traditions and how ready we were to encourage those who made the Talmudical study the aim of their existence.

With the assurance of the satisfactory results which will obtain to all Talmudical students by a perusal of this abridged Talmud.

I am very respectfully,

B. SZOLD.

Rev. Dr. K. Kohler,
Rabbi of the Cong. "Beth-El" of New York.

New York, Febr. 12th, 1895.

Dear Sir!

I gladly and heartily indorse the opinion expressed by Prof. Lazarus and the Rev. Drs. Jastrow, Mielziner and Szold, as to the merits of your planned edition of the Talmud. I also consider an abridged edition of the Talmud while omitting the many interpolations which tend to confuse the reader and facilitating the study by the addition of modern punctuation marks, would render the reading of the difficult passages a pleasure rather than a task, a benefit for the scholarly world both

Jews and Gentiles, and I can only recommend the undertaking of the work to the support of generous-hearted patrons of our so little subsidized Jewish literature.

Dr. K. KOHLER.

To Michael L. Rodkinson.

Rev. Dr. Felsenthal,
Rabbi of the Cong. "Zion" of Chicago.

Chicago, Febr'y 14, 1895.

Mr. Michael L. Rodkinson,
New York City.

Dear Sir:—

The fact cannot be denied that the Talmud, as it has been handed down to us, is very voluminous, and that furthermore, by the intricacies of the dialectics prevailing therein and by the labyrinthical methods pursued in the same, it cannot be fully mastered except by scholars who devote their lives, their days and their nights, almost exclusively to the study of this grand branch of ancient literature. In our present times and in countries where of necessity all students, rabbis included, have to pursue other branches of learning also, such an exclusive devotion to Talmudical studies is out of the question. For the majority of the students, and especially for those who, in colleges or in other ways, begin to study the Talmud, an abridgment of the same — such an abridgment by which the more important parts of the Talmud would be contracted into a narrower compass and many of its difficulties would be avoided — will be very desirable, especially if by the inserting of punctuation marks into the text and by explatory notes at the bottom of its pages or at the end of the various volumes the reading and the understanding of the talmudical extracts will be facilitated.

I would recommend therefore your intended publication of an epitomized Talmud to all friends of Jewish literature in general and to students of Theological Colleges especially. And may the wealthier ones among our coreligionists, even if they themselves are personally unable to read and enjoy such literature, nevertheless patronize your great undertaking and follow the example given by the wealthy merchants among the Zebulunites who supported the less wealthy students of our sacred literature belonging to the tribe of Issachar.

May you then succeed in furnishing us with an abridged Talmud in which especially the pedagogical requirements of a work of this kind will have been satisfied!

Respectfully,
B. FELSENTHAL.

Rev. M. Friedman,
Lector of the "Beth Hamedrash" of Vienna.

The Rev. M. L. Rodkinson,*)

Yours to hand, and I take this opportunity to inform you that I have read your article and heartily agree with you in most of your conclusions, although I beg to differ in regard to some omissions you made from my text, which I consider valuable and should have been left intact. However, the subject is of no importance and more of an academical than practical merit. As a rule, those who are rich in material wealth are poor in educational resources, and the rich in knowledge are poor in wordly possessions in verification of the Prophecy: for the wisdom of their wise men shall perish, and the understanding of their men shall be hid. (Isaiah, XXIX, 14.) and although you are not well versed in sacred mysteries(your own confession) yet you will I surmise readily understand the secret of "hid"

Yours very truly,
MEYER FRIEDMAN.

---

*) Translated from Hebrew which was published in the "Call" july 16, '85

As I am a stranger in America, I deem it advisable to give the opinion on my work expressed by European scholars ten years ago.

M. L. RODKINSON.

Letters from the celebrated physicist, Dr. A. Bernstein, founder of the Reform Congregation, and of "Das Volksblatt."

Dear Mr. Rodkinson :—

Accept my cordial thanks for your valuable work "Tefilla Lemoshe," which in many respects has given me valuable explanations of the development of the laws on "The wearing of the Tefillin."

I was exceedingly interested in your view on the influence of the Jewish Christian sect on the form of the "Tefillin," and the presentation of the laws relating to them. You would be doing signal service to science, if you were to continue your research on the Ebionites incidentally mentioned. The treatment of this theme would earn for you the gratitude of all men of science, and every layman should consider it a privilege to contribute to an undertaking of the kind.

Sincerely yours,
DR. A. BERNSTEIN.

Gr. Lichtenfeld, near Berlin,
23, 10, 1883.

Have you finished my "Abraham, Isaac and Jacob?" I should like to hear your opinion of it.

To Dr. Ritter, preacher of the Reform Congregation in Berlin.

Esteemed Sir:—

Many thanks for your New Year's sermon, the receipt of which pleased me the more, as I am unfortunately prevented by illness from leaving the house, and cannot hope to enjoy your addresses at first hand at the proper time and place. Permit me to address a question to you.

I have read "Tefilla Lemoshe," by Mr. Rodkinson, which you sent me, and find that since our Holdheim's most productive time no polemic work of such learning and judgment has appeared against orthodoxy. The author has planned other works of similar character, and I beg leave to ask you whether you do not consider it the duty of our congregation to support him in their execution.

It is a fact, of which I have been painfully aware since the last twenty years, that our congregation subsists on the "works of our fathers," without bearing in mind that our reason for existence is the promotion of the reform of Judaism. If we have come to a standstill in this endeavor, it continues to be our duty to support men who, like Mr. Rodkinson, fulfill their original mission by the aid of varied attainments and talents.

Were I not hindered by illness, I would plead his cause personally. At the end of my life I feel it more keenly than ever that I who was active in the matter from the first, must remember the saying, "To him who begins a work, we say, finish it."

I cherish the hope that you will succeed in obtaining at the proper place a realization of my wish.

With kindest regards,
Sincerely yours,
DR. A. BERNSTEIN.

Letter from the Rev. Dr. N. Brüll, Rabbi at Frankfort-on-the-Main.

Frankfort-on-the-Main,
August 4, 1883.

To Mr. M. L. Rodkinson, at Ems.

Esteemed Sir :—

I am in receipt of your valued letter addressed to me and my brothers, and take pleasure in saying the following in reply:

I have finished reading your valuable works on "Tefillin" from cover to cover with great attention. The novel and surprising views it contains will not fail to meet with careful consideration from the learned. It is a subject which latterly has been extensively treated by archæologists and historians, but by none so comprehensively and exhaustively as by yourself. Your plan and its mode of execution, your cautious use of the critical method, your precise analysis and profound understanding of the Talmudic passages and Mediæval literature applicable to the subject, the convenient arrangement of the material and the clear, excellent manner, might serve as models, for similar works. At present I must deny myself the pleasure of a detailed review, as I am very busy with literary work of different kinds. You may expect to see an exhaustive criticism of your book in the seventh volume of my "Jahrbuch" to appear early in 1884. In my brother's journal there will be a long notice in September or October, as all his space until then is occupied.

We have received Mr. L. Bing's work; it will receive a deserve by favorable notice.

I am with high regard,

DR. N. BRÜLL.

Letter of the Rev. Mr. Isidore, Chief Rabbi of France.

My dear Co-religionists:—

Mr. Rodkinson is a man of real merit, worthy of interest. His past and his present alike speak in his favor. He has written two works of permanent value, which throw light on two questions of prime importance to Judaism.

I should be glad to have him meet with a favorable reception at Paris.

ISIDORE,
Chief Rabbi of France.

P. S.—I have read with deep pleasure your work "Tefilla Lemoshe," and have taken three copies.

Letter of the learned philosopher and scholar, Dr. Steinthal, professor at the University of Berlin.

Berlin, W. Blumeshof 8,
21, 10, 1888.

Dear Sir:—

You wish to have my opinion on your work "Tefilla Lemoshe." I herewith give it to you gladly, and in so doing I do not believe myself guilty of judging matters with which I am not familiar.

I am particularly fond of works like yours, works, I mean, in which the meaning and history of religious thoughts and ceremonies are presented in a strictly scientific way. Such investigations are not only attracted from a psychologic, but also of the highest importance from a religious, point of view; they protest, or liberate us from superstition, and strengthen true religiousness.

Your work appears to me to be thorough; it shows how the Tefillin arose in the course of centuries, develops their history, and their changes in form. Whether you have quoted all the passages in our literature relating to Tefillin, I cannot say. But, in my opinion there are passages of such indisputable importance, that the meaning of all others depends upon theirs. A passage of that kind is the one you quote from the "Semag."

I wish to make one remark. According to my view, also, the "Tefillin" can be derived from no Biblical passage. The well-known verses supposed to refer to the Tefillin have only a symbolic meaning. The argument that *Uqshartem* is followed by *Ukhthabhtem* is not valid, for the latter is also to be taken symbolically. Or, has the law ever been written on doorposts in its entirety, or even Deuteronomy?

On doorposts as little as on hearts, but in hearts!

I wish your work this success: that henceforth a Jew who uses the phylacteries will not call one who does not use them an atheist; that he who obeys this custom hallowed by tradition does it, not as the fulfillment of a command, but as a voluntary clinging to a ceremony, by which he wishes to remind himself most impressively of the religious and moral principles that are to guide him.

May this, as well as all hopes cherished by you and me and all good Jews, be realized. Yours,

PROF. STEINTHAL.

NAMES OF SUBSCRIBERS.

We feel, at this issue, that we should publish a list of names of all who have thus far given us their aid, in the form of subscriptions to our undertakings. We cannot but feel that this edition of the Talmud is destined to become historic, and we are proud to perpetuate the names of those who extended us their warm support at the beginning of our vast enterprise. We regret that time has not permitted us to visit even our friends in New York, much less seek subscriptions there. The subscribers to date follow here, but subsequently we shall publish the names of all who contribute to this work.

PAID IN FULL FOR THE HEBREW AND ENGLISH COPIES.

Hon. Judge Sulzberger, (3 copies) $70.00
Rev. Dr. M. Jastrow, the late Simon Muhr, Philip Lewin, Charles J. Cohen, Morris Newberger, Simon B. Fleisher, Marks Bros., all of Philadelphia . . . 25.00 each
Rev. Dr. Isaac M. Wise (Cincinnati), Hon. Oscar Straus, Hon. Nathan Straus, Edward Lewison (New York), 25.00 each

PAID IN ADVANCE FOR ONE COPY OF HEBREW AND ENGLISH:

Rev. Dr. Jacob Vorsanger of San Francisco, William Rayner and Alfred Ullman (Baltimore), Moses Klein, S. L. Bloch, L. M. Leberman, A. Kaufman (Philadelphia), Rev. Henry Cohen (Galveston), I. B. Kleinert (New York) . . . . $10.00 each

SUBSCRIPTION PAID FOR THE ENGLISH TRANSLATION.

Rev. Dr. Krauskopf, Rev. Dr. Berkowitz, Rev. W. Loewenburg, Wm. B. Hackenburg, J. Kriger, Simon Miller, Morris Stern, H. B. Blumenthal, Henry Jonas, D. Teller, M. Mayer, J. Gerstley, Edwin Wolf, M.

B. Loeb, R. Blum, Herman Jonas, M. Pfaelzer, A. B. Loeb, D. W. Amram, J. Morwitz, W. Lichten, A. Hess, J. K. Arnold, M. H. Pulaski, J. Bacher, Dr. M. Franklin, Dr. L. W. Steinbach, Dr. J. L. Salinger, B. Kirschbaum, Dr. C. J. Spivak, M. Behal, E. Lederer, B. F. Greenewald, M. H. Stern, S. Klopfer, Morris Rosenberg (all of Philadelphia), $5.00 each

Rev. Dr. Szold, Rabbi T. Shanfarber, Rabbi Rosenau, Rev. A. Kaiser, Dr. A. B. Arnold, Isaac Strauss, Henry Sonnenberg, W. L. Wolf, A. Hantz Bros., Wm. Fisher, Mrs. G. Blum, J. Mann, G. Erlanger, Ph. Hamburger, Mrs. Joel Gutman, E. Greenbaum, D. Greenbaum, S. Frank, B. Cohen (all of Baltimore). . . . . 5.00 each

Rev. Dr. D. Philipson, Dr. M. Mielziner, Dr. G. Deutsch, M. Bettmann, Julius Freiberg (all of Cincinnati, O.) 5.00 each

Rev. Dr. K. Kohler, Dr. H. Baar, A. Solomon, Hon. M. Ellinger, Rev. Dr. M. H. Harris, Rev. Dr. S. H. Sonneschein, Rev. Dr. R. Grossman, C. Weingart, D. P. Hays, C. Sulzberger, Isaac Muslimer (all of New York). . . . . 5.00 each

We are also glad to be afforded a long awaited opportunity to express our heartfelt gratitude to the reverend gentlemen of the several cities visited by us during the year 1893, for their generous efforts in our behalf, both for their own subscriptions and also for soliciting the aid and support of their friends for our forthcoming works. In this connection we wish to inform our subscribers to the second revised edition of our History of Amulets that, owing to circumstances beyond our control, we are compelled to delay its publication for the present, although it is already in the hands of the printer, and shall, in its stead, forward to our subscribers this edition of the Talmud, subject, however, to their approval.

We take the pleasure to record the names of the following Rabbis and gentlemen with accounts received from them, with the assurance that we shall ever remember them with gratitude and thanks.

Rev. Dr. J. L. Leucht (New Orleans) and ten subscribers .	$110.00
Rev. Dr. M. Heller (New Orleans) and nine subscribers .	90.00
Rev. H. Cohen (Galveston) and seventeen subscribers . . .	101.00
Rev. Dr. Chapman (Dallas) and two subscribers	40.00
Rev. H. Bien (Vicksburg) and four subscribers	25.00
Rev. Saenger (Shreveport) and four subscribers	20.00
Rev. Dr. Samfield (Memphis) and four subscribers	25.00
Rev. C. Rubenstein (Little Rock) and ten subscribers . . .	52.00
Rev. Dr. Schulmann (Kansas City) and eight subscribers .	38.00
Per J. Half (Houston)	30.00

The address of the Editor is:

399 W. Sixth Street, CINCINNATI, O.

A FEW WORDS TO THE ENGLISH READER.

BY

MICHAEL L. RODKINSON.

The Hebrew edition of this work contains an elaborate introduction in three chapters, the translation of which does not appear here. Its contents include many important rules which we have followed in this work, but we do not feel called upon at this time to engross the time of the English reader by reciting them. We, however, deem it a duty to say a few words so that the reader may understand our position, and the reason that we have undertaken a work that cannot prove financially profitable, and that will probably be productive of much adverse criticism in certain quarters.

The fate of the Talmud has been the fate of the Jews. As soon as the Hebrew was born,* he was surrounded by enemies. His whole history has been one of struggle against persecution and attack. Defamation and deformation have been his lot. So, too, has it been with the Talmud. At the beginning of its formative period it was surrounded by such enemies as the Sadducees, the Boëthusians, and other sects. When its canon was fixed the Karaites tried to destroy or belittle its influence, and since that time it has been subjected to an experience of unvarying difficulty. Yet, with remarkable truth the words of Isaiah [xliii. 2] may be applied to both, "When thou passest through the waters, I will be with thee; and through the rivers, they shall not overflow thee; when thou walkest through the fire, thou shalt not be burned; neither shall the flame kindle upon thee." There is, however, one point concerning which this simile is not true. The Jew has advanced; the Talmud has remained stationary.

Since the time of Moses Mendelssohn the Jew has made vast strides forward. There is to-day no branch of human activity in which his influence is not felt. Interesting himself in the affairs of the world, he has been enabled to bring a degree of intelligence and

---

* Vide Genesis xliii. 32.

industry to bear upon modern life, that has challenged the admiration of the world. But with the Talmud, it is not so. That vast encyclopedia of Jewish lore remains as it was. No improvement has been possible; no progress has been made with it. Reprint after reprint has appeared, but it has always been called the Talmud Babli, as chaotic as it was when its canon was originally appointed.* Commentary upon commentary has appeared, yet the text of the Talmud has not received that heroic treatment that will alone enable us to say that the Talmud has been improved. Few books have ever received more attention than this vast storehouse of Jewish knowledge. Friends and enemies it has had. Attack after attack has been made upon it, and defence after defence made for it; yet whether its enemies or its defenders have done it more harm, it would be hard to tell. Not, forsooth, that we do not willingly recognize that there have been many learned and earnest spirits who have labored faithfully in its behalf, but for the most part, if the Talmud could speak it would say, "God save me from my friends!" For the friends have, generally, defended without due knowledge of the stupendous monument of Rabbinical lore; and the enemies have usually attacked it by using single phrases or epigrams disconnected from their context, and which could be used to prove anything. In both cases, ignorance has been fatal. For how many have read all the Talmud through and are, thus, competent to judge of its merits! Is it right to attack or defend without sufficient information? Is it not a proof of ignorance and unfairness to find fault, with that of which we are not able to give proper testimony?

If those, especially, who attacked the Talmud and hurled against it venomous vituperation, would have had an intimate knowledge of it, would they, for example, believe that a work that in one part said, "When one asks for food, no questions may be asked as to who he is, but he must immediately be given either food or money," could be guilty of teaching the monstrous doctrines it is so frequently charged with? Could a work be accused of frivolity and pettiness that defines wickedness to be "the action of a rich man who hears that a poor man is about to buy a piece of property, secretly overbids him (Qiddushin 59a)? Could there be a higher sense of true charity than that conveyed by the following incident? Mar Uqba used to support a poor man by sending him on the eve of each Day of Atonement four hundred zuz. When the Rabbi's son took the money on one occasion, he heard the poor man's wife say, "Which wine shall I put on the table? Which perfume shall I

* Vide Introduction.

sprinkle around the room?" The son, on hearing these remarks, returned with the money to his father and told him of what he had heard. Said Mar Uqba, "Was that poor man raised so daintily that he requires such luxuries? Go back to him and give him double the sum!" (Ketuboth 7a). This is not recorded by the Talmud as an exception; but it is the Talmudical estimate of charity. The Talmud is free from the narrowness and bigotry with which it is usually charged, and if phrases used out of their context, and in a sense the very reverse from that which their author intended, are quoted against it, we may be sure that those phrases never existed in the original Talmud, but are the later additions of its enemies and ignoramuses. When it is remembered that until it was first printed, that before the canon of the Talmud was fixed in the sixth century, it had been growing for more than six hundred years (the Talmud was in manuscript for eight centuries), that during the whole of that time it was beset by ignorant, unrelenting and bitter foes, that marginal notes were easily added and in after years easily embodied in the text by unintelligent printers, such a theory as here advanced seems not at all improbable. In fact in this very volume we have an instance which has been retained only because of its usefulness, as an example. In Chapter III, the question is asked, "What is the measure of the cornet sound?" In characteristic phrasing the answer is given that R. Simon b. Gamliel * explained (PIRESH) that, etc., etc. The term here used is altogether un-Talmudical, and this is an illustration of a marginal note, later incorporated in the text.

The attacks on the Talmud have not been made by the enemies of the Jews alone. Large numbers of Jews themselves repudiate it, denying that they are Talmud Jews, or that they have any sympathy with it. Yet there are only the few Karaites in Russia and Austria, and the still fewer Samaritans in Asia Minor, who are really not Talmud Jews. Radical and Reform, Conservative and Orthodox not only find their exact counterparts in the Talmud, but also follow in many important particulars the practices instituted through the Talmud, *e. g.*, New Year's Day, Pentecost (as far as its date and significance are concerned), the QADDISH, etc., etc. The modern Jew is the product of the Talmud, which we shall find is a work of the greatest sympathies, the most liberal impulses, and the widest humanitarianism. Even the Jewish defenders have played into the enemy's hands by their weak defences, of which such expressions as

---

* In the Talmud only the initials of the name, R. S. b. G., are given, and these could stand for a number of names. It is usual to interpret these letters, as is done in this accompanying translation, but we are sure that R. Simeon b. Gamliel is not the commentator referred to.

"Remember the age in which it was written" or "Christians are not meant by 'gentiles,' but only the Romans, or the people of Asia Minor, etc.," may be taken as a type.

Amid its bitter enemies, and weak friends the Talmud has suffered a martyrdom. Its eventful history is too well-known to require detailing here. We feel that every attack on it, is an attack upon the Jew. We feel that defence by the mere citation by phrases is useless, and at the best weak. To answer the attacks made upon it through ludicrous and garbled quotations were useless. There is only one defence that can be made in behalf of the Talmud. Let it plead its own cause in a modern language!

What is this Talmud of which we have said so much? What is that work on which so many essays and sketches, articles and books have been written? The best reply will be an answer in negative form. The Talmud is not a commentary on the Bible; nor should the vein of satire or humor that runs through it be taken for sober earnestness. Nor is the Talmud a legal code, for it clearly states that one must not derive a law for practical application from any halakhic statement, nor even from a precedent, unless in either case it be expressly said that the law or statement is intended as a practical rule [Baba Bathra 130 b]. Further: R. Issi asked of R. Jo'hanan: "What shall we do if you pronounce a law to be a Halakha?" to which R. Jo'hanan replied: "Do not act in accordance with it until you have heard from me, 'Go and practice.'" Neither is the Talmud a compilation of fixed regulations, although the Shul'han Arukh would make it appear so. Yet, even when the Shulkhan Arukh will be forgotten, the Talmud will receive the respect and honor of all who love liberty, both mental and religious. It lives and will live because of its adaptability to the necessities of every age, and if any proof were needed to show that it is not dead, the attacks that are with remarkable frequency made on it in Germany might be given as the strongest evidence. In its day the Talmud received, not the decisions, but the debates of the leaders of the people. It was an independent critic, as it were, adapting itself to the spirit of the times; adding, where necessary to the teachings of former days, and abrogating also what had become valueless in its day. In other words the Talmud was the embodiment of the spirit of the people, recording its words and thoughts, its hopes and aims, and its opinions on every branch of thought and action. Religion and Ethics, Education, Law, History, Geography, Medicine, Mathematics, etc., were all discussed. It dealt with living issues in the liveliest manner and, therefore, it is living, and in reading it we live over again the lives of its characters.

Nothing could be more unfair, nothing more unfortunate than to adopt the prevailing false notions about this ancient encyclopedia. Do not imagine it is the bigoted, immoral narrow work that its enemies have portrayed it to be. On the very contrary; it is as free as the bird in its statements. It permits no shackles, no fetters to be placed upon it. It knows no authority, but conscience and reason. It is the bitterest enemy of all superstition and all fanaticism.

But why speak for it? Let it open its mouth and speak in its own defence! How can it be done? The Talmud must be translated into the modern tongues, and urge its own plea. All that we have said for it would become apparent, if it were only read. Translation! that is the sole secret of defence! In translating it, however, we find our path bristling with difficulties. To reproduce it as it is in the original is in our judgment an impossible task.. Men like Pinner and Rawicz have tried to do so with individual tracts and have only succeeded in, at the best giving translations to the world, which are not only not correct, but also not readable. If it were translated from the original text one would not see the forest through the trees. For, as we said above, throughout the ages there have been added to the text marginal notes, explanatory words, whole phrases and sentences inserted in malice or ignorance by its enemies and its friends.* As it stands in the original it is, therefore, a tangled mass defying reproduction in a modern tongue. It has consequently occurred to us that in order to enable the Talmud to open its mouth, the text must be carefully edited. A modern book, coustructed on a supposed scientific plan, we cannot make of it, for that would not be the Talmud; but a readable, intelligible work it can be made. We have, therefore, carefully punctuated the Hebrew text with modern punctuation marks, and have re-edited it by omitting all such irrelevant matter as interrupted the clear and orderly arrangement of the various arguments. In this way, there disappears those unnecessary debates within debates, which only serve to confuse and never to enlighten on the question debated. Thus consecutiveness has been gained, but never at the expense of the Talmud, for in no case have we omitted one single statement that was necessary, or of any importance. In other words we have merely removed from the text those accretions that were added from outside sources, which have proven so fruitful a source of misunderstanding and misrepresentation.

* In other of our works we have named these interpolators.

It may be asked who and what are we that we undertake so colossal a task? We are simply a lover of the Talmud, who believe that we have discovered its spirit. The liberal, free, tolerant, broad humanitarian spirit that pervades that spiritual encyclopedia has been shamefully misrepresented and it cries out for rectification. Scholar after scholar has tried to improve matters by weighty commentaries that have only made the already intricate more difficult of comprehension. For ten years we have asked through letters, periodicals and books for a synod of scholars to judge of our work, and determine how to deal with this case. We have not had our request granted until now and so we have decided to proceed with our work alone. We realize that it is by no means perfect, nor beyond criticism. The enterprise is vast; and he who undertakes it is single-handed. The difficulties to be overcome are incalculable, one of the greatest being that the work is absolutely unendowed, and we must, in addition to the important work of editing, travel hither and thither to collect funds with which to continue publication.

We continue our labors in the full and certain hope that, "he who comes to purify, receives Divine help" and that in our task of removing the additions made by the enemies of the Talmud, we shall be purifying it from the most fruitful source of the attacks made on it and thereunto we hope for the help of Heaven. As we have already said we feel that this work will not be received everywhere with equal favor. We could not expect that it would. Jewish works of importance have most usually been given amid "lightning and thunder," and this is not likely to prove an exception. Yet this we ask, that the reader believe that we have been actuated only by the love of the Talmud, to save it from its cruel enemies and weak friends, and to put it in such a position that it can plead its own cause in its own defence.

INTRODUCTION TO TRACT ROSH HASHANA (NEW YEAR'S DAY).

NOTWITHSTANDING the fact that in the history of every nation, especially such as has ever attained to an established form of government, the calendar is a matter of great importance, the Scriptures do not in any manner treat of the Jewish calendar. There cannot even be found a fixed time whence the commencement of the year should be reckoned, although there is this passage in Exodus (xii. 2): "This month shall be unto you the chief of months: the first shall it be unto you of the months of the year." Doubtless this may be assumed to point to the month of Nissan (about April), as not only the most important month, but also as the beginning of the year.

In another passage (Exod. xxiii. 16), however, we find it written: "And the feast of ingathering (Tabernacles), at the conclusion of the year." This would be a palpable contradiction to the previous passage, were it not for the fact that the words "*Betze'th Hashana*" (rendered as "at the conclusion of the year") in the quoted passage can be, with perfect accuracy, translated "during the year." While such a translation would clear away all doubt as to Nissan being the beginning of the year, it could under no circumstances be applied to the Feast of Tabernacles, which is neither "at the conclusion" of the year nor "during the year" (in the sense "when the year has advanced"), if the beginning of the year be Tishri (about September). Hence the passage should be translated: "And the feast of the ingathering, which had been completed at the conclusion of the year"; *i.e.*, in the months preceding the month of Tishri.

In the face of these contradictory terms, we must revert to historical facts which would support one or the other of the above assertions, and we find, that not only the Egyptian rulers, but also the Jewish kings since the time of Solomon, counted the beginning of the year of their accession from the month of

Nissan, while other Eastern potentates, such as the Armenian and Chaldean kings, counted the commencement of their year of accession from Tishri.

It is not certain whether the Israelites, after their conquest of Canaan, computed their calendar in conformity with that of the country whence they came or with that of the country they had conquered; but it is plain that in the Mishnaic period, or after the erection of the second Temple, they counted the beginning of the year from Tishri. It may be, however, that their kings, following the example of their predecessors, commenced counting the year of their accession from Nissan, and in all civil contracts and state documents, according to the existing custom, used dates to agree with Nissan as the first month of the year.

On the other hand, the priestly tithes, during the days of the erection of the second Temple, were payable in Elul (about August), which was considered the expiring season of the year, in order to prevent the confusion which might arise from mixing one year's tithes with those of the other. The priestly tithing of fruits was, however, delayed until Shebhat (about February), the time when the fruits had already matured on the trees, in order that the various tithes should not be confused and to prevent the priests and Levites from unduly interfering with the affairs of the people.

The prehistoric Mishna, which always formed the law, in conformity with the existing custom, and not *vice versa*,* found four different New Year's days in four different months, and, with the object in view of making the custom uniform in all Jewish communities, taught its adherents to observe four distinct New Year's days, at the beginning of the four respective months in which certain duties were accomplished. Thus the text of the opening Mishna of this tract, prior to its revision by Rabbi Jehudah Hanassi, read as follows: "There are four different New Year's days; viz., the first day of Nissan, the first of Elul, the first of Tishri, and the first of Shebhat." The different purposes for which these days were established as New Year's days were well known at that time, and it was therefore deemed unnecessary to specify them. At the time

---

* Facts corroborating this statement will be found in our periodical *Bakay*, Vol. II., p. 20 *et seq.*

of the new edition of the Mishna, by Rabbi Jehudah Hanassi (the Prince), when the Temple was out of existence, and consequently tithes were no more biblically obligatory (the authority of the priests having been abrogated and reverted to the house of David, the great-grandfather of the editor), the latter referring to the first day of Nissan and the first day of Elul as New Year's days, added, by way of commentary, the words, "for kings and cattle-tithe."

He also cited the opinions of R. Eliezer and R. Simeon, that the New Year's Day for cattle-tithe should not be celebrated separately, but on the general New Year's Day; viz., on the first day of Tishri, as under the then existing circumstances there was no necessity to guard against the confusion of tithes accruing from one year to the other. From this it may be concluded that R. Jehudah Hanassi, in citing the above opinions, alluded to them as being in conformity with his own opinion. To that end he also cites the opinions of the schools of Shamai and Hillel respectively.

From the statement in the Mishna to the effect that "there are four periods in each year on which the world is judged," it appears that in the Mishnaic period the New Year's day was considered a day of repentance; and since the principal features of repentance are devotion to God and prayers for forgiveness of sin, Rabbi states, in the Mishna, that devotion is the only requirement during the days of penitence, *i.e.*, the days between New Year's Day and the Day of Atonement. The legend relating that on the New Year's day books (recording the future of each person) were opened was yet unknown in Rabbi's time.

The story told by R. Kruspedai in the name of R. Johanan, that "on New Year's Day books are opened," etc., is taken from the Boraitha which teaches: "Three books are opened on the day of judgment." This Boraitha, however, does not refer to the New Year's day, but to the day of final resurrection, as explained by Rashi, and that R. Kruspedai quotes his story in the name of R. Johanan proves nothing; for in many instances where teachers were desirous of adding weight to their opinions, they would quote some great teacher as their authority. R. Johanan himself permitted this method.

After Rabbi Jehudah Hanassi had completed the proper Mishnaic arrangement regarding the number of New Year's days, making the principal one "the Day of Memorial" (the first of Tishri); after treating upon the laws governing the sounding of the cornet in an exceedingly brief manner—he dwells upon the custom in vogue at the Temple of covering the mouth of the cornet or horn with gold, and declares the duty of sounding the cornet properly discharged if a person passing by the house of worship can hear it.

He arranges the prayers accompanying this ceremony in a few words, and then dilates at great length upon the Mishnayoth treating of the lunar movements by which alone the Jews were guided in the arrangement of their calendar, upon the manner of receiving the testimony of witnesses, concerning the lunar movements, and upon the phases of the moon as used by Rabban Gamaliel. He then elaborates upon the tradition handed down to him from his ancestors (meaning thereby the undisputably correct regulations), and also upon the statutes ordained by R. Johanan ben Zakkai, enacting that the sages of each generation are the sole arbiters of all regulations and ordinances, and may themselves promulgate decrees even though the bases for such be not found in the Mosaic code.

He also confirms the right of the chief Beth Din (supreme court of law), but not of a lower Beth Din, of each respective period, alone to arrange the order of the holidays, on account of the already apparent discontent of the masses, who were bent upon taking the management of these subjects into their own hands.

Thus he dilates upon this feature with the minutest exactness and supports his assertions with the decision of his grandfather Rabban Gamaliel, as well as with the decisions of Rabbi Dosa ben Harkhinas and Rabbi Jehoshua, to the effect that each generation has only to look for guidance to the Beth Din existing in its own time, and that the opinion rendered by such a Beth Din is as binding and decisive as that of Moses, even though it appear to be erroneous.

Such are the contents of this tract, certainly most important from an historical and archæological point of view. Proceed, then, and study!

SYNOPSIS OF SUBJECTS

OF

TRACT ROSH HASHANA*

CHAPTER I.

MISHNA I. The first Mishna ordains New Year's Days, viz.: For kings, for the cattle-tithe, for ordinary years, and for the planting of trees. A king who ascends the throne on the 29th of Adar must be considered to have reigned one year as soon as the first of Nissan comes. The Exodus from Egypt is reckoned from Nissan. When Aaron died Sihon was still living. He heard that Aaron was dead and that the clouds of glory had departed. The rule about Nissan only concerned the kings of Israel; but for the kings of other nations, they reckoned from Tishri. Cyrus was a most upright king, and the Hebrews reckoned his years as they did those of the kings of Israel. One is guilty of procrastination. Charity, tithes, the gleanings of the field, that which is forgotten to be gathered in the field, the produce of corners of the field.

One is culpable if he does not give forthwith that which he has vowed for charity. In the case of charity it must be given immediately, for the poor are always to be found. The Feast of Weeks falls on the fifth, sixth, or seventh of Sivan.

How the law against delay affects a woman. In which month is grain in the early stage of ripening? Only in the month of Nissan. It is also the New Year for leap-year and for giving the half-shekels. Congregational sacrifices brought on the first of Nissan should be purchased with the shekels raised for the New Year. He who lets a house to another for a year must count (the year) as twelve months from day to day; but if the lessee says (I rent this house) "for *this* year," even if the transaction takes place on the first of Adar, as soon as the first of Nissan arrives the year (of rental) has expired. The first of Tishri is the New Year for divine judgment. At the beginning of the year it is determined what shall be at the end of the year. The Supreme Court in Heaven does not enter into judgment until the Beth

---

* See introduction to synopsis of Tract Sabbath, Vol. I., p. xxix.

Din on earth proclaims the new moon. Israel enters for judgment first. If a king and a congregation have a lawsuit, the king enters first. From New Year's Day until the Day of Atonement, slaves used not to return to their (own) homes; neither did they serve their masters, but they ate and drank and rejoiced, with the crown of freedom on their heads. R. Eliezer says, that the world was created in Tishri. R. Joshua says, that the world was created in Nissan. Says R. Joshua, God grants the righteous the fulfilment of the years of their life to the very month and day. Sarah, Rachel, and Hannah were visited on New Year's Day. Joseph was released from prison on New Year's Day. On New Year's Day the bondage of our fathers in Egypt ceased. The Jewish sages fix the time of the flood according to R. Eliezer, and the solstices according to R. Joshua; but the sages of other nations fix the time of the flood also as R. Joshua does. Whoso vows to derive no benefit from his neighbor for a year must reckon (for the year) twelve months, from day to day; but if he said "for this year," if he made the vow even on the twenty-ninth of Elul, as soon as the first of Tishri comes that year is complete. The New Year for giving tithes is for a tree from the time the fruits form; for grain and olives, when they are one-third ripe; and for herbs, when they are gathered. R. Aqiba picked the fruit of a citron-tree on the first of Shebhat and gave two tithes of them, . 1–20

MISHNA II. At four periods in each year the world is judged. All are judged on New Year's Day and the sentence is fixed on the Day of Atonement. R. Nathan holds man is judged at all times. God said: "Offer before Me the first sheaf of produce on Passover, so that the standing grain may be blessed unto you. Recite before Me on New Year's Day the Malkhioth, that you proclaim Me King; the Zikhronoth, that your remembrance may come before Me, for good, and how (shall this be done)?" By the sounding of the cornet. Three circumstances cause a man to remember his sins. Four things avert the evil decree passed (by God) on man; viz., charity, prayer, change of name, and improvement. Some add to these four a fifth —change of location. Three books are opened on New Year's Day: one for the entirely wicked, one for the wholly good, and one for the average class of people. The school of Hillel says: The most compassionate inclines (the scale of justice) to the side of mercy. Who are those who inspire their fellowmen with dread of them? A leader of a community who causes the people to fear him over-much, without furthering thereby a high purpose. The legend how R. Joshua fell sick and R. Papa went to visit him. The Holy One, blessed be He, wrapped Himself, as does one who recites the prayers for a congregation, and pointing out to Moses the regular order of prayer, said to him: "Whenever Israel sins, let him pray to Me after this order, and I shall pardon him." Prayer is helpful for man before or after the decree has been pronounced. The legend of a certain family in Jerusalem whose members died at eighteen years of age. They came and informed R. Johanan ben Zakkai. The Creator sees all their hearts (at a glance) and (at once) understands all their works, . 20–28

MISHNA III. Messengers were sent out in the following six months: in Nissan, Abb, Elul, Tishri, Kislev, and in Adar. The legend of the king (of Syria who had earlier) issued a decree forbidding the study of the Torah among the Israelites, or to circumcise their sons, and compelling them to desecrate their Sabbath. Judah b. Shamua and his friends cried aloud: "O heavens! Are we not all brethren? Are we not all the children of one Father?" etc. Samuel said: "I can arrange the calendar for the whole captivity." Rabha used to fast two days for the Day of Atonement. Once it happened that he was right, ... 29-34

MISHNAS IV. to VII. For the sake of (the new moon), of the two months Nissan and Tishri, witnesses may profane the Sabbath. Formerly they profaned the Sabbath for all (new moons), but since the destruction of the Temple they instituted that (witnesses) might profane the Sabbath only on account of Nissan and Tishri. It once happened that more than forty pair (of witnesses) were on the highway (to Jerusalem) on the Sabbath. Shagbar, the superintendent of Gader, detained them, and (when) R. Gamaliel (heard of it, he) sent and dismissed him. It once happened, that Tobias the physician, his son, and his freed slave saw the new moon in Jerusalem. The explanation of the passage Exodus xii. 1, by R. Simeon and the rabbis. Who are incompetent witnesses? Gamblers with dice, etc., . . 34-36

CHAPTER II.

MISHNAS I. to IV. If the Beth Din did not know (the witness), another was sent with him to testify in his behalf. It once happened that R. Nehorai went to Usha on the Sabbath to testify (to the character) of one witness. The legend how the Boëthusians appointed false witnesses. Formerly bonfires were lighted (to announce the appearance of the new moon); but when the Cutheans practised their deceit it was ordained that messengers should be sent out. There are four kinds of cedars. The whole country looked like a blazing fire. Each Israelite took a torch in his hand and ascended to the roof of his house. Great feasts were made for (the witnesses) in order to induce them to come frequently. How were the witnesses examined? The sun never faces the concave of the crescent or the concave of a rainbow. (If the witnesses say) "We have seen the reflection (of the moon) in the water, or through a metal mirror, or in the clouds," "their testimony is not to be accepted." The chief of the Beth Din says: "It (the new moon) is consecrated," and all the people repeated after Him: "It is consecrated, it is consecrated." Pelimo teaches: "When the new moon appeared at its proper time, they used not to consecrate it," 37-42

MISHNAS V. and VI. R. Gamaliel had on a tablet, and on the wall of his upper room, illustrations of the various phases of the moon. Is this permitted? Yea, he had them made to teach by means of them. It happened once, that two witnesses came and said: "We saw the moon in the eastern part in the morning and in the western part in the evening." R. Johanan b. Nuri declared them to be false witnesses. Two other witnesses came and said: "We saw the moon on its proper day, but could not see it on the next evening." R. Gamaliel received them; but R. Dosa b. Harkhinas said: "They are false witnesses." R. Joshua approved his opinion. Upon this,

Gamaliel ordered the former to appear before him on the Day of Atonement, according to his computation, with his staff and with money. What R. Joshua did, and what R. Aqiba and R. Dosa b. Harkhinas said about it. What R. Hiyya said when he saw the old moon yet on the morning of the twenty-ninth day. Rabbi said to R. Hiyya: "Go to Entob and consecrate the month, and send back to me as a password, 'David the King of Israel still lives.'" The consecration of the moon cannot take place at a period less than twenty-nine and a half days, two-thirds and .0052 (*i.e.*, seventy-three Halaqim) of an hour. Even if the commonest of the common is appointed leader by a community, he must be considered as the noblest of the nobility. A judge is to be held, "in his days," equal in authority with the greatest of his antecedents. Gamaliel said to R. Joshua: "Happy is the generation in which the leaders listen to their followers, and through this the followers consider it so much the more their duty (to heed the teachings of the leaders)," 42–44

CHAPTER III.

MISHNA I. If the Beth Din and all Israel saw (the moon on the night of the thirtieth day), but there was no time to proclaim, "It is consecrated," before it has become dark, the month is intercalary. When three who formed a Beth Din saw it, two should stand up as witnesses and substitute two of their learned friends with the remaining one (to form a Beth Din). No greater authority than Moses, our master, yet God said to him that Aaron should act with him. No witness of a crime may act as judge, but in civil cases he may, ... 45–46

MISHNAS II. to IV. Concerning what kind of cornets may be used on New Year's and Jubilee days. Some words in the Scripture which the rabbis could not explain, until they heard the people speak among themselves. The cornet used on the New Year was a straight horn of a wild goat, the mouthpiece covered with gold. The Jubilee and the New Year's Day were alike in respect to the sounding (of the cornet) and the benedictions, but R. Jehudah's opinion was different. R. Jehudah holds that on New Year's Day the more bent in spirit a man is, and on the Day of Atonement the more upright he is (in his confessions), the better; but R. Levi holds the contrary. "On the fast days two crooked ram's-horns were used, their mouthpieces being covered with silver." According to whom do we nowadays pray: "This day celebrates the beginning of thy work, a memorial of the first day"? It is unlawful to use a cornet that has been split and afterwards joined together. If one should happen to pass by a synagogue, or live close by it and should hear the cornet, he will have complied with the requirements of the law. If one covered a cornet on the inside with gold it might not be used. If one heard a part of (the required number of) the sounds of the cornet in the pit, and the rest at the pit's mouth, he has done his duty. If one blew the first sound (Teqia), and prolonged the second (Teqia) as long as two, it is only reckoned as one. If one who listened (to the sounds of the cornet) paid the proper attention, but he that blew the cornet did not, or *vice versa*, they have not done their duty until both blower and listener pay proper attention. If special attention in fulfilling a commandment or doing a transgression is necessary or not. As long as Israel looked to Heaven for aid, and directed their hearts devoutly to their Father in Heaven, they prevailed; but when they ceased to do so, they failed. All are obliged to hear the sounding of the cornet, priests, Levites, and Israelites, proselytes, freed slaves, a monstrosity, a hermaphrodite, and one who is half-slave and half-free. One may not say the benediction over bread for guests unless he eats with them, but he may for the members of the family, to initiate them into their religious duties, ... 46-52

CHAPTER IV.

MISHNAS I. to IV. Regarding if the New Year fall on Sabbath. Where the shofer (cornet) should be blown after the Temple was destroyed. What was the difference between Jamnia and Jerusalem? Once it happened that New Year's Day fell on the Sabbath, and all the cities gathered together. Said R. Johanan b. Zakkai to the Benai Betherah: "Let us sound (the cornet)!" "First," said they, "let us discuss!" R. Johanan b. Zakkai ordained that the palm-branch should everywhere be taken seven days, in commemoration of the Temple. Since the destruction of the Temple, R. Johanan b. Zakkai *ordained* that it should be prohibited (to eat of the new produce) the whole of the day of waving (the sheaf-offering). Once the witnesses were delayed in coming, and they disturbed the song of the Levites. They then ordained that evidence should only be received until (the time of) the afternoon service. Concerning what songs the Levites had to sing every day from the Psalms. What did the Levites sing when the additional sacrifices were being offered on the Sabbath? What did they sing at the Sabbath afternoon service? According to tradition, a corresponding number of times was the Sanhedrin exiled. The witnesses need only go to the meeting place (of the Beth Din). Priests may not ascend the platform in sandals, to bless the people; and this is one of the nine ordinances instituted by R. Johanan b. Zakkai, ... 53-57

MISHNA V. Regarding the order of the benedictions on New Year's Day at the morning prayer, additional prayers, and at what time the cornet must be blown, etc. What passages from the Scriptures are selected for additional prayers on New Year's Day. To what do the ten scriptural passages used for the Malkhioth correspond? How many passages must be recited from Pentateuch, Prophets, and Hagiographa? We must not mention the remembrance of the individual (in the Zikhronoth), even if the passage speaks of pleasant things. What are the passages which must be said in the benediction of Malkhioth, Zikhronoth, and the Shophroth? R. Elazar b. R. Jose says: "The Vathiqin used to conclude with a passage from the Pentateuch." "Hear, O Israel, the Lord our God is our Lord," may be used in the Malkhioth. The second of those who act as ministers of the congregation on the Feast of New Year shall cause another to sound the cornet on days when the Hallel (Service of Praise, Ps. cxiii.-cxviii.) is read.

"NEW YEAR."

CHAPTER I.

MISHNA. There are four New Year days, viz: The first of Nisan is New Year for (the ascension of) Kings * and for (the regular rotation of) festivals; † the first of Elul is New Year for the cattle-tithe, ‡ but according to R. Eliezer and R. Simon, it is on the first of Tishri. The first of Tishri is New Year's day, for ordinary years, and for the reckoning of the sabbatic years, § and jubilees; and also for the planting of trees, || and for herbs.¶ On the first day of Shebhat is the New Year for trees,** according to the school of Shammai; but the school of Hillel says it is on the fifteenth of the same month ††

GEMARA. "FOR KINGS." Why is it necessary to appoint such a day? R. 'Hisda answered, On account of documents.‡‡ The Rabbis taught: A king who ascends the throne on the 29th of Adar must be considered to have reigned one year as soon as the first of Nisan comes, but if he ascends the throne on the first of Nisan, he is not considered to have reigned one year until the first of Nisan of the following year. From this we infer that only Nisan is the commencement of years for kings (or the civil New Year's);

* It mattered not according to the sages at what period of the year a Jewish king ascended the throne, his reign was always reckoned from the preceding first of Nisan. If, for instance, a Jewish king began to reign in Adar, the eleven months before would be considered one year of the reign of the king just deceased, and the month of Adar would be considered one year of the new king's reign. The next first of Nisan would be the beginning of the second year of the king's reign. This rule had to be observed in all documents in which the year of the king's reign was mentioned.

† This refers to the law concerning vows. If one made a vow it had to be fulfilled before the three festivals elapsed in the order of Passover, Pentecost and Tabernacles.

‡ A date had to be appointed in order to keep the tithes of animals born and products of the earth, distinct from year to year.

§ Vide Lev. xxv. and Deut. xv.

|| With regard to the prohibition of eating fruit of newly planted trees [Lev. xix. 23-25].

¶ So as not to mix the tithe on herbs from year to year.

** With regard to the tithe due on fruit trees.

†† The Gemara fully discusses the reasons for these institutions, but we deem it wise to anticipate, for the sake of clearness.

‡‡ So that in the case of mortgages, one may know which is the first and which is the second by means of the year of the king's reign mentioned in the documents.

that even a fraction of a year is considered a year; and that if a king ascends the throne on the first of Nisan, he is not considered to have reigned one year until the next first of Nisan, although he may have been elected in Adar. The Boraitha * teaches this, lest one might suppose that the year should be reckoned from the day of election and therefore the king would begin his second year (on the first of Nisan following).

The Rabbis taught: If a king die in Adar and his successor ascends the throne in Adar (documents may be dated either) the (last) year of the (dead) king, or the (first) year of the new king. If a king die in Nisan, and his successor ascends the throne in Nisan, the same is the case. But if a king die in Adar, and his successor does not ascend the throne until Nisan, then the year ending with Adar should be referred to as the year of the dead king, and from Nisan it should be referred to as that of his successor.†

R. Jo'hanan says: Whence do we deduce that we reckon the commencement of years (for the reign) of kings, only from Nisan? It is said [1 Kings vi. 1] "And it came to pass in the four hundred and eightieth year after the children of Israel were come out of the land of Egypt, in the fourth year of Solomon's reign over Israel, in the month Ziv, which is the second month, etc." He institutes the following analogy between "the reign of Solomon" and "the Exodus from Egypt" mentioned in this passage: As the Exodus from Egypt is reckoned from Nisan, so also is the reign of Solomon reckoned from Nisan. But how do we know that the Exodus *even* should be reckoned from Nisan? Perhaps we should reckon it from Tishri! The facts of the case do not support such a presumption, for it is written [Numbers xxxiii. 38] "And Aaron, the Priest, went up into Mount Hor at the commandment of the Lord, and died there, in the fortieth year after the children of Israel were come out of the land of Egypt on the first day of the fifth month;" and it is written [Deut. i. 3] "And it came to pass in the fortieth year, in the eleventh month, on the first day of the month, Moses spake, etc." Since he mentions the fifth month, which is certainly Abh, and he speaks of (Aaron's death as happening in) the fortieth year (and not the forty-first year), it is clear that Tishri is not the beginning of years (for kings). This argument is acceptable as far as the former (Aaron's)

---

* The word Boraitha is derived from a root meaning "*external, foreign*," etc. It means the traditions and opinions of Tanaim not embodied in the Mishna as compiled by R. Judah Hannasi.

† No reference should be made after the first of Nisan to the reign of the king just deceased. For instance: it was not permitted to speak of the year beginning with Nisan, as the second year after the death of the king.

case is concerned, for the text specifically mentions (forty years after) the Exodus; but in the latter (Moses') case, how can we tell that (the fortieth year) means from the Exodus? Perhaps it means (the fortieth year) from the raising of the Tabernacle in the wilderness! The terms "fortieth year" (mentioned in connection with both Aaron and Moses) are compared by analogy; as in the former case it means forty years from the time of the Exodus, so also in the latter case. But whence do we know that the incident that took place in Abh (the death of Aaron) happened before that which is related (the speech of Moses) as happening in Shebhat? Perhaps the Shebhat incident happened first! It is not reasonable to suppose this; for it is written [Deut. i. 4] "After he had slain Sihon the king of the Amorites," and when Aaron died Sihon was still living. Thus it is written [Numbers xxi. 1] "And the Canaanite, the King of Arad heard." What did he hear? He heard that Aaron was dead and that the clouds of glory had departed (and he thought that anyone might go up and fight against Israel). How can we make any such comparison? In the one place it speaks of the Canaanite, and in the other, of Sihon! Yes, we can, for a Boraitha says that Sihon, Arad and the Canaanite are identical. This opinion of R. Jo'hanan is quite correct, for we find that a Boraitha quotes all the verses that he quotes here, and arrives at the same conclusion.

R. 'Hisda says: They taught this rule about Nisan only concerning the kings of Israel, but for the kings of other nations, they reckon from Tishri. As it is said: [Nehem. i. 1] "The words of Nehemiah, the son of Hakhaliah. And it came to pass in the month of Kislev, in the twentieth year, Hanani, one of my brethren, came, he and certain men of Judah," and it is written: [ibid. ii. 1] "And it came to pass in the month Nisan, in the twentieth year of Artaxerxes the king, etc." Since Hanani stood before Nehemiah in Kislev, and the Bible speaks of it as the twentieth year, and since Nehemiah stood before the king in Nisan, and the Text calls it also the twentieth year, it is clear that the New Year (for the non-Jewish king, Artaxerxes) is not Nisan (or in the latter case he would have spoken of the twenty-first year). This argument is acceptable as far as the latter quotation is concerned, for it specifically mentions Artaxerxes, but in the former verse how do we know that he refers to Artaxerxes? Perhaps he refers to another event altogether! Says R. Papa: Since in the first passage we read "the twentieth year" and in the second we read "the twentieth year," we may deduce by analogy that as in the one case Artaxerxes is meant, so is he meant also in the other. But how do we know that the event, recorded as occurring in Kislev, and not the Nisan incident, happened first? Any other deduction would not accord with the facts of the case. For we have learnt in a Boraitha: The same words which Hanani said to Nehemiah in Kislev, the latter repeated to the king in Nisan, as it is said: [Nehem. i. 1-2] "The words of Nehemiah, son of Hakhaliah. And it came to pass in the month of Kislev, in the twentieth year, as I was in Shushan the palace, that Hanani, one of my brethren came, and certain men of Judah . . . . and the gates thereof are burned with fire." And it also said: [Nehem. ii. 1-6] "And it came to pass in the month of Nisan, in the twentieth year of Artaxerxes the king, that wine was before him . . . . so it pleased the king to send me; and I set him a time."

R. Joseph offered an objection: It is written [Haggai ii. 10] "In the twenty-fourth day of the sixth month, in the second year of Darius," and it is also written [ibid. 1] "In the second year, in the seventh month, in the one and twentieth day of the month." If the rule is that Tishri (the seventh month) is the beginning of years for non-Jewish kings, should not the Text read "in the third year of Darius" instead of the second year? R. Abahu answered: Cyrus* was a most upright king and the Hebrews reckoned his years as they did those of the kings of Israel (beginning with Nisan). R. Joseph again objected: If that were so there are texts that would contradict each other. First: it is written [Ezra vi. 15] "And this house was finished on the third day of the month Adar, which was in the sixth year of the reign of Darius the King." A Boraitha explains this to mean: At that same time in the following year Ezra and the children of the captivity went up from Babylon, and the Bible says about this [Ezra vii. 8] "And he came to Jerusalem in the fifth month in the seventh year of the king." But if the rule is (that for Cyrus the year began with Nisan and not Tishri) should not the Text say "the eighth year" (since the first day of Nisan, the beginning of another year, intervenes between the third of Adar, and the month of Abh)? And secondly: How can you compare these texts! In the one place it speaks of Cyrus, and in the other, of Darius! This remains unanswered.

"And for Festivals." Do then the festivals commence on the first of Nisan? Do they not begin on the fifteenth of that

---

* The Rabbis of the Talmud must have had a different reading in the book of Haggai from that which now exists There is no verse in Haggai that reads, as the one quoted here. There is therefore a great difficulty in understanding the discussion. Rashi even, is unable to enlighten us on this point. It is possible, however, that some of the Rabbis knew that "Darius" mentioned in Haggai referred to Cyrus, for all the Persian kings of the Achæmenidan dynasty were called Darius

month? R. 'Hisda answered: (The Mishna means that Nisan is) the month that contains that festival which is called the New Year for festivals (viz., Passover).

What difference does it make (in practice)? It makes a difference to one who has made a vow, because through this festival he becomes culpable of breaking the law, "Thou shalt not slack to pay."* And this is according to the opinion of R. Simon, who says: That (before one is guilty of delay) the three festivals must have passed by in their regular order, with Passover as the first (of the three).

The Rabbis taught: As soon as three festivals have passed by and the following duties (or vows) have not been fulfilled one is guilty of procrastination; and these are they, The vow of one who says "I will give the worth of myself (to the sanctuary)" or "I will give what I am estimated to be worth (in accordance with Lev. xxvii);" or objects, the use of which one has foresworn, or which one has consecrated (to the sanctuary) or sin-offerings, guilt-offerings, burnt-offerings, peace-offerings, charity, tithes, the firstlings, the paschal offerings, the gleanings of the field, that which is forgotten to be gathered in the field, the produce of corner of the field.† R. Simon says: The festivals must pass by in their regular order, with Passover as the first, and R. Meir says: As soon as even one festival has elapsed, and the vow has not been kept the law is infringed. R. Eliezer, b. Jacob, says: As soon as two festivals have elapsed, the law is infringed, but R. Elazar, b. Simon, says: Only the passing of the feast of Tabernacles causes the infringement of the law (whether or not any other festivals have passed by between the making and the fulfilling of the vow). What is the reason of the first Tana? Since in [Deut. xvi.] the Text has been speaking of the three festivals, why does it repeat "On the feast of Unleavened Bread, on the feast of Weeks and on the feast of Tabernacles?" It repeats these words to teach us (that the festivals must pass in the order just mentioned, before one is) guilty of procrastination. R. Simon says: It was not necessary to repeat "on the feast of Tabernacles," because the Text was speaking of that festival (when it mentioned the names of the three festivals). Why, then, does it repeat it? To teach us that Tabernacles shall be the last of the three festivals. R. Meir arrives at his opinion because it is mentioned of each festival "Thou shall come there (to Jerusalem) and ye shall bring there" (your

* This law of "Thou shalt not slack to pay," is known as "BAL TE'AHER;" i. e., the law against procrastination or delay.

† Lev. xxiii, 22.

vows; and this being said of each festival, if *one* elapses and the vow is not brought, then the law against delay is infringed). The reason of R. Eliezer, b. Jacob is that the passage [Numb. xxix. 39] runs: "These shall ye offer to the Lord on your appointed feasts," and the minimum of the plural word "feasts" is *two*. On what does R. Elazar b. Simon, base his opinion? We have learnt in a Boraitha: "The feast of Tabernacles" should not have been mentioned in [Deut. xvi. 16], since the preceding passages (of that chapter) were treating of that feast. Why, then, was it mentioned? To indicate that that particular feast (Tabernacles) is the one that causes the infringement of the law.

What do R. Meir and R. Elazar deduce from the superfluous passage "on the feast of Unleavened Bread, on the feast of Weeks, and on the feast of Tabernacles?" They use this verse, according to R. Elazar, who says in the name of R. Oshaya: Whence do we know that the law of compensation * applies to the feast of Weeks (although the feast is only one day)? For this very reason the Bible repeats the three festivals; and he institutes a comparison between the feast of weeks and the feast of unleavened bread; as the law of compensation applies to feast of unleavened bread for seven days, so also does it apply to the feast of Weeks for seven days. Why, then, does the Torah find it necessary to repeat the words, "In the feast of Tabernacles?" To compare it with the feast of Unleavened Bread; as, during the feast of Unleavened Bread it was obligatory to stay over night (in Jerusalem), so was it also necessary during the feast of Tabernacles. But how do we know that it was obligatory during the feast of Unleavened Bread? It is written [Deut. xvi. 7], "Thou shalt turn in the morning (after staying over night), and go unto thy tents." What are the sources of the above arguments? The Rabbis taught the following interpretation of Deut. xxiii. 21: "When thou shalt vow a vow unto the Lord thy God, thou shalt not slack to pay it." Perhaps these words only apply to a vow! How do we know that they may also be applied to a voluntary offering? In the passage just quoted we read "vow," and in another place [Lev. vii. 16], we find "but if the sacrifice of his offering be a vow or a voluntary offering;" as in the latter instance the Torah includes the "voluntary offering," so does it also in the former; "unto the Lord thy God," *i. e.*, offerings expressed by "I will give the value of myself" etc., and other objects mentioned above; "thou shalt not slack to pay it:" *i. e.*, the object promised must be given and not

* The privilege of bringing on one of the later days of a festival a sacrifice that should have been offered on the first day.

anything in exchange of it;* "for he will surely require it," *i. e.*, the sin- guilt- burnt- and peace-offerings; "the Lord thy God;" these words refer to offerings of charity, tithes, and firstlings; "of thee;" this refers to the gleanings, that which is forgotten in the field and the produce of the corner of the field; "and it would be sin in thee," *i. e.*, and not in thy sacrifice (which is not thereby invalidated).

The Rabbis taught: Deut. xxiii. 23; may be explained thus: "That which is gone out of thy lips" refers to the mandatory laws (of the Torah); "thou shalt keep" refers to the prohibitory laws; "and perform" is a warning to the Beth Din† (that they should enforce the laws); "according as thou hast vowed" refers to vows; "to the Lord thy God" refers to sin- guilt- burnt- and peace-offering: "a free-will offering" means just what it is; "which thou hast spoken," refers to the sanctified objects devoted to the Temple for repairs, etc.; "with thy mouth" refers to charity. Says Rabha: One is culpable if he does not give forthwith that which he has vowed for charity. Why so? Because there are always poor people (needing immediate help). Is not this self-evident? Aye, but one might suppose that, since the law prohibiting delay is found in connection with the duty of giving charity and also of bringing the various voluntary offerings, it would apply to both, and it would not be infringed until the three festivals had elapsed, therefore he teaches us (that charity and sacrifices are different): in the latter case, the infringement of the law depends on the festivals, but in the case of charity it must be given immediately, for the poor are always to be found. And Rabha further said: As soon as three festivals have passed (and one has not brought his offering), he daily transgresses the law against delay. Against this opinion the following objection was raised: As soon as a year, containing three festivals or not, has passed (he that does not bring his offering) be it a firstling or any of the holy offerings, transgresses daily the law against delay. It is quite possible that the three festivals may elapse and yet a year may not go by (*e. g.*, from Passover till Tabernacles is only seven months), but how can it happen that a year may pass and the three festivals should not occur (in that time)? It may happen according to those who say (that the three festivals must elapse) in their regular order, but according to those who do not say (that the three festivals must go by) in their regular order how can such a case

* Lev. xxvii. 32.

† The ecclesiastical and civil courts were called Beth Din, and consisted of an odd number of judges, so that in case of a division of opinion, a majority was always assured. The minimum number of judges required to form a court was three. In our translation we shall always use "Beth Din" instead of "court;" using it as an English term, as Sanhedrim.

happen? It is possible according to Rabbi (who holds that the intercalary month * is not a part of the year), and it occurs in a leap-year, when one consecrates anything (to the Temple) after the feast of Passover; for when the end of the second Adar has arrived, a year (of twelve months) has elapsed, yet the three festivals have not passed by in their regular order. But how can such a case occur according to the Rabbis? It can happen; as a Boraitha teaches: R. Shemaiah says, The feast of Weeks falls on the fifth, sixth, or seventh of Sivan. How is this possible? In a year when the months of Nisan and Iyar have thirty days each, Pentecost falls on the fifth of Sivan; when they each have twenty-nine days, Pentecost falls on the seventh of Sivan; but when the one has twenty-nine days and the other has thirty days, Pentecost falls on the sixth of Sivan.

R. Zera asked: How does the law against delay affect an heir? Shall we argue that the Torah says [Deut. xxiii. 21] "When *thou* shalt vow a vow" (*i. e.*, the testator has vowed), but the heir has not vowed (consequently, the law does not apply to him), or shall we argue from the passage [Deut. xii. 5, 6] "When ye be come . . . . then ye shall bring" and the heir (who is obliged to come) is also in duty bound to bring with him (the objects vowed by the testator)? Come and hear! R. 'Hiyya teaches: It is written in this connection "from thee" (*i. e.*, from the one who vowed) and this excludes the heir. But did we not say above that these words refer to the gleanings, etc.? The Torah uses the word ME'IMMOKH ("from thee"), which we can explain to mean both the successor and the gleanings, etc. (*i. e.*, all that comes "from thee").

R. Zera also asked: How does the law against delay affect a woman? Shall I say that since she is not obligated to appear (in Jerusalem) the law does not apply to her? or perhaps it is her duty to go there because she is included in the law "to rejoice." "Certainly," answered Abayi, "she is bound by this law because it is her duty to rejoice."

The schoolmen asked: From when do we count the beginning of the year for a firstling? Answered Abayi: From the moment it is born; but R. A'ha b. Jacob said: From the moment it is acceptable as an offering (*i. e.*, when it is eight days old, Lev. xxii. 27). These opinions are not contradictory, for the former Rabbi refers to an unblemished animal and the latter to one with a blemish. May, then, a blemished animal be eaten (on the day of its birth)? Yes, if we are sure it was born after the full period of gestation.

* Leap year occurs seven times in a cycle of nineteen years. On such occasions one month, the second Adar, is added to the twelve lunar months.

The Rabbis taught: The first of Nisan is the new year for (arranging the) months, for (appointing) leap-years, for giving the half-shekels, and, some say, also for the rental of houses. Whence do we know (that it is new year) for months? From Ex. xii. 2 where it is written, "This month shall be unto you the beginning of months; it shall be the first month of the year to you." It is also written [Deut. xvii. 1] "Observe the month of Abhibh" (early stage of ripening). In which month is grain in the early stage of ripening? I can say, only Nisan, and the Torah calls it the first. Could I not say Adar (when the grain begins to shoot up)? Nay, for the grain must be ripening during the major portion of the month (and in Adar it is not). Is it then written that the grain must be ripening the major portion of the month? Therefore, says Rabhina, the sages do not find (the rule of calling Nisan the first month) in the Torah, but in the Book of Esther, where it is clearly stated [Esth. iii. 7] "In the first month, that is, the month Nisan."

"For Leap-Years." Do we, then, count leap-years from Nisan? Does not a Boraitha teach us that Adar only is the intercalary month? Answered R. Na'hman b. Isaac: The words "FOR LEAP-YEARS" mean here the termination of leap-years* and our Tana † speaks of the beginning of the leap-year, and not the end.

"For Giving the Half-Shekels." And where is the scriptural text for this? R. Yashi answered: In Numb. xxviii. 14, "This is the burnt offering of the new moon each time it is renewed during the year." The Torah says *proclaim it a new month* and also bring a sacrifice from the new products; at the same time he makes a comparison between the words "year" used in this passage and in Ex. xii. 2, "it shall be the first month of the year to you," and he deduces that they both refer to Nisan.

R. Judah says in the name of Samuel: It is proper that the congregational sacrifices ‡ brought on the first of Nisan should be purchased with the shekels raised for the new year; but if one buys a sacrifice with the funds obtained from the former year's stock, it is acceptable, yet the law was but imperfectly complied with; also, if an individual offers from his own property (proper objects, for the congregational sacrifices), they are acceptable, but he must first present them to the congregation. Is this not self-evident? Nay, it may be feared that one will not give them to the congregation in the

* As soon as Nisan had been consecrated, there could be no further debate about making the past year intercalary, for once the new month had been called Nisan, it was forbidden to call it by any other name.

† The author of a Mishna The plural of the word is Tanaim.

‡ The Tamid or daily offering could not be presented to the Temple by an individual.

prescribed manner, and this, he teaches us, is not worthy of consideration. And the reason that our Tana does not mention that Nisan is a new year for the giving of shekels also, is because it is said above that if one has brought an offering (from the old stock) he has done his duty, therefore he could not make Nisan absolutely binding.

"And Some Say Also for the Rental of Houses." The Rabbis taught: He who lets a house to another for a year, must count (the year) as twelve months from day to day; but if the lessee says (I rent this house) "for this year," even if the transaction takes place on the first of Adar, as soon as the first of Nisan arrives, the year (of rental) has expired. Can you not say Tishri (is the beginning of the year for such transactions)? Nay, it is generally understood that if a man rents a house in the autumn he rents it for the whole of the rainy season (winter). And the Tana of the first part of the above Boraitha (who does not fix Nisan as the month for rentals) and also our Tana both are of the opinion that in Nisan too, bad weather sometimes prevails (and therefore Nisan and Tishri are alike in this respect).

"On the First of Elul is the New Year for the Cattle-Tithes." According to whose opinion is this? Says R. Joseph: It is according to Rabbi's own opinion which he formed according to the opinions of different Tanaïm. With regard to the festivals he holds the opinion of R. Simon and with regard to the cattle-tithe he holds the opinion of R. Meir. If that is so, are there not five beginnings of years, instead of four? Rabha answered that the Mishna mentioned only the four, which are not disputed by any-one; according to R. Meir there are four, if that "for the festivals" be excluded, and according to R. Simon there are four, if that "for the cattle-tithes" be excluded. R. Na'hman says: (No such explanation is needed); the Mishna means there are four (months) in which there are (or may be) many beginnings of years.

"According to R. Eliezer and R. Simon it is on the First of Tishri." R. Jo'hanan says: Both of them deduce their opinion by (various interpretations of) the same Scriptural passage. It is written [Ps. lxv. 13] "The pastures are clothed with flocks; the valleys also are covered with corn; they shout for joy, they also sing." R. Meir thinks (this is the interpretation) of these words: When are the pastures clothed with flocks? At the season when the valleys are covered with corn. And when are the valleys covered with corn? About (the time of) Adar. The flocks conceive in Adar and produce their young in Abh; consequently the beginning of the year (for the cattle-tithe) is Elul. R. Eliezer and R. Simon, however, say: When are the pastures clothed with flocks? At the season when they shout and sing. When do the ears of corn (seem to) send up a hymn of praise? In Nisan. Now, the sheep conceive in Nisan, and produce in Elul, consequently the beginning of the year (for their tithe) is Tishri. But Rabha says: All agree that only Adar is the time when the pastures are clothed with flocks, and the valleys are covered with corn. But they differ about this passage: [Deut. xiv. 22] "Thou shalt truly tithe" (*literally*, "Thou shalt tithe in tithing"), and we see that the Torah here speaks of two tithes, viz., of cattle and of grain. R. Meir thinks that this comparison may be instituted between the two; just as the tithe of grain must be given in the month nearest to the time it is reaped, so that of cattle must be given in the month nearest to the one in which they are born (Elul). R. Eliezer and R. Simon, however, are of the opinion that another comparison may be instituted between these tithes; just as the beginning of the year for giving the tithe of grain is Tishri, so also, is Tishri for that of cattle.

"THE FIRST OF TISHRI IS THE NEW YEAR'S DAY FOR ORDINARY YEARS." For what purpose is this rule? Answers R. Zera, to determine the equinoxes (and solstices); and this agrees with the opinion of R. Eliezer, who says that the world was created in Tishri; but R. Na'hman says (it is the new year) for divine judgment, as it is written [Deut. xi. 12] "From the beginning of the year till the end of the year," *i. e.*, at the beginning of the year it is determined what shall be at the end of the year. But whence do we know that this means Tishri? It is written [Ps. lxxxi. 3] "Blow up the cornet* in the new moon, in the time, it is hidden on our solemn feast day." What feast is it in which the moon is hidden? I can only say ROSH HASHANA (New Year's Day), and of this day it is written [ibid. v. 4] "For it is a statute unto Israel, a judgment (day) for the God of Jacob." The Rabbis taught: "It is a statute unto Israel," *i. e.*, the Supreme Court in Heaven does not enter into judgment until the Beth Din on earth proclaims the new moon. Another Boraitha teaches: It is written: "It is a statute unto Israel;" one might suppose that (New Year's Day is a day of judgment) only for Israel; whence do we know it is so also for other nations? Because it is written "it is the day of judgment of the *God* of Jacob" (the Universal God). Why, then, is "Israel" mentioned? To inform us that Israel enters for judgment first. This is the opinion of R. 'Hisda, who holds that if a king and a congregation have a law suit, the

* The word "cornet" will be used throughout this translation for the Hebrew word SHOPHAR.

king enters first, as it is said [1 Kings viii. 59] "The cause of his servant (King Solomon) and the cause of his people." Why so? Because it is not customary to let a king wait outside.

"FOR THE COMPUTATION OF SABBATIC YEARS." On what Scriptural passage is this based? On Lev. xxv. 4, which runs: "But in the seventh year shall be a sabbath of rest unto the land," and he deduces (that it means Tishri) by analogy from the word "year" in this passage and in the following: "From the beginning of the year" [Deut. xi. 12], which surely refers to Tishri.

"AND JUBILEES." Do, then, jubilees begin on the first of Tishri? Do they not begin on the tenth of Tishri, as it is written [Lev. xxv. 9], "In the Day of Atonement shall ye make the cornet sound throughout all your land?" Yea, but our Mishna agrees with the opinion of R. Ishmael b. Jo'hanan b. Beroqa; for a Boraitha teaches: It is written [Lev. xxv. 10], "Ye shall sanctify the year, the fiftieth *year*." Why was it necessary to repeat the word "year"? Because in the same connection it is said [ibid. 9], "On the day of atonement shall ye make the cornet sound," and one might suppose that the Jubilee is sanctified only from the Day of Atonement (and not before). Therefore the word "year" is repeated to teach us that by the words "ye shall sanctify the fiftieth year" is meant, that from the very beginning of the year the Jubilee commences to be consecrated. From this teaching R. Ishmael b. Jo'hanan b. Beroqa says: From New Year's Day until the Day of Atonement, slaves used not to return to their (own) homes; neither did they serve their masters, but they ate and drank and rejoiced with the crown of freedom on their heads. As soon as the Day of Atonement arrived the Beth Din ordered the cornet to be blown and the slaves returned to their own homes and fields reverted to their (original) owners.

We have learnt in another Boraitha: "It is a jubilee" (JOBHEL HI). What is meant by (these superfluous words)? Since it is said [Lev. xxv. 10], "And ye shall hallow the fiftieth year," one might think that, as at the beginning of the year the Jubilee commences to be sanctified so also it should continue to be consecrated after the end of the year; and be not surprised at such a teaching, since it is usual to add from the non-sanctified to the sanctified. Hence the necessity of the words, in the passage (next to that quoted above), [Lev. xxv. 11] "A jubilee shall that fiftieth year be unto you;" *i. e.*, the fiftieth year shall be hallowed, and not the fifty-first. But the Rabbis (who do not explain this passage according to the above Boraitha whence do they derive the regulation that the fifty-first year is not sanctified)? They say: One counts the fiftieth year and not the fifty-first; this excludes the opinion of R. Judah who holds that the jubilee year is added at the beginning and end.* The Rabbis taught "JOBHEL HI (it is a jubilee)," even if the people have not relinquished (their debts), even if the cornet is not sounded; shall we also say even if slaves are not released? Hence the word "HI" is used (to indicate that only when the slaves are released it is a jubilee), so says R. Judah. R. Jose says: "It is a jubilee," even if debts are not relinquished, and slaves are not released; shall we also say, even if the cornet is not sounded? Hence the word "HI" is used (and means the sounding of the cornet). Since one passage includes (all that is prescribed) and the other passage exempts (certain regulations), why should we say it is a jubilee even if they have not released slaves, but that it is not a jubilee if they failed to sound the cornet? Because it is possible, that sometimes (a jubilee may occur) and yet there are no (Hebrew) slaves to release, but a jubilee can never occur without the sounding of the cornet (for a cornet can always be found). Another explanation is that (the sounding of the cornet) is the duty of the Beth Din (and it will never fail to perform it), while (the releasing of slaves) is the duty of the individual, and we cannot be sure that he will perform it. (Is not the first explanation satisfactory) that he gives this additional explanation? (It may not be satisfactory to some who might say) that is impossible that not one (Hebrew) slave should be found somewhere, to be released. Therefore (the Boraitha adds) that the blowing of the cornet is the duty of the Beth Din (and they will not fail to attend to it) while the release of slaves is the duty of an individual (and we cannot) be sure that he will perform it.

R. 'Hiyya b. Abba, however, says in the name of R. Jo'hanan: The foregoing are the words of R. Judah and R. Jose; but the masters hold that all three conditions may prevent the fulfillment (of the law), because they hold that the word "HI" [Lev. xxv. 10] should be explained of the subjects mentioned in the passage in which it occurs, and in the preceding and the following passages also. What is the force of the words "throughout the land?" (They lead us to infer) that at the time when (under a Jewish government) liberty is proclaimed throughout the land (Palestine) it should be proclaimed outside the land; but if it is not proclaimed in the land, it need not be proclaimed outside the land.

"AND ALSO FOR THE PLANTING OF TREES." Whence do we

---

* *i. e.*, The Jubilee year is, at the same time, the fiftieth year of the last and the first of the coming series.

know this? From Lev. xix. 23 where it is written, "Three years shall it be as uncircumcised," and also, [ibid. 24] "But in the fourth year." We compare the term "year" used here with that of Deut. xi. 12, "from the beginning of the 'year,'" and deduce by analogy that they both mean Tishri. The Rabbis taught: For one who plants, slips or grafts (trees) in the sixth year (the year before the sabbatic year) thirty days before the New Year's day (as soon as the first of Tishri arrives) a year is considered to have passed, and he is permitted to use, during the sabbatic year (the fruits they may produce), but less than thirty days are not to be considered a year, and the fruits may not be used, but are prohibited until the fifteenth of Shebhat, whether it be because they come under the category of "uncircumcised" or under the category of "fourth year planting" [Lev. xix. 23, 24]. Whence do we deduce this? It is said in the name of R. Jo'hanan or R. Janai: The Torah says [Lev. xix. 24, 25], "And in the fourth year. . . . And in the fifth year," *i. e.*, it may happen that in the fourth year (from the planting, the fruit) is prohibited because it is still "uncircumcised," and in the fifth year (from the planting) because it is still the product of the fourth year.

We have learned: R. Eliezer says, In Tishri the world was created, the patriarchs (Abraham and Jacob) were born, and the three patriarchs died; Isaac was born on the Passover; on New Year's Day Sarah, Rachel and Hannah were visited with the blessing of children, Joseph was released from prison, and the bondage of our fathers in Egypt ceased; in Nisan our ancestors were redeemed from Egypt, and in Tishri we shall again be redeemed. R. Joshua says: In Nisan the world was created, and in the same month the patriarchs were born, and they also died; Isaac was born on the Passover; on New Year's day, Sarah, Rachel and Hannah were visited, Joseph was released from prison, and the bondage of our fathers in Egypt ceased. In Nisan our ancestors were redeemed from Egypt, and in the same month we shall again be redeemed.

We have learnt in a Boraitha: R. Eliezer says, Whence do we know that the world was created in *Tishri?* From the Scriptural verse in which it is written [Gen. i. 11] "And God said, let the earth bring forth grass, the herb yielding seed, and the fruit tree, etc." In what month does the earth bring forth grass, and at the same time the trees are *full* of fruit? Let us say, Tishri; and that time of the year (mentioned in Genesis), was the autumn: the rain descended and the fruits flourished, as it is written [Gen. ii. 6] "But there went up a mist from the earth, etc." R. Joshua says: Whence do we know that the world was created in *Nisan?* From the Scriptural verse in which it is written [Gen. i. 12] "And the earth brought forth grass, and herb yielding seed, and the tree yielding fruit, etc." In which month is the earth covered with grass (and at the same time) the trees *bring forth* fruit? Let us say, Nisan; and at that time animals, domestic and wild, and birds mate, as it is said [Psalm lxv. 14] "The pastures are clothed with flocks, etc." Further says R. Eliezer: Whence do we know that the patriarchs were born in Tishri? From the passage [1 Kings viii. 2] "And all the men of Israel assembled themselves unto King Solomon at the feast, in the month ETHANIM (strong), which is the seventh month; *i. e.*, the month in which ETHANIM, the strong ones of the earth (the patriarchs) were born. How do we know that the expression ETHAN means strength? It is written, [Numb. xxiv. 21] ETHAN MOSHABHEKHA "strong in thy dwelling place," and it is also written [Micah vi. 2] "Hear ye, O mountains, the Lord's controversy, and (VE-HAETHANIM) ye strong ones the foundation, etc."

Further says R. Joshua: Whence do we know that the patriarchs were born in Nisan? From 1 Kings vi. 1, where it says "in the fourth year, in the month ZIV (glory), which is the second month, etc.," which means in that month in which the "glorious ones" of the earth (the patriarchs), were already born. Whether the patriarchs were born in Nisan or Tishri, they died (in later years), in the same month as that in which they were born; as it is written [Deut. xxxi. 2] "Moses said I am one hundred and twenty years old to-day." The word "to-day" implies "just this day" my days and years are complete," for God grants the righteous the fulfillment of the years of their life to the very month and day, as it is said: "The number of thy days, I will fulfill," [Ex. xxiii. 26].

Isaac was born in Nisan. Whence do we know this? It is written [Gen. xviii. 14] "At the next *festival* I will return to thee, and Sarah will have a son." What festival was it when he said this? Shall I say it was Passover, and he referred to Pentecost? That cannot be for what woman bears children after fifty days gestation? If I say it was Pentecost, and he referred to Tishri, a similar objection might be raised, for who bears children after five months gestation? If I say it was Tabernacles, and he referred to Passover, a similar objection may be made, for who bears children in the sixth month of gestation? But we have learnt that that year was a leap-year, and Mar Zutra says that although a child born after nine months' gestation is never born during the month (but only at the end of the required time) still a seven months' child can be born before the seventh month is complete, as it is said [1 Samuel i. 20] "and it came to pass, LI-TEQUPHATH HA-YAMIM (when the time was come about);" the minimum of TEQUPHOTH * is two and of YAMIM is also two (*i. e.*, after six months and two days gestation, childbirth is possible). Whence do we know that Sarah, Rachel and Hannah were visited on New Year's Day? Says R. Elazar: By comparing the expression "visit," that occurs in one passage, with the word "visit" that occurs in another passage; and also by treating the expression "remember" in the same way. It is written concerning Rachel [Gen. xxx. 32] "And God remembered Rachel," and of Hannah it is written [1 Samuel i. 19] "And God remembered her." He institutes an analogy between the word "remember" used in these passages and in connection with New Year's Day which is called [Lev. xxiii. 24] "a Sabbath, a memorial (*literally*, a remembrance) of blowing of cornets." It is also written concerning Hannah [1 Sam. ii. 21] "And the Lord visited Hannah;" and of Sarah it is written [Gen. xxi. 1] "And the Lord visited Sarah," and by analogy all these events took place on the same day, New Year's Day. Whence do we know that Joseph was released from prison on New Year's Day? From Ps. lxxxi; in verses 3, 4, it is written, "Blow the trumpet, when the moon is hidden in the appointed time on our solemn feast day. For it is a statute for Israel." In verse 5 of the same Psalm it is written, "This he ordained (for the day) when Joseph went out, etc." On New Year's Day the bondage of our fathers in Egypt ceased. Whence do we know this? It is written [Ex. vi. 6] "I will bring you out from under the burdens of the Egyptians," and it is written in Ps. lxxxi. 6, "I removed his shoulder from the burden," (*i. e.*, I relieved Israel from the burden of Egypt on the day spoken of in the Psalm, *viz.*, New Year's Day). In Nisan they were redeemed, as it is recorded in the Bible. In Tishri we shall again be redeemed. This he deduces by analogy from the word "cornet" found in the following passages. In Ps. lxxxi. 3, it is stated, "Blow the cornet on the new moon" (*i. e.*, on New Year's Day) and in Isaiah xxviii, 13. it is written, "And in that day the great cornet shall be blown" (and as it means New Year's Day in the one place, so does it also in the other). R. Joshua says: "In Nisan they were redeemed and in that month we shall be redeemed again." Whence do we know

* TEQUPHA—Solstice or equinox; hence, the period of three months, which elapses between a solstice and the next equinox, is also called TEQUPHA. The Talmud reads the Biblical term as if it was plural.

this? From Ex. xii. 42, which says, "It is a night of special observance," *i. e.*, a night specially appointed, since the earliest times, for the final redemption of Israel. The Rabbis taught: The Jewish sages fix the time of the flood according to R. Eliezer, and the solstices according to R. Joshua, but the sages of other nations fix the time of the flood also as R. Joshua does.

"AND FOR HERBS." To this a Boraitha adds "tithes and vows." (Let us see.)! What does he mean by "herbs"? The tithe on herbs; but are not these included with other "tithes"? (Nay! for the tithe on herbs) is a Rabbinical institution, while the others are Biblical. If so, should he not teach the Biblical command first? (This is no question); because it was pleasing to him (to have discovered, that although the tithe of herbs is only a Rabbinical institution, yet it should have a special New Year, to prevent the mixing of tithes from year to year) he, therefore, gives it precedence. And the Tana of our Mishna teaches us the Rabbinical institution (viz., the New Year for herbs), leaving us to infer that if that must be observed so much the more must the Biblical law be followed.

The Rabbis taught: If one gathers herbs on the eve of New Year's Day before sunset, and gathers others after sunset, he must not give the heave-offering or the tithe from the one for the other, for it is prohibited to give the heave-offering or tithe from the product of the past year for that of the present, or *vice-versa*. If the second year from the last sabbatic year was just ending and the third year was just beginning, then, for the second year he must give the first and second tithes,* and for the third year he must give the first and the poor tithes. Whence do we deduce that (in the third year no second tithe was to be given)? R. Joshua b. Levi says: In Deut. xxvi. 12, it is written, "When thou hast made an end of tithing all the tithes of thine increase the third year, which is the year of the *tithe*," *i. e.*, the year in which only one tithe is to be given. What is to be understood (by *one* tithe)? The first and poor tithes, and the second tithe shall be abrogated. But perhaps it is not so (that the first and poor tithe are one tithe), but that the first tithe shall be also abrogated? This can not be so, for we read [Numb. xviii. 26] "The tithe which I have given you from them, for your inheritance.

*Tithes must be given even to-day, according to the Rabbinical law, throughout Palestine and Syria.

It was the duty of the Israelite to give of his produce the following offerings and tithes: (1) TRUMA a heave-offering to be given to the priest every year; the measure was not fixed by the Bible; (2) MAASER RISHON, or first tithe, to be given every year to the Levite; (3) MAASER SHENI, or second tithe, was to be taken in the second year to Jerusalem and eaten there, or to be converted into money, which was to be spent there; (4) MAASER ANI, or the poor tithe, to be given in the third year.

etc." (From this we see that) the Scripture compares this tithe to an inheritance; and as an inheritance is the perpetual property of the heir, so also is the first tithe an uninterrupted gift for the Levite.

"AND FOR VOWS." The Rabbis taught: whoso vows to derive no benefit from his neighbor for a year, must reckon (for the year) twelve months, from day to day; but if he said "for this year," if he made the vow even on the twenty-ninth of Elul, as soon as the first of Tishri comes, that year is complete, for he vowed to deny himself some pleasure and that purpose (even in so brief a period) has been fulfilled. But perhaps we should say Nisan (should be regarded as the new year in such a case)? Nay, in the matter of vows we follow the common practice among men (who generally regard Tishri as the New Year). We have learnt elsewhere: (We reckon the year for giving the tithe), for fenugreek as soon as it begins to grow; for grain and olives as soon as they are one-third ripe. What do you mean by "as soon as it begins to grow?" When it has put forth its blossoms. Whence do we know that we reckon the tithe on grain and olives when they are one-third ripe? R. Asi says in the name of R. Jo'hanan, and some think in the name of R. Jose of Galilee: The Bible says [Deut. xxxi. 10] "At the end of every seven years, in the solemnity of the year of release, in the feast of tabernacles." What has the year of release to do with Tabernacles; it is already the eighth year (because the Bible says "at the end of every seven years")? It is only to tell you that all grain which was one-third ripe before New Year's Day must be regarded even in the eighth year as the product of the sabbatic year. And for this we find support in a Boraitha: R. Jonathan b. Joseph says, It is written [Lev. xxv. 21] "And it shall bring forth fruit for three (LISHLOSH) years. Do not read LISHLOSH "for three," but in this case read LISHLISH "for a third" (*i. e.*, it is considered produce when it is a third ripe). We have learnt elsewhere: Rice, millet, poppies and lentils which have taken root before New Year's Day come under the category of tithes for the past year, and therefore one is permitted to use them during the sabbatic year; but if they have not (taken root), one is forbidden to use them during the sabbatic year, and they come under the category of tithes, of the following year.

Says Rabha: (Let us see)! The Rabbis say that the year (for giving tithes) begins as follows: "for a tree from the time the fruits form; for grain and olives when they are one-third ripe; and for herbs when they are gathered. Now under which head are the above (rice, etc.) classed? After consideration Rabha remarked: Since these do not all ripen simultaneously but are gathered little by little, the Rabbis are right when they say they are tithable from the time they take root. A Boraitha teaches: R. Jose of Galilee says that from the words [Deut. xvi. 13] "When thou hast gathered in thy corn and thy wine" we infer that as corn and wine, now being gathered, grow by means of the past year's rains, and are tithed as last year's (before New Year's Day) products; so every fruit that grows by the rain of last year is tithable as the last year's produce; but herbs do not come in this category, for they grow by means of the rains of the new year, and they are tithable in the coming year. R. Aqiba says that the words "when thou hast gathered in thy corn and thy wine" lead us to infer that as corn and grapes grow chiefly by means of rain and are tithed as last year's products, so all things that grow chiefly by rain, are tithed as belonging to the past year; but as herbs grow even by watering, they are tithed as the next year's products. In what case is this difference of opinion applicable? Answered Abbahu: In the cases of onions and Egyptian beans; for a Mishna says onions and Egyptian beans which have not been watered for thirty days before New Year's Day are tithed as last year's products, and are allowed to be used during the sabbatic year, but if they have been watered, then they are prohibited during the sabbatic year and are tithed as next year's products.

"On the First of Shebhat is the New Year for Trees." Why so? Said R. Elazar, in the name of R. Oshaia, because at that date, the greater part of the early rains have fallen, although the greater part of the Tequpha is yet to come. The Rabbis taught: It once happened that R. Aqiba picked the fruit of a citron tree, on the first of Shebhat and gave two tithes of them, one in accordance with the custom of the school of Shammai and one in accordance with the school of Hillel's custom. Says R. Jose b. Judah: Nay! Aqiba did not do this because of the custom of the school of Shammai or the school of Hillel, but because R. Gamliel* and R. Eliezer were accustomed to do so. Did he not follow the practice of Beth Shammai because it was the first of Shebhat? Answered R. 'Hanina and some say R. 'Hananya: The case here cited was one of a citron tree whose fruit was formed before the fifteenth of last Shebhat and he should have given the tithe of it even before the present first of Shebhat, but the case happened to be as cited. But Rabhina says: Put the foregoing together and read the (words of R. Jose) as follows: It did not happen on the first of Shebhat but on the fifteenth; and he did not follow the regulations of the school of Hillel or the school

* The opinion of R. Gamliel is stated a little further on.

of Shammai, but the custom of R. Gamliel and R. Eliezer. Rabbah b. Huna says: Although R. Gamliel holds that a citron tree is tithable from the time it is picked, as is the case with "herbs," nevertheless the new year for tithing it, is in Shebhat. R. Jo'hanan asked R. Janai: "When is the beginning of a year for (the tithe on) citrons?" "Shebhat," he answered. "Do you mean" said he, "the month Shebhat as fixed by the lunar year or by the solar year (from the winter solstice)?" "By the lunar year," he replied. Rabha asked R. Na'hman, "How is it in leap-years (when there are thirteen lunar months)?" "Shebhat, as in the majority of years," answered he. We have learnt: R. Jo'hanan and Resh Laqish both say that a citron that has grown in the sixth year and is unpicked at the entrance of the sabbatic year is always considered the product of the sixth year. When Rabhin came (from Palestine) he said, in the name of R. Jo'hanan; A citron that was as small as an olive in the sixth year but grew to the size of a (small) loaf of bread during the sabbatic year, if one used it without separating the tithe he is culpable because of TEBHEL.*

The Rabbis taught: A tree whose fruits formed before the fifteenth of Shebhat, must be tithed as the product of the past year, but if they formed after that, they are tithed during the coming year. R. Ne'hemiah says: This applies to a tree that bears two crops a year. How can there be two crops? It looks like two crops (as is the case with grapes); but in the case of a tree that produces but one crop, as for example, the palm, olive or carob, although their fruits may have formed before the fifteenth of Shebhat, they are tithed as the products of the coming year. R. Jo'hanan remarked that in the case of the carob, people follow the opinion of R. Ne'hemiah. Resh Laqish asked R. Jo'hanan: Since white figs take three years to grow fully ripe, must not the second year after the sabbatic year be regarded as the sabbatic year for them? R. Jo'hanan was silent.

MISHNA. At four periods in each year the world is judged; on Passover in respect to the growth of grain; on Pentecost in respect to the fruit of trees; on New Year's Day all human beings pass before God, as sheep before a shepherd; as it is said [Ps. xxx. 9] "He who hath fashioned all their hearts, understandeth all their works;"† and on Tabernacles judgment is given in regard to water (rain).

GEMARA. What grain (does the Divine judgment, affect on

---

* Produces, in that stage in which the separation of levitical and priestly shares is required before one can partake of them.

† Vide introduction.

the Passover)? Does it mean the grain now standing in the field (about to be reaped)? When then were all the accidents that have happened to it until that time appointed (by Divine will)? It does not mean standing grain but that just sown. Shall we say that only one judgment is passed upon it? Does not a Boraitha teach: If an accident or injury befall grain before Passover it was decreed on the last Passover, but if it happen (to the same grain) after Passover it was decreed on the most recent Passover; if an accident or misfortune befall a man before the Day of Atonement, it was decreed on the previous Day of Atonement, but if it happened after the Day of Atonement it was decreed on the most recent Day of Atonement? Answers Rabha: Learn from this that it is judged twice (in one year). Therefore says Abayi: When a man sees that the grain, which ripens slowly is thriving, he should as soon as possible sow such grain as ripens quickly, in order that before the time of the next judgment, it may already have begun to grow.*

With whose opinion does our Mishna agree? Certainly not with that of R. Meir, nor with that of R. Judah, nor with that of R. Jose, nor with that of R. Nathan, for they say as follows in a Boraitha: All are judged on New Year's Day and the sentence is fixed on the Day of Atonement; so says R. Meir. R. Judah says all are judged on New Year's Day but the sentence of each is sealed each at its special times, at Passover for grain, at Pentecost for the fruit of trees, at Tabernacles for rain, and man is judged on New Year's Day and his sentence is sealed on the Day of Atonement. R. Jose says man is judged every day as we read [Job vii. 18] "Thou rememberest him every morning;" and R. Nathan holds, man is judged at all times, for we read [ibid] "Thou triest him every moment." And if you should say that the Mishna agrees with the opinion of R. Judah and that by the expression "judgment" it means the "sealing of the decree," then there would be a difficulty about (the fate of) man. Says Rabha: The Tana of our Mishna is in harmony with the school of R. Ishmael, which says: At four periods is the world judged; at Passover in respect to grain; on Pentecost in regard to the fruit of trees; on Tabernacles in respect to rain, and on New Year's Day man is judged, but his decree is sealed on the Day of Atonement, and the Mishna speaks of the opening of judgment only (and not the final verdict). R. 'Hisda asked: Why does not R. Jose quote the same passage in support of his opinion as R. Nathan? You may say that "trying" means simply "probing." But does not "remembering" also convey the same idea? Therefore says R. 'Hisda,

* An example of Talmudical humor.

R. Jose bases his opinion on another passage, viz., [1 Kings viii. 59] "that God may pass judgment on his servant and on his people Israel every day." Says R. Joseph: According to whom do we pray nowadays for the sick, and for faint (scholars)? According to R. Jose.

A Boraitha says: R. Judah taught in the name of R. Aqiba: Why does the Torah command [Lev. xxiii. 10] a sheaf of the first fruits to be brought on the Passover? Because Passover is the period of judgment in respect to grain, and God said: Offer before Me the first sheaf of produce on Passover so that the standing grain may be blessed unto you; and why the two loaves [Lev. xxiii. 17] on the Pentecost? Because that is the time when judgment is passed on the fruit of trees, and because of the offering, blessings should ensue. Why was the ceremony of "the outpouring of water" (on the altar) performed on the feast of Tabernacles? God said: Perform the rite of "the outpouring of waters," that the rains may fall in due season; and He also said recite before Me on New Year's Day, the MALKHIOTH, ZIKHRONOTH and SHOPHROTH*; the Malkhioth, that you proclaim Me King; the Zikhronoth that your remembrance may come before Me, for good; and how (shall this be done)? By the sounding of the cornet. R. Abbahu asked why is the cornet made of a ram's horn? God said: Sound before me on a cornet made of a ram's horn, that I may remember, for your sake, the offering of Isaac, the son of Abraham [vide Gen. xxii. 13], and I shall consider you as worthy, as if you had shown an equal readiness to sacrifice yourselves to Me. R. Isaac says: A man is judged only according to his deeds at the time of sentence, as it is said [Gen. xxi. 17] "God heard the voice of the lad, as he *then* was," and the same Rabbi also remarked: Three circumstances cause a man to remember his sins, *viz.*: when he passes by an insecure wall, when he thinks deeply of the significance of his prayer, and when he invokes Divine judgment on his neighbor; for R. Abhin says: Whoso calls down Divine judgment on his neighbor is punished first, as we find in the case of Sarah, who said [Gen. xvi. 5] to Abraham, "My wrong be upon thee," and shortly after we read (that she died) "And Abraham came to mourn for Sarah

*These are the divisions of the Additional Service for the New Year's Day. The Malkhioth consist of ten scriptural passages in which God is proclaimed King. The Zikhronoth consist of an equal number of scriptural passages in which Divine remembrance is alluded to. The Shophroth are a similar series of selections in which the Shophar (cornet) is referred to. In chapter IV of this tract there is a discussion as to the composition of these selections. We retain the Hebrew names, because we feel that no translation or pharaphrase will adequately express what they mean

and to weep for her" [Gen. xxiii. 2] (And all this only applies to cases where appeal could have been made to a civil court). R. Isaac also said: Four things avert the evil decree passed (by God) on man, *viz.:* Charity, Prayer, Change of Name, and Improvement. Charity as it is written [Prov. x. 2] "Charity delivereth from death;" Prayer, in accordance with [Ps. cvii. 19] "They prayed unto the Lord in their trouble, and he saveth them out of their distresses;" Change of name, as it is written [Gen. xvii. 15] "As for Sarai, thy wife, thou shalt not call her name Sarai, but Sarah shall her name be," and the Text continues by saying [ibid. 16] "Then will I bless her and give thee a son also of her;" Improvement, we deduce from Jonah iii. 10, "And God saw their works that they turned from their evil ways," and the chapter continues and immediately adds "And God repented of the evil, he had said he would do unto them and he did it not;" Some add to these four, a fifth, Change of location, as we read [Gen. xii. 1 and 2] "And God said to Abraham, get thee out from thy land" (and afterwards) "I will make of thee a great nation."

R. Kruspedai * says in the name of R. Jo'hanan: Three books are opened on New Year's Day: one for the entirely wicked; one for the wholly good; and one for the average class of people. The wholly righteous are at once inscribed and sealed for life; the entirely wicked are at once inscribed and sealed for destruction; the average class are held in the balance from New Year's Day till the Day of Atonement; if they prove themselves worthy they are inscribed for life; if not they are inscribed for destruction. "Whence this teaching," asked R. Abhin? From Ps. lxix. 28 which reads "they shall be blotted out of the book of life and they shall not be inscribed with the righteous."

We have learned in a Boraitha: The school of Shammai says: There are three divisions of mankind at the Resurrection; the wholly righteous, the completely wicked, and the average class; the wholly righteous are at once inscribed and sealed for life; the entirely wicked are at once inscribed, and sealed for Gehinnom; as we read [Dan. xii. 2] "And many of them that sleep in the dust shall awake, some to everlasting life, and some to shame and everlasting contempt." The third class, the mean between the former two, descend to Gehinnom, but they weep and come up again, in accordance with the passage [Zech. xiii. 9] "And I will bring the third part through the fire, and I will refine them as silver is refined, and will try them as gold is tried; and he shall call on My Name, and I will answer him."

* Vide Introduction.

Concerning this last class of men Hannah says: [1 Sam. ii. 6] "The Lord causeth to die and maketh alive, he bringeth down to the grave and bringeth up again." The school of Hillel says: The Most Compassionate inclines (the scale of justice) to the side of mercy, and of this third class of men David says [Ps. cxvi. 1] "I would that God should hear my voice;" in fact David applies to them all that Psalm down to the words "I was brought low and he helped me."

Transgressors of Jewish birth and also of non-Jewish, who sin with their body descend to Gehinnom, and are judged there for twelve months; after that time, their bodies are destroyed and burnt and the winds scatter their ashes under the soles of the feet of the righteous, as we read, [Mal. iv. 3] "And ye shall tread down the wicked, for they shall be as ashes under the soles of your feet;" but as for Minim, informers, and skeptics who deny the existence of the Torah, or the Immortality of the soul or separate themselves from the congregation (of Israel), or who inspire their fellowmen with dread of them, or who sin and cause others to sin, as did Jeroboam the son of Nebat and his followers, they all descend to Gehinnom and are judged there from generation unto generation, as it is said [Isaiah lxvi. 24] "And they shall go forth and look upon the carcases of the men who have transgressed against me: for their worm shall not die, neither shall their fire be quenched;" "even when Gehinnom will be destroyed, they will not be consumed, as we read [Ps. xlix. 14] "And their forms shall endure even when the grave is no more." Why does so terrible a fate await the above? Because just such people stretched out their hands against the dwelling (of God, *i. e.* the temple at Jerusalem); as we read [ibid.] "because of what they did against His dwelling," and concerning them Hannah says, [1 Sam. ii. 10] "The adversaries of the Lord shall be broken to pieces." R. Isaac b. Abhin says: Their faces are black like the sides of a caldron; whilst Rabha remarked: Those who are now the handsomest of the people of Me'huza will yet be called the children of the nether-world.

What do you mean by Jews who transgress with their *body?* Says Rabh: The QARPAPHTA (frontal bone) on which are not placed the phylacteries.* And who are meant by non-Jews who transgress with the *body?* Those guilty of the sin (of adultery). Who are those who inspire their fellowmen with dread of them? A leader

* There were sects at that time who did not wear the phylacteries on the frontal bone, but on other places. The people here referred to are those mentioned in Mishna Megillah III. 5. Those who do not wear phylacteries at all are, under no circumstances, included under the head of these transgressors. (Vide Tosaphoth, ad.loc.) For fuller information the reader is referred to "The History of Amuleta," by the editor.

of a community who causes the people to fear him over-much, without furthering thereby a high purpose. R. Judah says in the name of Rabh: No such leader will ever have a learned son, as it is said [Job xxxvii. 24] "Men do therefore fear him: he will never see (in his family) any wise of heart."

The school of Hillel said above: He who is full of compassion will incline the scale of justice to the side of mercy. How does He do it? Says R. Eliezer: He *presses* on (the side containing our virtues) as it is said [Micah vii. 19] "He will turn again, he will have compassion upon us; he will suppress our iniquities." R. Jose says: He *lifts off* (the sins), as it is said [ibid. 18] "He removes iniquity and passeth by transgression," and it was taught in the school of R. Ishmael that this means that He removes each first sin (so that there is no second), and this is the correct interpretation. But, remarked Rabha, the sin itself is not blotted out, so that if one be found in later times with more sins (than virtues), the sin not blotted out will be added to the later ones; but, says Rabha, Whoso treats with indulgence one who has wronged him (forms an exception to this rule) for he will have *all* his sins forgiven, as it is said [Micah vii. 19] "He removes iniquity and passes by transgression:" from whom does He remove iniquity? From him who passes by transgression (committed against him by his neighbor). R. Huna b. R. Joshua fell sick and R. Papa went to visit him. The latter saw that the end was near, and said, to those present, "Make ready his provisions (shrouds)." Finally, he recovered, and R. Papa was ashamed to see him. "Why did you think him so sick," said they? "He was so, indeed," he replied, "but said God, since he was always indulgent (with every one), he shall be forgiven," as it is said, "He removes iniquity and passes by transgression." From whom does He remove iniquity? From him who passes by transgression.

R. A'ha says: The phrase "of the remnant of his inheritance" [Micah vii. 18] is like unto a fat tail (of an Arabian sheep) with a thorn through it (that will stick some that lay hold of it); (for He forgives) the *remnant* of His inheritance, and not all His inheritance. (What is meant by remnant)? Only those who deport themselves like a remnant (*i. e.*, modestly). R. Huna points out a contradiction in these passages: It is written [Ps. cxlv. 17] "The Lord is *just* in all his ways" and in the same passage, "and *pious* in all his works." It means, in the beginning He is only *just*, but in the end He is *pious*; (when He finds that strict justice is too severe on mankind He tempers justice with piety or mercy.) R. Elazar asked about the contradictory phrase in Ps. lxii. 12. "Unto thee, O Lord, belongeth *mercy*; for thou renderest to every man *according to his work*." This is explained as the above; in the beginning He rewards every man according to his works, but in the end He is merciful. Ilphi, or Ilpha asks a similar question about Ex. xxxiv. 6, where it is written, "abundant in goodness and truth," and gives a similar explanation.

"And the Lord passed by before him and proclaimed." R. Jo'hanan said: Had this passage not been written, it would have been impossible to have said it; for it teaches us that the Holy One, blessed be He, wrapped Himself, as does one who recites the prayers for a congregation, and pointing out to Moses the regular order of prayer, said to him: Whenever Israel sins, let him pray to me, after this order, and I shall pardon him.

"The Lord, the Lord" (these words mean), I am the same God before a man sins as I am after he sins and does repentance. "God, merciful and gracious;" R. Judah said (concerning these words): The covenant made through the thirteen attributes [Ex. xxxiv.] will never be made void, as it is said [ibid. 10] "Behold *I* make a covenant."

R. Jo'hanan says: Great is repentance! for it averts the (evil) decreed against a man, as it is said [Is. vi. 10] "Make the heart of this people fat. . . .and hear with their ears, and understand with their hearts, and *repent*, and be *healed*." R. Papa asked Abayi: Do not these last words, perhaps, mean before the (evil) decree has been pronounced? It is written, he replied, "be healed." What is that which requires healing? I can only say that, against which, judgment has been pronounced. Is this not contradictory to the rule: He who repents between (New Year's Day and the Day of Atonement) is forgiven, but if he does not repent, even though he offered the choicest sacrifices, he is not pardoned? There is no difficulty here; in the one case it refers to (the sins of) an individual, and in the other, to (those of) a community. Come and hear! It is written [Ps. cvii. 23-28] "They that go down to the sea in ships, that do business in great waters; these see the works of the Lord. . . . for he commandeth, and raiseth the stormy wind, which lifteth up the waves thereof, they reel to and fro, and stagger like a drunken man. . . . then they cry unto the Lord in their trouble, and he bringeth them out of their distresses; O, that men would praise the Lord for his goodness, etc." Signs are given, such as the words "but" and "only" in the Torah (which intimate limiting qualifications) to indicate that if they cried before the decree was pronounced, only then would they be answered; but if after, are they not answered? (Would not this be a contradiction to the words "to those of a community)? Nay, for those on a ship are not a community (but are considered as a unit).

Come and hear! The proselyte Beluria asked R. Gamliel (concerning the following apparent contradiction): It is written in your Torah [Deut. x. 17] "The Lord which regardeth not persons" (*literally*, who lifteth not up countenances); and it is also written [Numb. vi. 26] "May the Lord lift up his countenance." R. Jose, the priest, joined her, and said to her, "I will tell thee a parable. To what may this be compared? To one who lent money to his neighbor, and set a time for its repayment before the king; and (the borrower) swore by the king's life (to repay it on time). The time arrived and he did not pay and he came to appease the king. Said the king to him, 'I can forgive you only your offence against me, but I cannot forgive you your offence against your neighbor; go and ask *him* to forgive you.'" So also here; in the one place it means sins committed by a man against Himself; but in the other, it means sins committed by one man against another. Nevertheless, the Tanaim differ as to the decree pronounced against an individual, as we may see from the following Boraitha: R. Meir used to say, of two who fall sick with the same sickness, and of two who enter a tribunal (for judgment), on similar charges, one may recover, and one not, one may be acquitted, and one condemned. Why should one recover and one not, and one be acquitted and one condemned? Because the one prayed and was answered, and one prayed, and was not answered. Why should one be answered and the other not? The one prayed devoutly and was answered; the other did not pray devoutly and therefore was not answered; but R. Elazar says it was not because of prayer, but because the one prayed *before*, and the other *after* the decree was pronounced. R. Isaac says: Prayer is helpful for man before or after the decree has been pronounced. Is it then so, that the (evil) decree, pronounced against a congregation is averted (through the influence of prayer)? Does not one Scriptural verse [Jer. iv. 14] say, "Wash thine heart from wickedness, and another runs [ibid. ii. 22] "For though thou wash thee with nitre, and take thee much soap, yet thine iniquity is marked before me." Shall we not say in the one case it means [illegible] and in the other [illegible] the sentence has been pronounced? Nay; both refer (to a time) after the decree has been pronounced and there is no contradiction, for in one case it refers to a decree issued with an oath, and in the other, to a decree pronounced without an oath, as R. Samuel b. Ammi points out;

for he says in the name of R. Jonathan: Whence do we know that a decree, pronounced with an oath, cannot be averted? From [Sam. iii. 14] which says: "Therefore I have sworn unto the house of Eli, that the iniquity of Eli's house shall not be purged with sacrifice nor offering forever." Says Rabha: Even in such a case, it is only through *sacrifices* that sin cannot be purged, but by (the study of) the Torah it may be; and Abayi says: With sacrifice and offering it cannot be purged, but by (the study of) the Torah, and by active benevolence, it can. (Abayi based this opinion on his own experience for) he and (his master) Rabba were both descendants of the house of Eli; Rabba, who only studied the Torah, lived forty years, but Abayi, who both studied the Torah and performed acts of benevolence, lived sixty years. The Rabbis tell us also: There was a certain family in Jerusalem whose members died at eighteen years of age. They came and informed R. Jo'hanan b. Zakkai. Said he: "Perhaps you are descendants of Eli, of whom it is said 'all the increase of thy house shall die in the flower of their age'" [1 Sam. ii. 33]; "Go, then, study the Torah, and live!" They went and studied, and they lived, and they called that family R. Jo'hanan's. R. Samuel b. Inai says in the name of Rabh: Whence do we know, that if the decree against a community is even sealed, it may nevertheless be averted? From Deut. iv. 7 where it is written "as the Lord, our God, in *all* things that we call upon him for;" (but how can you harmonize that with the passage) [Is. lv. 6] "Seek ye the Lord while he may be found?" The latter passage refers to an individual, the former, to a community. When is that time that he will be found even by an individual? Answered Rabba b. Abhuha: During the ten days, from New Year's Day till the Day of Atonement.

"On New Year's Day all the Inhabitants of the World Pass Before Him Kibhne Maron (Like Sheep)." What does the Mishna mean by these last two words? "Like Sheep," as they are translated in Aramaic; but Resh Laqish says they mean "as the steps of the Temple" (*i. e.*, narrow, so that people ascended them one by one); R. Judah, however, says in the name of Samuel: (They mean) "like the armies of the house of David" (which were numbered one by one). Says Rabba b. Bar 'Hana in the name of R. Jo'hanan; Under any circumstances they are mustered at a glance. Said R. Na'hman b. Isaac: Thus also we understand the words of our Mishna: "He that fashioned all their hearts alike" [Ps. xxxiii. 15] *i. e.*, the Creator sees all their hearts (at a glance) and (at once) understands all their works.

MISHNA: Messengers were sent out* in the following six months; in Nisan, on account of the Passover; in Abh, on account of the fast; in Elul, on account of the New Year; in Tishri, on account of appointing the order the (remaining) festivals;† in Kislev, on account of the Feast of Dedication; in Adar, on account of the Feast of Esther; also in Iyar, when the Temple was in existence, on account of the minor (or second) Passover.‡

GEMARA: Why were they not also sent out in Tamuz and Tebheth (in which months there are also fasts)? Does not R. 'Hana b. Bizna, say in the name of R. Simon the pious: What is the meaning of the passage [Zech. viii. 19], "Thus saith the Lord of hosts; the fast of the fourth, and the fast of the fifth, and the fast of the seventh and the fast of the tenth, shall be to the house of Judah, joy and gladness" etc., that they are called fasts, and also days of joy and gladness? Are we not to understand that only in the time of peace (cessation of persecution) they shall be for joy and gladness, but in the time when there was not peace, they shall be fasts? Answered R. Papa it means this: When there was peace, these days should be for joy and gladness; in the time of persecution they shall be fasts; in times when there are neither persecution, nor peace, people may fast, or not, as they see fit. If that is so, surely then (messengers should not have been sent out) on account of the fast of Abh? Answered R. Papa: The fast (ninth day) of Abh is different, since many misfortunes occurred on that day, as the teacher says: On the ninth of Abh, the first and second Temples were destroyed, Bether was captured, and the city was razed to the ground.

A Boraitha teaches: R. Simon says, there are four matters that R. Aqiba expounded, but which I interpret differently; "the fast of the fourth" means the ninth of Tamuz on which the city was broken up, as it is said [Jer. lii. 6, 7] "in the fourth, in the ninth day of the month. . . .the city was broken up." What does he mean by fourth? The fourth of the months. "The fast of the fifth," means the ninth of Abh, on which the Temple of our God was burnt; and what does he mean by calling it, fifth? The fifth of the months. "The fast of the seventh" means the third of Tishri the day on which Gedaliah the son of Ahikam was slain (and we fast) because the death of the righteous is equal to the loss of the house of our

---

* The Beth Din sent them from Jerusalem to announce to other places the day which had been appointed New Moon, and thus to inform them whether it was the thirtieth or thirty-first day from the preceding New Moon.

† *e. g.* Tabernacles. This was necessary since the Beth Din might have made the month intercalary.

‡ Vide, Numb. ix. 10, 11.

God; and what does he mean by calling it the seventh? The seventh of the months. "The fast of the tenth," means the tenth of Tebheth, the day on which the king of Babylon set himself against Jerusalem, as it is said, [Ezek. xxiv. 1, 2] "Again in the ninth year, in the tenth month, in the tenth day of the month, the word of the Lord came unto me saying, Son of man write thee the name of the day, even of this same day; the king of Babylon set himself against Jerusalem;" and what does he mean by calling it the tenth? The tenth of the months; and actually this last event should have been placed first, (since it occurred first) and why is it placed here last in order? To mention the months in their regular order. However, (says R. Simon): I do not explain (the passage quoted above) in this manner, but as follows: "The fast of the tenth" means the fifth of Tebheth, on which day the news came to the exiles that the city was smitten, as it is said [Ezek. xxxiii. 21] "And it came to pass in the twelfth year of our captivity, in the tenth (month) in the fifth day of the month that one that had escaped out of Jerusalem came to me, saying, The city is smitten," and they held the day on which they received the news as the day (on which the Temple) was burnt. Moreover (says R. Simon) my opinion appears more satisfactory to me than R. Aqiba's, for I speak of the first, first, and of the last, last; while he speaks of the last, first, and of the first, last; he mentions them in the order of the months, whilst I mention them in the order in which the misfortunes occurred.

We have learnt: Rabh and R. 'Hanina say, The Book of Fasts (which contained the names of minor holidays on which it was prohibited to fast) is abrogated, but R. Jo'hanan and R. Joshua b. Levi say: It is not. When Rabh and R. 'Hanina say that it is abrogated they mean: In the time of peace, the (fast) days are days of joy and gladness; but, in the time of persecution they are fast days, and so also with other (days mentioned in the Book of Fasts); and when R. Jo'hanan and R. Joshua b. Levi say it is not abrogated (they mean) that those (four fasts mentioned in Zechariah) the Bible makes dependent on the rebuilding of the Temple; but those (mentioned in the Book of Fasts) remain as they are appointed. R. Tobi b. Matana asked a question: On the twenty-eighth of (Adar), the good news came to the Jews that they need no longer abstain from studying the Torah; for the king (of Syria had earlier) issued a decree, forbidding them to study the Torah, or to circumcise their sons, and compelling them to desecrate their Sabbath. What did Judah b. Shamua and his friends do? They went and took counsel of a certain matron, whose house the celebrated people of the city frequented. Said she to them, "Go and cry aloud at night." They did as she advised and cried aloud, "O heavens! Are we not all brethren? Are we not all the children of one Father? Are we not all the children of one mother? Why should we be treated differently from other nations, and from all people who speak other languages inasmuch as ye issue such cruel edicts against us?" The decrees were annulled, and the day (on which this happened) they appointed a holiday. But if it is true that the Book of Fasts has been abrogated, (*i. e.*, the former (feasts) have been all abrogated), may, then, new ones be added? The Tanaïm differ (on this question); for a Boraitha teaches: The days recorded in the Book of Fasts, whether during or after the existence of the Temple, are not permitted (to be kept as fasts), so says R. Meir; but R. Jose is of the opinion, so long as the Temple stood it was not permissible (to fast on them) because they were days of joy, but since the Temple fell it is allowed, because they are days of mourning. One rule says that they are abrogated; but another rule says they are not abrogated. There is a question here caused by one rule contradicting the other? There is no question; in the latter case it refers to the Feasts of Dedication and Esther (which are never to be abrogated): and in the former case, to all other (minor feast) days.

"IN ELUL ON ACCOUNT OF NEW YEAR'S DAY AND IN TISHRI ON ACCOUNT OF APPOINTING THE ORDER OF THE (REMAINING) FESTIVALS." Since (the messengers) were sent out on account of Elul, why need they go again on account of Tishri? Shall I say because (the Beth Din) desired to proclaim Elul an intercalary month? (That cannot be) for have we not learned that R. 'Hanina b. Kahana says in the name of Rabh: Since the time of Ezra we have not discovered that Elul was an intercalary month? We have not discovered it, because it was not necessary (to make it so). But if it will be necessary, shall we make it an intercalary month? This would disturb the position of New Year's Day! It is better that the position of New Year's Day alone should be disturbed, than that all the holidays should be disarranged. And the best evidence for this is that the Mishna says that the messengers were sent in Tishri on account of appointing the order of the festivals.

"AND IN KISLEV ON ACCOUNT OF THE FEAST OF DEDICATION AND IN ADAR ON ACCOUNT OF THE FEAST OF ESTHER." But the Mishna does not say if it be a leap-year, that the messengers were sent out in the second Adar on account of the Feast of Esther? From this we learn that the Mishna is not, according to Rabbi; for a

Boraitha teaches: Rabbi says: in a leap-year, messengers are sent out also in the second Adar on account of the Feast of Esther.

When Ulla came (from Palestine) he said: They have made Elul an intercalary month, and he also said: "Do my Babylonian comrades know the benefit we have gained through it?" Because of what is this a benefit? "Because of herbs,"* said Ulla. R. A'ha b. 'Hanina, however, said: "Because of dead bodies." † What difference is there between them? They differ concerning a holiday that falls immediately before or after the Sabbath (on the sixth or first day of the week). According to the one who says "because of herbs" we ought to add an intercalary day; but (it is not necessary) according to him who says "because of dead bodies," for we can employ non-Jews (to bury the dead for us on the holidays). If this is the explanation, why is this a benefit only for us (in Babylon); is it not also to the advantage of them (in Jerusalem)? Our climate is very hot, but theirs is not.

Is that so? Did not Rabba b. Samuel teach: One might suppose that as we intercalate the *year* when necessary, so we intercalate the *month* when necessary? Says the Torah [Ex. xii. 2], "This month shall be unto you the first of the months," which means as soon as you see (the new moon) as on this occasion, you must *consecrate* the month (whether or not it is necessary to *intercalate* it). (How then could they intercalate Elul, which had always only twenty-nine days)? To *intercalate* it (when necessary) was permitted; but to *consecrate* it, was not permitted; and Rabba's words should read: One might suppose that as it is permitted to *intercalate the year and the month* when necessary, so we may *consecrate the month* when necessary? Says the Torah [Ex. xii. 2], "This month shall be unto you, etc.," which means, only when the moon is seen as on this occasion, may you *consecrate* it.

Samuel said: "I can arrange the calendar for the whole captivity." Abba, the father of R. Simlai, said to him, "Do you know, sir, that which a certain Boraitha teaches, concerning the secret of the intercalary day, viz.: Whether the new moon appears before or after midday?" Answered he, "No." "Then, sir," said he, "if you do not know this, there may be other things which you do not

---

* By adding an intercalary day to Elul, the holiday (New Year or Atonement Day) was prevented from falling on Friday or Sunday, the intention being to separate the holiday by an intervening day from the Sabbath. Thus, herbs that were to be eaten fresh, and other foods, would not spoil, as they might, if kept from Thursday till after the Sabbath.

† A similar practice was followed with regard to the keeping of a dead body over the Day of Atonement and a Sabbath. Since it was impossible to keep the dead body two days, the Sabbath and the Atonement Day were separated by the means of the intercalated day.

know." When R. Zera went (to Palestine) he sent back word to his comrade (saying): The evening and the morning(following) must both belong to the month (*i. e.*, when the old moon has still been seen after dark on the twenty-ninth day of the month, the thirtieth evening and following day belong to the closing month). And this is what Abba, the father of R. Simlai, meant: We calculate only the beginning of the new moon; if it began before midday, it is certain that it was seen close upon the setting of the sun, but if it did not begin before midday, it is certain that it did not appear close upon the setting of the sun. What difference does it make (in practice)? Answered R. Ashi, to refute witnesses. R. Zera says in the name of R. Na'hman, in every case of doubt (about the holidays), we post-date but never antedate.* Does this mean to say that (in a case of doubt concerning the exact day on which Tabernacles begins) we observe the fifteenth and sixteenth but not the fourteenth; let us keep the fourteenth also; perhaps Abh and Elul have each only twenty-nine days? That two consecutive months should each have twenty-nine days is a matter that every one would know. Levi went to Babylon on the eleventh of Tishri. Said he, "Sweet is the food of Babylon, on the great Day (of Atonement now being held) in Palestine." They said to him, "Go and testify." Answered he, "I have not heard from the Beth Din the words, "It is consecrated,"" (and therefore I cannot testify). For R. Jo'hanan announced: In every place that the messengers sent in Nisan reached, but that the messengers sent in Tishri cannot reach, they must observe two days for the holidays; and they make this restriction for Nisan lest people would do in Tishri as in Nisan.† Rabha used to fast two days for the Day of Atonement.‡ Once it happened that he was right (because the Day of Atonement fell one day later in Palestine than in Babylon). R. Na'hman was once fasting on the Day of Atonement, and in the evening a certain man came and said to him, "To-morrow

---

* *i. e.* if there be a doubt about which day is the Passover or the feast of Tabernacles, the festival should be kept for two days; not, however, by *ante-dating* and keeping the *fourteenth* and fifteenth (of Nisan or Tishri) but by *post-dating* and keeping the fifteenth and *sixteenth* of either month.

† In Tishri, messengers might be delayed reaching distant places, to which they were sent to announce the date of the festival (Tabernacles), on account of New Year's Day and the Day of Atonement, on which they could not travel more than a short distance. In Nisan, however, they could, without delay, reach those places, and having announced the date of the festival, only one day was hallowed. Fearing that people might do, in regard to the Feast of Tabernacles what they did with regard to Passover, (*i. e.*, keep one day, even when in doubt about the date), the Rabbis instituted that both Tabernacles and Passover should have two days hallowed instead of one.

‡ He was in doubt whether the Beth Din at Jerusalem had made Elul intercalary or not, and as the messengers did not arrive until after the Day of Atonement, he fasted two days.

will be the Day of Atonement in Palestine." He angrily quoted. "Swift were our persecutors" [Lamen. iv. 19]. R. Na'hman said to certain sailors, "Ye who do not know the calendar take notice that when the moon still shines at dawn (it is full moon, and if it happens to be Nisan) destroy your leaven bread, (for it is then the fourteenth day).

MISHNA: For the sake of (the new moon) of the two months, Nisan and Tishri, witnesses may profane * the Sabbath, because in these months the messengers went to Syria, and the order of the festivals was arranged; when, however, the Temple † was in existence, they might profane the Sabbath in any month, in order to offer the (new moon) sacrifice in its proper time.

GEMARA: For the sake of these two months and not more? Against this I raise a question of contradiction: (Is it not said). For the sake of six months messengers were sent out? Answered Abayi: Thus he means: For all new moons, the messengers were sent out while it was still evening, but for Nisan and Tishri, they were not sent out until they heard from the lips of the Beth Din, the words "It (the new moon or month) is consecrated." The Rabbis taught: Whence do we know that for them we may profane the Sabbath? From [Lev. xxiii. 4] which runs "These are the feasts of the Lord, which ye shall proclaim in their seasons;" might not one suppose that as (witnesses) were permitted to profane the Sabbath until the new moons had been consecrated, so were messengers permitted to profane the Sabbath, until (the festivals) were introduced? Says the Torah: "which ye shall proclaim," *i. e.*, you may profane the Sabbath in order to proclaim them, but not to introduce them.

"When, However, the Temple Was in Existence, They Might Profane the Sabbath, in Any Month, in Order to Offer the (New Moon) Sacrifice, in Its Proper Time." The Rabbis taught: Formerly they profaned the Sabbath for all (new moons); but since the destruction of the Temple, said R. Jo'hanan b. Zakkai, have we any (new moon) sacrifice to offer? They then instituted that (witnesses) might profane the Sabbath only on account of Nisan and Tishri.

MISHNA: Whether the new moon had appeared clear to all or not, (the witnesses) were permitted to profane the Sabbath on its account. R. Jose says: If it appeared clear to everyone, ‡ the

* To travel to Jerusalem in order to inform the Beth Din might have necessitated walking more than the distance permitted on the Sabbath.

† The Temple in Jerusalem.

‡ It might then be presumed that everyone had seen it, and it was therefore unnecessary for anyone to go to Jerusalem to announce it to the Beth Din.

Sabbath should not be profaned (by witnesses). It once happened that more than forty pair (of witnesses) were on the highway (to Jerusalem) on the Sabbath, when R. Aqiba detained them at Lydda. R. Gamliel then sent word saying, "If thou thus detainest the people, thou wilt be the cause of their erring in the future (*i. e.*, they may refuse to come and testify).

GEMARA: The Rabbis taught: The words [Eccles. xii. 10] "Qoheleth sought to find out acceptable words," mean, that Qoheleth sought to invent laws, without the aid of witnesses or warning. An echo was heard saying, [Eccles xii. 10], "Let that which is written be upright, even words of truth" (which meant that) by means of two witnesses (should the words of truth be established).

"It Once Happened That More Than Forty Pair (of Witnesses) Were on the Highway (to Jerusalem) and R. Aqiba Detained Them, etc." A Boraitha teaches: R. Judah says, God forbid that R. Aqiba should have detained them: it was Shazpar, the superintendent of Gader who detained them, and (and when) R. Gamliel (heard of it, he) sent and dismissed him.

MISHNA: When a father and son have seen the new moon, they must both go to the Beth Din, not that they may act together as witnesses, but in order that, should the evidence of either of them be invalidated, the other may join to give evidence with another witness. R. Simon says: Father and son, and relatives in any degree may be accepted as competent witnesses to give evidence as to the appearance of the new moon. R. Jose says: It once happened that Tobias the physician, his son, and his freed slave, saw the new moon in Jerusalem (and when they tendered their evidence), the priests accepted his evidence and that of his son, but invalidated that of his freed slave; but when they appeared before the (Beth Din) they received his evidence, and that of his freed slave, but invalidated that of his son.

GEMARA: Asks R. Levi: What is the reason for R. Simon's opinion? It is written [Ex. xii. 1] "And the Lord spake unto Moses and Aaron saying: This month shall be *unto you*, "which means, this evidence shall be acceptable from you (although you are brothers). And how do the *Rabbis* explain it? They say it means: This testimony shall be given into your hands (*i. e.*, the Beth Din's). Says Mar Uqba in the name of Samuel the rule is according to R. Simon.

MISHNA: The following are considered incompetent to be witnesses: gamblers with dice, usurers, pigeon-breeders,* those who

* Those who breed and train pigeons for racing.

deal with the produce of the sabbatic year, and slaves. This is the rule: All evidence that cannot be received from a woman cannot be received from any of the above. One who has seen the new moon, but is unable to go (to give evidence), must be brought (if unable to walk) mounted on an ass, or even in a bed.* Persons afraid of an attack by robbers may take sticks with them;* and if they have a long way to go, it will be lawful for them to provide themselves with, and carry their food.* Whenever (witnesses) must be on the road a day and a night, it will be lawful to profane the Sabbath to travel thereon, to give their evidence as to the appearance of the moon. For thus it is written [Lev. xxiii. 4] "These are the feasts of the Lord, the holy convocations, which ye shall proclaim *in their appointed seasons.*"

* Even on the Sabbath, when under ordinary circumstances this might not be done.

CHAPTER II.

MISHNA: If the Beth Din did not know him (the witness) another was sent with him to testify in his behalf. In former times they would receive evidence (about the appearance of the moon) from any one; but when the Boëthusians used their corrupt practices the rule was made, that evidence would only be received from those who were known (to be reputable).

GEMARA: What is meant by "another" (in the above Mishna)? Another pair (of witnesses). This is proved by the following reasoning: If you do not say so, then what is the meaning of "him," in the words of the Mishna "If the Beth Din did not know *him?*" Shall I say it means one (witness)! Surely the evidence of one was not received, for this transaction was called "judgment" [Ps. lxxxi] (and two witnesses are necessary)? What then does "him" mean? That pair; so also here, "another" means another pair. Is then the evidence of one not accepted? Does not a Boraitha state: It once happened that R. Nehorai went to Usha on the Sabbath to testify (to the character) of one witness? He knew, that there was one witness in Usha and he went to add his evidence (and thus make two witnesses). If that is so, why need it tell us (that R. Nehorai went on the Sabbath)? One might suppose that, as there was a doubt (that he might not meet the other witness), he ought not to have profaned the Sabbath (by traveling to Usha as a single witness); therefore he teaches us (that even in such a case of doubt the Sabbath might be profaned).

When Ulla came (to Babylon, from Palestine), he said: They have already consecrated the New Moon in Palestine. Said R. Kahana: (In such a case) not only Ulla, who is a renowned man, is to be believed, but even an ordinary man. Why so? Because men will not lie about a matter, that will become known to every one.

"IN FORMER TIMES THEY WOULD RECEIVE EVIDENCE FROM ANY ONE, ETC." The Rabbis taught: What corruption did the Boëthusians practice? They once sought to deceive the sages, and they bribed, with four hundred zuz (silver coins), two men, one belonging to their party and one to ours. The former gave his evidence and went out; to the latter, they (the Beth Din) said, "Tell us what was the appearance of the moon?" "I went up, replied he," to Maale Adumim,* and I saw it crouching between two rocks. Its head was like a calf, its ears like a goat, its horns like a stag, and its tail was lying across its thigh. I gazed upon it and shuddered, and fell backwards; and if you do not believe me, behold, here I have two hundred zuz bound up in my cloth. "Who induced you to do this" they asked? "I heard," he replied, "that the Boëthusians wished to deceive the sages; so, I said to myself, I will go and inform them, lest some unworthy person may (accept their bribe) and come and deceive the sages." Then, said the sages, "The two hundred zuz may be retained by you as a reward, and he who bribed you, shall be taken to the whipping-post (and be punished)." Then and there they ordained that testimony should be received only from those who were known (to be of good character).

MISHNA: Formerly bon-fires were lighted (to announce the appearance of the new moon); but when the Cutheans † practiced their deceit it was ordained that messengers should be sent out. How were these bon-fires lighted? They brought long staves of cedar wood, canes, and branches of the olive tree, and bundles of tow which were tied on with twine; with these they went to the top of the mountain, and lighted them, and kept waving them to and fro, upward and downward, till they could perceive the same repeated by another person on the next mountain, and thus, on the third mountain, etc. Whence did these bon-fires commence? From the mount of Olives to Sartabha, from Sartabha to Grophinah, from Grophinah to Hoveran, from Hoveran to Beth Baltin; they did not cease waving the burning torches at Beth Baltin, to and fro, upward and downward, until the whole country of the captivity appeared like a blazing fire.

GEMARA: The Rabbis taught: Bon-fires were only lighted to announce the new moon that appeared and was consecrated at the proper time (after twenty-nine days). And when were they lighted? On the evening of the thirtieth day. Does this mean to say that for a month of twenty-nine days the bon-fires *were* lighted, but *not* for a month of thirty days? It should have been done for a month of thirty days, and not at all for a month of twenty-nine days. Says Abayi: That would cause the people a loss of work for two days (because they would wait to see if the bon-fires would be lit or not and thus lose a second day).‡

* The name of a place between Jerusalem and Jericho.

† A sect of Samaritans.

‡ The thirtieth day from the last New Moon was always New Moon, but in intercalary months the thirty-first day was also New Moon (second day); In the latter case the thirtieth day (first day of New Moon) belonged to the passing month, and the second day of New Moon

"How Were These Bon-Fires Lighted? They Brought Long Staves of Cedar Wood, etc." R. Judah says: There are four kinds of cedars: the common cedar, the Qetros, the olive tree, and the cypress. Qetros says Rabh, is (in Aramaic) Adara or a species of cedar. Every cedar, says R. Jo'hanan, that was carried away from Jerusalem, God will in future times, restore, as it is said [Is. xli. 19], "I will plant in the wilderness the cedar tree," and by "wilderness" He means Jerusalem, as it is said, [Is. lxiv. 10], "Zion is (become) a wilderness." Further says R. Jo'hanan, "Woe to the Romans, for whom there will be no substitution," for it is said [Is. lx. 17], "For brass, I will bring gold, and for iron, I will bring silver, and for wood, brass and for stones, iron;" but what can He bring for R. Aqiba and his comrades (who were destroyed by Rome)? Of them He says [Joel iii. 21], "I will cleanse them, (but for) *their* (Aqiba's and his comrades') blood, I will not cleanse them."

"And Whence Did These Bon-Fires Commence?" From Beth Baltin. What is Beth Baltin? "Biram," answered Rabh What (does the Mishna) mean by the captivity? Says R. Joseph. "Pombeditha." And how was it that the whole country looked like a blazing fire? We learn that each Israelite took a torch in his hand and ascended to the roof of his house.

MISHNA: There was a large court in Jerusalem, called Beth Ya'azeq, where all the witnesses met, and where they were examined by the Beth Din. Great feasts were made there for (the witnesses) in order to induce them to come frequently. At first, they did not stir from there all day (on the Sabbath),* till R. Gamliel, the Elder, ordained that they might go two thousand cubits on every side; and not only these (witnesses) but also a midwife, going to perform her professional duties, and those who go to assist others in case of conflagration, or of an attack of robbers, or of flood, or (of rescuing people) from the ruins (of a fallen building) are considered (for the time being) as inhabitants of that place, and may go (thence on the Sabbath) two thousand cubits on every side. How were the witnesses examined? The first pair were examined first. The elder was introduced first, and they said to him: Tell us, in what form you

was the first day of the new month. Bonfires were always lighted on the night of the thirtieth day, *i. e.*, on the night after new moon; and if no bonfires were lighted then there were two days New Moon. In the case of the month of Elul they would, after twenty-nine days observe New Year's Day. Now if that month happened to be intercalary (*i. e.* have thirty days) and bonfires would have been lighted, the next day would have had to be observed as New Year's Day again, and the people would consequently have lost a second day.

* For if they had already traveled two thousand cubits, they were prohibited from journeying more than four cubits more.

saw the moon; was it before or behind the sun? Was it to the north or the south (of the sun)? What was its elevation on the horizon? Towards which side was its inclination? What was the width of her disk? If he answered, before the sun, his evidence was worthless. After this they introduced the younger (witness) and he was examined; if their evidence was found to agree, their testimony was accepted as valid; the remaining pairs (of witnesses) were asked leading questions, not because their testimony was necessary, but only to prevent them departing, disappointed, and to induce them to come again often.

GEMARA: Do not the questions (asked by the Mishna), "was it before or behind the sun?" and "was it to the north or to the south?" mean the same thing? Answered Abayi: (The Mishna asks) whether the concave of the crescent was before or behind the sun, and if (the witness said) it was before the sun, his evidence was worthless; for R. Jo'hanan says: What is the meaning of the passage [Job xxv. 2] "Dominion and fear are with him; he maketh peace in his high places?" It means that the sun never faces the concave of the crescent or the concave of a rainbow.

"What Was its Elevation on the Horizon? Towards Which Side Was its Inclination?" In one Boraitha we have learnt: If (the witness) said "towards the north," his evidence was valid, but if he said, "towards the south," it was worthless; does not another Boraitha (which says the following) teach the very opposite: If (the witness) said "towards the south," his testimony was accepted, but if he said "towards the north" it was valueless? There is no difficulty here; in the latter case it speaks of the summer, while in the former it refers to the winter. The Rabbis taught: If one (witness) said its elevation appeared about as high as two ox-goads and another said about as high as three, their testimony was invalid, but either might be taken in conjunction with a subsequent witness (who offered similar testimony). The Rabbis taught: (If the witnesses say) "we have seen the reflection (of the moon) in the water, or through a metal mirror, or in the clouds," their testimony is not to be accepted; or (if they say we have seen) "half of it in the water, and half of it in the heavens, or half of it in the clouds," their evidence carries no weight. Must they then see the new moon again (before their testimony can be accepted)? Answered Abayi: This is their meaning, if the witnesses testify that they saw the moon, accidentally, and they then returned purposely and looked for it, but they saw it not, their evidence is worthless. Why so? Because one might say they saw a patch of white clouds (and they thought it was the moon).

MISHNA: The chief of the Beth Din says "It (the new moon) is consecrated," and all the people repeated after him "It is consecrated, it is consecrated." Whether the new moon was seen at its proper time (after twenty-nine days) or not, they used to consecrate it. R. Elazar b. Zadok said: If it had not been sent at its proper time it was not consecrated, because it had already been consecrated in heaven (*i. e.*, of itself).

GEMARA: Whence do we know that the (chief of the Beth Din must say "It is consecrated")? Answered R. 'Hiyya b. Gamda in the name of Rabbi: The Torah says [Lev. xxiii. 44], "Moses declared unto the children of Israel the feasts of the Lord" from which we deduce that (as Moses, who was the chief in Israel, declared the feasts to Israel, so also does) the chief of the Beth Din announce the words "It is consecrated."

"ALL THE PEOPLE REPEATED AFTER HIM "IT IS CONSECRATED, IT IS CONSECRATED." Whence do we know this? Answered R. Papa: The Torah says [Lev. xxiii. 2], "Which *ye* shall proclaim," *i. e.*, which ye, all the people shall proclaim; but R. Na'hman b. Isaac says: We know it from the words [ibid.] "*These* are my feasts," *i. e.* (*these people*) shall announce my feasts. Why are the words "It is consecrated" repeated twice? Because in the Scriptural verse just quoted we find it written "holy convocations" (*literally*, announcements, and the minimum of the plural expression is two).

"R. ELAZAR B. ZADOK SAID: IF IT HAD NOT BEEN SEEN AT ITS PROPER TIME, IT WAS NOT CONSECRATED, ETC." Pelimo* teaches in a Boraitha: When the new moon appears at its proper time, they used not to consecrate it, but when it appears out of its proper time, they used to consecrate it. R. Eliezer, however, says: In neither case used they to consecrate it, for it is written [Lev. xxv. 10] "And ye shall consecrate the fiftieth year;" *years* should be consecrated, but not *months*. R. Judah says in the name of Samuel: The law is according to R. Elazer b. Zadok. Abayi says: We have also a Mishna to the same effect, viz.: If the Beth Din and all Israel saw the new moon (on the thirtieth day) and if the examination of the witnesses had already taken place, and it had become dark before they had time to announce "It is consecrated," the month (just passing) is intercalary. That (the month) is intercalary is mentioned (by the Mishna), but not that they said "It is consecrated?"

* The name of a Tana, a contemporary of Rabbi.

It is not clear that this is a support for Abayi's argument, for it was necessary to say that it was intercalary, or we would not have known that the next day was the intercalary day. One might have thought since the Beth Din and all Israel saw the new moon, that it was apparent to all, and that the month does not become intercalary, therefore he teaches us that (nevertheless the month becomes intercalary).

MISHNA: R. Gamliel had on a tablet, and on the wall of his upper room, illustrations of the various phases of the moon, which he showed to the common people, saying, "Did you see the moon like this figure or like this?"

GEMARA: Is this permitted? Does not a Boraitha teach that the words "Ye shall not make with me" [Ex. xx. 23] mean, ye shall not make pictures of my ministers that minister before me, such as the sun, moon, stars or planets? It was different with R. Gamliel, for others made it for him. But others made one for R. Judah, yet Samuel said to him "Thou, sagacious one, destroy that figure!" * In the latter case the figure was embossed, and he was afraid that one might suspect the owner (of using it as an idol). Need one be afraid of such suspicion? Did not that synagogue in Shephithibh of Nehardea have a statue (of the king), yet Rabh, Samuel, and Samuel's father and Levi went there to pray and were not afraid of being suspected (of idolatry)? It is a different case when there are many. Yet, R. Gamliel was only one? Yea, but he was a prince, and there were always many with him; and if you wish you may say that he had them made to teach by means of them; and that which is written [Deut. xviii. 9] "thou shalt not learn to do," means but thou mayest learn, in order to understand and to teach.

MISHNA: It happened once, that two witnesses came and said: We saw the moon in the eastern part of the heavens in the morning, and in the western part in the evening. R. Jo'hanan b. Nuri declared them to be false witnesses; but when they came to Jamnia, Gamliel received their evidence as valid. (On another occasion) two other witnesses came and said: We saw the moon on its proper day, but could not see it on the next evening of the intercalary day; R. Gamliel received them; but R. Dosa b. Harkhinas, said: They are false witnesses; for how can they testify of a woman being delivered (on a certain day), when, on the next day, she appears to be pregnant? Then R. Joshua said unto him: I approve your opinion. Upon this Gamliel sent him (R. Joshua) word, saying, "I order

* literally "put out the eyes of that figure"

you to appear before me on the Day of Atonement, according to your computation, with your staff and with money. R. Aqiba went to him (R. Joshua), and found him grieving; he then said to him, I can prove that all Gamliel has done is proper for it is said, "These are the feasts of the Lord, holy convocations which ye shall proclaim," either at their proper time, or not at their proper time, only *their* convocations are to be considered as holy festivals. When he (R. Joshua) came to R. Dosa b. Harkhinas, the latter told him, "If we are to reinvestigate the decisions of the Beth Din of Gamliel, we must also reinvestigate the decisions of all the Beth Dins which have existed from the time of Moses till the present day; for it is said [Ex. xxiv. 9], "Moses, Aaron, Nadab, Abihu, and seventy elders went up (to the Mount)." Why were not the names of the elders also specified? To teach us, that every three men in Israel that form a Beth Din are to be respected in an equal degree with the Beth Din of Moses. Then did R. Joshua take his staff and money in his hand, and went to Jamnia, to Gamliel, on the very day on which the Day of Atonement would have been according to his computation: when Gamliel arose, and kissed him on his forehead, saying, "Enter in peace, my master and disciple! My master—in knowledge; and my disciple—since thou didst obey my injunction."

GEMARA: A Boraitha teaches us: that R. Gamliel said to the sages, thus it has been handed down to me from the house of my grandfather (Hillel), that sometimes the new moon appears elongated and sometimes diminished. R. 'Hiyya saw the old moon yet on the morning of the twenty-ninth day, and threw clods of earth at it, saying, "We should consecrate thee in the evening, and thou art seen now? Go, hide thyself!"

Said Rabbi to R. 'Hiyya: "Go to Entob and consecrate the month and send back to me as a password* 'David, the King of Israel still lives.'" The Rabbis taught: Once it happened that the heavens were thick with clouds and the form of the moon was seen on the twenty-ninth of the month (of Elul), so that the people thought that New Year's Day should be then proclaimed, and they (the Beth Din) were about to consecrate it. Said R. Gamliel to them: Thus it has been handed down to me by tradition, from the house of my grandfather, the consecration of the moon cannot take place at a period less than twenty-nine and a half days, two-thirds and .0052 (*i. e.*, seventy-three 'Halaqim) of an hour. On that self-same day the mother of Ben Zaza died and R. Gamliel delivered a great funeral

* This device was resorted to because, in the days of Rabbi, the Romans had prohibited the Jews, under penalty of death, to consecrate the moon.

oration,* not because she specially deserved it, but in order that the people might know that the new moon had not yet been consecrated by the Beth Din.

"WHEN HE (RABBI JOSHUA) CAME TO R. DOSA B. HARKHINAS, ETC." The Rabbis taught: The reason that the names of those elders are not mentioned, is in order that one should not say: Is So-and-so like Moses and Aaron? Is So-and-so like Nadabh and Abihu? Is So-and-so like Eldad and Medad? (And how do we know that one should not ask thus)? Because, it is written [1 Sam. xii. 6], "And Samuel said unto the people the Lord that appointed Moses and Aaron" and in the same connection it is said [ibid. 11.], "And the Lord sent Jerubaal and Bedan and Jephtha and Samuel." Jerubaal is Gideon; and why is he named Jerubaal? Because he strove against Baal; Bedan is Samson; and why is he named Bedan? Because he came from Dan. Jephtha means just what it is (*i. e.*, he had no surname or attribute). It is said [Ps. xcix. 6] "Moses and Aaron among his priests, and Samuel, among them that called upon his name;" the sacred text regards the three common people equal with the three noblest, to teach us that Jerubaal was in his generation like Moses in his; Bedan in his generation was like Aaron in his; Jephtha in his generation was like Samuel in his generation. From all this one must learn, that if, even the commonest of the commoners is appointed leader by a community, he must be considered as the noblest of the nobility, for it is said [Deut. xvii. 9] "And thou shalt come unto the priests, the Levites, and unto the judge that shall be in those days." (Why does the Torah say "in those days"?) Can you imagine that one could go to a judge who was not in his days? (Surely not! but by these words Scripture teaches us that a judge is to be held "in his days" equal in authority with the greatest of his antecedents). We find a similar teaching in Eccles. vii. 10: "Say not thou, that the former days were better than these!"

"HE TOOK HIS STAFF, ETC." The Rabbis taught: (Gamliel said to R. Joshua): Happy is the generation in which the leaders listen to their followers, and through this the followers consider it so much the more their duty (to heed the teachings of the leaders).

---

* No funerals or funeral orations were, or are, permitted on the holidays.

CHAPTER III.

MISHNA: If the Beth Din, and all Israel saw (the moon on the night of the thirtieth day), or, if the witness had been examined, but there was no time to proclaim "It is consecrated" before it has become dark, the month is intercalary. If the Beth Din alone saw it, two of its members should stand and give the testimony before the others, who shall then say "It is consecrated, It is consecrated." When three who formed a Beth Din saw it, two should stand and conjoining some of their learned friends with the remaining one, give their testimony before them, who should proclaim "It is consecrated, It is consecrated," for one (member of a Beth Din) has not this right by himself alone.

GEMARA: "If the Beth Din Alone Saw It, Two of Its Members Should Stand and Give Their Testimony Before the Others, etc." Why so? Surely hearsay evidence is not better than the testimony of an eye-witness! Says R. Zera: It refers to a case where they saw it at night (and on the next day they could not consecrate the new moon until they had heard the evidence of two witnesses).

"When Three, Who Formed a Beth Din, Saw it, Two Should Stand and Conjoining Some of Their Learned Friends With the Remaining One, etc." Why so? Here also we may say, surely hearsay evidence is not better than the testimony of an eye-witness! And if you should object that this also means where they saw it at night, is this not, then, the same case? The case is the same, but he needs to state the above, because of the concluding words, "one (member of a Beth Din) has not the right by himself alone;" for you might possibly think that we say, since in civil cases three (are required to constitute a Beth Din), but where he is well known (as a learned authority) one judge may act alone, so here we may consecrate (the new moon) on the authority of one judge, therefore, he teaches us (that three are required). Perhaps I should, nevertheless, say here (that one learned authority is sufficient)? Nay, for there is no greater authority than Moses, our master, yet God said to him, that Aaron should act with him, as it is written [Ex. xii. 1, 2]. "And the Lord spake unto Moses and Aaron, in the land of Egypt, saying: This month shall be unto *you* the beginning of months."

Does this mean to say that a witness may act as judge? And shall I then say that the above Mishna is not according to R. Aqiba, for a Boraitha teaches: If the members of the Sanhedrin saw a man commit murder, part of them may act as witnesses and part as judges, according to R. Tarphon; but according to R. Aqiba all of them are witnesses, and no witness (of a crime) may act as judge? You may state (that the Mishna is) according to R. Aqiba even. In the latter instance R. Aqiba only refers to capital cases, for the Torah says [Numb. xxxv. 24, 25] "Then the congregation shall judge . . . .and the congregation shall deliver," and since they saw him commit murder, they will not be able to urge any plea in his favor; but here (concerning the new moon) even R. Aqiba assents (that a witness may act as judge).

MISHNA: Every kind of cornet may be used (on New Year's Day) except those made of cow-horn, because they are called "horn" (QEREN) and not "cornet" (SHOPHAR). R. Jose says: Are not all cornets called "horn," as *e. g.*, it is said [Josh. vi. 5] "And it came to pass that when they made a long blast with the horn."

GEMARA: How comes it that the word JOBHEL means ram? A Boraitha teaches: R. Aqiba says, When I went to Arabia, I found they called a ram "Yubla." The Rabbis did not know the meaning of the word SALSELEHO in the passage [Prov. iv. 8] "Salseleho and she shall promote thee." One day they heard Rabbi's maidservant say to a certain man who was (conceitedly) playing with his hair, "How long wilt thou MESALSEL (twist up) thy hair?" The Rabbis did not know the meaning of the word YEHABHEKHA in the passage [Ps. lv. 22] "Cast YEHABHEKHA (burden) upon the Lord." Says Rabba b. Bar 'Hana, "One day I went with a certain Arabian caravan merchant and I was carrying a burden. Said he to me, 'Take down YEHABHEKH (thy burden) and put it on my camel.'"

MISHNA: The cornet used on the New Year was a straight horn of a wild goat: the mouth-piece was covered with gold. The two trumpets were stationed one on each side: the sound of the cornet was prolonged, while that of the trumpet was short, because the special duty of the day was the sounding of the cornet. On the fast days two crooked ram's-horns were used, their mouth-pieces being covered with silver, and the two trumpets were stationed in the middle between them: the sound of the cornet was shortened while that of the trumpets was prolonged, because the special duty of the day was the sounding of the trumpets. The Jubilee and New Year's Day were alike in respect to the sounding (of the cornet) and the benedictions, but R. Judah says on the New Year we blow (a cornet) made of ram's-horn, and on the Jubilee one made of the horn of a wild goat.

GEMARA: R. Levi says: It is a duty on New Year's Day and the Day of Atonement to use a bent cornet, but during the rest of the year a straight one. But have we not learned that the cornet used on the New Year must be the "*straight* horn of a wild goat? He (R. Levi) supports his opinion with the following Boraitha which teaches that R. Judah says: On New Year's Day they used to blow (a cornet) made of a straight ram's-horn and on the Jubilees, one made of wild goat's horn. About what do they dispute? R. Judah holds that on New Year's the more bent in spirit a man is, and on the Day of Atonement, the more upright he is (in his confessions), the better: but R. Levi holds the more upright a man is on New Year's Day and the more bowed in spirit on the Fast Days, the better.

"THE MOUTH-PIECE WAS COVERED WITH GOLD." Does not a Boraitha teach, however, that if one covers the place to which the mouth was put the cornet may not be used; but if (he covers) another place it may be used? Answered Abayi: Our Mishna also means, a place to which the mouth was not put.

"THE TWO TRUMPETS WERE STATIONED ONE ON EACH SIDE." Could the two sounds be easily distinguished? Nay; and therefore the sound of the cornet was prolonged to indicate that the special duty of the day was the sounding of the cornet.

"ON THE FAST-DAYS TWO CROOKED RAM'S-HORNS WERE USED, THEIR MOUTH-PIECES BEING COVERED WITH SILVER." Why was the cornet used in the one case covered with gold and in the other, with silver? All (signals for) assemblies were blown on horns made with silver as it is written [Numb. x. 2] "Make unto thee two trumpets of silver . . . that thou mayest use them for the calling of the assembly, etc." R. Papa b. Samuel was about to follow the practice laid down by the Mishna: said Rabha to him, that was only customary so long as the Temple was in existence. A Boraitha also teaches this applies only to the Temple; but in the country (outside of Jerusalem) in a place where they use the trumpet, they do not use the cornet, and *vice-versa*. And so also did R. 'Halaphta, in Sepphoris and so too did R. 'Hanina b. Teradjon in Si'hni, when the matter was brought to the attention of the sages, they said: That was the custom, only at the eastern gates or the Temple Mount. Rabha, but some say R. Joshua b. Levi asked: From which Scriptural verse is this deduced? From Ps. xcviii. 6 which runs, "With trumpets and sound of cornet, make a joyful noise before the Lord, the King;" *i. e.*, before the Lord, the King (in the Temple) we need both the trumpets and the cornet, but not elsewhere.

"THE JUBILEE, AND THE NEW YEAR WERE ALIKE IN RESPECT TO THE SOUNDING (OF THE CORNET), AND THE BLESSINGS." R. Samuel b. Isaac said: According to whom do we now-a-days pray: "This day celebrates the beginning of thy work, a memorial of the first day?" According to R. Eliezer who says: The world was created in Tishri. R. Ina asked a question: Did we not learn in our Mishna that the Jubilee and New Year are alike in respect to the sounding (of the cornet), and the benedictions, and now how can that be so when we say "This day celebrates the beginning of thy work, a memorial of the first day," which is said on New Year but not on the Jubilee? (That which we have learnt in our Mishna that they are alike means) in every other respect but this.

MISHNA: It is unlawful to use a cornet that has been split and afterwards joined together; or one made of several pieces joined together. If a cornet had a hole that had been stopped up, and prevented (the production) of the proper sound, it might not be used; but if it does not affect the proper sound, it might be used. If one should blow the cornet inside a pit, a cistern or a vat and the sound of the cornet was (plainly) heard (by one listening to it) he will have done his duty (to hear the cornet on the New Year), but not if he heard only an indistinct sound. Thus also, if one should happen to pass by a synagogue, or live close by it and should hear the cornet (on the New Year) or the reading of the Book of Esther (on the Feast of Esther), he will have complied with the requirements of the law, if he listened with proper attention but not otherwise; and although the one heard it as well as the other, yet the difference (on which everything depends) is, that the one listened with proper attention, and the other did not.

GEMARA: The Rabbis taught: If a cornet was long and they shortened it, it might be used; if one scraped it and reduced it to its due size, it might be used; if one covered it on the inside, with gold, it might not be used; if on the outside and it changed the tone from what it originally was, it might not be used, but if not, it might be used; if a cornet had a hole in it and they closed it up, and thereby prevented (the production) of the proper sound, it might not be used, but if not it might be used; if one placed one cornet inside another and the sound heard (by a listener) was produced from the inner one he has complied with the requirements of the law, but if from the outer one, he has not.

"OR ONE MADE OF SEVERAL PIECES JOINED TOGETHER." The Rabbis taught: If one added to a cornet never so small a piece, whether it be of the same kind of horn or not, it might not be used. If a cornet had a hole, whether one stopped it up with a piece of the same kind (of horn) or not, it might not be used, but R. Nathan held (only when repaired with material) *not* of the same kind, it might not be used, but otherwise it might. (To which) R. Judah, added: That is, if the greater part of a cornet was broken. From this we may prove that if repaired with material of the same kind, although the greater part was broken, it may, nevertheless be used.

"If one covered a cornet on the inside with gold it might not be used; if on the outside, and it changed the tone from what it originally was, it might not be used, but if not, it might be used." If a cornet had been split lengthwise, it might not be used, but if crosswise, yet enough remained with which to produce the sound, it might be used, but if not, it might not be used. [And how much is that? R. Simon b. Gamliel explains it to be as much as we may hold in our closed hand, and yet on either side a portion is visible].* If its tone was thin, or heavy or harsh, it might be used, for all tones were considered proper in a cornet. The schoolmen sent a message to the father of Samuel: (One has complied with the requirements of the law if he bored a hole in a horn and blew it. That is self-evident! for in every cornet a hole must surely be bored. Says R. Ashi: If one bored a hole through the bony substance inside the horn (which ought to be removed), are we to suppose that one substance causes an interposition with another of the same nature, (and that, therefore it might not be used)? Therefore they sent to say that this is no objection.

"IF ONE SHOULD BLOW THE CORNET INSIDE A PIT OR A CISTERN, ETC." R. Huna says: They taught this only in the case of those who stood at the pit's mouth, but those who were in the pit comply with the requirements of the law. If one heard a part of (the required number of) the sounds of the cornet in the pit, and the rest at the pit's mouth, he has done his duty; but if he heard a part before the dawn of day, and the rest after the dawn, he has not complied with the requirements of the law. Asked Abayi: Why in the latter case (should he not have done his duty, because he did not hear the whole of the sounds at the time when the duty should be performed), yet, in the former case (he is considered to have done

* The opinion of the editor is that this parenthesis is a fair illustration of the interpolations in the Talmud. The term PIRASH is not Talmudical and was only used in later times. It has only been left here because the explanation happens to be correct.

.his duty) under similar circumstances? How can you compare these cases? In the latter case, *the night is not* the time of performing the obligation at all, while in the former case, *a pit is* a place where the duty may be performed for those who are in it! Shall we say that Rabba held: If one heard the end of the sounding (of the cornet), without having heard the beginning he complied with the requirements of the law, and from these words we must understand that if he heard the beginning, without the end he has also done his duty? Come and hear! If one blew the first sound (TEQIA) and prolonged the second (TEQIA) as long as two, it is only reckoned as one; and (if Rabba's opinion is correct) why should you reckon it as two? (This is no question)! If he heard a half the sounds, he has done his duty, but when one blows one sound on the cornet, we may not consider it two halves. Rabha says: One who vows to receive no benefit from his neighbor, may blow for him the obligatory sounds (of the cornet); one who vows refusal of any benefit from a cornet, may blow on it the obligatory sounds. Furthermore says Rabha: One who vows to refuse any benefit from his neighbor may sprinkle on him the waters of a sin-offering in the winter, but not in the summer. One who vows to receive no benefit from a spring, may take in it an obligatory bath in the winter, but not in the summer. The schoolmen sent a message to the father of Samuel: If one had been compelled to eat unleavened bread (on the first night of Passover, *i. e.*, he had not done so of his own accord) he has also done his duty. Who compelled him? Answered R. Ashi, Persians. Rabha remarked: From this statement we can prove that if one plays a song on the cornet, he complies with the requirements of the law. It is self-understood! The cases are similar? But one might suppose that in the former case, the Torah commanded him to *eat* (unleavened bread) and he *ate* it, but in the former case the Torah speaks of "a *remembrance* of blowing the cornet" [Lev. xxiii. 24], and (when he plays a song he does not *remember* his duty for) he is engaged in a worldly occupation! Therefore he teaches us that even under such circumstances he *does* comply with the requirements of the law. To this an objection was raised. We have learnt: If one who listened (to the sounds of the cornet) paid the proper attention, but he that blew the cornet did not, or *vice-versa*, they have not done their duty, until both blower and listener pay proper attention. This is all right as far as the case where the blower, but not the listener, pays the proper attention, for it is possible that the listener imagines he hears the noise of an animal: but how can it happen that the listener should pay due attention and the one who blows (the cornet) should not, except he was only playing a song (by which he does not do his duty)? (It is possible) if he only produced a dull sound; (*i. e.* and not, for example a Teqia).

Said Abayi to him: But now, according to your conclusion (that a duty performed without due attention is the same as if performed with due attention) will you say that he who sleeps in a tabernacle on the eighth day of the feast of Tabernacles receive stripes (because he had no right to observe the law for more than seven day)? Answered he: I say that one cannot infringe a command except at the time when it should be performed. R. Shamen b. Abba raised an objection: Whence do we know that a priest who ascended the platform (to pronounce the priestly benediction) must not say: Since the Torah has given me the right to bless Israel, I will supplement (the benedictions Numb. vi. 24-26) by one of my own, as for example [Deut. i. 11] "May the Lord God of your fathers make you a thousand times so many more as ye are?" From the Torah which says [Deut. iv. 2] "Ye shall not *add* unto the word." And in this case as soon as he has finished the benedictions, the time for performing that duty has gone by, still if he add a blessing of his own he is guilty of infringing the law which says "Ye shall not add?" Said Rabha: (I mean). To fulfill the requirements of the law one need not pay attention; to transgress the law against supplementing, at the time prescribed for performing it, also, does not require one's special attention; but to transgress the law against supplementing at the time not prescribed for performance, needs one's special attention. R. Zira said to his attendant: "Pay attention, and sound (the cornet) for me!" Do we not thus see that he holds that to fulfill the requirements of the law the act is not enough and one must pay attention? This is a disputed question among the Tanaim, for a Boraitha teaches: One who hears (the blowing of the cornet) must himself listen in order to perform his duty, and he who blows (the cornet) blows after his usual manner. R. Jose says: These words are said only in the case of the officiant for a congregation; but an individual does not comply with the requirements of the law unless both he that hears and he that blows pay proper attention.

MISHNA: (It is written in Ex. xvii. 11 that) "When Moses held up his hand, Israel prevailed, etc." Could then the hands of Moses cause war to be waged or to cease? (Nay); but it means that as long as Israel looked to Heaven for aid, and directed their hearts devoutly to their Father in Heaven, they prevailed; but when they ceased to do so, they failed. We find a similar instance also in [Numb. xxi. 8] "Make unto thee a fiery serpent and set it on a pole, and every one that is bitten, when he looketh upon it shall

6

live." Could then the serpent kill or bring to life? (Nay); but it means when the Israelites looked (upward) to Heaven for aid and subjected their will to that of their Father in Heaven they were healed, but when they did not, they perished. A deaf mute, an idiot, or a child cannot act in behalf of the assembled congregation. This is the general rule whosoever is not obliged to perform a duty, cannot act in behalf of the assembled congregation (for that duty).

GEMARA: The Rabbis taught: All are obliged to hear the sounding of the cornet, Priests, Levites and Israelites, Proselytes, Freed-Slaves, a monstrosity, a hermaphrodite, and one who is half slave and half free. A monstrosity cannot act in behalf of those like or unlike itself, but a hermaphrodite can act in behalf of those of the same class, but not of any other. The teacher says: It is said, All are obliged to hear the sounding of the cornet, Priests, Levites and Israelites. This is self understood, for if these are not obliged, who are? It was necessary to mention priests here, for one might have supposed, that since we have learnt, "the Jubilee and New Year's Day are alike with regard to the sounding of the cornet and the benedictions," that only those who are included under the rule of Jubilee are included in the duties of New Year's Day; and as the priests are not included in the rule of Jubilee (for they have no lands to lie fallow, etc.), might we not therefore say that they are not bound by the duties of New Year's Day? Therefore he teaches us (that they must hear the sounding of the cornet).

Ahabha, the son of R. Zera teaches: With regard to all the benedictions, although one has already done his duty he may nevertheless act for others, with the exception of the blessings over bread and wine; concerning which, if he has not yet done his duty, he may act for others, but if he has done his duty, he may not act for others. Rabha asked: What is the rule in the case of the benediction of the unleavened bread, and the wine used at the sanctification of a festival? Since these are special duties, may one act for others, or perhaps the (duty is only the eating of the unleavened bread and the drinking of the sanctification wine) but the benediction is not a duty, and therefore he cannot act for others? Come and hear! R. Ashi says: When we were at the home of R. Papa, he said the blessing of sanctification for us, and when his field-laborer came from work he said the blessing for him. The Rabbis taught: One may not say the benediction over bread for guests, unless he eats with them, but he may for the members of the family, to initiate them into their religious duties; with regard to the Service of Praise [HALLEL Ps. cxiii-cxviii.] and the reading of the Book of Esther, although one has already done his duty, he may, nevertheless, act for others.

CHAPTER IV.

MISHNA: When the feast of New Year happened to fall on the Sabbath, they used to sound (the cornet) in the Temple, but not outside of it. After the destruction of the Temple R. Jo'hanan b. Zakkai ordained that they should sound (the cornet) in every place in which there was a Beth Din. R. Elazar says that R. Jo'hanan b. Zakkai instituted that for Jamnia alone; but they (the sages) say the rule applied both to Jamnia and every place in which there was a Beth Din. And in this respect also was Jerusalem privileged more than Jamnia, that every city, from which Jerusalem could be seen, or the sounding (of the cornet) could be heard, which was near enough, and to which it was allowed to go on the Sabbath, might sound the (cornet) on the Sabbath but in Jamnia they sounded (the cornet) before the Beth Din only.

GEMARA: Whence do we learn these things? Says Rabha: The Rabbis issued a decree concerning them according to Rabba; for Rabba says, Although the duty of sounding (the cornet) is obligatory upon all, yet all are not skilled in sounding (it), therefore they feared lest one might take (the cornet) in his hand, and go to an expert and carry it more than four cubits on the New Year. The same rule applies to the palm branch (LULABH) and also to the scroll (on which is written the) Book of Esther.

"AFTER THE DESTRUCTION OF THE TEMPLE, R. JO'HANAN B. ZAKKAI ORDAINED, ETC." The Rabbis taught: Once it happened that New Year's Day fell on the Sabbath, and all the cities gathered together. Said R. Jo'hanan b. Zakkai to the Benai Betherah:* "Let us sound (the cornet)!" "First," said they, "let us discuss!" "Let us sound it," replied he, "and then we will discuss!" After they had sounded (the cornet) they said to him "Now let us discuss!" He answered "The cornet has now been heard in Jamnia, and we cannot retract after the act has been performed."

"BUT THEY (THE SAGES) SAY THE RULE APPLIED BOTH TO JAMNIA AND EVERY PLACE IN WHICH THERE IS A BETH DIN." Says R. Huna, that means, in the presence of the Beth Din. Does this preclude people from sounding (the cornet) out of the presence of the Beth Din? And, when R. Isaac b. Joseph came (from

* A scholarly family of Babylonian descent, much favored by Herod.

Jamnia) did he not say: When the officiant appointed by the congregation in Jamnia had finished sounding (the cornet) one could not hear his own voice on account of the sounds (of the cornets) used by individuals? (Even individuals) used to sound (the cornet) in the presence of the Beth Din. We have also been taught: Rabbi says, We may only sound (the cornet) during the time that the Beth Din is accustomed to sit.

"JERUSALEM WAS PRIVILEGED MORE THAN JAMNIA, ETC." (When the Mishna speaks of) "Every city from which Jerusalem could be seen," it means with the exception of a city located in the valley (from which it could be seen only by ascending to an elevated spot); by "the sounding (of the cornet) could be heard," it means to except a city located on the top of a mountain; by, "which was near enough," it means to exclude a city outside the prescribed limit (of a Sabbath journey); and by, "and to which it was allowed to go" it means to exclude a city (even near by) but divided (from Jerusalem) by a river.

MISHNA: Formerly the palm-branch (LULABH) was taken to the Temple seven days, but in cities outside (of Jerusalem) it was taken (to the synagogue) one day. Since the destruction of the Temple, R. Jo'hanan b. Zakkai ordained that the palm-branch should everywhere be taken seven days, in commemoration of the Temple, and also that it should be prohibited (to eat the new produce) the whole day of waving (the sheaf-offering; vide Lev. xxiii. 11-15).

GEMARA: Whence do we know that we do this in commemoration of the Temple? The Scriptures say [Jer. xxx. 17] "For I will restore health unto thee, and I will heal thee of thy wounds, saith the Lord, because they called thee an outcast, saying, This is Zion whom no man seeketh after." By implication (we see) it (Zion or the Temple) needs being sought after (or commemorated).

"AND THAT IT SHOULD BE PROHIBITED TO EAT . . . ON THE WHOLE DAY OF WAVING (THE SHEAF-OFFERING) ETC." R. Na'hman b. Isaac remarks: R. Jo'hanan b. Zakkai says this according to the opinion of R. Judah, for it is said [Lev. xxiii. 14] "And ye shall eat neither parched corn . . . until the selfsame day," *i. e.*, until the very day itself, and he holds that whenever the expression "until" (ADH) occurs it is inclusive. How can you say the above according to (R. Judah); surely he differs from him? For we have learnt: Since the destruction of the Temple R. Jo'hanan b. Zakkai *ordained* that it should be prohibited (to eat of the new produce) the whole of the day of waving (the sheaf-offering)! Says R. Judah: Is this not prohibited by the Torah which says: "Until the self-same day?" R. Judah was mistaken; he thought that R. Jo'hanan b. Zakkai taught that (the prohibition) was Rabbinical, and it was not so, for R. Jo'hanan also said it was Biblical. But does the Mishna not say "he ordained?" Aye; but what does it mean by "he ordained?" (It means), he explained the ordinance.

MISHNA: Formerly they received evidence as to the appearance of the new moon the whole (of the thirtieth) day. Once, the witnesses were delayed in coming, and they disturbed the song of the Levites. They then ordained that evidence should only be received until (the time of) the afternoon service, and if witnesses came after that time both that and the following day were consecrated. After the destruction of the Temple, R. Jo'hanan b. Zakkai ordained that evidence (as to the appearance) of the new moon should be received all day.

GEMARA: What disturbance did they cause to the Songs of the Levites? Said R. Zera to Ahabha his son: Go and construe (the Mishna) thus: They ordained that evidence as to the appearance of the new moon should not be received, only that there might be time during the day to offer the continual and the additional sacrifices and their drink offerings, and to chant the (daily) song without disturbing the order. A Boraitha teaches: R. Judah says in the name of R. Aqiba, what (song) did (the Levites) chant on the first day of the week? "The earth is the Lord's and the fullness thereof" [Ps. xxiv.], because he is the Creator, the Providence and the Ruler of the Universe. What did they sing on the second day? "Great is the Lord and greatly to be praised" [Ps. xlviii.], because He distributed His works and reigned over them. On the third day they sang "God standeth in the congregation of the mighty" [Ps. lxxxii.], because He, in his wisdom made the earth appear and prepared the world for its occupants. On the fourth day they sang "O Lord, to whom retribution belongeth" [Ps. xciv.], because (on that day) He created the sun and moon, and (determined) to punish in the future those who would worship them. On the fifth day they sang "Sing aloud unto God our strength" [Ps. lxxxi.], because (on that day) He created birds and fish to praise Him. On the sixth day they sang "The Lord reigneth, He is clothed with majesty" [Ps. xciii.], because (on that day) He finished His works and reigned over them. On the seventh day they sang "A Psalm or Song for the Sabbath Day" [Ps. xcii.], for the day that is wholly Sabbath. R. Nehemiah asked:

Why did the sages make a distinction between these sections (for the last refers to a future event, while all the others refer to the past)? It *should* have been said, that they sang that Psalm on the Sabbath day because He rested!

What did the Levites sing when the additional sacrifices were being offered on the Sabbath? R. Anan b. Rabha says in the name of Rabh: Six sections of Deut. xxxii.* R. 'Hanan b. Rabha also says in the name of Rabh, as these sections were divided (by the Levites) so they are divided for the reading of the Torah (on the Sabbath on which they are read). What did they sing at the Sabbath afternoon service? Says R. Jo'hanan, a portion of the song of Moses [Ex. xv. 1-10]; the conclusion of that song [ibid. 11-19] and the song of Israel [Numb. xxi. 17]. The schoolmen asked: Did they sing all these on one Sabbath, or did they, perhaps, sing one section on each Sabbath? Come and hear! A Boraitha teaches: During the time that the first choir of (Levites who sang at the time of the additional sacrifice) sang their sections once, the second choir (that sang at that time of the afternoon sacrifice) had sung theirs twice; from this we may deduce that they sang but one section on each Sabbath.

R. Judah b. Idi says in the name of R. Jo'hanan: According to the Rabbinical explanation of certain Scriptural passages, the Shekhinah made ten journeys; and according to tradition, a corresponding number of times was the Sanhedrin exiled, viz.: from the cell of Gazith (in the Temple) to the market-place; from the market-place to Jerusalem; from Jerusalem to Jamnia; from Jamnia to Usha; from Usha (back again) to Jamnia; from Jamnia (back again) to Usha; from Usha to Shapram; from Shapram to Beth Shearim; from Beth Shearim to Sepphoris; from Sepphoris to Tiberias, and Tiberias was the saddest of them all.

R. Elazar says they were exiled six times as it is said [Is. xxvi. 5]. "For he bringeth down them that dwell on high; the lofty city he layeth low; he layeth it low even to the ground; he bringeth it even to the dust." Says R. Jo'hanan: And thence (from the dust) they will in future be redeemed, as it is said [Is. lii. 2] "Shake thyself from the dust; arise, and sit down, etc."

MISHNA: R. Joshua b. Qar'ha says: This also did R. Jo'hanan b. Zakkai ordain: that it mattered not where the chief of the Beth Din might be, the witnesses need only go to the meeting-place (of the Beth Din).

---

*i-vii; viii-xiii; xiv-xix; xx-xxvii; xxviii-xxxvi, xxxvii-xliv. These passages are called HAZYV LAKH because the initial letters are H, Z, Y, V, L, KH.

GEMARA: A certain woman was summoned for judgment before Amemar in Nehardea. Amemar went away to Me'huzá, but she did not follow him, and he then excommunicated her. Said R. Ashi to Amemar: Have we not learned that it mattered not where the chief of the Beth Din might be, the witnesses need only go to the meeting-place (of the Beth Din)? Answered Amemar: That is true in respect to evidence for the new moon; but with regard to my action "The borrower is servant to the lender" [Prov. xxii. 7]. The Rabbis taught: Priests may not ascend the platform in sandals, to bless the people; and this is one of the nine ordinances instituted by R. Jo'hanan b. Zakkai; six are to be found in this chapter, one in the first chapter; another one is, if one become a proselyte now-a-days, he must pay a quarter of a shekel for a sacrifice of a bird, (so that if the Temple should be rebuilt the authorities would have a contribution from him towards the daily sacrifices). R. Simon b. Elazar said, that R. Jo'hanan had already withdrawn this regulation and annuled it, because it easily led to the sin (of using the money for different purposes). And what is the ninth (ordinance of R. Jo'hanan)? R. Papa and R. Na'hman b. Isaac dispute about this; R. Papa says it was with regard to a vineyard of the fourth year's crop; but R. Na'hman b. Isaac says it was with regard to the crimson colored strap (displayed on the Day of Atonement).

MISHNA: The order of the benedictions (to be said on New Year is as follows): The blessings referring to the Patriarchs (ABHOTH), to the mighty power of God (GEBHURОTH), and the sanctification of the Holy name; to these he adds the selection in which God is proclaimed King (MALKHIOTH), after which he does not sound the cornet; then the blessing referring to the sanctification of the day, after which the cornet is sounded; then the Biblical selections referring to God's remembrance of his creatures (ZIKHRONOTH) after which the cornet is again sounded; then the Biblical selections referring to the sounding of the cornet (SHOPHROTH), after which the cornet is again sounded; he then recites the blessings referring to the restoration of the Temple, the adoration of God, the benediction of the priests; such is the opinion of R. Jo'hanan b. Nuri. R. Aqiba said to him, if the cornet is not to be sounded after the Malkhioth, why are they mentioned? But the proper order is the following: The blessings referring to the Patriarchs (Abhoth), to the mighty power of God (Gebhuroth), and the sanctification of the Holy name; to this last, the Biblical selections referring to the proclamation of God as King (Malkhioth) are joined and then he sounds the cornet; then the Biblical selections referring to God's remembrance of His creatures (Zikhronoth), and he then sounds the cornet; then the Biblical selections referring to the sounding of the cornet (Shophroth), and he again sounds the cornet; then he says the blessings referring to the restoration of the Temple, the adoration of God, and the priestly benedictions.

GEMARA: The Rabbis taught: Whence do we know that we should recite the Malkhioth, Zikhronoth, and Shophroth? Answered R. Eliezer: From the passage [Lev. xxiii. 24] in which it is written "Ye shall have a Sabbath, a memorial of blowing cornets, a holy convocation," the word "Sabbath" refers to the consecration of the day; "a memorial" refers to the Zikhronoth; "blowing of cornets" refers to the Shophroth; "a holy convocation" means the hallowing of the day in order to prohibit servile work. R. Aqiba said to him: Why is not the word "Sabbath" construed to mean the prohibition of servile work, since the passage (quoted above) begins with that? And then, let the passage be interpreted thus: "Sabbath" means the hallowing of the day and the prohibition of servile work; "memorial" refers to the Zikhronoth; "blowing of the cornets" refers to the Shophroth; "a holy convocation" means the consecration of the day. Whence do we know that we should recite the MALKHIOTH? A Boraitha teaches: The words, "I am the Lord, your God; and in the seventh month" [Lev. xxiii. 22, 24] may be interpreted to refer to the proclamation of God as King. R. Jose says it is not necessary to cite this passage; for the Torah says [Numbers x. 10] "that they may be to you for a memorial, before your God: I am the Lord your God." These concluding words "I am the Lord, your God" are entirely superfluous, but since they are used, of what import are they? They form a general rule, that in every selection, in which (God's) remembrance of His creatures is mentioned there should also be found the thought that He is the King of the Universe.

MISHNA: Not less than ten Scriptural passages should be used for the Malkhioth, ten for the Zikronoth and ten for the Shophroth. R. Jo'hanan b. Nuri says the requirements of the law will be fully complied with, if but three of each class have been used.

GEMARA: To what do the ten Scriptural passages used for the Malkhioth correspond? Answered Rabbi: To the ten expressions of praise used by David in the Psalms. But there are more expressions of praise found? Only those are meant, in conjunction with which it is written "praise him with the sound of the cornet," [Psalm ci. 3]. R. Joseph says they correspond to the ten commandments that were proclaimed to Moses on Sinai. R. Jo'hanan says they correspond to the ten words with which the universe was created.

"THE REQUIREMENTS OF THE LAW WILL BE FULLY COMPLIED WITH IF BUT THREE OF EACH CLASS HAVE BEEN SAID." The schoolmen asked: Does he mean three from the Pentateuch, three from the Prophets and three from the Hagiographa, which would make nine, and they differ about one (passage)? or perhaps one from the Pentateuch and one from the Prophets and one from the Hagiographa, which would make three, and they differ about many passages? Come and hear! A Boraitha teaches: Not less than ten Scriptural passages should be used for the Malkhioth, ten for the Zikhronoth, and ten for the Shophroth; but if seven of them all were recited, corresponding to the seven heavens, the law has been complied with. R. Jose b. Nuri remarked: He that recites less (than ten of each) should not, however, recite less than seven, but if he recited but three, corresponding to the Pentateuch, Prophets, and Hagiographa, but some say corresponding to the Priests, Levites and Israelites, the requirements of the law have been fulfilled. R. Huna b. Samuel says the rule is according to R. Jo'hanan b. Nuri.

MISHNA: We do not cite Scriptural passages for the above three series that contain predictions of punishment. The passages from the Pentateuch are to be recited first, and those from the Prophets last. R. Jose, however, says if the concluding passage is from the Pentateuch the requirements of the law are fulfilled.

GEMARA: Passages, proclaiming the kingdom of God that should not be used, (because of the above) are such as the following [Ezekiel xx. 33]: "As I live, saith the Lord God, surely with a mighty hand, and with a stretched out arm, and with fury poured out, I will rule over you," and although as R. Na'hman says (of this passage): Let Him be angry with us, but let Him take us out of captivity, still, since it refers to anger, we should not mention "anger," at the beginning of the year. An example of the same idea being found in conjunction with the Zikhronoth is to be read in [Ps. lxxviii. 3]. "For he remembered they were but flesh; and in conjunction with the Shophroth an example is found in Hosea v. 8. "Blow ye the cornet in Gibeah, etc." We must not mention the remembrance of the individual (in the Zikhronoth) even if the passage speaks of pleasant things, as, for example [Ps. cvi. 4], "Remember me, O Lord, with the favor that thou bearest unto thy people." According to R. Jose passages that contain the expression of "visiting" may be used in the Zikhronoth, *e. g.*, "And the Lord visited Sarah [Gen. xxi. 1] or "I have surely visited you"

[Ex. iii. 16] so says R. Jose; but R. Judah says, they may not. But even if we agree to what R. Jose says (shall we say that) the passage "and the Lord visited Sarah" speaks of an individual (and therefore it should not be used)? Nay; since many descended from her, she is regarded as many and therefore that passage though speaking of one only, is regarded as though it spoke of many.

(In the Malkhioth, they used Ps. xxiv. 7-10, which is divided into two parts). The first part can be used as two of the required passages, and the second as three, so says R. Jose; but R. Judah says: The first part can be used only for one, and the second for two.* So too [Ps. xlvii. 6, 7] "Sing praises to God, sing praises, sing praises to our King, sing praises; for God is the King of all the earth;" R. Jose says: This may be used for two of the Malkhioth; but R. Judah says it is to be reckoned as one only.† Both, however, agree that the next verse of the same Psalm "God is King over the nations; God sitteth upon the throne of his holiness," is to be used for one only. A passage containing a reference to God's remembrance of His creatures and also to the cornet as, for instance [Lev. xxiii. 24] "Ye shall have a Sabbath, a memorial of blowing of cornets" may be used in the Zikhronoth and the Shophroth; so says R. Jose; but R. Judah says: It can only be used in the Zikhronoth. A passage in which God is proclaimed King, containing also a reference to the cornet, as for instance [Numb. xxiii. 21] "The Lord his God is with him, and the shout (TERUATH) of a king is among them," may be used in the Malkhioth and in the Shophroth, says R. Jose; but R. Judah says: It may only be used in the Malkhioth. A passage containing a reference to the cornet, and nothing else, as for instance [Numb. xxix. 1] "It is a day of blowing the cornet;" may not be used at all.

"THE PASSAGES FROM THE PENTATEUCH ARE TO BE RECITED FIRST AND THOSE FROM THE PROPHETS LAST." R. Jose says: We should conclude with a passage from the Pentateuch, but if one concluded with a passage from the Prophets, the law has been complied with. We have also learnt: R. Elazar b. R. Jose says, The Vathiqin used to conclude with a passage from the Pentateuch. That is all very well as far as Zikhronoth and Shophroth are concerned for there are many such passages; but as for the Malkhioth there are but three in the Pentateuch, viz.: "The Lord his God is with him, and the shout of a King is among them" [Numb. xxiii. 21]; "And he

* He excludes the two interrogative sentences "who is the king of glory?"

† He rejects one, because the words "our king," referring to one people only, was not a sufficiently broad expression of praise for Him, who is the King of the universe.

was king in Jeshurun" [Deut. xxxiii. 5]; and "The Lord shall reign forever" [Ex. xv. 18], but we require ten and there are not so many? Said R. Huna: We have learned that, according to R. Jose, the passage, "Hear, O Israel, the Lord our God, is one Lord" [Deut. vi. 4], may be used in the Malkhioth, but R. Judah says it may not; so also they hold with regard to the passages, "Know, therefore, this day, and consider it in thine heart, that the Lord, he is God there is more else" [Deut. iv. 39], and "Unto thee it was shewed, that thou mightest know that the Lord, he is God; there is none else beside him." (Deut. IV. 35).

MISHNA: The second of those who act as ministers of the congregation on the feast of New Year shall cause another to sound the cornet; on days when the HALLEL (Service of Praise, Ps. cxiii-cxviii) is read, the first (minister) must read it. In order to sound the cornet on New Year's Day it is not permitted to go beyond the Sabbath limit, to remove a heap of stones to ascend a tree, to ride on an animal, to swim over the waters, nor to cut it (the cornet) with anything prohibited either by the (Rabbinical) laws against servile work or by the Biblical laws; but if one wishes to put water or wine in a cornet (to cleanse it) he is allowed to. Children may not be prevented from sounding the cornet, but on the contrary we are permitted to occupy ourselves with teaching them until they learn to sound it; but one who thus teaches, as also others who listen to sounds thus produced, do not thereby fulfill the requirements of the law.

GEMARA: Why are the above prohibitions made? Because the sounding of the cornet is a mandatory law; now, the observance of a festival involves both mandatory and prohibitory laws, and the mandatory do not render the prohibitory laws inoperative.

"CHILDREN MAY NOT BE PREVENTED FROM SOUNDING THE CORNET, ETC." May then women be prevented? Does not a Boraitha teach: Neither women nor children may be prevented from sounding the cornet on the New Year's Day? Answered Abayi: There is no difficulty here; the one is the opinion of R. Judah and the other of R. Jose and R. Simon, who say that as women are permitted (in the case of sacrifices) to lay their hands on the animals, so here, if they desire to sound the cornet, they may.

"UNTIL THEY LEARN." R. Elazar says: Even on the Sabbath; so also does a Boraitha teach: We are permitted to occupy ourselves with teaching (children) until they learn (to sound the cornet) even on the Sabbath; (and if we do not prevent them doing this on the Sabbath) how much less do we, on the feast (of New Year). Our

Mishna says, "we do not prevent them" (but it does not say that we should tell a child to go and sound the cornet). Is this then prohibited? No; a child already initiated in the performance of religious duties is not prohibited, but we do not tell a child, not yet initiated, to go and sound the cornet; yet, if he sounds it of his own accord, no law has been infringed.

MISHNA: The order of sounding the cornet is three times three. The length of a TEQIA is equal to that of three TERUOTH, and that of each Terua as three moans (YABABHOTH). If a person sounded a Teqia and prolonged it equal to two, it is only reckoned as one Teqia.* He who has just finished reading the benedictions (in the additional service for the New Year) and only at that time obtained a cornet, should then blow on the cornet the three sounds three times. As the Reader of the congregation is in duty bound (to sound the cornet) so too is each individual; but, says R. Gamliel, the Reader can act for the congregation.

GEMARA: But we have learnt in a Boraitha that the length of a Teqia is the same as that of a Terua. Says Abayi: Our Mishna speaks of the three series, and means that the length of all the Teqioth is the same as that of all the Teruoth. But the Boraitha speaks of only one series and says that one Teqia is equal to one Terua (which is the same thing).

"EACH TERUA IS (AS LONG AS) THREE MOANS." But we have learnt in a Boraitha, a Terua is as long as three broken (staccato) tones (SHEBHARIM). Says Abayi: About this they do indeed differ, for it is written [Numb. xxix. 1] "It is a day of blowing the cornet" which in the (Aramaic) translation of the Pentateuch is "It is a day of sounding the alarm (YABABHA); Now it is written concerning the mother of Sisera [Judg. v. 28] "The mother of Sisera . . . . moaned" (VAT'YABETH); this word, one explains to mean a protracted groan, and another to mean a short wail. The Rabbis taught: Whence do we know (that one must sound) with a cornet? From the passage in which [Lev. xxv. 9] "Thou shalt cause *the cornet* . . . . to sound, etc." Whence do we know that (after the Terua) there should be one Teqia? Therefore it is said (later in the same verse) "Ye shall make the cornet sound." † But perhaps this

---

*The cornet is sounded three times, corresponding to the Malkhioth, Zikhronoth and Shophroth. The order of the sounds is Teqia, Terua, Teqia; Teqia, Terua, Teqia, etc. The case here supposed is that the one who sounded the cornet sustained the second Teqia as long as two Teqioth, intending thereby to sound the second and third Teqioth. This, we see, is not permitted

† The Hebrew words UTHEQATEM TERUA are interpreted to mean that first a Teqia should be sounded, and then a Terua.

only refers to the Jubilee. Whence do we know that it refers also to New Year's Day? Because it says (in the same verse) "in the seventh month." These words are superfluous; for what purpose then does the Torah use them? To teach us that all the sounds of the cornet during the seventh month should be like each other. Whence do we know that the sounds are to be three times three? From the three passages, "Thou shalt cause the cornet . . . to sound" [Lev. xxv. 9]; "A Sabbath, a memorial of blowing of cornets" [Lev. xxiii. 24]; "It is a day of blowing the cornet" [Numb. xxix. 1]. But the following Tana deduces it by analogy from (the rules given in) the wilderness [Numb. x. 1-10]; for a Boraitha teaches: The words "When ye sound an alarm" [Numb. x. 5] means one Teqia and one Terua. Do you mean one of each, or do you mean that both together should constitute one? Since the Torah says [ibid. 7] "But when the congregation is to be gathered together, ye shall blow but ye shall not sound an alarm," we deduce that (in the first citation) it means one of each. But whence do we know that there should be one Teqia before the Terua. From the words [ibid. 5] "When ye sound an alarm" (*i. e.*, first a "sound," or Teqia, and then an "alarm," or Terua). And whence do we know that there should be one after the Terua? From the words [ibid. 6] "An alarm shall they sound!" R. Ishmael, the son of R. Jo'hanan b. Beroqa, says: It is not necessary (to deduce it from these passages, but from the following), in which the Torah says, "When ye sound an alarm the second time" [ibid. 6]. The words "a second time" are unnecessary, but since they are used, what do they signify? They form a general rule that on every occasion, on which "alarm" (Terua) is mentioned, a sound (Teqia) must be used with it as a second (or following) tone. Possibly all this only refers to the practices followed in the wilderness, but how do we know that they refer to New Year's Day also? We learn it by analogy from the use of the word "cornet" (*sic!* Terua), which is found in the three passages, [Lev. xxiii. 24] "A sabbath, a memorial of cornets;" [Numb. xxix. 1] "It is a day of blowing of cornets;" and [Lev. xxv. 9] "Thou shalt cause the cornet. . . .to sound;" and as for each Terua there are two Teqioth, we, therefore, learn that on New Year's Day there are sounded three Teruoth and six Teqioth. R. Abbahu enacted in Cæsarea that the order should be first a Teqia* then three single staccato sounds, or Shebharim, then a Terua, and then again a Teqia. What are we to think of that? If by Terua is

* The Teqia is a long tone produced by sounding the cornet. The Terua is long tremulous sound. The SHEBHARIM consists of three short staccato sounds.

meant "a protracted groan" then he should have instituted the order to be a Teqia, a Terua and then a Teqia; and if it means "a short wail" then he should have instituted the order to be, a Teqia then Shebharim (three single broken sounds) and then again a Teqia? He was in doubt whether it meant one or the other (and therefore he enacted that both should be sounded).

"IF A PERSON SOUNDED A TEQIA AND PROLONGED IT EQUAL TO TWO, ETC." R. Jo'hanan says: If one heard the nine sounds at nine different hours during the day, the requirements of the law are fulfilled and we have also learnt: If one heard the nine sounds at nine different hours of the day the requirements of the law are fulfilled, and if he heard from nine men at one time, a Teqia from one and a Terua from another, etc., the law has been complied with even if he heard them intermittently, and even during the whole day or any part of the day. The Rabbis taught: (Generally) the soundings of the cornet do not obviate each other, nor do the benedictions; but on New Year's Day and the Day of Atonement they do.

"HE WHO HAS JUST FINISHED READING (THE ADDITIONAL SERVICE) AND ONLY AT THAT TIME OBTAINED A CORNET SHALL SOUND ON THE CORNET THE THREE SOUNDS THREE TIMES." This means, only when he did not have a cornet at the beginning (of the service); but if he had one at the beginning of the service when the sounds of the cornet are heard, they must he heard in the order ot the benedictions of the day. R. Papa b. Samuel rose to recite his prayers. Said he to his attendant, When I nod to you, sound (the cornet) for me." Rabha said to him: This may only be done in the congregation. A Boraitha also teaches: When one hears these sounds, he should hear them, both in their order, and in the order of the benedictions (in the additional service of the New Year). These words only apply to a congregation, but one need hear them in the order of the benedictions only, if he is not in a congregation; and a private individual who has not sounded the cornet (or heard it sounded) can have a friend sound it for him; but a private individual who has not recited the benedictions cannot have a friend say them for him; and the duty to hear the cornet sounded is greater than that of reciting the blessings. How so? If there be two cities (to which a person may go) and in one city they are about to sound the cornet and in the other to recite the benedictions, he should go to the city in which they are about to sound the cornet; and not to that in which they are about to recite the benedictions. This is self-evident! for is not one a duty prescribed by the Torah and the other by the Rabbis? (It is not so self-evident as one might suppose); but it is needed to tell us that in the case in which one is *sure* that they have not recited the benedictions in one city, and with regard to the other he is in *doubt* (whether they have sounded the cornet or not, he must nevertheless go to the place where they are about to sound the cornet.)

"JUST AS THE READER OF THE CONGREGATION IS IN DUTY BOUND (TO SOUND THE CORNET) SO TOO IS EACH INDIVIDUAL." A Boraitha teaches: The schoolmen said to R. Gamliel, why according to your opinion should the congregation pray? Answered he: In order to enable the Reader of the congregation to arrange his prayer. Said R. Gamliel to them: But why, according to your opinion, should the Reader pray? Answered they: In order to enable those who are not expert, to fulfill the requirements of the law. Just as he enables those who are not expert, said he, so too he causes those who are expert, to fulfill the requirements of the law. R. Bar b. 'Hana said in the name of R. Jo'hanan: The sages accept the opinion of R. Gamliel; but Rabh says there is still a dispute between them; could (the same) R. Jo'hanan say this? Have we not heard that R. 'Hana of Sepphoris said in the name of R. Jo'hanan: The rule is according to R. Gamliel: from these words ("the rule is according to R. Gamliel") we see that there must have been some that disputed with him! Says R. Na'hman b. Isaac: It is perfectly clear; by the words, "the sages accept the opinion of R. Gamliel," R. Meir is meant, and the rule arrived at through those who disputed with him (was arrived at) through other Rabbis; for a Boraitha teaches: R. Meir holds that with regard to the benedictions of New Year's Day and the Day of Atonement, the Reader can act for the congregation; but the other Rabbis say: Just as the Reader is in duty bound, so too is each individual. Why, only for these benedictions (and no others)? Shall I say it is because of the many Biblical selections used? Does not R. 'Hannanel say in the name of Rabh: As soon as one has said (the passages beginning with) the words, "And in thy law it is written," he need say no more? It is because there are many (more and longer) benedictions (than usual). We have also learnt, R. Joshua b. Levi says: Both the private individual and the congregation as soon as they say (the passages beginning) with the words, "And in thy law it is written," need say no more. R. Elazar says: A man should always first prepare himself for prayer and then pray; concerning this R. Abba says: The remarks of R. Elazar clearly apply to the benedictions of New Year's Day and the Day of Atonement, and to the various holidays, but not to the whole year. It is not so; for did not R. Judah prepare himself (even on a week day) before his prayers and then offer them? R. Judah was an exception, for since he prayed only once in thirty days, it was like a Holiday. When Rabhin came (from Palestine) he said that R. Jacob b. Idi said in the name of R. Simon the pious: R. Gamliel did not excuse from public service any but field-laborers! What is the difference (between them and others)? They would be forced to lose their work (if they went to a synagogue) but people in a city must go (to the House of Prayer).

הוצאה החדשה

של

תלמוד בבלי

תוכן מחדש, נסדר ונסמן בסמני הנקודות של השפות החיות

ונתתרגם בשפת אנגליש

מאת

מיכאל ל. ראדקינסאן.

מסכתות

שקלים עם פירוש רמ״ל

וראש השנה עם פרש״י ותורה אור.

חלק רביעי (מהוצאה האנגליש).

בהוצאה החברה מדפיסי התלמוד

54 East 106th Street.

נויארק,

תרנ״ז.

מסכת
שקלים

בכל מקום בש״ס שהגמרא תפרש את המשנה ותדקדק אחריה בכל מלה וגם בכל אות, הנה המשניות מבוארים והגמרא במקום שפירושה צריך ביאור ולא יובן בלעדו, אפרשנו בפירוש רש״י על מקומו בפנים, שכמעט בכל מקום דבריו אשר יוסיף, הנם לא בתור „פירוש״ ורק כמשלים את החסר בפנים למען יובנו דבריהם, אבל פה שאין גמרא כלל וישנם מקומות במשניות הללו הצריכים פירוש וביאור ולא רק להשלים את החסר, ולכן הביאור נחוץ מאד להיות ל ב ד ו למען תובן כונת המשנה.

מובן מאליו, כי חדושים משלי בביאורי, מעטים המה, וכולו מיוסד על פירוש הגמרא הירושלמית, המימוני והברטנורא, הר״ר ישראל ליפשיטץ, וגם על הפירושים הנמצאים פה ושם בש״ס הבבלי (כמו בביאור ענין הקלבן אחזתי פרוש רש״י בחולין ונתתי לו היתרון נגד שארי הפרושים אשר נטו ממנו, וכמוהם עוד באיזה מקומן) ובכן אחשוב למותר לבקש ח ס ד מאת המבקרים, כי לא ימהרו להוציא משפט טרם יתבוננו היטב בכל הפרושים הנ״ל ובטרם יעמיקו ג״כ בפירושי שצריך התבוננות מפני קיצורו; כי הישרים בלבותם והחכמים המבינים, יעשו כזאת מבלעדי אבקשם, ולהחצופים, הבורים ועמי הארץ, הרגילים לקרא תגר על דברי, לדייף, ולהגיד בשמי או מפי כתבי, דברים אשר לא עלו על דעתי לעולם, הלא לא יועילו בקשותי; וכשם ש ר ק ד ו כנגד כל מה אשר כתבתי וערכתי עד כה, ולא נגעו ולא פגעו בכבודי ובכבוד מלאכתי אפילו כמלא נימה, כן ירקודו, ינהמו יכרכרו וינעיו כנגד מלאכתי החדשה הזאת, ואקוה כי גם עתה לא יפגעו בי לרעה, ולא אשים לב לדבריהם. חלומותיהם תביחתם. כאשר כן עשיתי עד כה, כי באמת אני בתומי אלך, אינע ולא א י ע ף למצא חן בעיני אלהים ו א ד ם אך לא בעיני בורים חצופים, ועמי הארץ, אשר כל מגמתם בנעייתם נגדי היא, רק למען יורע כי בראים כמותם עוד נמצאים בעולם, ומה איפוא לי ולהם?

קראתי לפרושי הזה „פירוש רמ״ל״ שהיא הראשי תיבות משמי ראדקינסאן מיכאל ל. ולא ר׳ מיכאל ל. והנני מודיע זאת מפורש, לבל יאשימוני כי לקחתי לעצמי תואר „רבי״, כי כשם שאיני מתגדר במלאכת אחרים כן איני חפץ שתהיה מלאכתי בת בלי שם, כי הודות לה׳ לא אבוש בשמי ואקוה כי לא יכלמו בי אוהבי גם מפרושי החדש.

ובה׳ הנותן ליעף כח אבטח ולא אפחד, כי הוא יאזרני חיל, ינחני במעגלי צדק ויעזרני לגמור את המלאכה הגדולה והכבדה הזאת להגדיל תורת התלמוד להאדירה ולהרגמה כיד ה׳ הטובה עלי, ומשנאי ומשניאי יראו ויבושו, אמן.

נ ו י א ר ק, בחדש אייר, תרת״ז.

מיכאל ל. ראדקינסאן.

הקדמת העורך והמפרש.

בשם השם!

מלאכתי הכבדה, ההערכה והוצאה החדשה של התלמוד בבלי ותרגומו בשפת אנגליש, הביאתני למלאכה ח ד ש ה אשר לא נסיתי עד כה והיא, להיות גם מפרש את המשניות של המסכתות שהגמרא הבבלית חסרה להן; כי לחסר את המסכת הזאת מן סדר מועד לא יתכן, מפני שכל המשניות הללו יסודתן בהררי קודש, קורות ההיכל ועבודת הכהנים בו, בזמן שהיה קים, דבר הצריך לימוד, ידיעה וקריאה, כמו במקורן העברי כן בתרגומן. אבל לתרגם את המשניות הללו על פי אחד הפירושים שכבר נדפסו הוא כמעט דבר שאי אפשר, כי שונים המה הפירושים זה מזה וכולם ארוכים ומפולפלים, ואם אמנם טובים המה ורצוים לעם לא יכולתי להשתמש בם בתרגומי, הנקי מכל פלפול צדדי, זולת פלפולי הגמרא בעצמה. ובאמת עד כמה שלא יהיו טובים ומתוקנים כל הפירושים למס׳ הזאת, לא נוכל בשום אופן לדמותם עם פירוש רש״י ז״ל כמו בקצורו, כן בסגנון לשונו, המפרש כל דבר על מקומו בלי שום פלפול צדדי, ומבלי שום נטיה לענין אחר זולת הענין שהוא עסוק בו; ואך פירוש כזה מוכשר ומתוקן לתרגם בשפת חיה. ואני נזהר מאד בהוצאה הזאת שיכיל התרגום את המקור הנדפס ולא ינרע ממנו ולא יוסיף עליו, למצער במקום שאפשר, ולא יהיה בזה מה שאין בזה. שעל כן עסלתי לי לפרש את המסכת הזאת בפירוש קצר, היינו לבאר כל משנה הצריכה פירוש וביאור, והשייך רק למסכת הזאת; מבלי כל פרושים לדברים שנשנו ונתפרשו במסכתות אחרות, ומבלי כל נטיה צדדית ופלפול זר בהלכה או בסברא, כאשר כן דרכי בכל ההוצאה הזאת, וינעתי ומצאתי תאמין.

במדומה לי, אחי הקורא, שעלתה בידי לפרש את כל המסכת, במלות קצרות ומובנות, עד שגם הקורא שיקרא את המשניות האלו בפעם הראשונה, לא יחסרו לו ביאור המלות וכן הבנת הענין הדק היטב בכל שמנה פרקיה; ולכן שמתי כו מקום במדור התחתון לכל צד במקום הצריך ביאור ופירוש, וכה עשיתי גם בתרגום האנגלי׳ הדפסתי את הפירוש מלמטה בציונים. לא כמו שאני עושה בתרגומן של מסכתות אחרות עם פירוש רש״י שהנני מסגירו בפנים בשני חצאי לבנה, מטעם משום מאד, והוא:

מסכת שקלים.

א) באחד באדר משמיעין על השקלים ועל הכלאים, בחמשה עשר בו, קורין את המגילה בכרכין ומתקנין את הדרכים, ואת הרחובות ואת מקואות המים, ועושין כל צרכי הרבים, ומציינין את הקברות ויוצאין אף על הכלאים.

ב) אמר רבי יהודה, בראשונה היו עוקרין ומשליכין לפניהם, משרבו עוברי עבירה, היו עוקרין ומשליכין על הדרכים, התקינו שיהו מפקירין כל השדה כולה.

ג) בחמשה עשר בו, שולחנות היו יושבין במדינה; בעשרים

פירוש רמ״ל

א) **באחד באדר משמיעין על השקלים**, שיתרומו אותם באחד בניסן, זמן נתינת השקלים, שנאמר, ויהי בחדש הראשון באחד לחדש הוקם המשכן (שמות מ׳), והני עלה (בירושלמי), ביום שהוקם המשכן בו ביום נתרמה תרומה. **ועל הכלאים**, מכריזין להזהר מתערובות, מפני שבעת הזאת זמן הזריעה קרוב לבוא. **בט״ו בו קורין את המגילה בכרכים**, אבל בפרזות קורין בי״ד. ולא היה צורך להזכיר זאת במשנה מפני שרוב הערים אינן מוקפות חומה ולא חיישינן לשכחה, אבל בערים המוקפות חומה שהנה מעטות וקרוב לשכחה, לפיכך הזכיר זאת במשנה שידעו בכרכים את זמן קריאת המגילה, כי אם גם קראו אותה בי״ד חייב לקרותה עוד הפעם בט״ו כאשר כן היא ההלכה פסוקה בירושלמי „אמר ר׳ מני ויאות״ כו׳, ואולם אחרי כל הדוחקים שדחקו עצמם המפרשים החדשים לפרש את מאמר התלמוד בירושלמי שהמשנה באה ללמדנו, שכל המצות הנוהגות באדר שני, אינן נוהגות באדר ראשון, איני יודע איככה מוכח זאת מהמשנה. **ומתקנין את הדרכים**, אחרי שעברו ימות הגשמים ונתקלקלו, ובפלשתינא זמן גשמים הוא רק עד אדר, הוא הטעם לרחובות ומקואות, שהרחובות נתקלקלו ובמקואות נפל הרפש, וצריכין לנקותן, למען יוכלו לטהר עצמם לפני הרגל. **ועושין כל צרכי הרבים**, אומר בירושלמי שבעת ההיא הב״ד מתאסף לדון דיני ממונות, דיני נפשות, דיני מכות, ופודין ערכין, תרומות והקדשות, ומשקין את הסוטה, ועורפין עגלה ערופה, ושורפין את הפרה, ורוצעין עבד עברי ומטהרין את המצורע, ועוד כמו אלה שנתנו בעת ההיא. **ומציינין את הקברות**, שנתקלקלו בימות הגשמים, בסיד; ובירושלמי אומר שמציינין את הקברות למען לא יטמאו בהם העוברים, ומוכיח זאת מקרא (ויקרא י״ג) וטמא טמא יקרא, שהיא הטומאה קוראת ואומרת „פרוש ממני״. **ויוצאין אף על הכלאים**, מפני חומר האיסור לא היו מסתפקין בהכרזה בלבד, כי אם היו שולחים לבקר את השדות.

ב) ר׳ יהודה בא לבאר מה שהיו עושין השלוחים אם מצאו כי לא נזהרו בכלאים; ובירושלמי מוכיח מנין להפקר ב״ד שהוא הפקר מן עזרא (י׳ 8) „וכל אשר לא יבוא לשלשת הימים יחרם״. **לפניהם**, על השדה משרבו עוברי עבירה, שהשתמשו בהם.

ג) **שולחנות**. מפני שהשולחנים היו נושאים אתם שולחנות לתת עליהם את המטבעות, יאמר, כי היו משימים השולחנות עד חמשה ועשרים באדר במדינה, להקל על העם שיחליפו את מעותיהם על חצי השקל הכתוב בתורה, שמחויב כל אחד לתת; ואך מן חמש ועשרים בו היו יושבין במקדש להמציא שם את החצי שקל לבאי מבחוץ הוד לא שקלו את שקליהם; ומשישבו במקדש, התחילו למשכן גם בחוץ לארץ את אלה אשר לא הביאו שקליהם, למען יביאו את תרומתם טרם יבוא אחד בניסן, כי גם במדינה היו שופרות למטרה הזאת. וגם הכהנים חייבים היו בשקלים אשר עקרם לקרבנות ציבור, אבל הם מצאו עלילה להפטר מזה כדלקמן. ומפני שהיו הכהנים בזמן המקדש רבים לא היו ממשכנים אותם, מפני דרכי שלום.

וחמשה ישבו במקדש. משישבו במקדש התחילו למשכן. את מי ממשכנין? לוים וישראלים, גרים ועבדים משוחררים, אבל לא נשים ועבדים וקטנים. כל קטן שהתחיל אביו לשקול על ידו, שוב אינו פוסק, אין ממשכנין את הכהנים מפני דרכי שלום.

ד) **א**מר רבי יהודה העיד בן בוכרי ביבנה: כל כהן ששוקל אינו חוטא, אמר לו רבי יוחנן בן זכאי לא כי, אלא כל כהן שאינו שוקל חוטא, אלא שהכהנים דורשים מקרא זה לעצמן (ויקרא ו): .וכל מנחת כהן כליל תהיה לא תאכל׳, הואיל ועומר ושתי הלחם ולחם הפנים שלנו, היאך נאכלים?

ה) **א**ף על פי שאמרו אין ממשכנין נשים ועבדים וקטנים, אם שקלו מקבלין מידן, העכו״ם והכותים ששקלו אין מקבלין מהן, ואין מקבלין (מידן) קיני זבים וקיני זבות וקיני יולדות חטאות ואשמות, (אבל נדרים ונדבות מקבלין מידן), זה הכלל: כל שנידר ונידב מקבלין מידן, כל שאין נידר ונידב אין מקבלין מידן. וכן הוא מפורש על ידי עזרא, שנאמר (עזרא ד): .לא לכם ולנו לבנות בית לאלהינו׳.

ו) **ו**אלו שחייבין בקלבון: לוים וישראלים, גרים ועבדים משוחררים, אבל לא כהנים ונשים ועבדים וקטנים. השוקל על ידי כהן, על ידי אשה, על ידי עבד, על ידי קטן פטור, ואם שקל על ידו ועל יד חברו, חייב בקלבון אחד; רבי מאיר אומר שני קלבנות. הנותן סלע ונוטל שקל חייב שני קלבנות.

ז) **ה**שוקל על ידי עני ועל יד שכנו ועל יד בן עירו פטור, ואם הלוון חייב. האחין והשותפין שחייבין בקלבון פטורין ממעשר

פירוש רמ״ל

ד) שלנו, כלומר יש לנו חלק בהם, היאך היינו יכולים לאכול אותם? ובאמת היתה הטענה הזאת שוא, מפני שהכל הולך אחר הרוב ורובא דעלמא אינם כהנים; אבל הכה היו המושלים ודרשו לטובת עצמם ומפני דרכי שלום הניחו אותם.

ה) ואין מקבלין מידן קיני זבים, כלומר על הכותים (שמרונים) לבד (כן ירוש בירושלמי ורמב״ם). לא לכם ולנו לבנות בית לאלהינו, ומפני שהשקלים היה גם לבדק הבית לא רצו כי יהיה להם חלק בבית המקדש, אבל נדרים, עולות לקרבן, או חטאות ואשמות שמקריבין אותם בשבילם לכפרה להם, מקבלים מהם, שבזה אין הבדל בין איש לאיש.

ו) קלבון, השקל הנזכר בתורה הוא הסלע הנזכר במשנה, והיה שוה שני שקלים הנקראים במשנה, ומפני שהתה יד הקדש תמיד על העליונה, והחשו שמא אין משקל השקל של המשנה שוה למשקלו של חצאי שקל האמור בתורה (לדעת הרמב״ם לא פחות מן 192 גרעיני שעורה) לכן הצריכו שיתן הכרע מעט לכל חצי שקל, וההכרע הזה נקרא קלבון מן יונית „קאלאבוס״, וכל השוקל רק ממדות חסידות ולא מפני שהוא חייב עפ״י דין, אינו נותן אותו קלבון, והכהנים שהיו אומרים שאינם חייבים בשקלים, והחסידים שבהם שהיו נותנים, לא היו לוקחין מהם את הקלבונות, מפני דרכי שלום.

ז) השוקל על ידי עני, ר״ל נותן מתנה בשבילו, שזהו רק מדת חסידות ולא חיוב, לכן פטור מקלבון. האחין והשותפין וכו׳, מעשר בהמה יותן אך מהנולד אצלו, אך אם קנה

בהמה, וכשחייבין במעשר בהמה פטורין מן הקלבון; וכמה הוא קלבון? מעה כסף, דברי רבי מאיר, וחכמים אומרים חצי (מעה.)

פירוש רמ״ל

ולדות מאדם אחר, או גם אם חלק בנכסי אביו וקבל את הולדות מעזבונו אינו חייב במעשר מפני שאנו חושבין את הולדות כאלו כל אחד מהאחים קנה אותם מאחיו, (כן השותפים רק אז חייבים במעשר בהמה בעת שהמה שותפים אבל כאשר נתחלקו יחשבו הולדות כאלו כל אחד קנה אותם משותפו,) ומובן מאליו שבעת שהאחים המה ביחד יחשבו כאדם אחד, שע״ל כן אינם חייבים בקלבון אם נותנים סלע בעד שניהם, מפני כי כספם הוא של אביהם ולא של עצמם כ״ז שלא חלקו ויחשב פה כאלו אביהם שוקל בעדם, שאז הוא פטור מקלבון.

פרק שני.

א) מצרפין שקלים לדרכונות מפני משוי הדרך. כשם שהיו שופרות במקדש, כך היו שופרות במדינה. בני העיר ששקלו את שקליהן ונגנבו או שאבדו, אם נתרמה תרומה נשבעין לגזברים ואם לאו נשבעין לבני העיר, ובני העיר שוקלין תחתיהן. נמצאו, או שהחזירום הגנבים, אלו ואלו שקלים ואין עולין להם לשנה הבאה.

ב) הנותן שקלו לחבירו לשקול על ידו, ושקלו על ידי עצמו, אם נתרמה תרומה מעל; השוקל שקלו ממעות הקדש, אם נתרמה התרומה וקרבה הבהמה מעל, מדמי מעשר שני ומדמי שביעית יאכל כנגדן.

ג) המכנס מעות ואומר: "הרי אלו לשקלי", בית שמאי אומרים מותרן נדבה, ובית הלל אומרים מותרן חולין; "שאביא מהן לשקלי", שוין שהמותר חולין; "אלו לחטאת", שוין שהמותר נדבה, "שאביא מהן לחטאת", שוין שהמותר חולין.

ד) אמר רבי שמעון מה בין שקלים לחטאת? לשקלים יש

פירוש רמ"ל

פרק שני.

א) מצרפין שקלים לדרכנות, הדרכון היה מטבע של זהב משקל שני סלעים ונקרא בל' יון "דאריקאס", והתיבות היו כעין שופרות קצר מצד אחד ורחב מצד השני, מפני שהיו נותנין לתם את התיבות סגורות ובצד העליון היה רק נקב כגודל הדרכון בעביו ולא ברחבו והיו מטילין שם הדרכונות אך לא היו יכולים לקחתם משם בעת שהיו סגורות. ואמרו "מצרפין" ר"ל שאם בני העיר החליפו את שקליהם בדרכונות אינם חייבים בקלבונות; כי מפני טורח הדרך היו הגזברים מחויבים לעשות כן ולכן אין מזה נזק להקדש. אם נתרמה תרומה, ר"ל אם כבר הוציאו חלק מכסף השקלים על קרבנות או בדק הבית, שאז נחשבו גם אלו השקלים כאלו היו בין אלה שהוציאו (כי כן היה התנאי ביניהם שמכל שקל יש חלק מכל אחד ואחד הנותן שקלים למען יהיה לכל אחד חלק בהקרבן או בדק הבית), ולכן אם כבר הוציאו מכלל השקלים שהיו מתחלקים לג' קופות והיו משתמשים בקופה אחת לכל דבר הצריך עד שתתם הקופה כדלקמן. אז נשבעים לגזברים, כי השקלים כבר המה שייכים להם גם אם לא הגיעו לידם, אבל אם לא נתרמה התרומה, אז יחשבו השקלים של בני העיר עד שיגיעו ליד הגזברים, והטעם הזה הוא גם במשנה שלאחריה שאם נתן לו דברו לשקול ושקל על ידי עצמו מעל בהקדש, מפני שהיו מקריבין גם על העתיד לבוא כי היו ממשכנין על השקלים אף את העניים שבישראל, (רמב"ם).

ב) יאכל כנגדן, ר"ל יקח מכסף החולין שלו את הסכום מעות שהיו בידו מהמעשר ויאמר: הרי אלו תחת אלה השקלים שלקחתי מהם למחצית השקל, ויעשה בהם את חובתו.

ג) המכנס וכו', תוכן המשנה הזאת הוא: במי שמתחיל לקבץ פרוטות על יד, ואומר "מהכסף הזה אקח לשקלי" שלדעת בית הלל אחרי שכבר שקל את המותר מהסכום הנקבץ, המותר חולין; ולדעת ב"ש גם אז אם רק יחד אותם לכונת משאר הכסף, מותרן נדבה, אבל במי שאוחז בידו כסף רב ואומר הרי א ל ו לשקלי, מותרן נדבה אפילו לבית הלל, (ירושלמי ורמב"ם).

ד) אמר ר' שמעון, נותן טעם לדברי ב"ה שגם לדעתם בחטאת אם גם קובץ על יד מותרן נדבה, מפני שאין קצבה לחטאת ויכול לקנות גם במאה סלעים, משא"כ שקלים יש להם קצבה

להן קצבה, לחטאת אין לה קצבה; רבי יהודה אומר אף לשקלים אין להן קצבה, שכשעלו ישראל מן הגולה היו שוקלין דרכונות, חזרו לשקול סלעים, חזרו לשקול טבעין, ובקשו לשקול דינרין; אמר רבי שמעון, אף על פי כן יד כולן שוה, אבל חטאת, זה מביא בסלע, זה מביא בשתים, וזה מביא בשלש.

ה) מותר שקלים חולין, מותר עשירית האיפה, מותר קיני זבין, קיני זבות וקיני יולדות וחטאות ואשמות, מותריהן נדבה. זה הכלל, כל שהוא בא לשם חטא ולשם אשמה מותריהן נדבה, מותר עולה לעולה, מותר מנחה למנחה, מותר שלמים לשלמים, מותר פסח לשלמים, מותר נזירים לנזירים, מותר נזיר לנדבה, מותר עניים לעניים, מותר עני לאותו עני, מותר שבוים לשבוים, מותר שבוי לאותו שבוי, מותר המתים למתים, מותר המת ליורשיו. רבי מאיר אומר מותר המת יהא מונח עד שיבא אליהו; רבי נתן אומר מותר המת בונין לו נפש על קברו.

פירוש רמ״ל

„והעשיר לא ירבה כתיב״, ור׳ יהודה חולק ואומר שגם לשקלים אין להם קצבה כי הכל לפי כח המדינה ואם תחליפו בדעתם לשקול דרכון תחת חצי שקל הרשות בידם, אבל ע״ז השיב ר׳ שמעון מענה נכוחה, שגם אז יש להם קצבה כי כולם אינן רשאים לשקול רק במטבע שהוחלטה, משא״כ חטאת שאין לו כל מטבע, וכ״א כפח שירצה יקריב.

ה) מותר קיני כו׳, אחרי שהביא המסדר את המשנה את דעת ב״ה וב״ש וידוע הוא שהלכה כב״ה, יביא את המשנה הזאת שסתמה כב״ה שמותר השקלים הוא חולין; ומפרש הדין כן הנותר על כל דבר שבצדקה שכולם מסכימים ורק על מותר המת, ר״ל מה שהקדישו בעדו לקבורתו, יערער ר״מ ויאמר כי יהא מונח עד שיבא אליהו, מפני כי הכסף הזה לא נתן בשביל היורשים והמת כבר נקבר, ור״נ אומר כי בנין הציון הוא ג״כ כבוד המת, ואולם כל הדברים הללו המה אם היה הכסף של יחיד, אבל אם היה ממעות העיר, הפרנסים ברוב דעות, יוכלו לשנות את את כסף הצדקה כמו משבוים לעניים ולהיפך.

פרק שלישי.

א) בשלשה פרקים בשנה תורמין את הלשכה, בפרוס הפסח בפרוס עצרת, בפרוס החג, והן גרנות למעשר בהמה, דברי רבי עקיבא; בן עזאי אומר בעשרים ותשעה באדר, ואחד בסיון, ובעשרים ותשעה באב, רבי אלעזר ורבי שמעון אומרים באחד בניסן, באחד בסיון, בעשרים ותשעה באלול. מפני מה אמרו בעשרים ותשעה ולא אמרו באחד בתשרי? מפני שהוא יום טוב, ואי אפשר לעשר ביום טוב לפיכך הקדימוהו לעשרים ותשעה באלול.

ב) בשלש קופות, של שלש שלש סאין תורמין את הלשכה, וכתוב בהן: אלף, בית, גימל; רבי ישמעאל אומר, יונית כתוב בהן: אלפא, ביתא, גמלא. אין התורם נכנס, לא בפרגוד חפות, ולא במנעל, ולא בסנדל, ולא בתפילין, ולא בקמיע, שמא יעני,

---

פירוש רמ״ל

פרק שלישי.

א) בשלשה פרקים כו', ענין הפרק הזה הוא סדר תוצאות השקלים על הקרבנות שהיו משתדלים לערבב את כסף השקלים שיהיה לכל אחד מישראל חלק בקרבנות ציבור לבד התנאי שהותנה כדלעיל, וכן היו עושין: שאחרי שכבר גבו את כל השקלים בתחילת ניסן היו ממלאים מהכסף הזה שלש תביות גדולות, ערך תשעה סאין כל אחת, והיו מכסין אותן במטפחות, ואח״כ היו מביאין שלש קופות קטנות כל אחת ג' סאין והיו ממלאין את הקופות הקטנות שהיו מסומנות בשלש אותיות א. ב. ג. בעברית או ביונית, כל אחת ואחת מהתביות הגדולות, ומהקופות הקטנות היו מוציאין את הכסף לקנות בהן קרבנות ציבור; והמילוי פעם הראשונה היתה בט״ו בניסן שהוא חצי החדש קודם הפסח, וכן היו עושין ט״ו ימים לפני חג השבועות, אך בעת אשר מלאו אותם שנית התחילו מן התביות האחרונה שמשם מלאו בפעם הראשונה את הקופה המסומנת באות ג', מלאו עתה את הקופה המסומנת באות א. ואח״כ מלאו מן השנית שהיתה קודם ראשונה לקופה המסומנת באות ב. ומן השלישית שהיתה מקודם שניה לקופה המסומנת באות ג. ועשו זאת כדי לערבב הכספים שיהיה לכל אחד חלק בקרבנות ציבור או בבדק הבית, שלכן בכל פעם בבואו לשלישית לא היה מכנה אותה לסימן, שמסתמא יתחיל לעתיד, ותרם את הראשונה לשם ארץ ישראל הקרובה יותר לירושלים והשניה לשם הכרכים המוקפות חומה הרחוקות מארץ ישראל, והשלישית בשביל כל מדינות הרחוקות מפני שכל הקרוב קרוב קודם; אך עכ״ז היו המעות מעורבין והיה לכ״א מישראל חלק בהם, וכ״ז היו עושים בפרהסיא גדול למען לא יהיה שום חשד על הגבאים, והתורם או גם כל הנכנס ללשכת שבה היה הכסף, היו מחויבין להסיר מהם כל הבגדים שיש בהם איזה כיס וגם לא במנעל וסנדל או אזמקאות מקום שיכולים להסתיר הכסף ולא גם בתפילין ובקמיע שיש בהם קמטים ותיבות קטנות ששמה יכולים להסתיר הכסף, והכל בשביל הכתוב והייתם נקיים וגו'. **בפרוס עצרת בפרוס החג,** מפני שהקרבנות בשבעת ימי הפסח רבו לכן היו מוכרחים לפתוח את הקופה השנית בט״ו באייר, אבל חג השבועות שהוא רק יום אחד ולא רבו הקרבנות מכסף הצבור, לכן היו מעות הקופה השנית מספיקות עד חצי אלול שאך אז פתחו את הקופה השלישית. **והן גרנות למעשר בהמה,** כלומר הזמנים הללו והולדות של בהמות הם כמו עומדות בגורן ואסור לשחטן ולאכול מהן טרם תופרש המעשר, אבל בין הזמנים הללו רשאים היו לאכילה גם קודם הפרשת המעשר. והטעם שקבעו את אלו הזמנים למעשרות, הוא מפני שאז החלו עולי רגלים לעלות לירושלים ורצו בשבילם שיהיו הבהמות מצוים להם לקניה. **בן עזאי אומר,** בן עזאי ור״א ור״ש חולקים בזה רק מפני גרנות המעשר, שלדעתם המעשר ינתן רק אז.

ויאמרו מעון הלשכה העני, או שמא יעשיר, ויאמרו מתרומת הלשכה העשיר, לפי שאדם צריך לצאת ידי המקום, כדרך שצריך לצאת ידי הבריות, שנאמר: "והייתם נקיים מה׳ ומישראל" (במדבר ל״ב) ואומר: "ומצא חן ושכל טוב בעיני אלהים ואדם" (משלי ג).

ג) **ש**ל ב.ת רבן גמליאל נכנס, ושקלו בין אצבעותיו, וזורקו לפני התורם, והתורם מתכוין ודוחפו לקופה. אין התורם תורם, עד שיאמר להם: אתרום? והן אומרים לו: תרום! תרום! תרום! שלש פעמים.

ד) **ת**רם את הראשונה ומחפה בקטבלאות, שניה ומחפה בקטבלאות, שלישית לא היה מחפה, שמא ישכח את התרום ויתרום את דבר התרום. תרם את הראשונה לשם ארץ ישראל, והשניה לשום כרכים המוקפין לה, שלישית לשום בבל, ולשום מדי, ולשום מדינות הרחוקות.

פירוש רמ״ל

ג) של בית ר״ג נכנס, כלומר כל אחד מבית ר״ג בעת שהיה נותן שקליו היה מתנהג כן.

ד) ויתרום את דבר התרום, כלומר מן הקופה הראשונה שכבר התחיל ממנה בפעם הראשונה.

פרק רביעי.

א) התרומה מה היו עושין בה? לוקחין בה תמידין, מוספין ונסכיהם, העומר, ושתי הלחם, ולחם הפנים, וכל קרבנות הציבור. שומרי ספיחים בשביעית, נוטלין שכרן מתרומת הלשכה; רבי יוסי אומר, אף הרוצה מתנדב שומר חנם; אמרו לו, אף אתה אומר שאין באין אלא משל ציבור.

ב) פרה ושעיר המשתלח ולשון של זהורית באין מתרומת הלשכה. כבש פרה, וכבש שעיר המשתלח, ולשון שבין קרניו, ואמת המים, וחומת העיר ומגדלותיה, וכל צורכי העיר באין משירי הלשכה; אבא שאול אומר: כבש פרה כהנים גדולים עושין אותן משל עצמן.

ג) מותר שירי הלשכה מה היו עושין בהן? לוקחין בהן יינות שמנים וסלתות, והשכר להקדש, דברי רבי ישמעאל; רבי עקיבא אומר, אין משתכרין בשל הקדש, ולא בשל עניים.

ד) מותר התרומה מה היו עושין בה? רקועי זהב ציפוי לבית

פירוש רמ"ל

פרק רביעי.

א) שומרי ספיחים בשביעית, העומר ושתי הלחם אשר דינם, כי יבואו רק מארץ ישראל ודוקא מן תבואה החדשה שגדלה בזו השנה, מאין היו לוקחים אותם בשנת השביעית שאז לא זרעו ולא קצרו? היו שולחים תרים לראות באיזה מקום גדלים תבואה מה שנזרעה בשנה הקודמת שנקראת בלשון המקרא (ויקרא כ"ה) ספיח ולשמור אותה שלא תשלוט בה יד אחר לעקרה קודם שיבוא הקרבן ממנה, מפני שבשנת השביעית הכל הוא הפקר ואין רשות לבעל השדה לבלי להניח אחרים ליתלוש את הצמחים והתבואה. התרים והשומרים הללו היו מקבלים שכרם מתרומת הלשכה, ובכסף הזה נחשב כאלו קנו בו את התבואה שיש לכל אחד חלק בהם. ור' יוסי האומר שמתנדב אדם להיות שומר חנם סובר שקרבן יחיד מתנת להיות של ציבור אם הוא מנדב אותו אבל אין הלכה כמוהו בעומר ושתי הלחם, אם כי בשאר קרבנות מותר לקחת משל יחיד אם הוא מנדב אותם לציבור בעין יפה (ראה ר"ה).

ב) פרה ולשון של זהורית, מותר הכסף שלא היה נכנס לשלש רביות הגדולות שזכרנו למעלה, נקרא שירי הלשכה והיו נותנין אותו במקום גבוה, שהיו עולים עליו ע"י אלמנאק ב"א מעלות; ומהכסף הזה היו עושים כבש לפרה אדומה, שדינו יתבאר במסכת פרה אדומה, וכן הכבש לשעיר המשתלח לעזאזל וללשון שבין קרניו שדינם יתבארו ביומא, וכן לאמת המים והחומת העיר ירושלים אם היו צריכים תיקון.

ג) מותר שירי הלשכה, ר"ל אם אחר כל אלה עוד נשאר כסף תוך ללשכה מה היו עושין בו? לוקחין יינות, כל מי שמביא קרבן, עליו לנסך על המזבח וסולת ושמן למנחה, וכל אלה היו קונים בעזרה בכספם, והסחורה הזאת אסורה, כי בעד מותר הכסף של שירי הלשכה, היו קונין יין שמנים וסלתות למכירה להמקריבים, למען ירויחו מעות להקדש, אבל ר"ע חולק ואומר, שאסור לעשות סחורה במעות הקדש וכן במעות של עניים. ובירושלמי חושב דברים רבים מה שעשו במותר כסף השקלים כמו שכר לימוד הלכות שחיטה, הלכות קרבנות, וכן לבקר את מומי הקרבנות שכל אלה היו לוקחין ממעות שירי הלשכה; ועוד כמו אלה, (ראה שם הלכה ד' בזה הפרק).

ד) מותר התרומה, ר"ל אם הגיע אחד בניסן שכבר יש תרומה חדשה משקלים שבאו

קדשי הקדשים; רבי ישמעאל אומר, מותר הפירות קייץ למזבח ומותר התרומה לכלי שרת; רבי עקיבא אומר, מותר התרומה קייץ למזבח, ומותר נסכים לכלי שרת; רבי חנינא סגן הכהנים אומר, מותר נסכים קייץ למזבח, ומותר התרומה לכלי שרת; זה וזה לא היו מודים בפירות.

ה) מותר הקטורת מה היו עושין בה? מפרישין ממנה שכר האומנין, ומחללין אותה על שכר האומנין, ונותנין לאומנין בשכרן, וחוזרין ולוקחין אותה מתרומה חדשה; אם בא החדש בזמנו, לוקחין אותה מתרומה חדשה, ואם לאו מן הישנה.

ו) המקדיש נכסיו, והיו בהן דברים ראויין לקרבנות הציבור ינתנו לאומנין בשכרן, דברי רבי עקיבא; אמר לו בן עזאי אינה היא המדה, אלא מפרישין מהן שכר האומנין, ומחללין אותה על מעות האומנין, ונותנין אותן לאומנין בשכרן, וחוזרין ולוקחין אותן מתרומה חדשה.

ז) המקדיש נכסיו, והיתה בהן בהמה ראויה לגבי המזבח, זכרים ונקבות, רבי אליעזר אומר, זכרים ימכרו לצרכי עולות,

---

פירוש רמ״ל

השנה, אם נשאר בכסף משנה שעברה מה עושים בה? מותר הפירות, עתה יצא ויתן בדבר שאלה חדשה מה היו עושין בהרוחה שהרויחו מהנסכים כבמשנה הקודמת, ואומר ר' ישמעאל שהיו קונין קרבנות אם קרה כה שהיה המזבח עומד בטל באין קרבנות היחידים, אבל ר"ע האומר שאסור להרויח ממעות הקדש אומר כי לקיץ המזבח היו לוקחין ממותר הכסף משנה שעברה, ומותר נסכים ר"ל מה שנשאר ממיצוי המדות של נסכים, (כי היו לוקחין במדה גדושה ומקריבין מדה מחוקה) לכלי שרת, ור"ח סגן הכהנים דעת אחרת לו בזה. והנה מן המשנה הזאת (ורבות דומות לה בכל המשניות) נראה כי בזמן המקדש היו הכהנים הממונים מדוקים כל דבר בסוד ולא נודע דבר איך התנהגו, כי לולא זאת לא היתה המחלוקת מצוית תיכף אחר החורבן, ועוד יותר שר' ישמעאל היה כהן ואבותיו אלישע וישמעאל היו כהנים חשובים בזמן המקדש וכן ר' חנינא סגן הכהנים היה מן הכהנים החשובים, וגם הם לא ידעו את המנהג ואך חלקו בסברות. ושמור הכלל הזה בבואך לבחון משניות שחלוקות בדבר המנהג ואין אחת מהן אומרת מפי הנסיון.

ה) מותר הקטורת, ר"ל הנשאר בבוא השנה משנה שעברה ומשנת התרומה היו משתמשים בקטורת הנקנות משקלים החדשים, ויען כי מדת הקטורת היא מלא חפניו ואין הידים בגודלן ורחבן שוות, וכהן שהיד שלו קטנה היה ג"כ נוטל רק מלא חפניו, היה נשאר בכל שנה איזה מדות מסממני הקטרת.

ו) כל המקדיש נכסיו, סתם הקדש יאמר ר"ע הוא לבדק הבית ולכן סיקל אם גם היו בין חפצי ההקדש דברים הראוים למזבח, כמו סממני הקטרת ולא הצריכם להיות קרבים על המזבח, ואולם בדברים חיים הראוים למזבח וכן גם יינות ידובר בזה בהמשניות לקמן, ואולם בן עזאי מחמיר גם בסממני הקטרת. כדעתו, כי דעת המקדיש נכסיו בודאי נוטה יותר שיקרבו דברים הראוים למזבח, על המזבח עצמו; אשר לכן מבקש חילולם על מעות האומנין וחוזרין ולוקחין אותה מתרומה חדשה [illegible] לצרכי המקדש.

ז) זכרים ימכרו לצרכי עולות, גם ר"א סובר כי סתם הקדש הוא לבדק הבית, אבל עכ"ז ירמה כי הדברים עצמם הראוין למזבח לא יצאו מיד המזבח אם גם שדם יעלה לבדק הבית שלכן מצריך למוכרם לצורך המזבח עצמו. ואך ר' יהושע הסובר כבן עזאי בזה, יאמר

ונקבות ימכרו לצרכי זבחי שלמים, (ודמיהן יפלו עם שאר נכסים לבדק הבית); רבי יהושע אומר, זכרים עצמן יקרבו עולות, ונקבות ימכרו לצרכי זבחי שלמים, ויביאו בדמיהן עולות, ושאר נכסים יפלו לבדק הבית; רבי עקיבא אומר, רואה אני את דברי רבי אליעזר מדברי רבי יהושע, שרבי אליעזר השוה את מדתו, ורבי יהושע חלק; אמר רבי פפיים, שמעתי כדברי שניהן: המקדיש בפירוש, כדברי רבי אליעזר, והמקדיש סתם, כדברי רבי יהושע.

ח) המקדיש נכסיו, והיו בהן דברים ראויין על גבי המזבח: יינות, שמנים ועופות, רבי אליעזר אומר, ימכרו לצורכי אותו המין, ויביא בדמיהן עולות; ושאר נכסים יפלו לבדק הבית.

ט) אחת לשלשים יום משערין את הלשכה; כל המקבל עליו לספק סלתות מארבעה, עמדו משלש, יספק מארבעה; משלש ועמדו מארבעה, יספק מארבעה, שיד הקדש על העליונה; ואם התליעה סולת, התליעה לו, ואם החמיץ יין, החמיץ לו; ואינו מקבל את מעותיו, עד שיהא המזבח מרצה.

פירוש רמ״ל

כי דעת המקדיש הוא, אם גם סתם דבריו, כי למזבח יותר טוב מן בדק הבית שלכן הזכרים יקרבו לעולה בשם המנדב אבל נקבות הראויות רק לשלמים ואינו יכולין להקריב בשם המנדב, אם איננו בעת ההקרבה, לכן ימכרו לצורך הזה לאחר ובדמיהן יקרבו עולות בשם המנדב. ור״ע שדעתו לענין סתם הקדש כר״א, יאמר כי הוא רואה את דברי ר״א, אבל ר׳ פפיים כמכריע יאמר שאם הקדיש כל נכסיו סתם וביניהם היו בהמות למזבח ולא קראם בשם, אז כונתו כי כל אחד יקרב למקום הראוי לו, ויקרבו כדברי ר׳ יהושע, אבל אם פירש ואמר: „הנכסים והבהמות שלי כולם הקדש" ולא אמר מפורש כי הבהמות יוקרבו למזבח, גלה בזה דעתו שכל נכסיו קדושה אחת הן, לבדק הבית; כי אם לא כן, כיון שקרא הבהמות בשם, היה לו להוסיף עוד מלה אחת „למזבח". ובמשנה שאחריה סתם כר״א, מפני שיינות שמנים ועופות אין להם פדיון ולכן יקרבו בדמיהם עולות וכו׳.

ט) אחד לשלשים יום, ענין זאת המשנה, שבכל חודש היו קורין את המוכרים שיסכמו את המחיר על כל דבר הנצרך למזבח ולבדק הבית על כל החודש, ולכל המסכם מחירו היו נותנין את הקדימה שיפקיד אותן למזבח ולבדק הבית; והמקחים שהיו קוצבים אותם היו על כל החודש, באופן שאם נתיקרו הדברים, היו סובלים המוכרים את הנזק, אבל אם הוזל השער, יד ההקדש על העליונה; והרשות היה לגבאים שלא לשלם רק כפי השער הזול, אם המוכרים הקדימו להם קצת זול. ומה שאומרת ואם התליע, התליע להמוכרים, ר״ל אם גם קבלו את המעות היה עוד אחריותן עליהן, אבל בירושלמי אומר, כי המה היו מקבלין את המעות מיד, והכהנים זריזין הם ולא הניחו את הסולת להתליע ואת היין להחמיץ.

פרק חמישי.

א) **אלו** הן הממונין שהיו במקדש: יוחנן בן פנחס על החותמות אחיה על הנסכים, מתתיה בן שמואל על הפייסות, פתחיה על הקינין. פתחיה זה מרדכי; למה נקרא שמו פתחיה? שהיה פותח בדברים ודורשן ויודע שבעים לשון. בן אחיה על חולי מעיים, נחוניה חופר שיחין, גביני כרוז, בן גבר על נעילת שערים, בן בביי על הפקיע, בן ארזא על הצלצל, הוגרוס בן לוי על השיר, בית גרמו על מעשה לחם הפנים, בית אבטינס על מעשה הקטורת, אלעזר על הפרוכת ופנחס על המלבוש.

פירוש רמ"ל

פרק חמישי.

א) **אלו הן הממונין,** לא בזמן אחד היו הממונין שהוא חושב במשנה, כ"א דורות רבים הפרידו ביניהן, אבל המשנה מזכרת רק הטובים והחכירים שהיו ממונין בכל דור, וענין החותמות יתבאר במשנה ד'. **הפייסות,** רן: שהיו הכהנים מטילין גורל ביניהם מי יעלה לעבוד עבודה זו ומי עבודה זו, והיו צריכין לממונה להחזיק הסדר ושיהיה רשום אצלו מי יעלה לפיים היום ומי למחר. **קינין** הן הקרבנות שכל אשה יולדת היתה צריכה להקריב ומפני שהיו רבות צריכין היו לממונין גם בזו להחזיק הסדר, שכל הבאה קודם תקריב קודם ושיתנו לה את הקינין במחיר הקצוב ולא ירבו עליהן, וגם היו מתערבין מפני ריבוי המביאין וחכמה רבה נצרכה להורות דיני תערובות האלה, עיין בפירוש תפארת ישראל. **חולי מעיים** היה דבר הרגיל מאד במקדש, מפני שהיו הכהנים נושאים עליהם בעת העבודה רק הארבעה בגדים קריב, והיו הולכים יחפים על הרצפה של שיש ובין כה מוכרחים היו לאכול את בשר הקרבנות שלא יביאו קדשים לידי נותר, ולכן נחלו תמיד בחולי מעיים, והממונים היו רואים על כל אחר שנחלה להביאו למקום הרפואה ולמנות אחרים תחתיהם, ולכן היו ממונים רבים לזה, וזה נחשב מכל המדריגות רק הממונה הראשי שהכל היה נעשה הרת השגחתו. **חופר שיחין,** לא רק במקדש וירושלים כ"א בכל הארץ ובסוריא, להכין מים לעולי לרגל ולבאי מקדש. **כרוז,** הוא הממונה שהיה מכריז בעצמו, או מצוה להכריז, כל עבודה ועבודה בזמנה. **נעילת שערים,** גם לזה היו ממונים הרבה, לנעול כל שער ולשמור את המקדש, כי כן היתה המצוה לשמור את המקדש אף שלא בעת מלחמה וסכנה, כאשר יתבאר במס' תמיד, והממונים היו מעמידים כל שומר על מקומו שלא יישן ושילך סביב סביב במקום שהוגבל לו, ואם היו מוצאין את אחד מהם ישן, היו מלקין אותו ושורפין את כסותו וזה היה נקרא **פקיע** שהיו לזה ממונים אחרים לבד הממונים על נעילת שערים. **צלצל,** המה התופים שהיו מכים בהם להשמיע בעת הקרבת הקרבנות, וכן היו מלוים את אחיהם הלוים בנגנם בכלי זמר את המזמורים הראויים בעת הקרבת הקרבנית, ואף המנצח על השירים „קאפעלל-מייסטער" היה ממונה אחר, לבד הממונים על התופים והמצלתים. **מעשה הקטורת,** שהיה נצריכת שתי פעמים, בכל יום והיקותה תותה ענין ועסק גדול להרכיבה ולערבה מכמה סממנים ושיעור כל אחד ואחד, ואיך שיהיה ענן הקטורת עולה, ומן האומנין המצוינים בזה היו **בית אבטינס,** וכן **לחם הפנים** שהיו עושין י"ב חלות בכל שבת היו צריכין לאומנין שלא יתקררו מהרה בעת שהיו מונחים על שולחן של שיש, וגם צורתם ותבניתם, המבואר במס' תמיד, ולזה היה הממונין **בית גרמו** דורות הרבה שהיו מוכרין את אומנתם לבניהם, גם **להפרוכת** שהיו מחליפין אותו תדיר היה ממונה מיוחד לקבל אותו מהמגרבים ולראות אומנתו ונקיותו ומלאכתו. גם היו אנשים רבים עסוקים בהלבשת הכהנים בבגדיהם ומשגיחים שיהיו נקיים מפני הולי המעיים התגילה במקדש, וכובסי הבגדים, שעל כולם היו ממונים מיוחדים. ולשכות רבות היו במקדש שהיו מיוחדות רק לבגדי הכהנים.

ב) אין פוחתין משלשה גזברין ומשבעה אמרכלין, ואין עושין שררה על הציבור בממון פחות משנים, חוץ מבן אחיה, שעל חולי מעיים, ואלעזר שעל הפרוכת, שאותן קבלו רוב הציבור עליהן.

ג) ארבעה חותמות היו במקדש, וכתוב עליהן: עגל, זכר, גדי, חוטא; בן עזאי אומר, חמשה היו וארמית כתוב עליהן: עגל, זכר, גדי, חוטא דל, וחוטא עשיר. עגל, משמש עם נסכי בקר, גדולים וקטנים זכרים ונקבות; גדי, משמש עם נסכי צאן, גדולים וקטנים, זכרים ונקבות, חוץ משל אילים; זכר, משמש עם נסכי אילים בלבד; חוטא, משמש עם נסכי שלש בהמות של מצורעים.

ד) מי שהוא מבקש נסכים, הולך לו אצל יוחנן, שהוא ממונה על החותמות, נותן לו מעות, ומקבל ממנו חותם; בא לו אצל אחיה, שהוא ממונה על הנסכים, נותן לו חותם, ומקבל ממנו נסכים, ולערב באין זה אצל זה, ואחיה מוציא את החותמות, ומקבל כנגדן מעות, ואם הותירו הותירו להקדש, ואם פחתו, ישלם יוחנן מביתו, שיד הקדש על העליונה.

פירוש רמ״ל

והנה המשנה אינה מזכרת אם היו הממונים כהנים, לוים, או גם ישראלים היו ביניהם, וכבר דברו בזה הרבה חכמי זמננו, ואולם הרוצה לדעת את תכונת הכהנים והממונים האלו, סיבם ומצבם בארוכה, עליו לעיין בספר Die Priester und der Cultus von Prof. Buchler Wien, 1895 ושמה יראה כי מספר הכהנים לבד עלו לא למאות ולא לאלפים, כי אם לעשרות אלפים, וכן מספר הלוים היה רב מאד, וכן על איזה דברים היו הממונים רק מהכהנים ועל איזה דברים גם מלוים וישראלים, ראה שם מצד 47-67, ואנחנו דברנו עוד מזה בסוף מס׳ שבת בדבר הי״ח גזירות שגזרו חכמים על הכהנים ועל התרומה.

ב) **אין פוחתין**, סדר הנשיאות במקדש היו כן: המלך ואחריו הכהן גדול, ואחריו הסגן, ואחריו הקתליקין שהיו שנים, אחריהם האמרכלין שהיו שבעה, ואחריהם הגזברין שהיו רבים וגם תחתיהם היו ממונים רבים. והנה משמרת כל אחד מהם מבואר במס׳ תמיד ויומא ובפרט בהספר הנזכר למעלה.

ג) **ארבעה חותמות**, הנסכים לכל קרבן שונים היו בידוע, ולכל הנסכים היה מחיר קצוב במקדש, והנה נסכי כבשים ועזים גם הזכרים שבהם שוים היו והותם „גדי" היה מספיק גם להמביא קרבנו כבש, אבל לאילים היה נסך מיוחד גדול ממנו ולכן השתמשו בחותם „זכר" שהיה סמן לפי שקרבנו „איל", אבל בבקרים שוין הזכרים והנקבות הגדולים והקטנים ולכן השתמשו בחותם „עגל" למי שקרבנו מן הבקר. ועל קרבן המצורעים השתמשו בחותם „חוטא" (לרמז שהצרעת באה מפני החטא) שעל העשירים היה להביא שני אלים וכבשה אחת ונסכיהם, היה החותם ח ו ט א מספיק לתת להם את הנסכים שהוזכרו בתורה, אבל על העניים המצורעים שלא היה להם להביא רק כבש אחד ושתי תורים, ורק עשרון אחד סולת ולוג שמן בלא יין, אמרו חכמים, כי לא היה צריך לסמן מיוחד; ובן עזאי היה אומר, כי חמשה חותמות היו שעל החמישי היה כתוב ח ו ט א ־ ד ל להבדילו משאר גדי הצריך גם יין ואומר שהיה כתוב עליהן ארמית ולא עברית ובלי ספק היתה קבלה בידו, כי כל הסמנים שבמקדש היו ארמית וכן נראה מן המשנה עצמה בכל הסמנים (וזמן רב אחרי עלותם מבבל דברו הכהנים רק ארמית וכן האשכולות עד אחר הלל ושמאי, וגם בעדיות קבלו עדותם בארמית והציגו בלשונם, וראה בספר ביכנער הנ״ל).

ה) **מי** שאבד ממנו חותמו, ממתינין לו עד הערב, אם מצאו לו כדי חותמו, נותנין לו, ואם לאו, לא היו נותנים לו, ושם היום כתוב עליהן מפני הרמאין.

ו) **שתי** לשכות היו במקדש: אחת לשכת חשאים, ואחת לשכת הכלים; לשכת חשאים, יראי חטא נותנין לתוכה בחשאי, ועניים בני טובים מתפרנסין מתוכה בחשאי; לשכת הכלים, כל מי שהוא מתנדב כלי, זורקו לתוכה, ואחד לשלשים יום, גזברין פותחין אותה, וכל כלי שמצאו בו צורך לבדק הבית, מניחין אותו, והשאר נמכרין בדמיה ונופלין ללשכת בדק הבית.

פירוש רמ״ל

ה) מי שאבד ממנו חותמו, אם אבד חותם לא אמרו שיהיה יד הקדש על העליונה והמאבד חותמו לא ישיג כלום, כ״א בקרת היו עושים בהכסף הנפרה ואם היה הכסף יתר על החותמות שביד הנותן נסכים והסכום שלו שוה עם המעות שנתן הקונה בעד חותמו, היו נותנין לו נסכים ועל החותם לא היו מקפידין אותו למצוא, כי היה כתוב עליו שם היום ואינו מועיל ליום אחר.

ו) שתי לשכות, בתלמוד ירושלמי מביא ציורים יפים מן לשכת חשאים ויספר דברים רבים ממעשה הצדקה הזאת. והנה לשכות רבות היו במקדש בשמות מיוחדים אשר לא יחשבם פה, ואך לחשיבות שתי לשכות הללו יבקבם.

פרק ששי.

א) **ש**לשה עשר שופרות, שלשה עשר שולחנות, שלש עשרה השתחויות היו במקדש; של בית רבן גמליאל ושל בית רבי חנינא סגן הכהנים היו משתחוים ארבע עשרה; והיכן היתה יתירה? כנגד דיר העצים, שכן מסורת בידם מאבותיהם, ששם הארון נגנז.

ב) **מ**עשה בכהן אחד, שהיה מתעסק, וראה הרצפה שהיא משונה מחברותיה, בא ואמר לחבירו, לא הספיק לגמור את הדבר עד שיצתה נשמתו, וידעו ביחוד ששם הארון נגנז.

ג) **ו**היכן היו משתחוים? ארבע בצפון, וארבע בדרום, שלש במזרח ושתים במערב, כנגד י״ג שערים. דרומים, סמוכין למערב: שער העליון, שער הדלק, שער הבכורה, שער המים; ולמה נקרא שמו שער המים? שבו מכניסין צלוחית של נסוך מים בחג. רבי אליעזר בן יעקב אומר: בו המים מפכין, ועתידין להיות יוצאין מתחת מפתן הבית.

ד) **ל**עומתן בצפון סמוכין למערב: שער יכניה, שער קרבן,

פירוש רמ״ל

פרק ששי.

א) **שלשה עשר שופרות,** כבר אמרנו שהתיבות שהיו בהם נכנס השקלים או הנדבות נקראים שופרות מפני שהיו קצרים מלמעלה ורחבים מלמטה שלא תוכל יד לכנס בתוכה, וכן היו עקומים מטעם זה, המשנה הזאת תספור את כל מה שהיה במקדש במספר שלשה עשר המספר הקדוש להם, (כנגד שלש עשרה מדות הרחמים הנזכרים במקרא, ושכנגדם התקין ר׳ ישמעאל שלשה עשרה מדות לדרוש בהם את התורה), ובמשנה ה׳ תפרש מה היו הי״ג שופרות משמשין, וכן תפרש באיזה מקומן היו ההשתחויות. (כן תוכן המשנה הזאת נראה, כי ידעו מלימודי פיטאגארום בדבר המספרים והמספר 13 היה נחשב לאי־צולח גם בימים הקדמונים, ולמען הסיר מלב ההמון את האמונה הטפלה הזאת, תקנו דברים קדושים במספר הזה, או אולי כונו בזה להמתיק רוע מזלו של המשתמש במספר 13 בזה שנתנוהו לדברים קדושים; וגם בזמננו נוסדה חברה בשם "Thirteen-Club" המשתמשים כל הדברים רק במספר 13 להראות להמון שאין כל חשש וסכנה בו.) ובמס׳ מדות יתבאר איפוא היה דיר העצים.

ב) **מעשה בכהן,** הכהן היה בעל מום ופסול לעבודת הקרבנות ורק היה מתעסק לבור העצים שהמתולעים או הנרקבים היו פסולים; וכן היו מצלין את העצים מן העור שעליהן למזבח; והארון נגנז עוד במקדש ראשון כאשר ראו שאין עוד תקוה שתנצל העיר והמקדש מידי הכשדים, והכהן הזה מת, מפני שרצה לגלות את הסוד הזה; ועיין בספרנו The Pen-tateuch etc., Chicago, 1894.

ג) **והיכן היו משתחוים,** האומר כי י״ג שערים היו במקדש, הוא אבא יוסי בן יוחנן, מר מן הכהנים הגדולים שהיו במקדש שני, אבל לדעת החכמים רק שבעה שערים היו וההשתחויות היו כנגד י״ג פרצות שפרצו היונים בבהמ״ק ובית חשמונאי גדרום; שלכן גזרו ההשתחויות כנגד הפרצות האלה כעין הודיה, וארו״ם תמכנת אשר תחשוב תשעה בשמותם ושנים בלא שם מיוחד ואומרת איפוא היו בארם, נראה כי כרכרית כן היה (והחכמים חלקו רק מהמשנה ולא מהקבלה, וראה בתפא״י על המשניות, ופירושו בשם אביו קשה להולמו).

ד) **פשפשין,** נקראים דלתות קטנות בתוך הגדולות, כי הגדולות היו כבדין וקשין לפתוח

שער נשים, שער השיר. ולמה נקרא שמו שער יכניה? שבו יצא יכניה בגלותו. במזרח: שער ניקנור, ושתי פשפשין היו לו: אחד מימינו, ואחד משמאלו, ושנים במערב, שלא היה להן שם. שלשה עשר שולחנות היו במקדש: שמונה של שיש בבית המטבחים, שעליהן מדיחין את הקרביים, ושנים במערב הכבש, אחד של שיש, ואחד של כסף; על של שיש, היו נותנים את האיברים, על של כסף, כלי שרת; ושנים באולם מבחוץ על פתח הבית: אחד של שיש, ואחד של זהב; על של שיש, נותנין לחם הפנים בכניסתו, ועל של זהב, ביציאתו, שמעלין בקודש ולא מורידין; ואחד של זהב מבפנים, שעליו לחם הפנים תמיד.

ה) שלשה עשר שופרות היו במקדש, וכתוב עליהם: תקלין חדתין, תקלין עתיקין, קינין, וגוזלי עולה, עצים, ולבונה, זהב לכפורת, וששה לנדבה. תקלין חדתין, שבכל שנה ושנה, ועתיקין, מי שלא שקל אישתקד שוקל לשנה הבאה; קינין, הן תורין, וגוזלי עולה, הן בני יונה, כולן עולות, דברי רבי יהודה; וחכמים אומרים: קינין, אחד חטאת ואחד עולה, וגוזלי עולה, כולן עולות.

ו) האומר: „הרי עלי עצים", לא יפחות משני גיזרין; „לבונה", לא יפחות מקומץ; „זהב", לא יפחות מדינר זהב, ששה

פירוש רמ״ל

וכתנים או לוים רבים היו מתכנכין לפתוח או לסגור אחד הדלתות. וענין השולחנות מבואר, ואמרו: „מעלין בקדש" הוא, מפני שלחם הפנים היה מונח בפנים על שולחן של זהב, הצריכו לו שולחן כזה גם בצאתו מן הקדש.

ה) שלשה עשר שופרות, השופר הראשון היה כתוב עליו „תקלין חדתין" ר״ל בו צריכין להשליך את השקלים משנת זו בפני הגזבר, והשני היה כתוב עליו „תקלין עתיקין" לאמר: בו ישליכו השקלים שלא נגבו בשנת העברה ג״כ בפני הגזבר והוא מקבל מכנו קבלה, שיחזירו לו את עבוטו. השלישי היה כתוב עליו קינין, לאמר כי החפץ לנדב על „קינין" ישליך נדבתו בו. הרביעי „גוזלי עולה" ר״ל בו ישליכו המנדבים בעד תורים ובני יונה למזבח לצרכי עולה את נדבותיהם, החמישי „עצים" בו יקובל נדבות על העצים למערכה, הששי כתוב עליו „לבונה" בשביל המנדבים נדבות על הלבונה, השביעי „זהב לכפורת" כי בו היו הנדבות שהתנדבו בשביל קדש הקדשים והכפורת שהיה שם. אלה המה השבעה שופרות הראשונים, והששה שהיו לשם נדבה, גם עליהם היו חרותים שמות מיוחדים (לדעת הרמב״ם) והם: על הראשון „מותר חטאת", ר״ל מי שהקדיש מעות לחטאת ואחרי קנותו נשארו לו עוד מהם היה משליכם בשופר הזה למען שמן הכסף הזה לא יוקח רק לצרכי חטאת, השני „מותר אשם", השלישי „מותר קיני זבין וזבות ויולדות", הרביעי „למותר קרבנות נזיר", והחמישי „מותר קרבן מצורע" שזהו כנ״ל, אם הפריש מעות למטרת אחד מהם ונשארו בידו אחרי שהוציא מהם למטרת נדבתו ישליך המותר כל אחד במקום המסומן לטעמו, ועל הששי היה כתוב „נדבה" כתם המעות היו לוקחין לכל הנצרך למקדש או למזבח. ובדבר הפלוגתא שבין החכמים לר״י הוא כי החכמים סוברים שדעת המנדבים לקינין היא, שמכספם יקנו דבר שיעלה על המזבח כולו כליל, והרמב״ם אומר שהלכה כחכמים.

ו) האומר הרי עלי, אחרי שנתבארו ענין השופרות השונים שהיו משתמשים לנדבות שונות תבאר, כי רק אז מותר להשליך להשופרות כמה שיחפוץ ואפילו כל שהוא, גם אינו משלם

לנדבה. נדבה מה היו עושין בה? לוקחין בה עולות, הבשר לשם, והעורות לכהנים; זהו מדרש דרש יהוידע כהן גדול: ·אשם הוא אשם אשם לה׳ (ויקרא ה׳) זה הכלל, כל שהוא בא משום חטא ומשום אשמה, ילקח בו עולות, הבשר לשם, והעורות לכהנים; נמצאו שני כתובים קיימים: אשם לה׳ ואשם לכהנים, ואומר ·כסף אשם וכסף חטאות לא יובא בית ה׳ לכהנים יהיו·. (מלכים ב׳ י״ב)

פירוש רמ״ל

את נדרו אשר נדר קודם, אבל אם נדר ואמר הרי עלי איזה דבר, אז יש שיעור קצוב שלא יפחות מזה, ואגב תשמיענו המשנה כי העורות של כל הקרבנות היו לכהנים, ובספרו של Buchler הנ״ל, ימצא הקורא כמה כהנים היו מתעסקים בזה והעשירות הגדולה שהיתה להכהנים מהעורות, וכמה לשכות מיוחדות שהיו בשביל זה במקדש, וכן מתי נתחלקו להכהנים ושהכהנים בעלי הזרוע גזלו את הכהנים העניים בלקחם לעצמם בזרוע את החלק היותר גדול, אם שהיו מששים עצמם מעבודת הקרבנות שהיתה עבודה קשה מאד, והכום העורות היה רב מאד, (עיי״ש ותמצאם).

פרק שביעי.

א) מעות שנמצאו בין השקלים לנדבה, קרוב לשקלים יפלו לשקלים, לנדבה יפלו לנדבה, מחצה למחצה, יפלו לנדבה; בין עצים ללבונה, קרוב לעצים יפלו לעצים, ללבונה יפלו ללבונה, מחצה למחצה יפלו ללבונה; בין קינין לגוזלי עולה, קרוב לקינין יפלו לקינין, לגוזלי עולה, יפלו לגוזלי עולה; מחצה למחצה יפלו לגוזלי עולה; בין חולין למעשר שני, קרוב לחולין יפלו לחולין, למעשר שני יפלו למעשר שני, מחצה למחצה יפלו למעשר שני. זה הכלל, הולכין אחר הקרוב להקל, מחצה למחצה להחמיר.

ב) מעות שנמצאו לפני סוחרי בהמה, לעולם מעשר; בהר הבית, חולין; בירושלים בשעת הרגל, מעשר, ובשאר כל ימות השנה חולין.

ג) בשר שנמצא בעזרה, איברין עולות; חתיכות חטאות; בירושלים זבחי שלמים; זה וזה תעובר צורתו ויצא לבית השריפה, נמצא בגבולין איברין נבילות, חתיכות מותרות; בשעת הרגל שהבשר מרובה, אף איברין מותרין.

פירוש רמ"ל

פרק שביעי.

א) מעות שנמצאו, לפי שיש הבדל בין קדושה לקדושה בקרבנות ובנכסים, ומהחובה שלא יחליפו לקנות מן מעות שנתרמו לקדושה חמורה דברים שהמה רק קדושה קלה, לכן אומר שאם נמצא הכסף בשיעור שוה משני הדברים, היינו שנמצא הרצפה מן הכסף לתיבת השקלים ולתיבת הנדבה שוה הנהו, אז מחשש שמא המה מעות נדבה שמהם קונין רק עולות וחמת קדושה חמורה מן כסף השקלים שבדמיהם קונין כל דבר וגם נותנין לאומנין, לכן יקנו בכסף הזה דבר שבו קדושה חמורה מן כסף השקלים, וכן הדבר עם עצים ולבונה שהלבונה קדושה מהעצים מפני שהלבונה היא קרבן והעצים רק מכשירי קרבן, וכן הוא הדין בכל אשר תחשוב המשנה הלאה שהשנית קדושה יותר מהראשונה, ולכן בית ספק תזכה תמיד החמורה מן הקלה. וזה אומרת „להחמיר", ר"ל לקנות בהכסף דבר שבו קדושה חמורה מהצד שכנגדה, ובדבר עמידתם של המעות הספק ראה בפירוש תפא"י.

ב) לפני סוחרי בהמה, הכסף שנמצא בהר הבית שרוב ההולכים בו המה כהנים, יש לשער כי הכסף נפל מאתם והמה חולין, מפני כי כסף הקדשים לא ישאו הכהנים בצלחתם ואם גבלוהו מן התיבה למטרת הקרבן, בלי ספק כבר חללו אותו על הבהמה בעודו בלשכה, וממילא יצא הכסף לחולין; משא"כ אם נמצא הכסף במקום אחר לפני סוחרי הבהמות היא בלתי ספק ממעות מעשר שני, אשר רוב הקונים אך בכסף מעשר שני יקנו, ולכן נחשב כן בכל ימות השנה. ומטעם הזה הכסף הנמצא בכל מקום בחוצות ירושלם בשעת הרגל, שכל ישראל יעלו שמה לרגל ויביאו אתם את כסף מעשר שני, הולכים אחר הרוב שנאבד מאחד מהאורחים, אבל בכל ימות השנה, זולת שוק הבהמות, הכסף חולין.

ג) יען כי זבחי השלמים נאכלין בכל העיר לכל אדם, לכן אם נמצא בשר ברחוב נחשוב אותו לשלמים, ויען כי יכול להיות שהוא נותר (ר"ל יותר משני ימים ולילה אחד), לכן יחזיקוהו בספק עוד לילה אחד למען יוכלו להוציאו לבית השריפה כודאי נותר. ובעזרה שהעולה היתה

ד) בהמה שנמצאת מירושלים ועד מגדל עדר, וכמידתה לכל רוח, זכרים עולות, נקבות זבחי שלמים; רבי יהודה אומר, הראוי לפסחים פסחים, קודם לרגל שלשים יום.

ה) בראשונה היו ממשכנין את מוצאיה עד שהוא מביא נסכיה, חזרו להיות מניחין אותה ובורחין, התקינו שיהו נסכיה באין משל ציבור.

ו) אמר רבי שמעון, שבעה דברים התקינו בית דין, וזה אחד מהן: נכרי ששלח עולתו ממדינת הים, ושלח עמה נסכים, קריבין משלו, ואם לאו, קריבין משל ציבור; וכן גר שמת, והניח זבחים, אם יש לו נסכים קריבין משלו, ואם לאו, קריבין משל ציבור; ותנאי בית דין הוא על כהן גדול שמת שתהא מנחתו קריבה משל ציבור. רבי יהודה אומר, משל יורשין ושלימה היתה קריבה.

ז) על המלח, ועל העצים, שיהו הכהנים ניאותין בהן; ועל הפרה שלא יהו מועלין באפרה, ועל הקינין הפסולות שיהו באות משל ציבור; רבי יוסי אומר, המספיק את הקינין מספיק את הפסולות.

פירוש רמ"ל

עולה כליל על המזבח ולא היו מנתחים אותה לנתחים רק לאברים שלמים, לכן אם נמצא אבר שלם ידענו שהוא עולה, אבל החטאת, שממנה היו הכהנים אוכלין, היו מנתחין לנתחים ולכן חוששין שמא חטאת היא, ואם אמנם לא היו אוכלים כלל את הנמצאות מחשש נותר, היתה צריך להשמיענו את דין הבשר הנמצא, למען נדע הדין אם עבר אחד ואכלו, שאז בירושלם לא היה חייב שום אדם על האכילה ההיא, וכן בעזרה לא היינו יכולים לחייב את הכהן בעד איזה חתיכה מפני שהיא היתה בודאי דבר הנאכל לכהנים, כי מהעולות לא היה חתיכות, אבל אם אכל אבר שלם, אז חייב שמא מעולה היא שמשפטה להיות כולה כליל. ואגב תבאר את הדין בבשר חולין שנמצא בכל ערי ישראל שאם אך חתיכה היא ולא אבר, הולכין אחר הרוב שהוא מבשר שחוטה, אך על אבר שלם יש לחוש שמא לא חשבו לחתכו מפני שהיא נבלה ועזבו אותו לחית השדה כמו שהוא ולכן אסור בכל ימות השנה; אך ברגל, שהבשר מרובה, הולכין גם באברים אחר הרוב שהוא מבשר שחוטה, במקום שרוב אנשי העיר ישראל המה.

ד) בהמה שנמצאת וכו', ר' יהודא יצדק בהשקפתו על בהמות הזכרים שנמצאו קרוב לפסח, העת שכל ישראל מקריבין את פסחיהן שקרוב לודאי הוא כי הוא אחד מן הפסחים שנאבדו לבעליהן, אבל כונתו דוקא על זכר בן שנה ולא על בהמה שנראת שיש לו יותר מן שנת אחת, אך החכמים מחמירין גם בזה ואומרים כי יוקרב לעולה שהיא כולה כליל, פן מן העולות היא ומעלין בקדש ולא מורידין.

ו) כהן גדול שמת, מנחת כהן היא הנאמר בויקרא ו, 13.

ז) מועלין באפרה, אם כי מן התורה אין בה לא קדושה ולא מעילה גזרו החכמים, מפני שהיו הכהנים משתמשים באפרה, ועיקר הדבר שהמשנה מזכרת את, חמה הקינין הפסולות, ר"ל אם נמצאו פסולות אחר שהגזבר שלם בעדם ולקחם מהמוכר, שבלי ספק נפסלו בעת היותם כבר תחת יד הגזבר שאז אין אחריותה על המוכר ואחרים יקרבו תחתיה משל צבור, ויען כי יד ההקדש תמיד על העליונה, והדבר הזה היה מן הדברים שרוב המוכרים לא יכלו לעמוד בו, לכן הוצרכו לתקן זאת בתקנה מיוחדת, ור' יוסי חולק גם בזה, אך אין הלכה כמותו. ופרטי הדינים מקינים יתבארו במקומם.

פרק שמיני.

א) כל הרוקין הנמצאין בירושלים טהורין, חוץ משל שוק העליון, דברי רבי מאיר; וחכמים אומרים בשאר ימות השנה, שבאמצע טמאין, ושבצדדין טהורין, ובשעת הרגל, שבאמצע טהורין, ושבצדדין טמאין, שמפני שהן מועטין, מסתלקין לצדדין.

ב) כל הכלים שנמצאין בירושלים, דרך ירידה לבית הטבילה, טמאין, דרך עליה, טהורין; שלא כדרך ירידתן, עליתן, דברי רבי מאיר; רבי יוסי אומר, כולן טהורין, חוץ מן הסל, ומן המגריפה, והמריצה, המיוחדין לקברות.

ג) סכין שנמצאת בארבעה עשר, שוחט בה מיד, בשלשה עשר שונה ומטביל; וקופיץ, בין בזה ובין בזה שונה ומטביל; חל ארבעה עשר להיות בשבת, שוחט בה מיד, בחמשה עשר שוחט בה מיד, נמצאת קשורה לסכין, הרי זו כסכין.

ד) פרוכת שנטמאה בולד הטומאה, מטבילין אותה בפנים ומכניסין אותה מיד, ואת שנטמאה באב הטומאה, מטבילין אותה בחוץ, ושוטחין אותה בחיל, ואם היתה חדשה שוטחין אותה על גג האיצטבא, כדי שיראו העם את מלאכתן שהיא נאה.

פירוש רמ״ל

פרק שמיני.

א) כל הרוקין, רוק הזב הנזכר בתורה (ויקרא ט״ו 8) ידוע הוא שהוא טמא, ויען כי אי אפשר שלא היו זבין בין העם הרב שבא בירושלם יום יום, ואי אפשר שלא יגעו טהורים ברוקי של הזב בעת מהלכם ברחובות ירושלם, תשמיענו המשנה את המנהג, איככה נהגו בהיות ירושלם בשלוהה והמ״ק על מכונו. והנה ר״מ אמר שכל טמאי זיבה הלכו לטו בשוק העליון ולא בשוקים וברחובות אחרים למען לא יטמאו את הטהורים, אבל חכמים אומרים, כי בשעת הרגל קבעו למהלך הטמאים את צדי הדרכים וכל הטהורים הלכו באמצע, ובחול להיפך, ומובן מאליו שאין יחוש להרוק שנמצא במקום שהטהורים מהלכים, וכן אין ספק שהרוק הנמצא במקום שהטמאים מהלכים, שהוא טמא.

ב) כל הכלים, כזאת המשנה למדנו כי שני דרכים היו לבית הטבילה אחת לירידה ואחת לעלית, שלא יגעו הטהורים בעת עלייתן את הטמאים ויתטמאו שנית, ולכן הנהגו הולכים אחרי הרוב כלומר כל דפריש מרובא פריש, ובירידה שהיו כל הכלים טמאין הנמצא טמא ובעליית שהיו טהורין הנמצא טהור, ואף על הכלים שמיוחדין לטומאה גזרו גם נמצאו בדרך העליית, מפני שאין מוציאין כלי מחזקתו; והטעם הזה גם בסכין במשנה שלאחר זאת, ואך הקופץ שלא נתנו לשחוט בו שונה הוא, כי אינו פריש מרובא. הר״ר יאסף תרגם על פי פירוש המימוני את המשנה הזאת והוא רחוק מאד, ולכן פרשנו את המשנה בפשוטה, ואחרי כתבנו זאת ראינו גם בפירוש תפארת ישראל, שגם הוא מכון כפירושנו.

ד) פרוכת שנטמאה, ענין ולד הטומאה פר״ל „ראשון לטומאה״ יקרא מי שנגע באב הטומאה, וסדר מחלקותם היא: „גוית מת״ היא נקראת „אבי אבות הטומאה״, הנוגע בה הוא „אב הטומאה״ והנוגע בו הוא „ראשון״, הנוגע בראשון יקרא „שני לטומאה, וכן „שלישי, וכן „רביעי״, ופרטי דינם יתבארו בסדר טהרות.

ה) רבי שמעון בן גמליאל אומר משום רבי שמעון בן הסגן, פרוכת עביה טפח, ועל שבעים ושנים נימין נארגת, ועל כל נימא ונימא עשרים וארבע חוטין, ארכה ארבעים אמה ורחבה עשרים אמה, ומשמנה ושתי רבוא נעשית, ושתים עושין בכל שנה, ושלש מאות כהנים מטבילין אותה.

ו) בשר קדשי קדשים שנטמא, בין באב הטומאה בין בולד הטומאה, בין בפנים, בין בחוץ, בית שמאי אומרים הכל ישרף בפנים, חוץ מי שנטמא באב הטומאה בחוץ; בית הלל אומרים הכל ישרף בחוץ, חוץ מי שנטמא בולד הטומאה בפנים.

ז) רבי אליעזר אומר, את שנטמא באב הטומאה, בין בפנים, בין בחוץ, ישרף בפנים; רבי עקיבא אומר מקום טמאתו, שם שריפתו.

ח) אברי התמיד ניתנין מחצי כבש ולמטה במזרח, ושל מוספין ניתנין מחצי כבש ולמטה במערב, ושל ראשי חדשים ניתנין מתחת כרכוב המזבח מלמטה. השקלים והבכורים אין נוהגין אלא בפני הבית, אבל מעשר דגן ומעשר בהמה והבכורות נוהגין בין בפני הבית, בין שלא בפני הבית. המקדיש שקלים ובכורים, הרי זה קדש; רבי שמעון אומר, האומר בכורים קדש, אינן קדש.

הדרן עלך מסכת שקלים.

פירוש רמ"ל

ה) רשב"ג, בדבר הפרכת יאמר בירושלמי כי המשנה דברה בלשון הבאי, וגם בבבלי (חולין צ:) יחשוב את המשנה הזו וגם מה שהשקו את התמיד בכוס של זהב מן דברי הבאי, ואולם תראה בספר Buchler שזכרנו לעיל, יראה כי ריבוי הכהנים המטבילין אותו אינו גוזמא, כי לא מצאנו את המשנה תספר גוזמאות ותהיקש לערים גדולות ובצורות בשמים, וכן לותבקע הארץ לקולם אינו דומה כלל, כי כבר אמר ר' ישמעאל גם בהלכה שדברה תורה כלשון בני אדם, משא"כ פה שהמספר מצומצם, וגם להשקות את התמיד בכלי זהב איננו מן דברים המפליאים, לפי רובי העשירות וכלי זהב שהיו במקדש, ועי"ג, (ראה בתפא"י מ"ט בשם הגאון מווילנא), וגם הסך שקצבה להוצאת הפרוכת יכול להיות כי היה מטבע קטנה כהאיסטר עתה במדינת השולחן או כהסוּ בצרפת; כי בדרך כלל לא מצאנו שהמשנה תספר גוזמאות.

ו, ז) הכל ישרף בפנים. מקום טומאתו, במסכת תמיד יתבארו שתי המשניות האלו, כי שם מקומן.

ח) ענין הכרכוב שהוא לענין מוספי ר"ח יתבאר במס' מדות. מעשר והבכורות נהגו גם שלא בפני הבית יכלכל את המון הלוים, שלא היה להם כל נחלה כאבותיהם.

מסכת

ראש השנה

פרוזדור להכנס לטרקלין (ובו ג׳ פתחים).

פתח ראשון

ענף אחד קטן מענפי האילן הגדול והחזק אשר גבהו שחקים וברחבו יסוב את כל העולם ויקשר ויאחד את כל בית ישראל בארבע כנפות הארץ, הוא התלמוד בבלי, שנחתם לנו זה כשתים עשרה מאות שנה, הנהו לפניכם קוראים נבונים, במסכתא „ראש השנה״ הזאת עם העתקתה בשפה חיה אשר תאיר אורה ראשונה; ואחריה תבאנה חברותיה המסכתות הקודמות לפניה והמאוחרות בסדר הש״ס, כי כבר ערוכים בידנו ושמורים אתנו כל המסכתות מסדרי זרעים מועד נשים, כמוה וכמתכונתה, ואם יחיינו ה׳ בחסדו עוד שנה אחת, תהינה כל המסכתות כסדרי נזיקין קדשים כה ית פצוהם, בידינו.

קנקן חדש הוא, אם כי מלא ישן על כל גדותיו הנהו, שעל כן חובתנו היא להתיצב בפתח שעריו להסיף מלים אחדים בראשית ההוצאה החדשה הזאת לאמר: מה ראינו על ככה ומה הגיע אותנו לגשת אל המלאכה הגדולה והנכבדה הזאת, ומה היא התועלת אשר תצא ממנה לבית ישראל, ולכל העולם כולו?

חובתנו הזאת הננו ממלאים בשמחה, ובתודה לאל עליון הגומר עלינו, ונאמר: „לעולם יצפה אדם לחלום טוב עד כ״ב שנה״, אמרו חז״ל ואנחנו חלום נעים חלמנו, רעיוננו על משכבנו סלקנו זה כשתים עשרה שנה, ועוד בשנת תרמ״ב הואנו לדעת בספרנו „לבקר משפט״, כי מגדי התלמוד ומלעיזיו הכניסו בו דברים רבים נגד רצונם ודעתם של מאספי התלמוד, ובשנת תרמ״ה פרסמנו את החלום הזה ברוב ענין, במאמרים גדולים אשר הקדשנו בהקול 300, 99, 208, וגם בחוברות מיוחדות „אגרת פתוחה לכל התורנים והרבנים״ „ואגרת התלמוד השנית״ ועד כה לא מצאנו לו פתרונים אם כי משיבי החלום הזה נמצאו אז רבים גדולים וכן שלמים: ולמען ידעו דורותנו והבאים אחרינו את כל חליפי הדברים שהיו בין חכמי הזמן ובינינו, עשר שנים לפנים, בענין הזה, נחשוב לא למותר לברר את עקרי הדברים ולשומם לפני קוראנו החדשים בארץ החדשה. כה היו ראשית דברנו בהקול 298:

א״ר״א א״ר ח אלמלא לא חטאו ישראל לא נתן להם אלא חמשת חומשי תורה וספר יהושע בלבד וגו׳ שנ׳ כי ברב חכמת רב כעס (נדרים כב). יותר מהמה בני הזהר עשות ספרים הרבה וגו׳ שכל המכניס אותם לתוך ביתו מהומה הוא מכניס לביתו (מדרש קהלת).

הדברים האלה, אחי ורעי, נאמרו עשר מאות שנה לפנים! ואנחנו היושבים בדור הזה מה נענה אבתרייהו? אם חז״ל משיבי רואי אמרו בזאת על ספרי הנביאים, על כתבי הקדש, ועל קדש הקדשים כשיר השירים, על המשנה והתלמוד שבימיהם, מה נאמר אנחנו על הספרות התלמודית והרבנית אשר פרצה ורבה וכה צפונה ונגבה, ועוד תפרוץ תתגדל ותתרחב מיום אל יום? אם בעיניהם היתה ספרותם חטאת הקהל וכל המכניסה לתוך ביתו הכניס מהומה בביתו, מה תהיה ספרותנו הרבנית בעינינו? ואיזה שם נכנה אנחנו להספרים הרבים אשר נולדו, ויצצו חדשים לבקרים בדבר התלמוד וספרות הרבנית, מהמחייבים והמזכים, כהמקטרגים והמליצים? הן גם המה שטפו ועברו כל גבול ואם נאספם חד אל אחד ימלאו בית גדול ורחב ידים, תחתים שנים ושלישים באין מקום להכניס בו מחט כדקית! ואם בעינים הודרות נבים את כל הנאמר והנדפס, תשאל האם נפתרה גם אחת מן השאלות שעליהן ידונו הספרים הרבים, אם באו בדבר אחד למצער לכלל דעה אחת והחליטו המסכנה ואמרו

כן יקום? נשתוממו לראות, כי השאלות תלויות ועומדות גם עתה במקדם בלי כל פתרון *), כי הדעות שונות הנה ומשונות גם עתה והפוכה על שתי הסעיפים, פוסח גם עתה ויפסח גם הלאה עד שתצא נפשו; וכל הספרים הרבים, השאלות והתשובות, הוכוחים, והרשבאטען, המה רק גל של עצמות יבשות גדול, גל עד על חטאת הדור ועל משובתו!

שבתי הסכתי בדברי חז"ל האלו ושמתי עיני ולבי על הספרות של כל עם ועם ועל ספרותנו עתה, וראיתי כי דבריהם חיים וקימים המה בלי כל הפלגה ובלי כל גוזמא כי באמת אנחנו היהודים אשמנו מכל עם ברשנו מכל דור בספרותנו הגדולה והרחבה, שהיא כמעט כולה רק דתית כהעצלאנית, קאזואיסטית וכו', וספרים מעטים אשר השיעור וההגיון יסודם והחדש וחנסיון יוכלו לחרוץ משפטיהם על הדבר הנידון כשני פעמים שנים שהם ארבעה, לא נתחברו מאתנו כלל, או רק מעט מזער אשר העתיקו מספרי חכמי העמים, וכל עסקנו אנחנו הוא בפרושים, בהגהות, בהערות, בהיפאטעז ובאפיטכוס בדבר הכתוב בתלמוד ובספרי הרבנים שלאחריו, ומכל אלה אנחנו מחברים ספרים חדשים סביב התלמוד ומחוברים לו וגם נפרדים כמנו, הרבה מאד, ואם לא נאמר כי חסרי התועלת המה כולם, הנה לא נפרוץ על המדה אם נאמר כי תועלתם, גם של הטובים שבהם, מעטה מאד ויועילו רק לאחד בעיר ושנים במשפחת המלומדים ועוסקים בתורת הספרות, אך תועלת כללית לא תבוא כלל, גם להדבר שהמה מינעים עצמם להועיל.

נקח נא לדוגמא את ספרי הגאונים האחרונים (ונניח את ספרי ההלכות מהראשונים אשר כל אחד ואחד כנה במה לעצמו מפני שקינא בחברו או לא ישר בעיניו דברי שקדמו אשר כבר דברנו מזה במקום אחר) כהגר"א מווילנא, ר"ע איגער ר"י פיק, ועוד ועוד, אשר המה החלו להגיה את התלמוד ולדקדק במלותיו נקודותיו וטעמיו, ומה עשו? האם הדפיסו המה את התלמוד בהגהותיהם, האם הסירו ממנו את המלות אשר לא ישרו בעיניהם ושמו אחרות תחתיהן? לא! המה כתבו הגהותיהם על ספר לאמר „כן צריך להיות" והמדפיסים למען שבח מקחם הכניסום בשולי התלמוד ויעשו לו זר סביב מהגהות רבות ושונות מאד, וכה ירפיסו המדפיסים בכל שנה ושנה את הש"ס עם הגהות חדשות, עם הערות שונות ופרושים משונים אשר יוסיפו תורני הדור המתחקים לעשות כמעשה הגאונים האחרונים, ויגדל ויכבד התלמוד ומן שנים עשרה כרכים עבים ורחבים נעשו כ"ד כרכים גדולים דפוס ווילנא ומרוב העצים לא נראה את היער! לא נראה את התלמוד הבטל במיעוטו מרוב העוטרים אותו והמלא גם בתיבנו מאותיות שונים ומשונים, ציונים, כוכבים, ענולים ומרובעת מסגרים בחצי לבנה, בתיבות מרובעות וכוי הטורים כל אחד לעין בזר הזהב סביבו ואם נחפוץ ללמוד את התלמוד ולהבין בו עם כל פירושיו והגהותיו או הספק לנו מסכת אחת על כל ימי חיינו הפלא אפוא כי רוב העם אין לו כל מושג כהתלמוד?! האם נתפלא איפוא שגם בין החכמים המצוינים המתעלאנים והפלוסופים נמצא אך מעט מן המעט אשר קראו ולמדו את כל התלמוד כולו? ומה הועילו לנו איפוא המגיהים ברגהותידם והמפרשים בפירושיהם? הן הכה רק גדרו בעדו — ואין בא ואין יוצא לתוכו ומכנו.

ובן לאירך נישא מה עשו לנו המשכילים אשר עברו על התלמוד בעין בקרת

*) לא יכבד השאלות והוכוחים שנשאלו מאת האנטיסמיטים והשמטים בדבר התלמוד והשו"ע לא נתפתרו עד כה, כי גם שאלות ותשובות בדבר ענינות, מים שאין להם סוף, דוחים, חליצות, כרלנה קוהות וקיסות ומחכות לפתרון הרבנים, אם כי כבר כפרי „שאלות ותשובות" יגיעו לאלפים. האין זה פלא השמיני בתבל?

חדה לדעתם, והראו לנו על מקומות רבים כי המה נתוספו בדורות שלאחריהם מרבנן סבוראי מהגאונים והמפרשים אם בזדון או בשגגה, מה הועילו לנו החכמים מן המאספים עד החלוצים עד ראה״ו ור״י הלבן בבית מדרשיהם האחרונים אשר כתבו ספרים רבים בענינים כאלה? האם השליכו המה את המאמרים שאינם מן התלמוד החתצה, ויתנו לנו תלמוד נקי אשר נוכל לקרא ולהבין בו? הן גם המה רק חברו ספרים והגהות כהרבנים, והעירו ויעוררו מה שהעירו, נ״כ רק לאוצר הספרים אשר כפריהם יאסף אל תוכו 1), וכה יודפס התלמוד עם כל שבושיו וטעותיו אשר כאלה כן אלה מודים בהם, באין משים לב לנקותו ולטהרו ולהחליף שמלותיו אשר בלו מרוב שנים.

וכמעשה הרבנים הגאונים עם התלמוד כן עשו הפוסקים האחרונים גם שולחן הערוך אשר על פיו צריכים אנו לחיות ולהתנהג, גם אותו סבבו כדבורים, ויעטרו לו עטרות ואת תוכו מלאו בציונים, אותיות, כוכבים, ועגולים, כפלו את ארבעת חלקיו ויעשו מהם שמונה ספרים גדולים ארוכים ורחבים ולבד אשר הוסיפו בספרים מיוחדים עד כי גם הלכה אחת ממנו עם כל מפרשיו פוסקיו ושינויו תספיק לנו לכל ימי היינו וגם אז לא נמצא בו ידינו ורגלינו כי זה אוסר וזה מתיר, זה מכשיר וזה פוסל, זה מיקל וזה מחמיר 2) וכה אם יקרה לפנינו מקרה אשר תצא מסדר היום — זולת כף חולבת שנתחבה בקדירה של בשר, צריכים אנחנו לרבנינו כי המה יפסקו לנו את הדין — אך המה מתונים המה בדין ולא ימהרו לחרוץ משפט. ולכן ישאלו אחד מחבירו וישיבו כל אחד לחבירו עם אגרת שלומם וכל מכול הם אחד לא נעדר — וכהם יצאו לנו „שאלות ותשובות" בכל ענפי החיים (!) והמכחור, המדות הטובות והרעות אשר יפרו ירבו וישרצו בכל שנה עד כי רשימת שמותיהם כחזקים ספרים שלמים — וזאת היא ספרותנו אשר נוצרה באשמתנו, זאת היא חטאתנו החרותה בעט ברזל לחרפתנו ולבשתנו מזכרת נצח — ואנחנו מרחיבים אותה, מפארים אותה בפארי אלילים ופסילים — ותחפרון כי נהיה ככל האדם ?!

וכה אנחנו היהודים התלמודים 3) שאין לנו — בעולמנו הדתי ובהשם הזה אשר בו נקרא את עצמנו ובו נקרא מפי אוהבינו ושונאינו — אלא ד׳ אבות של התלמוד בלבד, לא נדע את התלמוד, ואין לנו ממנו גם מרחב קטן! אין אנו יודעים מה הוא התלמוד בכל הכתוב והנדפס ומה היא אינו כן התלמוד ולא רק המון עמנו בלבד אינם יודעים מה להבר ומה לזרות ממנו שע״כ המה מהדרשים ומעריצים אותו כולו עם כל הנספח לו והדבוק והקשור בו למראה עיניהם, כ״א גם חכמינו מורינו ופלוסופינו אינם

---

1) הנה תקנתה כן הוא, כי הספרים היותר טובים והיותר מועילים, אשר החכמים יקנו אותם בנפש חפצה, יקרבום רבה ויתנו אותם מצד אל צד יראו ממנו איזה ענינים אשר מסבבם יש להם נטיה להם, ואת כ יעמידוהו אל אוצר הספרים ושם לא יגע בו יד עדי ביאת הגואל.

2) על הלכות שחיטה וטריפות תמצא חמשים ספרים אשר השו״ע שבולים גבוהי קומה וכבדי חמרם ולקטנים מהם אין מספר, מן ספק אחד נעשו ספקות רבים להצטרף לענין ספק ספקא, ומריעותא אחת נעשו ריעותות רבות מאד לסמך תזפיצתה לענין תרתי ריעותא, עד כי נהיה לספל בעיני החכמים אם תרצה לאכול בשר כשר עליך לאכול גידי הסמים, ועכ״ז עוד לא יניחו השוחטים את ידיהם בעליתם ויחברו ספרים קצרים וארוכים בענייני שחיטות ובדיקה.

3) כל היהודים לבד הקראים תלמודים המה, וגם אלה אשר כבר פסקו מביעות גדולות ויחללו את יום השבת ביום א׳, ואשר כבר בטלו את כל המנהגים הדתיים, גם המה אך תלמודים הנה וזה לך האות כי חוגגים המה את חג השבועות בששי בסיון אשר רשם לנו רק התלמוד, ובתורה אנו קוראים ממחרת השבת ובאיזה יום לא נכון, לבד אשר יתנהגו כמותו בדיני אבלות, וכו׳ במאמרנו: מה הוא התלמוד, במאמרנו The Pentateuch etc. ובהערה אחרונה במאמרנו: Is the Jewish religion non dogmatic?

יודעים מאומה ממנו ובכל המון בית ישראל גם המה אינם יודעים מה לרחק ומה לקרב! הראיתם חזיון מעציב כזה בכל העמים השונים לארציהם ולמשפחותיהם? ואין חולה מאתנו על הדבר הזה אין מי ידאג להשיב לנו את תורתנו וכבודנו, אין משים לב לדבר הגדול הזה להחזיר עטרה ליושנה; ועד מתי תהיה כזאת בבית ישראל?

אליכם אישים אקרא! אליכם חכמי ישראל, רבניו, ראשיו, מנהליו, סופריו גאוניו ופליסופיו, אזעק ואשוע לאמר: „הבו לנו את תורתנו! הבו לנו את התלמוד צרוף ונקי בספר מיוחד אשר נוכל לקרא בו ולשום אליו לבנו, תורתנו הוא וללמדו אנו צריכים, הן בכם הדבר תלוי לנקותו ולטהרו ולתתו לנו למורשה! כי מי יבא אחריכם אחרי אשר כבר תעשו? מי יביא אתכם בדין? ומי יהרהר אחרי מעשיכם אם תהיו כולכם באגודה ובעצה אחת?

ידעתי אמנם גם ידעתי עד מאד כי קול קריאתי לא יהיה אף כקול קורא במדבר הוא ישוב אלי טרם יגיע לאזניכם, כי ידעתי אתכם ויודע אני את תנואותיכם, אהם לא תשימו לבבכם לדברי איש אשר לא בצל הכסף ישכון, ואם חכמת המסכן בזויה, קיו קריאתו ובקשתו, וקיו בן בנו של קיו עצתו ודברו, ולעולם לא תתאספו באגודה ובעצה אחת לטובת ישראל ותורתו, ואם קראתי אליכם, לא קראתי אלא כדי לצאת ידי חובתי לעצמי, כדי להראות לכם כי קולי קול גדול הוא אם גם אין שומע לו, אבל הפעם אחלי ארוני שמעו נא לי ואתודה לפניכם על כל מעשי, (וידוי שאין בו חרטה) אגלה לפניכם את כל מחשבותי, ולא בידים ריקניות אבוא לפניכם כי גם אציע לפניכם הצעה אחת אשר אם אך תחפצו לקבלה תראו ברכה בה.

שמעו נא ואספרה!

אחד הסופרים אנכי, אחד מאלה הנני מודה ומתודה המוסיפים חטא על פשע בספרות העברית, הנני כותב ומדפיס זה שנים רבות ספרים ומאמרים רבים אשר לפי ראות עיני, ככל איש הרואה את בניו ואת ילדי רוחו דרך זכוכית מגדלת, טובים המה ומועילים לכשירצו חכמי הדור, וגם אם שוגה אנני ראיתי כי כבר הביאו תועלת לאחרים המלומדים אשר יתאימו את דרכי ומחשבותי, וגם זכיתי לראות כי ספרי נכרכים ועומדים באוצרות הספרים אשר לא תגע בהן יד, אבל הנני מצטער כל ימי להביא תועלת לעמי, תועלת מוחשית, תועלת בפועל ולא תועלת לימודית אשר כבר הביאו ויביאו אותה חכמים רבים — ולא אכחד, לא לעמי לבדו רפצתי להיות לתועלת כי־א גם לכל מין האדם הישר והנני חושב, הנני מתבונן, הנני מעמיק ברעיוני: איככה להשיב את התלמוד להעם והעם אל התלמוד בפועל ולא באומר לבד, כי לוא יהיה כזאת, כי אז תהיה התועלת לא לעם ישראל בלבד, כי־א גם אל כל האנשים הישרים בלבותם אשר ישמחו על דבר אמת — וכבר יעצתי בלבי עצות שונות ומשונות, אבל אחרי שמתי עליהם עין בקרת ראיתי כי הבל המה ורעות רוח.

אבל רעיוני הזה לא יתן לי מנוח, הוא שיחתי והגיוני כל היום וגם בלילה לא ינוח לבי, על משכבי בלילות אתהפך מצד אל צד ואבקש התחבולות איך להוציא את חפצי זה אל הפועל, ומתחלה אמרתי בלבי לאסוף את כל המאמרים אשר מצאתים כי נתוספו בו, אם מהשונים ואם ממנגדי התלמוד ומלעיגיו, אל מקום אחד על ספר מיוחד ולהרסם על נס, בראיות מוצקות ובמופתים חותכים לעיני כל ישראל ולעיני כל העמים, וכל הנשאר יהיו כולו קודש לה׳ ולישראל; ובזה אמרתי לגול את חרפת התלמוד מעל ישראל ולהצדיקו בעיני מנגדיו, וכמעט שמחתי על עצתי הזאת ואמרתי לגשת אל המלאכה, אבל אחרי התבוננתי מאד, והעברתי גם אותה תחת שבט הבקרת, מצאתי ראיתי כי גם זה הבל, גם מלאכתי הזאת אשר אולי אצטרך להקדיש לה כל

שארית ימי לא תוביל אל המטרה הדרושה, ואם אחבר ספר כזה, יתוסף רק באוצר הספרים אבל לא יזיז ולא יניע אף א.ת אחר מכל הש״ס ואם גם יטב בעיני רבים, ואם גם יכירו וידעו את כל המאמרים שבלי כל תפונה לא נאמרו מבעלי התלמוד ומאספיו, לא יוסרו מהתלמוד, המדפיסים לא יזרום הלאה, וכנגדי התלמוד ינדוהו גם אז כמקדם טרם הופיע ספרי; ואלה שאינם יודעים אותו לא ידעוהו גם אז. כי מי הוא הפתי אשר יקח ספרי בידו בעת אשר יבא להגות בתלמוד, ועפ״י ספרי ידלג על המאמרים שאינם מן התלמוד? מה גם כי הקנאים הפונעים אשר גם מבלעדי זאת ירדפו אותי באף ובחמה שפוכה, אשר גם עתה ינבלו שמי ויציקו לי עד דכא, הנה אז חיים יבלעוני, ולמה איפוא ארע לנפשי, מבלי היסב למכרתי אף בקוצו של יוד?

הנה כי כן נתקו מבני מזמותי ולא ידעתי איככה לכונן מורשי לבבי, ולא אכחד, כי כבר עלה הרעיון על לבבי לקצר את התלמוד, היינו להתחיל מחדש להעתיק את כל הנראה לי מהתלמוד לבדו ולהניח את כל המאמרים אשר אדע מראש כי לא להתלמוד המה, או גם אלה אשר אפק בם וכה יצא התלמוד נקי וכלול בהדרו, לבצער אלה המאמרים אשר אין לי בהם כל תפונה; אבל ראיתי כי המלאכה כבדה וקשה מאד, היא תחמיס ממני את כל מבחרי עתותי וסוף כל סוף אפונה אם יעלה זאת בידי לבדה, לגומרה לתקנה ולשכללה ברוח בער ובאר ולהעלוהה על כזבח הדפוס, ובמעט אמרתי נואש גם לזאת, לולא הקרה המקרה קונטרס קטן לידי אשר מדי ראיתיו והתבוננתי בו, הרגשתי כנפשי כמו ניצוץ של אש בחבית מלאה אבק שרפה, היא הרתיח כמצולה את כל דמי לבבי, בו ראיתי אור גדול עד אשר כמעט כהו עיני לנשא אותו: ויהי אף הרגעתי את רוחי, אך שבו דופקי עורקי למרוצתם המורגה, בינותי בלבי, חשבתי, העמקתי עצה, והחלכתי לגשת אל המלאכה, אם ימצאון עוזרים ה״י טוב ואם לא אשען על מאחז״ל „במקום שאין אנשים השתדל להיות איש, ועם בר קפרא אקרא: זלת קפרן קנה באתר, ובאתר דלית גבר תהוי גבר (ברכות) אנסה, בחי לבדי ויעבור עלי מה!

הקונטרס הקטן אשר לקח את כל לבבי זה שמו „דבר על אודות התלמוד״ ואותו כתבו ידי הרב החריף בעל עין טובה ובוחנת ר׳ מאיר איש שלום, לכבוד רעו ואמתו ה״ב המובהק ר׳ א״ה וו״ס ליום מלאת לו שבעים שנה (וימסרנו לי בידו ביום הנ״ל ובבית האחרון) והובנו מכיל רק 5 עלים או 10 צד. והנה דוגמאות שהים שהן ארבע: שתים בהלכה ושתים בהגדה שבהדוגמאות האלו יראה לכל את כל הנמצא בהם מעקר התלמוד ואשר נתוספו בו אם בדרך אגב. או בדרך קושיא ופירוש, והם פרושי הדברים, שאם נסלקם יהיה מרוצת הענין נקי וב״י בלא ערבוב ובלבול ואז יצא לנו גם התרגום, וכה הוא מסיים את דבריו:״ ובדרך אגב נעיר באן שאם נדקדק בסגנון הלשונות שבתלמוד אז מיד ותיכף נוכל להכיר מה שהוא מעקר הסוגיא ומה שנתוסף בה, וגם אותו התוספות נכירם מה שנתוסף זה אחר זה, ומזה תשובה גדולה על אותם הסוברים שלא היה התלמוד כתוב ומונח״ דבריו אלו כנים ונכונים ואין צריכים חזוק לכל מי שיש לו חוש ההרגש והיודע ומכיר את סגנון התלמוד. והנה הוא מצא בהדוגמא האחרונה ההלכה בריש מס׳ פסחים מן המעקסט המכיל 4½ צד את התלמוד העקרי לא יותר מן 60 שורות שמהן רבות רחבות; ואני הסרותי בתקוני שתקנתי אז עוד 25 שורות עד שנשאר הטעקסט הנקי מכל הארבע וחצי צד, רק כצד אחד קטן ועל כל זה לא יחסר לנו מאומה, לא כלום! מכל תוכן הענין האמיר בו והסכימו על ידי הרב המלומד היותר גדול בזמנו הר״ר לאנדוא ז״ל כאשר יראה הקורא במכתבו ואתו חכמים רבים וגם הוא בעצמו אם אמנם לא הזר מדעתו אחרי

רואו את תקוני, לא התריז עליהם מאד. כאשר יראה הקורא במכתבו שנדפס אז בהקול בעתו). וכה אם נעתיק את המעתקסט מכל הש"ס אשר שני שלישים או גם יותר נתוספו בו לפי הדוגמא ההיא. הנה ישאר לנו כפר קטן בכמותו ורב מאד באיכותו. התורה שבע"פ שלמה תהיה אתנו ולא יחסר כל בה, והיא תהיה מסורה בידנו ונוכל להגביה ולהראותה בגאון לעיני כל האדם כמו שאנו מגביהין את תורת משה בכל שבת וקוראים ואומרים: „וזאת היא התורה אשר שם משה לעיני כל ישראל“.

אמנם כן, ידעתי גם ידעתי כי קצור התלמוד המדובר שאנחנו נקרא אותו: התלמוד העקרי „דער עכטער תלמוד“ ראוי הוא להעשות רק ע"י אספת חכמים גדולים „געלעהרטע קאללעגיום“ אשר יבררו אותו עפ"י הכללים אשר יניחו במלאכתם ורק מהסכמת כולם יפורסם בבית הדפוס, ולא לאיש אחד לעשותו ולתקנו אם גם יהיה מלומד גדול מן הראשונים שבדור, אבל אדוני הן רק זאת חפצי ומגמתי כי מלאכתי תובא לפני אספת החכמים אשר היא תחרוץ עליהם משפט. וגם זאת אני עשה רק מפני שארע עד מאד, כי אין גם אחד מן החכמים שבדור שיחפוץ לקבל עליו מלאכה כבדה ועצומה כזאת, ואם נבא לקרא ולבקש את החכמים, יעברו שנים רבות טרם יתאחדו בדעותיהם בענין הזה, ואם גם יתאחדו תתמשך המלאכה שנים רבות טרם תצא לפועל, כי יודע אני ומכיר את חכמי דורנו הגדולים עם הקטנים: רובם ככולם אינם פנוים ועתותם ספורות, כל אחד ואחד יש לו מלאכה מיוחדה שהוא עוסק בה שתקח כל עתו, והרבנים שבהם עסוקים בדרשותיהם ובעבודתם לעדתם. ובדרך כלל נוכל להגיד כי לא רבים מוכשרים למלאכה הזאת ואולי ימצאון רק מעטים מן המעטים, כי במלאכה הזאת לא החכמה היא העקר כ"א המעשה, למלאכה הגדולה הזאת צריכים אנו רק לאלה היודעים היטב את התלמוד וסגנון לשונו הבבלית והירושלמית, כגנון לשונה של המשנה, התוספתא והברייתא, וסגנון לשונם של המדרשים ובעלי ההגדה, ולא יחליפו ולא ימירו את זה בזה. למלאכה הזאת נצרכה עין חדה ואזן שומעת אשר תבחן מלים ולב מבין להבדיל בין קודש לחול, בין מאמר אשר אומרו כון בו ללמד ולהשכיל ובין מאמר אשר אומרו כון בו רק להתל ולדבר בלשון ערומים; וכל איש אשר אלה לו ראוי הוא למלאכה הזאת עם גם לא קבל חכמתו מבית מדרש המדעים. אם גם לא נסמך לדוקטור ולפראפעססאר: ועם גם איננו מבין השפות רומית יונית על בוריין; ויען כי מאלה האחרונים. — יודע אני ומרגיש אני בנפשי ולא לשפת יתר התחשב לי זאת — אמנה גם אנכי ונוסף לי עליהם רצון חזק ומתוק. רגיל בזקן לנשא עמל ומתלאה, ולסבול עד ב"ה שבח הסבל יוכל שאת. שלא יפרענו מכלאכתי ורצוני. הנני מקבל עלי לגשת אל המלאכה הזאת טרם יבקשוני ונמצאתי טרם ידרשוני; שאם יחפצו חכמי ישראל לבקר את מלאכתי ולשום עינם עליהם טרם תצא לפרסום מובן אני להגישה לפניהם בלא שום בקשת שכר ופרס,-- וגם טובת הנאה, כי שכר המלאכה תהיה לי מלאכתי בעצמה ופעולתי זה שכרי.

כל הדברים האלה נדפסו אז בהקול ובאגרת פתוחה ובמקום הזה עשיתי למבחן את הדוגמא מסכ' פסחים ושני מאמרים הגדה מ"גלות ומזבחים. דבריתי בבקשת גם מכל החכמים, ומתועלת הגדולה אשר תצא ממנה לכל העולם כלו; לאיזה מטרה פרסמתי את המאמר טרם גשתי אל המלאכה ומה שאעשה אח"כ כאשר תגמר המלאכה ברצות ה'; וגם בקשתי את כל חכמי הדור כי בחכמם יכבדוני לשלוח לי חות דעתם וכו' וכו' והחפץ לדעתם ימצא אותם בהקול שנה ששית סדר 235—231. ובאגרת פתוחה בכתפות. וגם מכתבים מיוחדים תריצותי לאחרים מחכמי הזמן ועל זה קבלתי תשובות מחכמים הגדולים: הרה"ג דר' לאנדוא ז"ל, הרב הג"מ דר' מ. לאזערוס, והרה"ג ר' מאיר איש שלום, גם המה נדפסו בעתם (וחשוב להדפיסם גם בסוף מאמרי זה) ובחמשים מכתבים אחרים בדעות שונות ובהסכמות

כולם אשר לא נתנו אז לדפוס ורק נזכרו בהקול No 300 ובאגרת התלמוד הבנית להגנע מוצא לנחוץ לתת עקרי הדברים פה, מפני ששמת מבואר היטב סדרי המלאכה ותכליתה, אשר לא שניתי רבות גם עתה אחרי שעברו עלי עשר שנים שלא עסקתי בענין הזה ואת הקורא אבקש כי ישים לבו לדברי שאינם דברים של מה בכך ואלו הם:

פתח שני.

אם אתם מקבלים את התורה מוטב!

„ויתיצבו בתחתית ההר" א״ר אבדימא בר חמא מלמד שכפה הקב״ה עליהם את ההר כגיגית ואמר להם אם אתם מקבלים את התורה מוטב ואם לאו שם תהא קבורתכם. א״ר אחא בר יעקב מכאן מודעא רבה לאורייתא. אמר רבא אעפ״כ הדור קבלוה בימי אחשורוש דכתיב קימו וקבלו, קימו מה שקבלו כבר. (שבת פ״ח).

ומי מצו למימר הכי (שהקב״ה לא נתן את התורה לאומות העולם) והכתיב „ויאמר ה׳ מסיני בא וזרח משעיר למו, אלוה מתימן יבא וגו׳" מאי בעי בשעיר ומאי בעי בפארן? א״ר יוחנן מלמד שהחזיר הקב״ה את התורה על כל אומה ולשון ולא קבלוה עד שבא אצל ישראל וקבלוה? אלא הכי אמרי „כלום קבלנוה ולא קיימנוה" כו׳ אלא הכי אמרי „כלום כפית עלינו הר כגיגית ולא קבלנוה כמו שעשית לישראל" כו׳. (ע״ז א׳).

אחי ואדוני! אך שבועות אחדים עברו מאת גליתי רעיוני בדבר התלמוד, ולשמחת לבבי הגיעוני מכתבים רבים אשר יברכו וישבחו את הרעיון הזה בכלל, כולם מודים ואומרים כי הדבר הזה ר״ל „קצור התלמוד" נחוץ לנו מאד, וכולם מתאוננים על האינדיפערענטיזמוס השוררת בין בני עמינו ואשר לכן יפוגו רובם אם יעלה בידי לגמור את המלאכה הכבדה הזו. והאדון הפראפעססאר לאצארוס בברלין אשר הקדיש את כל ימיו לטובת היהדות וספרותה, יאמר גם זאת שאחרי אשר קרא את מאמרי בשום לב ובהתבוננות ובעליצת נפשו, אחותו גם הוגה חרישית כאשר לא יאמין כי עוד בחייו יזכה לראות את הדבר יוצא לפעולתו ומתאונן מאד אשר הוא לבדו כבר עסוק הנהו עבודה רבה אשר אין בכחו להזניחה ולכלותה בכח והנה, ולמצא קא־לעגיום לא יקוה מפני האינדיפערענטיזם וכו׳ וכו׳.

ועוד יותר מכה שקבלתי בכתובים שמעו אזני מאנשים רבים השונים בדעותיהם ובמפעליהם אשר דברתי אתם אודות הרעיון הגדול הזה ובתוכם גם עם גאון אחד רב ואב״ד בכרך גדול ברוסיא אשר נהירין ליה שבילי הש״ס כשבילי עירו, וכולם מסכימים לעצם המלאכה, כולם יבינו את נחיצות הש״ס הקצר" אשר יפקח את עיני רבים להבין ולהשכיל בו, ואף דעותיהם שונות הנה בסדור המלאכה, זה יחפוץ להניח פירוש רש״י על הקיצור הנדפס, וזה יאמר כי הנוספות אשים בן הצד ואראה עליהם, באצבע לאמר: „ראה זה חדש תוכף הוא". ועוד פרטים אחדים שאינן כדאי לפורבם אבל כולם באחד מסופקים א) אם יהיה לאל ידי לגמור לבדי את המלאכה בלא עזרת רבים או יחידים, ב) לא יהא כדברי כי אחל ואכלה את מלאכתי, אם יקבל הספר הזה לכל עדת ישראל אם יהיה אך כאיש אחד לבדו, ג) אם תהיה תפארת המלאכה הזאת להקרא שמי עליה, אחרי כי כבר יודעים ומכירים אותי כחבורי, שהנני עושה את החקירה חפשית בישראל, ד) ישאלו אחדים מדוע פרסמתי את הדבר הזה מראש למען העיר ריבת רבים? ולדעתם בטוחים הנה שאם הייתי עושה את מלאכתי בחשאי והייתי גומרה ומדפיסה כליל, אז לא היה ע״ז שום פוצה פה אף מן הקנאים.

הדברים האלה עוררוני לפרסם שנית באר היטב בדבר המלאכה הזאת, להגיד מפורש בכמה כחי גדול לגשת אל המלאכה, וכמה הנה תקותי כי עשה אעשה וגם יכול אוכל. אבל טרם אעשה זאת הנני מוכרח לשוב ולהבים לאחור על השתלשלות

התורה הכתובה והמסורה מראשיתן עד היום הזה, ולהתבונן על המאמרים הנפלאים המספרים לנו סדר קבלת תורתנו אשר הצגתים בראש מאמרי הזה, ואומר:

כל איש אשר לו מח בקדקדו יבין עד מאד, כי מדיוקי הכתובים לבדם לא היו יכולים ר׳ יוחנן ור׳ אבדימי דמן חיפא ללמד את הגדותיהם המפליאות שהמה בענין הוצאת לעז על התורה שאינה שוה להתקבל לכל אומה ולשון, וגם לישראל עצמם לולא כפו עליהם את ההר, ועוד יותר לא היו מתקבלים הגדותיהם האלו כדבר ברור נכון וקים לכל חכמי האגדה עד שר׳ אחא ב״י אמר מכאן מודעה רבה כו׳ ורבא הצטרך לחפש בהשתלשלות התורה זמן אחר שקימו מה שקבלו כבר (גם שם הלא באונס היה) ומסדרי הש״ס התפלאו על אוה״ע ומי מצו למימר הכי? מפני „המלמד" שברא ר׳ יוחנן כי החזיר הקב״ה את התורה ולא קבלוה! — כאלו גם אוה״ע מוכרחים הטה לשמוע בקול המלמד הזה; ואחרוני המסדרים שנו את ההגדה הראשונה בשיטתה מן „כלום נתת לנו ולא קבלנוה", על „כלום כפית עלינו את ההר," ורק מפני „המלמד" של ר׳ אבדימי? ובמה יפה כחם של „המלמדים" האלו מכל „מלמדי" ההגדה אשר מצבם רעוע ורופף מאד ואין שואלין בהם ואין משיבין עלידם?!

אבל האמת תעיד על עצמה, כי ההגדות האלו אינן הגדות היוצאות רק מפי המלמדים האלו כ״א היו מסורות בפי החכמים וקבועות בלבם ולא היה להם לפון אף וגע באמתתן — ר׳ יוחנן הזה אשר היה ממוקירי ומרחיבי דתורה שבע״פ, הוא אשר היה העד כי רבנו הקדוש סדר את המשנה לבדו בלא אספת חכמים המסכימים אתו (אדרבה הוא סדר אותה נגד דעתם של רוב החכמים ראה בדו״ד ודורשיו) והוא ר׳ יוחנן עצמו אשר מצא לנחוץ לחזק את התורה הזאת ולשום אותה לחוק על העם בזמנו (מפני שראה בעין פקוחה כי לולא זאת שהבולל והערב הגם בין הגוים שבפיהם בזמנו באשר פרצה ונתגדלה התורה המשיחית) ושם כללים מפליאים לאמר: „אם יכול אדם לשלשל את השמועה עד משה, שלשלה (ירושלמי שבת פ״א ה״ב) אם באה הלכה תחת ידך ואין אתה יודע מה טיבה אל תפליגנה לדבר אחר שכמה הלכות למ״מ קבועות במשנה [שכר רבי], (שם באה פ״ז) כל מ״א דלא מחוורא כמבינן לה מאתרין כנ״אן" (שם ברכות פ״ב עירובין פ״י) והוא ראה כי דבריו מצאו מסלות בלבב העם ותורתו נתקבלה ונתקדשה. האם היה יכול לדרוש אדרת בשבח ישראל כי רק בני ישראל עלולים ומוכשרים לקבל הלכות שאינם יודעין מה טיבן, ואין לך כל אומה ולשון בעולם שתקבל הלכות כמו אלו? האם לא נאה דורש אשר גם נפי „המלמד" שלו כי הקב״ה החזיר את תורתו לכל האומות ולכל הלשונות (גירסת ע״י יעקב) ולא רצו לקבלה? כי עד כמה שהיה כחו רב בהלכה להחזיקה ולקיימה ולשלשלה עד למשה מסיני כן היה גדול כחו באגדה לגלות טפח והסתיר דבר אשר כל החכמים יבינו את אמתתו ולא ישתו בו —.

ואולם ר׳ אבדימי דמן חיפא גלה טפחיים. הוא בא לגלות על תורתנו הכתובה והמסורה כי מעולם לא נתקבלה אצלנו אלא בכפיה ובאונס. כי באמת התורה הכתובה והמסורה תסייעו, בקבלת התורה היו קולות וברקים, ענן כבד, קול שופר חזק, הר סיני עשן כולו, ויחרד כל העם ויאמר נעשה ונשמע" ובתורה המסורה „דודים דברי סופרים מדברי תורה", „כל העובר על דברי חכמים חייב מיתה", „מכין אותו מכות מרדות עד שתצא נפשו", 1) וגם „כל הפורץ גדר שגדרו חכמים לימוקיה חויא דרבנן דלית ליה אסותא"! אבל בגלותו את הדבר הזה גלה גם את טעמו לאמור: „אם תקבלו את

1) מה שהקשו כן בימים הרחוקות מאד להעובר על דברי תורת משה את בעדים ובהתראות, עד כי קראו את הסנהדרין שהרגו לסירוגין אחת בשבעים שנה בשם סנהדרין קטלנית. המחבר.

התורה מוטב, תהיו לעם בין העמים, ואם לא שם תהא קבורתכם, הוא לא אמר פה תהא קבורתכם תחת ההר כאשר היה צריך לומר אם היתה כונתו שישארו קבורים תחת ההר אם לא יקבלוה, כ״א: שם! שם בין האומות הרבים תהא קבורתכם שאם לא תקבלו את התורה תתערבו ותתבוללו ביניהם ותחדלו מלהיות לעם ולא יזכר שם ישראל עוד. — והנה אנו ראים כי „המלמד״ של ר׳ אבדימי דמן חיפא הוא באמת מלמד גדול ונכבד מאד, הוא מלמד זכות כמו על כלל ישראל כי לא נופלים המה מיתר האומות לקבל דבר שלא ידעו מה טיבה, תם להם לב כמוהם, כן על הכופים עליהם את ההר שמפני שקטן יעקב ודל הוא הנהו מוכרח לקבל את תורתו בכפיה ובאונס, למען יחיה, ולמען לא יקבר בין יתר העמים — ועד כמה כנים ונאמנים דבריו אלה יבין כל איש כי לולא תורתנו שעמדה לנו האם נשאר לנו כל זכר? לולא כפיית ההר כנינית בכל דור ודור אפוא היינו כולנו?

כן הוא, אחי ואדוני! הננו מקבלים את תורתנו בכפיה בכל דור ודור, בכל עת וזמן וכל איש היודע אף מעט את סדר השתלשלות תורתנו, מימות משה עד עזרא ונחמיה אשר נקבצו כל ישראל לקול החרם הגדול (מרעידים על הדבר ומהגשמים, עזרא י׳) עד המשנה בשררתו של רבנו הנשיא, עד התלמוד שגזרו רבנן סבוראי ואמרו: עליו אין להוסיף וממנו אין לגרוע (מחמת המינים ובתוה אחרות), עד ספרי הגאונים שמשלו בממשלה בלתי מגבלה, עד ספרי הרבנים שאחריהם שהחלו להגיד כי דבריהם קבלו מן השמים (הראב״ד הסמ״ג ספר התרומה, ר׳ יעקב מקורביל ועוד ועוד) עד ספרי הפוסקים הראשונים והאחרונים שגזרו „ואין לשנות״, יראה את ההר כפוף ועומד עלינו גם עתה מלמעלה ואומר „אם תקבלו את התורה מוטב ואם לאו״ . . . .

ואולם אם הכופים הראשונים שכונתם היתה באמת לקיום האומה, עשתה כפיתם הגדולה פרי רב, והחזיקה את הלאום עד היום הזה (אם כי הפריזו על המדה כאשר התאוננו חז״ל בעצמם ואמרו משרבו תלמידי שמאי והלל נעשתה התורה כשתי תורות, וביום שגזרו על הדברים המיתרים אמרו „והיה קשה לישראל כיום שנעשה בו העגל״) הנה הכופים האחרונים גדשו את הסאה ובכפיתם עזרו לרעה הרבה מאד כי רבים המה מאד מאד אשר יצאו לרגלם מתחת ההר הכפוי ולא יראו עוד לא את ההר ולא את היער ולא את הדוב — ואף גם זאת עשו האחרונים שתחת אשר תורת הראשונים עד שנחתם התלמוד, שאם אמנם היה מסדר הספר לרוב איש אחר לבדו, נוען עב״ם עם בני גילו ועם תלמידיו את מה לזרות ואת מה להבר, הנה באו האחרונים ובנו להם כל אחד במה לעצמו עפ״י דעתו וסברתו לבדה, חבר ספר ויכפה את ההר כי יקבלוהו, עד במה היתה כפיתו של כל מחבר כפר. כי ספרו יתקבל ויתקדש, לא פה המקום לבאר, (כי יתארך ויתרחב המאמר מאד וכבר יצאתי כמעט ממסורתי) אבל זאת יכול כל איש לראות בתוכן כפרי הראשונים, ובהסכמות של הרבנים על ספרי האחרונים, וגם מעת חדלו ההסכמות להיות למנהג בישראל. לא חדלו המבקרים והבקירים במכתבי העתים והמודעות השונות הרבות המפליאות את הספר לכפות את ההר וכו׳ וכו׳. והמחברים העניים אשר אין להם לא זה ולא זאת מחזירים על הפתחים עם ספריהם וכופים גם המה את ההר, עד כמה שיש ביכולתם, שיקבלו ספריהם, כללו של דבר אם נסתכל בעין טובה וחודרת נראה כי אין לך ספר וספר בכפרות ישראל שלא כפו בעדו את ההר אם מעט ואם הרבה, ובלתי זאת לא היה לו כל זכר בעולם. ואולם אין רע בלי טוב כי בין הכפרים הנתנים בכפיה ישנם גם אלה אשר יפיצו אור רב ויועילו מאד לקיום לאומיות ישראל.

הנה כי כן שונה היא ספרות ישראל מהספרות של כל עם ועם. שתחת שלכל העמים והלשונות ישנם סוחרי ספרים אנשים חכמים וידועים הקונים את פרי עטם של החכמים וידפיסום על חשבון עצמם, ואשר טרם יוציאו את כספם יתבונו מאד במהות הספר, בהצטרכותו לעם, בטובתו וברעתו. הנה לנו, עם בנ״י, אין לנו סוחרי ספרים כאלה ולא אנשים חכמים וידועים אשר יתעסקו בהרחבת ספרותנו, כמעט כל המחברים מדפיסים את ספריהם על חשבון עצמם. או בסלות אחרות על חשבון הקהל מבלי ישאלו את פיו, והמדפיסים שבנו, מדפיסים או את ספרי המחברים על חשבונם, או את התלמוד וספרי הדת עם הוספות על מה שלפניהם על חשבון עצמם למען שבח מקחם; או סדורי תפלות עם הוספות ופירושים ותחינות ומעמדות וסמני הקאפיטלין תהלים ליולדות לחולה וכו׳ וכו׳, ודברי ר׳ יוחנן וגם דברי ר׳ אבדימי דכן חיפה נצבים וקימים לעד ומזהירים עלינו כביום נאמרו.

אך לא בזה לבד נפלינו מכל העמים בכל המדינות כ״א גם בזה אשר לפי ערך מספרנו נגד כל העמים, תוגדל ספרותנו אלף פעמים ואולי גם רבבות פעמים מספרותו של כל עם ועם, כי עם חכם ונבון אנחנו באמת מלידה ומבטן ואין אנו צריכים כלל לידיעת בית מדרש המדעים, לידיעת בית הספר הכללי, וגם לידיעת התלמוד וכפרושיו לחבר ספר מועיל, די לנו אם נבין מעט את שפת קדשנו, ואם גם לא נבינה מה בכך? יש לנו שפות רבות בנות ובני בנות שפתנו הקדושה ויש לנו ספרים רבים הצריכים ביאור, וגם ביאורים רבים צריכים ביאור, וכל מבאר ומחבר יניח מקום לבניו להתגדר בו לחבר ביאור לביאורו. ואם גם כבר נדפסו פרושים וביאורים עד בלי די, הלא יש לנו שבעים פנים לתורה, תורתנו ארוכה מארץ מדה ורחבה מני ים והיא מעט המחזקת את המרובה, רבבות פירושים ואלפי אלפים טעמים קבלנו בבפיה ובכל אלה תורת ה׳ עודנה תמימה היא ולא נגע בה עוד יד כל איש! וע״כ מגודל היער לא נראה את העצים ומרוב העצים לא נראה את היער, ותורתינו הכתובות והמסורית חתוכות הנן לנו כביום שנתנו לנו כי נתקימה בנו קללת רשב״י שאמר: „אלא מה אני מקיים ישוטטו לבקש דבר ה׳ ולא ימצאו שלא ימצאו הלכה ברורה ומשנה ברורה במקום אחד״ (שבת קל״ט.) ור״ל אפי׳ במקום אחד וד״ל.

אמנם כן נתאמת בנו מאחז״ל הזה במדה גדושה מאד. וכאשר אמרו במ״א ישראל חבאו בבפרים ולקו בבפלים, כי מעט כפו עלינו את ההר ונזרו ואמרו: עליו אין להוסיף וממנו אין לגרוע״ אשר נתקים רק החצי השני שלא גרעו כמנו אבל הוסיפו עליו הרבה מאד בכל דור ודור בזדון ובשגגה. (כאשר יבאר הדבר ביום שכל הרב הראה ו ברודר ח״נ) לא לבד שאין לנו הלכה ומשנה ברורה עד שחוברי ספרים למאות להמציא ההלכה לנו, אלא שגם משטני התלמוד ומנגדיו רבו מאד וכפעם בפעם ירימו על גם את מאמריו להראית משטנתו, אי־סבלנותו, הדוחיו והבליו, וממאמריו האלה חותכים את גזר דינו לכליה ולשרפה. ודברים כאלה רואים אנו בכל דור ודור מימות ענן, רשאול, וואלטער, אייזענמענגער, פפעפערקארן עד ראהלינג הממקער בדור הזה, אך מה עושים מצדיקי התלמוד? המה מאספים מאמרים אחרים המכילים בקרבם מדות ישרות, אהבת אדם במדה גדושה, סבלנות רבה, וכו׳ וכו׳ ועיקום לעומת המאמרים הנ״ל, ובדבר המאמרים אשר ירימו שונאי התלמוד יתנצלו „את מי אין כמו אלה״? כי אם נחפש בחוקי הגוים הקדמונים, באגדותיהם ודרשותיהם נמצא דברים רבים מאד הגרועים יותר רב ממאמרי התלמוד, והטענה הזאת יכולה היתה באמת להיות טענה חזקה ואמתית אלו היו התלמוד אגדותיו ודרשיו מונחים בארכיונו כמו שמונחים חוקי הגוים הקדמונים, אגדותיהם ודרשותיהם, הבליהם והזיותיהם

בארביוע ואין משים לב עליהם, אבל מה כחה של הטענה הזו ומה טעמה, בעת שההבדל הגדול בולט ונראה? ספרי העמים הקדמונים מונחים בארכיונים ולא יראו רק להפילאלאגן ודורשי קדמוניות, והתלמוד עם כל מה שבתוכו נדפס בכל שנה ושנה לאלפים! העיני האנשים ההם תנקר לקבל את הטענה הזאת ולהצדיק את התלמוד ואותנו המחזיקים בו? אותנו, אשר גם אנחנו מודים ואומרים כי יהודים תלמודים נחנו!?

ולא זו בלבד. אלא שהמפרשים את האגדות הזרות וההלכות שאין אנחנו יודעין מה טיבן, באללאגארית מדומית, בחקירות כזבות, בפילוסופיא של הכל ובהזיות הקבלה והכמה נסתרה, שגם המה נספחים אל התלמיד, ירעו ויציקו לנו מאד [1]), כי בזה המה מקדישים את התלמוד כולו ומחזקים את טענת המנגדים, אשר אינם יכולים ואינם צריכים להאמין בסודות התלמוד כמו שאינם מאמינים בסודות של ספרי הקדמונים, כי הלא ישאל ישאלו בנו „אם אין ממש בכל הדברים החסרי טעם האלו, ואין בם מועיל, וכבר בלו מזוקן מדוע לא תבירו אתם כהתלמוד אשר אתם מדפיסים ללמוד וללמד?! ואם עודכם מחזיקים בם ואומרים כי דבריהם ממולאים בסודות שאין לכם בעצמכם כל מושג מהם, הלא בעלי הזיה שאין כמוכם בכל העולם אתם?!"

והסגנה הזאת, מורי ורבותי, תעשה רושם גדול וחזק לא בעיני העמים האחרים, כ"א על היהודים עצמם שרובם אינם יודעים את התלמוד, ואינם יכולים לדעתו בכמותו שהוא עתה, כי המה שמעים את הכתוב בתלמוד רק מפי שונאיו ואת טענת מצדיקיו אינם יכולים להכניס בלבם, ואשר על כן נחלקו לשלש מפלגות: האחת תעשה את התלמוד כולו לקדש קדשים ואומרה כי הוא מלא סודות, רמזים, צירופי שמות וחכמה נסתרה על כל גדותיו, (המה מפרשים „ביצה" ברית י"ב צירופי הויה, „בית שמאי" מלשון במתא שמאי ר"ל בית המושל על כל העולם, „בית הלל" הבית שמהללים ומשבחים את הרבש"ע), את כל המצית עשה יקחו לסרסרים ולשושבינים ליחד בהם את קוב"ה ושכינתיה ואת הל"ת יקחו לכלי זין ללחום בם נגד הסטרא אחרא נגד הס"ם, השטן, לילית וכל כת דילה, או להיפוך; השנית אשר נכנסה בלבה טענת המנגדים ועל ידם השמיטו ידיהם מן התלמוד שופכים את מי הרחצה עם הילד, הכה אשר אבדו את התלמוד חיי רוחם ויסוד אמונתם, נשארו בלא כל אמונה, והמה נקראים יהודים רק מפני שנולדו מאבותם היהודים; והשלישית אשר לא תוכל לשרש מלבה את שורש האמונה, ולא תוכל לחבל את נטיתה להאמין באיזה דבר, תעבור את זרם המים, המה מטהרים במים את בשרם ובזה יפטרו בפעם אחת מהתלמוד ומכל מה שבתוכו אבל לא מהאמונה. במה חללים הפיל התלמוד מעת החלו מגדיו להעלים את טובו להראות את חסרונותיו? אם את הדבר הזה תחפצו לדעת עליכם להסתכל בעין חודרת ולהבים על מספר בני ישראל בכל מקום שהם, על מספרם הכולל שלא ישדיף בשום אופן על שבעה מיליאנען, בעת שעם ישראל הוא העם הזקן והקדום מכל העמים הנמצאים בעת, בעת שהמה פרים ורבים יתר על כל העמים, מתים פחות מהם (ואולי יתמן הטוען כי מבנ"י נהרגו לאלפים וכו' וכו' יראה נא בהערתי על מכתב ש"ל בהקול נ"ו 285 יד 26) ומה היא הסבה האמתית והנכונה כי מספרנו לא יתרבה ולא יתגדל אם לא זאת „שלא נמלאה צור אלא מחורבנה של ירושלם"?! כי לדאבון נפשנו כבר ראינו ונוכחנו לדעת, שכל אשר יצא מדת התלמוד, לא שב אליה עוד.

---

[1]) ומה נאמנו דברי החכם המנוח „דובש" בהחלוץ שאמר על מפרשי „רבה בר בר חנה" בפרושים כאלו: „גבלה נא ביד רבה בב"ח וביד מפרשיו כל אפולת."

ובכן אקוה כי כל ההוגה דעות והמתבונן יבין וידע כי אין עצה ואין תרופה אחרת כ א לטהר את התלמוד, לנקותו ולהפרידו, לקבל את כל מאמריו הקרוכים, את כל ההלכות והאגדות שאין בהם כל נפתל ועקש ולהדפיסם לבדנה, ולהרים אותם על נס לעיני כל ישראל ולעיני כל שונאינו ומנדינו לאמר: „זאת היא התורה שבע״פ אשר שמו לנו חז״ל בעלי התלמוד, והשאר מונח בארכיונו, כרוכה ומונחה בקרן זוית וכל הרוצה ליטול יבא ויטול, ובזה ידע ישראל את התלמוד אשר לא ידע עד כה, לא יירא עוד ללמדו לבניו, ולא עוד יבוש בו ישראל, וגם משנאינו יתנו בעפר פיהם כי את האחריות מהמאמרים שנשארו מונחים בארכיונו לא יוכלו לשום עלינו כי אז הלא נאמר להם עד שאתם אומרים לנו טול קיסם מבין שיניך, אומרים אנחנו לכם כול קורה מבין עיניך.

ועתה אדוני! אחרי הודעתי לכם באגרתי הראשונה כי אחרי ההסתכלות וההתבוננות על ספרותנו הזאת לא נתן לי הרעיון מנוח יומם ולילה להקריב להעם את התלמיד והתלמוד להעם, אחרי ההתבוננתי וראיתי כי הירא ורך הלבב עבודתו פסולה. ואחרי אשר לקחתי לי למשען את עצת חז״ל במקום שאין אנשים השתדל, ואחרי אשר אני רואה כי רעיוני מצא מסלות בלבבכם והבינו את נחיצת המעשה והמלאכה, אשוב לפרש לפניכם את כל מחשבותי בזה ואת כל פרטי עבודתי אשר אומר לגשת אליה בקרב הימים בעזרת אלקי אבותי, ואענה על אחרון ראשון ועל ראשון אחרון:

מודה אני כי לוא יכלתי לעשות את מלאכתי בחשאי ולא גליתי ממנה עדי תהיה כולה מוכנת בידי, כי עתה יותר טוב היה ל פ נ י בפרטים אחדים, וגם בפרטים אחדים להמלאכה בעצמה כי את הנעשה כבר א ן להשיב, ואם אמנם לא נתקבל אצלנו שום ספר בלא קולות וברקים, מיום נתנה התורה לנו, הנה הקולות לא יחדלון גם אז כאשר כבר יצא הספר מבית הדפוס; ממינים ומשמאלים, מזכים ומחייבים, לא יחסרו לנו גם בעת ההיא, ולכן יותר טוב היה הדבר לוא היה ביכולתי, לשבת במנוחה שלש שנים למצער ולא לעסוק בשום דבר זולת מלאכתי הזאת. אבל מפני שאין בכחי לעשות את הדבר הזה, ומפני שבאמת חפצתי לשמוע דעת החכמים והתורנים על עצם הרעיון ועל נחיצת המלאכה ראיתי כי לא נכון לבטל את המלאכה ולבלות את הרעיון מפני פרסומו.

וע״ד אשר יחושו אחדים כי שמי, שם יחידי, יזיק לקבלת הספר, או גם לראשית המלאכה, הנה שתי תשובות בדבר, א) להדפיס את הספר בלא שם המחבר יזיק מאד, כי מעת החלה המסיאן האנגלית והאשכנזית יהפיץ ספרי עברים בהעלמת שם המחבר, יוטל החשד על כל ספר אשר יופיע בהעלמת השם אם גם מטרתו הוא נגד המיסיאן, וגם המזיק בדעותיו להמיסיאן רב יתר מאשר יזיק לדעות הקנאים איננו יוצא מן החשד הזה. ואם אמנם גם החשד הזה איננו מונע את החכמים לקרא את הספר ולהבין בו, אבל המון העם ינתעו ממנו ויעמדו מרחוק ואז לא יוכל הספר להשיג את מטרתו; ואת שנית, שאם אמנם אינני רודף אחר הכבוד[1]) אבל גם אינני בורח ממנו, מפני שלא אחפוץ שהוא ירדוף אחרי; כי החסר רודפים אני מבלעדי? ולכן אם יהיה ה׳ בעזרי ואגמור את המלאכה הזו אחפוץ כי יקרא שמי עליה, כי הן זהו שכרי מכל

---

1) לא מפני שאשנא אותו או שאינו יקר בעיני אך מפני שבטבעי א י נ נ י מ ן ה ר ו ד פ י ם ולא קוד שנם א ת ע ב את הרודפים, ובאמת מלא אוכל להתפאר כי אינני מן הרודפים א ח ר י ש ו ם ד ב ר ב ע ו ל ם, גם לא אחרי החכמה בעת שאוכל להיות מבלעדו ובפרוטות — כי גם שונאי היותר גדולים לא ימציאון עלי את החסרון הזה כי הנני מהרודפים אחרי איזה דבר מגונה או משובח.

עמלי! מה גם כי אחרי יודע מהות הספר, אחרי יוכחו כי לא נוסף בו אות אחד מכל הנכתב והנדפס בכל הש״ס כבר ואף יחסרון בו מאמרים הנמצאים בכל הש״ס, לא יעלה ולא יוריד שם המסדר את הש״ס מערכו אף כמלא נימא, וגם הקנאים היותר גדולים אם אך יודע להם כי אין בהספר הזה אלא דברי התלמוד בעצמו ולא חסר ממנו גם ענין אחד בהלכה ואגדה, ורק הדברים הטפלים נחסרו בו, לא ימנעו את עצמם מללמוד בו וללמדו, כי גם המה אוהבים את עצמם וחפצים לקחת מן הכוכן בלא עמל ויגיעה, מלעמול ולינע את עצמם חנם..., ומכאן אמנם תשובה גם להשאלה השניה אם יקובל הספר לעם אם יהיה רק מאיש אחד, אבל נוסף לזאת נשאל גם אנחנו: ההכבן הסכין העם לקרא בספרים אשר נתחברו מסחברים רבים? או הנמצא ספר כזה? הן מעת שהנחיל הקב״ה את תורתנו הקדושה למשה מורשה, ואמר ,זכרו תורת משה עבדי׳, נקבו כל הספרים בשם כחבריהם האחד, והמספר היותר גדול הוא השנים: המשנה נקראת ע״ש רבנו הקדוש, התוספתא ע״ש ר׳ חייא ור׳ אושעיא, הש״ס ע״ש רבינא ורב אשי, 1) המדרש ע״ש ר׳ חייא רבה, הספרי ע״ש רב וכו׳. ומאז והלאה נקראים הספרים ע״ש מחבריהם היחידים, השאלתות ע״ש רב אחאי. ההלכות גדולות ע״ש ר״ג מקיירא, וגם המחברים המאוחרים אשר חברו ספרים ויתפרצו כי יקובל ספרם קראו עליהם את שם אחד מן הגדולים כמו פרקי דר״א, אבות דר׳ נתן ועוד ועוד. ואין עוד לדבר מספרי הרבנים אשר כל אחד ואחד נתחבר רק מאיש אחד אם גם ספר דתי הוא להלכה ולמעשה, ומעולם לא נתחבר ספר דתי כאספת חכמים ע״י ישיבת אקארעמיע ועפ״י רוב דעות בישראל, ואיפוא א״כ יקח לו ההמון את הרעיון לבקש ספר שיצא מסוד חכמים ונבונים יושבי בישבת תחכמוני? וכה לא נשאר לי אלא לפרש במה כחי גדול אשר אדמה בנפשי לגשת אל המלאכה לבדי ואיככה אוכל להעיר זמן עשית המלאכה לא יותר מן שלש שנים בעת אשר לבאורה הזמן הזה נצרך גם לאיש מלומד לעבור על כל הש״ס עם מפרשיו ונושאי כליהם? ואיה היא המלאכה הקשה והכבדה מאד. מלאכת ההעתקה מן הש״ס אשר גם לזה לא אקבל שום עוזר מפני שאין ידי משגת לשלם להם, ומפני שנסיתי כבר בעסקי בעבודתי אצל האדון הפראפ. לאצארוס כי ההגהה למלאכת המעתיק לקחה ממני עתותי יותר מאשר העתקתי בעצמי. ואיך אפוא אקבל עלי מלאכה כזו לגמרה כליל במשך שלש שנים, אם יחייני ה׳, גם מבית הדפוס?

יודע אני אדוני את כל אלה, וחלילה לי לחשוב על עצמי, כי הנני מהיר במלאכתי יותר מכל חכמי הדור, או כי מן המלומדים בגילי, תכ״ז הקצבתי הזמן בהתבוננות רבה ובמתינות. והנני רואה כי הזמן הזה הוא היותר גדול הנצרך למלאכה הזאת וגם אז אם אעבוד רק חמש, שש שעות בכל יום, ששה ימים בשבוע. ולמען יאמינו לי קוראי אפרש את סדר המלאכה ואגלה את סודה, כי כבר כתב עלי החכם מא״ש שאינני מבעלי הסוד, ואז יראו הכל, כי לא מגזם ולא מתפאר אני.

קוראי „הקול" חמש שנים לפנים כבר ידעו כי בקי אני במלאכת השבעת הפולסס וכבר גליתי את סודה (בגליון 14 או 16 שנה חמישית בו. כי איננו בידי בודכי לעיין בו) אבל אחי, הוספתי חמש שנים ולמדתי עוד מלאכה אחת אשר גם בה ישתמשו סופרים רבים והוא מלאכת ה מ ס פ ר י ם ואת המלאכה הזאת אשר אני אומר לגשת אליה לא בקולמסי ולא בעטי אעבוד אך בשכלי הדל ובמספרים האחרים שיהיו בידי.

אני אעשה את מלאכתי בשתי ששי״ן האחר יהיה ש״ס גדול עם כל המפרשים

1) יעיין כ״ז בספר דור דור ח״ג בפרקי השבעה עשר והשמונה עשר.

ונושאי כליו, עם האלפסי והאשר״י וכל ההגהות אשר נתוספו בו גם מהאחרונים, וכו אלמוד בשקידה ובעין חודרת ולא אניח אי״ה שום מפורש, מניה, מראה המקומות השייכים לעניני וגם את אלפסי והרא״ש אקרא וכן גם את הש״ס ירושלמי אקרא במקום שישנו, ואחרי אתבונן ואחליט מה לזרות ומה להבר, ארשום בעט עופרת בהש״ס הקטן את אשר החלטתי להשאיר לי, מהפנים ומרש״י ובזה עשיתי את מלאכתי, כי בפנים הספר לא אוסיף אפילו אות אחד משלי. ורק את אשר אמצא להעיר או לפרש להקוראים מדוע עזבתי את המאמר או ההגדה ההיא ארשום בסמנים מיוחדים אשר אוכל לקרות בם רק אני לבדי בספר מיוחד, ואת הספר ההוא לא אשלימו עד אשר אכלה את מלאכתי כולה מכל הש״ס. ויען כי לפי ידיעתי הברורה ד״ה היא לפני שעה אחת לדף גמרא אחד עם כל מפרשיו ונושאי כליו הנצרכים למלאכתי בלי שום פלפול צדדי שאינו נוגע לעניני, מפני שכבר קראתי אותו כולו וגם כל הירושלמי תוספתא ומשניות בחורף 84—83, וישנם דפים כאלה אשר גם שעה תמימה לא אצטרך להם וגם חצי שעה תספיק להם, הנה יהיה בכחי ללמוד ולהבין בכל יום עכ״פ חמשה דפין גמרא אשר יהיו מוכנים לדפוס, וכה נצרך לי למלאכתי רק ערך 550 ימים אשר אעבוד בהם חמשה שעות בכל יום כי לערך 2570 דפים (זולת המשניות) גמרא ישנם בכל הש״ס בבלי.

ואחרי כל אלה אם גם המצא תמצא איזה שגיאה במלאכתי, היינו אם אחרי כל ההתבוננות אשמים איזה דבר אשר החכמים ימצאו אותו משקר התלמוד, או כי אבנים דבר אשר החכמים ימצאוהו שאינו מיקרר התלמוד. הנה לא ארצה בזה בגבעית כלה, כי את החסר יוכלו להשלים בכל עת והנוסף יוכלו להכרו, העקר הוא כי הרשיון יצא לפועל והמלאכה הראשונה תוגמר; והשלימה לפארה ולכללה עוד יש עת רבה ועוד לא תמו חכמים מן הארץ, ומוקירי התלמוד עוד ישנם, אנכי אעשה מה שמוטל עלי ובכל כחותי וכשרונות נפשי אעבוד את העבודה הזאת, אבל לא אומר כי לא אשגה, או כי „קבלו דעתי" אני יודע את עצמי הודות לה׳, יודע אני את חברי ויודע אני את רבותי, אני אתבונן במה שהרשתי ואעשה את שלי, והמה יעשו את המוטל עליהם והתלמוד הקצר יהיה אי״ה לנס ולברכה לכל ישראל ולכל הגוים אשר יראו אותו בקצורו בהדרתו ובהעתקתו.

ועתה אתם בני ישראל כל אלה אשר מצא הרעיון מסלות בלבבכם, כל איש אשר יקר בעיניו תורתנו הקדושה והטהורה. כל החפץ בטובת עמו דתו ותורתו, תמכוני, עזרוני! תנו ידכם לדבר הגדול הזה, עמדו לימיני ותמכו עלי בחסדכם, והיו נכונים לקבל את תורתנו שבע״פ הקדושה הישנה והטהורה על ידי איש דך ונכאב אשר הקדיש את חייו למסרה הזאת, והתברכו מן השמים.

פתח שלישי:

התמונה המבארת את דברי הלל הזקן.

הרים וגבעות, שמים וארץ, חמה ולבנה, כוכבים ומזלות, בקשו עלי רחמים! עד שמבקש עליך נבקש על עצמנו! אמר: אין הדבר תלוי אלא בי! הניח ראשו בין ברכיו וכו׳, יצאת בת קול כו׳ מזומן לחיי עולם הבא, בכה רבי כו׳ ואמר לא דיין שמקבלים אותם אלא גם שקוראים אותם. (ע״ז י״ז במעשה דבן דורדיא).

חכמי חרשים קרבו הנה, ציירים אמנים גשו נא והתבוננו במה כחכם גדול לצייר לפנינו תמונה זו שהתוו לפניכם חכמנו ז״ל בכפור חול ובקתר כלים, כעשר מאות שנה לפנים, התעשו גם תוכלו? העל היריעה הפרושה לפניכם תתארו אותה

בישר, או כי חרש פסל תעשוה ? אפונה !.... אמנם כן בנסיון יסודה, ובתבונת האנשים וסדרי התבל מקורה, אבל ארמה כי הגיל לא יכילנה, היריעה תקצר מהשתרע וגם המעצד והמקדח אין אתים המה לפסול למו לוחות התמונה הזאת.

התמונה הזאת אשר יצירו לנו חכמינו בשכלם החד, לא חדשה המה מדעתם, כי זה באלפים שנה הנה אותה ראש נשיאנו הלל הזקן ברוחו, לאמר: אם אין אני לי, מי לי? אם לא עכשיו אימתי? אבל קולו היה קול קורא במדבר, והחיים בעיר ובשדה לא שמו לבם אליו; ואף חז״ל בעוסק בינתם, ובעזת רוחם ירדו לסוף דעתו של נשיאנו זה, ולפרש ולבאר את שיחו ואת הגיונו בראו למו תמונה נאמנה שבה תארו לפנינו בשרד את עומק דעתו ורחבי בינתו, את שיחו ואת הגיונו; אך חז״ל האחרונים שהקדישו את כל ימיהם ללמד את תכונת האדם, לתכן את רוחם ולדעת סדרי התבל, אך המה אשר למדו לדעת את גבהות הלב של בעלי הכסף והזרוע, ואת מרת נפש העני האובד המבקש עתידות לו בין רעיוניו אשר יוליכוהו בישימון דרך, אך למו, הורה נסיונם למצא תמונה כזאת מאיש מסכן המקריב את עצמו על מזבח האידעע שלו ואשר יאמר לתקן בו את העולם כולו וגם למצוא בו אחרית ושם לו בהעתיד הקרוב. אשר בשם עולם הבא יכנוהו.

בשניותו וברוחו חמר יראת המסכן; כי חכמתו בזויה, כי להוציא מחשבה כזו אל הפועל אין לאל ידו בלתי עזרת מרום העם הירשב בהר, והנהו פתה אליו ומבקש רחמים כי יתמוך בידו; הנהו קורא לישע את אלי הזהב שיזהירו בעולם החשוך כזהר הרקיע, הנהו מחלה את פני החכמים שבשמים ירחו הגם בעיניו, או כי בעיניהם, כי ישימו לו לב, הנהו פורש כפיו אל בעלי המזלות שבין הכוכבים ישימו קינם וההתחרות והספיקולציה יסודתם, כי יקחו את האידעע שלו למשחק למו וינסו בו את כחם, אך כולם באחד ישחקו ילעגו לו יבוזו לו בפניו ובשחוק גלוי על שפתם וכעס אצור בלבם, יענו לו: הלמסכן להתחכם ? הלעני לבקש עתידות, הגם איבד בין האידעעיסטים ? סוב פנה לך אל הדוסים לך ! כי עד שנעתר לבקשתך, נבקש רחמים על עצמנו כי מי כמונו ההרים הרמים, הגבעות הנשאים אשר לשמים ישלו שיאנו ובין כוכבים נשים קננו בעלי אידעעים? הן כולנו מחשבים אנחנו אחרי עתידותנו, כולנו חפצים בעולם הבא, כולנו עסוקים בו, אך עוד לא עלה בידינו אף חצי תאותנו, ומי אתה כי תקרב אלינו ?! ברח לך איפוא, עני וכואב, אל מקומך, בשפל תשב שם תנוח ושמה תקבר אתה ואידעעותיך ומאתנו הרף ואל תפריע את מחשבותנו כי יש לנו רב״.

אך האובד הזה, לא לבד שלא נפלה רוחו בדברם אליו בה, כ״א התאזר ויעשה חיל, כי אך ראה שתוחלתו בם נכזבה, אך התבונן כי חנם עבר שבעה נהרות, שוא שקד לעלות ההרה, להבל כלה כחו לדלג שור מחמה ללבנה ולקפץ מכוכב זה אל מזל אחר, התחזק ויעמד על עמדו ויאמר אל לבו: מה נואלתי בשומי מבטחי על ההרים הרמים, מה שגיתי בחשבי שאת האידעע שהריתי והגיתי שנים רבות, שכלה שארי ולבבי, ימציאו לי זרים! שוא לכם גבורי הכסף, חבל עליכם חכמים בעיניכם שלהטיב לא תדעו, ברשני מדבריכם כוכבי חושך, ספיקולנטען אשר לא תבינו באידעעים ולא תדעו מה לזרות ומה להבר, לא בכם הדבר תלוי, אין האידעע תלוי אלא בי ! בי לבדי, כי האם אין עזרתה בי ?! ובדברו כזאת נהפך ויהי לאיש כביר כח ורב אונים, ויחטר עת לשום ראשו בין ברכי עצמו; ואם כי במעט לא נותרה בו נשמה, לא זז משם עד שהשיג את מטרתו, עד שאחז בקצה החבל שבו יטפס ויעלה אל על, אל ראש האידעע השוכן בקרבו. בו יאחז ולא ירפנו ובכל יום ויום הנהו מטפס ועולה ומתקרב אל מטרתו ואיננה עוד ממנו והלאה ! או אז תשמענה אזניו מאחריו גם

„בת קול“ קוראת בקול, כי הוא איננו עוד „בן־בלי־עזר“ כ״א אלי־עזר המזומן ומוכן לחיי עולם הבא, ויושבי מרום אשר נפקחו עיניהם לראות את העני האובד הזה מטפס ועולה ומפסע בינו ובין מטרתו ואין עוד בכחם לעמוד כנגדו, התחלו גם המה להאיר פניהם אליו אם כי עיניהם תזלנה דמעות ובשחוק מר יענו ויאמרו: לא דיים לבעלי מחשבות ותשובות האלו שמתקבלין, כ״א גם „רבי“ יתקראון, ו„חכם“ יתכנון.

זאת היא התמונה אשר עמדה לנגד עיני בעת כמעט אמרתי נואש לכל אשר הגה רוחי בעולם הישן והחדש אשר נדחתי גם בו מדחי אל דחי: כי כאשר נגלו לפני שערי ארץ החדשה, נגלו לפני גם שמים חדשים גם תלאות חדשות גם צרות חדשות, גם אויבים חדשים אשר סבוני כדבורים ויעקצוני כשועלים, ולא מצאתי מנוח לי וכמעט לא האמנתי בחיי, אבל רעיוני הלוני בכל מקום ובכל עת, בשכבי, בקומי ובלכתי בדרך, ולא בושתי לגלות לבי לפני חכמים בבקשת עזר וכעד אשר כמצחק הייתי בעיניהם, עד אשר במילים מעטים האיר והעיר את רוחו השופט החכם המבין ויודע תושיה מאיר סולצבערגער מעיר „אהבת אחים“ אשר אמר לי: „רב לך חולם חלומות מאשר יש בכחך להבין ולרקוח, הוציא מתחת ידך אשר עשית ואשר כוננת והנח לפנינו; והיה אם נראה כי יש ממש בה נהיה לך מעיר לעזור“ לדבריו אלה הקיצותי ואף סבותי את שכמי מטעונו קניתי לי גמרא והחלותי לעשות את מלאכתי ואז ראיתי כי חפץ ה׳ יצליח בידי; ואף אז קניתי לי ש״ס קטן וגדול והדוגמא הראשונה מונחת לפניכם.

ואתם חכמי לב, אנשי אמת, וכל אשר לו עין בקרת וחודרת, הואילו נא לעבור על המסכתא הזאת כולה בעת אשר תהיה הגמרא הישנה פתוחה לפניכם, ואל תמהרו להוציא משפט, טרם תסתכלו היטב בכל החבור פה, ובטובכם תדקדקו היטב ללמוד את המאמרים השלימים, מקצתם וגם מלות אחדות אשר לא תמצאו פה; וגם תעיינו במסורת הש״ס בצדה ואז, אמרו נא את אשר בלבבכם, גלוי, לעין כל.

לא לנו, אחי ואדוני, לא לנו, כ״א לשם התלמוד, לשם „תורתנו שבע״פ“, חיי רוחינו ונשמת אפינו, תנו כבוד! הדעת והתבונה, האמת והצדק, תהינה לכם לרוח משפט ולקו בקרת על המלאכה וכשרון המעשה. והיה אם תמצאו כי היא דורשת תיקון, באיזה מקומות או בכולה, השמיעוני נא והנני מוכן לשמוע לקולכם. כי יהיה בשם ולשם האמת. אך לבקרת הצופה ולדברי בח. הנני מגיד מראש, לא אשים לב ולא יעשו שום רושם עלי...

בספר מיוחד, ארשום בכתב אמת את הסיבה והטעם, שהכריחו אותי לחסר את הדברים שנחסרו בכל הש״ס, כל אחד ואחד טעמו בצדו; אם תהינה עתותי בידי, אחרי יזכני השם לראות, כי כבר יצא התלמוד הקצר מבית הדפוס, ואניחו באחד מבתי אוצר הספרים שיד רבים ממשמשים בהם בבריטעש מוזעאום בלאנדאן, אבל הנני מוצא את עצמי מחויב לתת גם פה כללים אחדים שעל פיהם הנני עושה את מלאכתי, גם פה, והמה:

א) בכל מקום שנכפלו הדברים בין בלי שנוי ובין גם בשינוי לשון קצת, בין על מקומם ובין במקומות מפוזרים בכל הש״ס, יבואו רק פעם אחת ב מ ק ו ם ה ר א ו י ל ה ם.

ב) שקלות וטריות, בתוך השקלות וטריות, שנתוספו במאות האחרונות להרחבת התלמוד, שאינן מ ו ס י פ י ן שום חדוש בההלכה עצמה או במשאה ומתנה, וכן בהגדה, יחסרו; ורק המסקנא תבוא במקום שהיא צריכה.

ג) את אשר הכניסו בו היהודים המשיחים בזדון וכן אשר הכניסו רבים בבלי

דעת דברים שהמה נגד דעת בעלי התלמוד ומטרתם הכללית, יוסרו באין חמלה.1)

ד) לפעמים יצאתי גם מאלו הכללים במקום שראיתי כי במעט אין באפשרי זאת להעתיק בשפה חיה, כמו: „הנותן מטתו בין צפון לדרום הוין ליה בנים זכרים שנא' „וצפונך תמלא בטנם" אשר יקשה מאד להעתיק מלת וצפונך במובנה פה „נארד" מפני שמובן המלה בכתוב יש לו הוראה אחרת וגם אז אין שום ראיה מהכתוב, כי הבטן תמלא גם מנקבות — שעל כן הנחתי המאמר ואת הראיה מקרא החסרתי. וכן במסכת הזאת (כא.) מהיכן את? מדמהריא,2) דם תהא אחריתו. שכל העיר לא נבראה אלא למשל הזה שאין לנו ממנו כל תועלת והמעתיק לא יהיה בכחו להעתיק אף אחרי הזיעה שתטיף משערותיו. כל הדומים לזה החסרתי מבלי לנגוע בהענין עצמו.

ה) ציינתי בכל צד וצד את הדף שבגמרות הישנות, להקל על הקורא אם יאבה לקרא גם את החסר, ובסמן הכולל (ב.) (ב:) שר"ל ב. עמוד א', ב' עמוד ב וכן כולם.

ו) את פירוש רש"י כמו שהוא הנחתי במקום שנצרך ואם אמנם גרעתי ממנו רב במקום שיוכל הקורא להבין את הגמרא מבלעדי פירושו. על כל זה לקח ממני כמעט מחצית הגליון בכל עמוד, והאמת לא אכחד, כי לא כן היתה מחשבתי מתחלה כאשר יראה הקורא בפתח שני, אבל יען הרב המלומד היותר גדול בזמנו לאנדא ז"ל העירני ע"ז במכתבו ואני הבטחתי לו לשמוע לקול דברו, קימתי הבטחתי אם כי נרמה לי נזק רב, כי במס' ברכות כבר החלותי להדפיס הרש"י בצדו, מלאכה אשר לא הורגלה בה מסדרי האותיות במדינה הזאת.3)

---

1) הנני מוציא את עצמי מ"ח להראות דוגמא אחת לקוראי וישפטו עליה וסמנת: בברכות (י.) יאמר רשב"ח בשם ר' יונתן (בש"ס גרסס יוחנן והוא שבוש גמור כי רשב"ח יאמרם בכ"מ אך בשם ר' יונתן). כל פרשה שהיתה חביבה על דוד פתח בה באשרי וסיים באשרי דכתיב אשרי האיש וסיים באשרי כל חוסי בו. ופרשה אחרת כזאת לא נמצא בכל התהלים ועיין תוספת שדחקו עצמם ויישב אך לא עלתה בידם. והנה פרשה „למה רגשו" לפי דעת המפרשים מדברת רק מגדולתו של המשיח, „בני אתה", „נשקו בר פן יאנף", „אשרי כל חוסי בו", ואת דעת רשב"ח בדבר המשיח ימצא הקורא בכבודו של ר' משה הרישון פ' ויצא ל. בספרו של הרר. וויגשע הנקרא בשם „יסודי המשיח" וביחוקות משיחו להאברבנאל בשינוי נוסח מעט כפי הכתוב בירושלמי. ולבל אאריך הנה להציג לשונו פה, הנני רק להעיר שהוא רשב"ח אומר: שנגלה לו מפי אליהו שהמשיח נולד בבית לחם יהודה, והוא אליהו מחכה עליו ליום הדין הגדול". אותו מצאתי אומר (בשבת קטז.) כי שבקה ספרי תורה לנו ולא חמשה חומשי תורה (לא כמקום האומר כי „ויהי בנסוע הארון" הוא ספר מיוחד יעיין נא הקורא היטב). אותו מצאתי מדבר בסגנון הזה במקומות רבים מאד בתלמוד וכולם מונים אצלי (אחרי נתתי ציונם להפ"ס הגדול לאצרות בספרי לו ציוני הש"ס); בהתצאותי התבייתי מאמרים כאלה, ולא אכחד כי חשוד בעיני הסופר „למה רגשו" למעשה ידי המפרשים; ואשר כמהם נמצאו עוד, הראני החכם המדקדק הד"ר ר"מ רייכערזאן ורשני אמנם להרם אותם על גם בשמו הגם הראות לי חתימות „שאול" על אחד מהם, אבל לא זה היא המקום. מה גם כי תודות להי' הוא רייכערזאן והקוראים יוכלו לדרוש ממנו אך זאת אחשוב לי לחובה להגיד כי מתחלה נג לבי להאמין לו ואח"כ הודותי לו בלבי, מפני ראיה חזקה אחת אשר מצאתיה אח"כ ונקבע הדבר בלבי.

2) ראה התהלים ז. בדבר השמות זהמאי דואי וכו', כי נכונת דבר.

3) (וגם מלאכה כבדה היא באכת לשער מקודם כמה יהיו שורות רחבות במקום שהרש"י עודף על הגמרא, וכמה קצרות במקום שפרש"י עודף ובעת ההיא לשמור את הסדר שיהיה פרש"י במקומו; כי מהש"ס היכן נקל לעיות את מפני שחרפים מכל הגמרות שרם הנה מסא"כ פה שנצרך למדד ולדייק, וע"כ עלה כולו קשיותים. בשני דפוסים הדפסתי מס' ברכות האחר פשט את הרגל בכלותו פרק ראשון, ולא קבלתי מאומה. והשני הוכרח לקלקל כנירים לוחות על קבוצ טיים

ז) בחרתי במס׳ „ראש השנה״ לתתה קודם משני טעמים א) מאשר המס׳ ברכות היא ביד המעתיק כמו שהיא ואשר נדפס עד כעת נתקלקל וב) כי מפני שהיא תכיל הרבה חפצתי לתתה עם ההעתקה ביחד, להקל על המבקר שיוכל לבקר את הטעקסט וההעתקה גם יחד. זולת זאת המסכתא הזאת לבד ההלכה, תכיל ענין גדול ונחוץ במנין שנות החמה והלבנה ובענין קידוש החודש תקנת ריב״ז ועדותם השוה לכל נפש חוקר ומעיין ברחז״ל.

ח) עוד אחת הנני להבטיח ולעשות לטובת כל הלומדים והמשכילים, והוא להעמיד כל הדברים שהובאו במשניות ובגמרא כ״א על מקומם הראוי ביחוד; במסכתא הזאת ימצא זאת הקורא בענין סופר דין לשמים, והוא מצער. אבל במקום שיבאו משניות שלמות והגמרא להם שלא במקומם הראוי לענין המדובר בהמסכת, אעביר אותו להמסכתא ההיא אשר עקרה ידובר בענין הזה, וכה תדבר כל מסכתא ומסכתא רק מענין ששמה מוכיח. ובקדושין אשר תופיע תיכף אחרי זאת המסכתא, ימצא הקורא דוגמא גדולה מזה וידין מהם על השאר; וזהו תועלת גדולה להסדר הנכון ואקוה להפיק רצון בזה מאת כל המפלגות בעמנו, כי אם לא יאבו אחדים להכיר את מלאכתי לתלמוד הקדום, הלא על כרחם יודו, כי הנהו „קיצור התלמוד״ כההלכה והאגדה וכל המשא ומתן בהם לא נחסר, וכי הוקל מאד לכל מעיין אשר יאבה לקרות בגמרא, שעד כה היה לפניו כספר החתום.

ט) הרה״ג דר. מילצינער העיר אותי במכתב מיוחד על המראה מקומות מהש״ס שנשמטו בברכות ועוד על דברים אחרים; שמעתי גם לו ונתתי את הספר „תורה אור״ על מקומו לפני כל מקרא ומקרא שהובא מהתנך אבל אינני מקבל אחריותו עלי כי אם אמנם מצאתי באיזה מקומות שהמ״אה מקום נשתבש, לא לקחתי עלי את המלאכה לחפש ולעיין אחריו כי רב המלאכה לפני מבלעדה, ולכן הנחתיו כמו שהוא בגמרות הישנות, וגם על יתר הדברים שהעירני החכם הנ״ל שמתי לבי והנני מודה לו על יגיעתו לקרא פרק אחד מסדורי בעין פקוחה חודרת ובוקרת. כן הנני מודה להרבנים הגדולים עיני ישראל הרה״ג דר. מ. יאסטראוו והרה״ג דר. ב. סאלד שנעתרו לבקשתי לעבור על חלק מסוים ממלאכתי בעין בקרת ולחות את דעתם גלוי לעיני כל ישראל והעמים, ומקרב ולב עמוק אברך את זקן בית ישראל את הרב הגדול המאירי. ראש בית המדרש לרבנים בסינסינאטי ועורך את העתון הנודע לשם **American Israelite** אשר לא יניח את ידו להטיב אתי בכל אשר אך יוכל בנפשו ובמאדו; יהי נועם ה׳ על כולם להאריך ימיהם ושנותיהם לתפארת ולטובת בית ישראל.

כן יקרה בעיני עצת החכם המלומד הר״ק קאהלער לקצר כל מה דאפשר, כי דעתו היא שכל אשר יקטן בכמותו תגדל איכותו, וכן כתבתי אני זה עשר שנים לפנים. אבל לדאבון נפשי לא אוכל לקצץ בנטיעת כלי האפנים שעליהם תסוב מלאכתי. יהי שם הרב קאהלער מבורך בעבור יגיעתו ועמלו בשביל היהדות והיהודים, כי הוא היה הראשון אשר זה שלש שנים לפנים התנדב לי את שמו רצוני להדפיס מכתבי כובבים

מהעמודים הנדפסים מפני שהיו משובשים עד כי אין באפשרי להשתמש בם. שלכן בחרתי בגמ׳ הזאת לתתה עם פרש״י בשולי היריעה מתחת, אם כי המראה מקום סמני הקריאה והשאלה הנקודות המפסיקות ופרש״י לקחו יותר ממחצה הגליון בכל עמוד, ואולי גם שלשה רבעים, דבר אשר לא דמיתי מראש, ואם אמנם גם פה נפלו איזה שגיאות הדפוס מאותות הרומות, אבל בכלל טובה היא ההגהה, כי בדפוס רב משכיל ובקי בתלמוד הדפסתי והוא קבל עליו מלאכת ההג״הה, ונשתדל ביתר המסכתות כי לא תהינה שגיאות בכלל.

בשמן לבקש תמיכה על מלאכתי זאת, אך אני יראתי פן לא תעלה בידי ושמו יהיה לבוז לבן חרלתי. עתה הגיעני מכתב תהלה בשפת אשכנז וחות דעתו בשפת אנגלית מהרב הגדול הישיש שקנה חכמה. דר. פסלזמהאל. שהנני נותן את דעתו לפני הקוראים וגם לפניו היו 10 עלים מסס״ ראש השנה, וישמח לבי מאד כי גם דעת החכם הזה מסכמת עם החכמים שקדשוהו ויהי גם שמו מבורך. לאחרונה הנני אתן תודה להמעתיק החכם הרב לעאנרד לוי נ״י שמלבד שעשה זאת בלי כל תשלום גמול, הנה הואיל בטובו לקבל עליו את הטרחא היתירה לקרא לפני כל מלה ומלה, טרם נתן לדפוס; ואין דבר בכל העתקתו אשר לא שמתי עיני במו וראיתי כי היא מתאמת את תאריגינאל.

נם החכמים קראסקאפף ובעריקאוויץ יקבלו תודתם שהשתדלו בכל אשר יכלו לתמוך את ידי בחתומים אשר שלמו כסף מראש למען אוכל לגשת אל מלאכתי, והנני מודיע בזה לכל אלה אשר יתמכו את ידי ויעזרו לי בין בכחם בין באתם, בין בעשה ובין במעשה, כי לבד זאת ששכרם יהיה כפול מן השמים יברך דור אחרון את שמם, כי שמם יזכר ויפקד לעתידים ותומכים בשערי המסכתות הבאים. ובזה אצא מאת פני הקורא, לא בקידה והשתחויה, כ״א בשלש פסיעות לאחורי, מרכין ראש, למזרח. צפון ודרום ואומר: שלום, שלום לרחוק ולקרוב. וה׳ יברך את עמו בשלום.

נויארק יום שהוכפל בו כי טוב כ״ד שבט תרנ״ה לפק.

מיכאל. ל. בהרב החסיד ר׳ אלכסנדר ז״ל ב ן-ר א ד ק ת.

מכתבי תהלה.

ואלה המה המכתבים שכבדוני בהם גדולי הדור עשר שנה לפנים והיום, שהנני נותן אותם. בסדר יום כתיבתם. בתודה. הכתובים בשפות החיות העתקתי לשפת עבר, והכתובים בשפת עבר העתקתים לאנגליש למען ירוץ בם כל קורא:

מכתב הרב הגדול המורה בבית מדרש המדעים בברלין ויועץ הממשלה וכו׳ שמו נודע למשגב הר״ר משה לאצארוס נ״י.

Berlin, den 20 July. 1885.

ראדקינסאן אדני הנכבד!

למענה על מכתבו היקר מיום י״ד לח״ז הנני להגיד:

בשום לב ובשמחה קראתי את מאמרו הראשי בהקול נר 298, אבל גם תנה הרשית לקחת לבבי אחרי התבוננתי בדבריו.

שמחתי כי הרעיון הנשא הזה הנוצץ ברוחו של עולם היהדות פורש בשום שכל בהקול אבל גם צר לי כאשר לבי לא יתנני להאמין, כי אראה את מחשבתך יוצאת לפעולות אדם בימי בחיים חיותי.

אין כל ספק בלבי כי באיזה מקום ובאיזה זמן יצאו דבריך אל הפועל, כי המה נחוצים ונצרכים, אבל המלאכה הזאת הוכל להעשות רק ע״י אספת ועדי חכמים מובהקים, שגם המה יהיה להם על מה שיסמוכו, כי יקבלו תמיכה להוצאות הדבר הגדול הזה מיחידים עשירים ונדיבים.

אבל באלה כן אלה רואים אנחנו שהאינטרעססען שהיה בם ויאבד בם כל רגש טוב תשגב לטובת התלמוד והיהדות כלה; ואולם בין אלה אשר יחשבו את התלמוד לסקור חכמתם או כי שאר דבריו גר לרגלם, כרובם הם מבעלי קוצר רוח וקטנות המוח תשתרר בם, אשר על כן יחסר להם מבט ישר על קורות העתים ועל הדעות והמגמות אשר תצאנה לנו מן ההיסטוריה אשר אך על ידי ההתבוננות עמוקה בהם נוכל לעכב עצה ולחבר כפר כזה.

ואולם גם על התחלת העבודה וההכנות להמלאכה ישמח לבי מאד והנני מוכן לתת ידי לחן.

אמנם עד כמה שקצרה לי לבלי תת ידי לדבר הזה ולהשיב פניה, לא אוכל, עם כל חפצי, לקחת על עצמי מלאכה כזו או גם אף להשתתף בה. בעבור עמוסה עלי עבודה רבת בצרכי צבור שהנני רובץ תחת משאי ולא אוכל להעמיס עלי עבודה חדשה הצריכה עמל ויגיעה רבה, ובעת שלא אוכל לקוות על תמיכת חכמי הדור שיקחו חלק בזה. בכגב כזה יחסר לי תקוה תם רגשיה לזה. מקרב לבי אברכו ברגשות שלמות,

הנני המכבדו

לאצארוס.

ז) בחרתי במס׳ „ראש השנה״ לתתה קודם משני טעמים א) מאשר המס׳ ברכות היא ביד המעתיק כמו שהיא ואשר נדפס עד כעת נתקלקל וב) כי מפני שהיא תכיל הרבה חפצתי לתתה עם ההעתקה ביחד, להקל על המבקר שיוכל לבקר את הטעקסט וההעתקה גם יחד. חולת זאת המסכתא הזאת לבד ההלכה, תכיל ענין גדול ונחוץ במנין שנות החמה והלבנה ובענין קידוש החודש תקנת ריב״ז ועדותם השוה לכל נפש חוקר ומעיין בדחז״ל.

ח) עוד אחת הנני להבטיח ולעשות לטובת כל הלומדים והמשכילים, והוא להעמיד כל הדברים שהובאו במשניות ובגמרא כ״א על מקומם הראוי ביחוד; במסכתא הזאת ימצא זאת הקורא בענין מוסר דין לשמים, והוא מצער. אבל במקום שיבאו משניות שלמות והגמרא להם שלא במקומם הראוי לענין המדובר בהמסכת, אעביר אותו להמסכתא ההיא אשר עקרה ידובר בענין הזה, וכה תדבר כל מסכתא ומסכתא רק מענין ששמה מוכיח. ובקדושין אשר תופיע תיכף אחרי זאת המסכתא, ימצא הקורא דוגמא גדולה מזה וידין מהם על השאר; וזהו תועלת גדולה להסדר הנכון ואקוה להפיק רצון בזה מאת כל המפלגות בעמנו, כי אם לא יאבו אחרים להכיר את מלאכת, לתלמוד הקדום, הלא על כרחם יודו, כי הנהו „קיצור התלמוד״ כההלכה והאגדה וכל המשא ומתן בהם לא נחסר, וכי הוקל מאד לכל מעיין אשר יאבה לקרות בגמרא, שעד כה היה לפניו כספר החתום.

ט) הרה״ג דר. מילצינער העיר אותי במכתב מיוחד על המראה מקומות מהש״ס שנשמטו בברכות ועוד על דברים אחדים; שמעתי גם לו ונתתי את הספר „תורה אור״ על מקומו לפני כל מקרא ומקרא שהובא מהת נך אבל איני מקבל אהריותו עלי כי אם אמנם מצאתי באיזה מקומות שהמ״אה מקום נשתבש, לא לקחתי עלי את המלאכה לחפש ולעיין אחריו כי רב המלאכה לפני מבלעדה, ולכן הנחתיו כמו שהוא בגמרות הישנות, וגם על יתר הדברים שהעירני החכם הנ״ל שמתי לבי והנני מודה לו על יגיעתו לקרא פרק אחד מסדורי בעין פקוחה חודרת ובוקרת. כן הנני מודה להרבנים הגדולים עיני ישראל הרה״ג דר. מ. יאסטראוו והרה״ג דר. ב. סאלד שנעתרו לבקשתי לעבור על חלק מסוים ממלאכתי בעין בקרת ולחות את דעתם גלוי לעיני כל ישראל והעמים, ומקרב ולב עמוק אברך את זקן בית ישראל את הרב הגדול המאירי. ראש בית המדרש לרבנים בסינסינאטי ועורך את העתון הנודע לשם American Israelite אשר לא יניח את ידו להטיב אתי בכל אשר אך יוכל בנפשו ובמאדו; יהי נועם ה׳ על כולם להאריך ימיהם ושנותיהם לתפארת ולטובת בית ישראל.

כן יקרה בעיני עצת החכם המלומד הר״ק קאהלער לקצר כל כה דאפשר, כי דעתו היא שכל אשר יקטן בכמותו תגדל איכותו, וכן כתבתי אני זה עשר שנים לפנים. אבל לדאבון נפשי לא אוכל לקצץ בנטיעת כללי האפנים שעליהם תסוב מלאכתי. יהי שם הרב קאהלער מבורך בעבור יגיעתו ועמלו בשביל היהדות והיהודים, כי הוא היה הראשון אשר זה שלש שנים לפנים התנדב לי את שמו ויצתי להדפיס מכתבי כוכבים

מהעמודים הנדפסים מפני שהיו משובשים עד כי אין באפשרי להשתמש בם. שלכן בחרתי במס׳ הזאת לתתה עם פרש״י בשולי היריעה מתחת, אם כי המראה מקום סמני הקריאה והשאלה תקודות המפסיקות ופרש״י לקחו יותר ממחצה הגליון בכל עמוד, ואולי גם שלשה רבעים, דבר אשר לא דמיתי מראש, ואם אמנם גם פה נפלו איזה שגיאות הדפוס מאותות הרומות, אבל בכלל טובה היא ההגהה, כי ברפוס רב משכיל ובקי בתלמוד הדפסתי והוא קבל עליו מלאכת ההג״הה, ונשתדל ביתר המסכתות כי לא תהיינה שגיאות כלל.

בשמן לבקש תמיכה על מלאכתי זאת, אך אני יראתי פן לא תעלה בידי ושמו יהיה לבוז לכן חדלתי. עתה הגיעני מכתב תהלה בשפת אשכנז וחות דעתו בשפת אנגלית מהרב הגדול הישיש שקנה חכמה. דר. פעלזענטהאל. שהנני נותן את דעתו לפני הקוראים וגם לפניו היו 10 עלים ממס" ראש השנה, וישמח לבי מאד כי גם דעת החכם הזה מסכמת עם החכמים שקדשוהו ויהי גם שמו מבורך. לאחרונה הנני אתן תודה להמעתיק החכם הרב לעאנרד לוי נ"י שמלבד שעשה זאת בלי כל תשלום גמול, הנה הואיל בטובו לקבל עליו את הטרחא היתירה לקרא לפני כל מלה ומלה, טרם נתנו לדפוס; ואין דבר בכל העתקתו אשר לא שמתי עיני במו וראיתי כי היא מתאמת את האריגינאל.

גם החכמים קראסקאפף ובעררקאוויץ יקבלו תודתם שהשתדלו בכל אשר יכלו לתמוך את ידי בהתומים אשר שלמו כסף מראש למען אוכל לגשת אל מלאכתי, והנני מודיע בזה לכל אלה אשר יתמכו את ידי ויעזרו לי בין בכחם בין באותם, בין בעשה ובין במעשה, כי לבד זאת ששכרם יהיה כפול מן השמים יברך דור אחרון את שמם, כי שמם יזכר ויפקד לעתרים ותומכים בשערי המסכת'ת הבאים. ובזה אצא מאת פני הקורא, לא בקידה והשתחויה, כ"א בשלש פסיעות לאחורי, מרכין ראש, למזרח. צפון ודרום ואומר: שלום, שלום לרחוק ולקרוב. וה' יברך את עמו בשלום.

נויארק יום שהוכפל בו כי טוב כ"ד שבט תרנ"ה לפק.

מיכאל. ל. בהרב החסיד ר' אלכסנדר ז"ל ב ן - ר א ד ק ה.

מכתבי תהלה.

ואלה המה המכתבים שכבדוני בהם גדולי הדור עשר שנה לפנים והיום, שהנני נותן אותם. בסדר יום כתיבתם, בתורה. הכתובים בשפות החיות העתקתי לשפת עבר, והכתובים בשפת עבר העתקתים לאנגליש למען ירוץ בם כל קורא:

מכתב הרב הגדול המורה בבית מדרש המדעים בברלין ויועץ הממשלה וכו' שמו נודע למשגב הר"ר משה לאצארוס נ"י.

Berlin, den 20 July, 1885.

ראדקינזאן אדוני הנכבד!

למענה על מכתבו היקר מיום י"ד לח"ז הנני להגיד:

בשום לב ובשמחה קראתי את מאמרו הראשי בהקול נר 298, אבל גם תחת הרשית לקחת לבבי אחרי התבוננתי בדבריו.

שמחתי כי הרעיון הנשא הזה הנוצץ במוחו של עולם היהדות פורש בשום שכל בהקול אבל גם צר לי מאשר לבי לא יתנני להאמין, כי אראה את מחשבתך יוצאת לפעולות אומן בקרוב בחיים חיותי.

אין כל ספק בלבי כי באיזה מקום ובאיזה זמן יצאו הדברים אל הפועל, כי המה נחוצים ונצרכים, אבל המלאכה הזאת הגדולה תוכל להעשות רק ע"י אספת ומועצי חכמים מובהקים, וגם המה יהיה להם על מה שיסמוכו, כי יקבלו תמיכה להוצאות הדבר הגדול הזה מיחידים עשירים ונדיבים.

אבל כאלה כן אלה ראשים אנחנו שהשגרת, פקידתנביזמוס שודר בם ויאבד בם כל רגש טוב תשגב לטובת התלמוד והיהדות כלה; ואולם בין אלה אשר יחשבו את התלמוד למקור חכמתם או כי שאף דבריו נר לרגלם, כרובם הם מבעלי קוצר רוח וקטנות המוח תשתרר בם, אשר על כן יחסר להם מבט ישר על קורות העתים ועל הדעות הנשגבות אשר תצאנה לנו מן הפילוסופיה אשר אך על ידי התבוננות עמוקה בהם נוכל לשבם קצת ולחבר ספר כזה.

ואולם גם על התחלת העבודה והתכונת להמלאכה ישמח לבי מאד והנני מוכן לתת ידי להן.

אמנם עד כמה שקשה לי לבלי תת ידי לדבר הזה ולהשיב פניך, לא אוכל, עם כל חפצי, לקחת על עצמי מלאכה כזו או גם אף להשתתף בה. בהיותי עמוס על עבודה רבת בצרכי צבור שהנני רובץ תחת משאי ולא אוכל להקים על עבודה דרושה הצריכה עמל ויגיעה רבה, ובעת שלא אוכל לקוות על תמיכת חכמי הדור שיקחו חלק בזה. במכתב בזה יחסר לי העוז וגם הנטיה לזה. מקרב לבי אברכו ברשואה שלמה,

הנני המכבדו

לאצארוס.

מכתב הרב הגדול החו״ב נודע בכל תפוצות ישראל בחבוריו הנפלאים „מאיר עין״ מורה בבית המדרש שבווין הר״ר מאיר פרידמאן נ״י.

ה׳ לפ״ דברים כרת״ת לפ״ק,
16 יולי, 1885, ווינא.

לכבוד המו״ל את הקול הרב החכם מו״ה מיכאל לוי ראדקינזאן נ״י

את מכתבך קבלתי והנני להודיעך כי קראתי את מאמרך בהסכמת הלב ברוב ענייניו, אם כי לא אסכים בכל שאתה מוצא להסכים במה שהגרתי שאין אני רואה ד״ם להסכים מיתבי מאמתי וכו׳ וכו׳. שבכולם באה מלת אור בכוון אורתא ושייכים הם לעקר הענין ובפרט מיתבי מר זוטרא וכו׳. ששמו נקרא עליו, אבל איך שיהיה כך או כך, אין הדבר נ״א להלכה ולא למעשה ר״ל אקאדעמיש, כי בעלי חכמת אינם בעלי כסף ובעלי כסף אינם בעלי חכמה וע״ב נתקים בנו: „ואבדה חכמת חכמיו ובינת נבוניו תסתתר״, ואעפ״י שאינני מבעלי הסוד תבין הסוד של הסתתר, והאמן לי כי לא מצאתי לי פנאי ועת למלאות דברי לשנות על כערך בענין התפילין כי השונת שאלת האוכל לבני ביתי קודמת לכל התשובות,

המוקירך והמכבדך מאיר איש שלום. *)

מכתב הרב הגדול המנוח שהיה המלומד היותר גדול בזמנו מכל הרבנים שבהודו בתלמוד ומפרשיו ומצוין במדותיו האב״ד ד״ק דרעזדן והמדינה רב בנימין זאב וואלף דר. לאנדויא ז״ל.

ב״ה דרעזדען יום ד׳ י׳ אב לשנת והוא ישר א׳ר׳ח׳ו׳ת׳י׳ד׳ לפ״ק.

שלום לכבוד הרב החכם והחוקר הנכבד כ״ש כ״ה ר׳ מיכאל לוי ראדקינזאהן נ״י.

שמעתי את הקול מדבר מבין פרחי נגד אשר נטעת בו עלים לתרופה לכבוד תורתנו ולהרים קרן חכמת ישראל כי נתת את לבך לקרב אל המלאכה הגדולה והיקרה מאוד לשום לפני בני ישראל את התורה שבעל פה בתמונתה הראשונה טרם התערבו בה במשך הזמן כמה וכמה תוספות מחיבנים סבוראים ומהגאונים, מבלתי נגעת חרש בעקר ההלכה, גם להסיר מן התלמוד כמה וכמה אגרות שנכנסו אליו מפי חמאותיים, ובתוכם דברים אשר אין להם שחר ולא לכבוד הם לחכמינו ז״ל. שמעתי וישמח לבי כמוצא שלל רב. ומה אוסיף לדבר על גדול התועלת אשר תצא ממלאכתך לכל לומדי תורה כי ימצא להם ספרך אשר קראת בשם: „התלמוד הישן והקצר״ מנוקה מכל תוספות, ותחת השנות הדברים עשר פעמים בכל המקומות הנוגעים בהם יצויין רק מראה מקום המסכתי והדף אשר בא זכרונם ראשונה, והי׳ לנו, ככל עם ועם ובכל מדע ומדע, ספר כולל כל דברי תורה שבע״פ בקצור למען ירוץ קורא בו. הלא בטוב טעם הצעת כל אלה במאמרך בהקול נו׳ 298. אך יהיה ה׳ בעזרך ויישר כחך וחילך לשאת עול המשא הכבד הזה על שכמך ויפתח לבך ויאר עיניך לבוא אל מסורת האמת ולא תחטיא. כי הלא דבר הוא לחקר בענין תורת לברר ולהוציא חדש מפני ישן, ויפה אמרת בהתחברך עם הכמים מובהקים אשר יש להם יד ושם בתורה וגם נתן ה׳ להם לב לדעת ועינים לראות את החדש (קריטיק). ואולם תמהתי על כל החרדה אשר חרדת מפני חמת מוציאי דבה לאמר כי מקצץ בנטיעות אתה; הנה לא באת לפגע חרש בפסק הלכה וגם לא באת לרחק הדברים מן העולם רק לקרב הקוראים אל הספר והדברים הנוספים גם רבה ימצאו כמאז גם היום בתלמוד הארוך ושם יקראון. והלא כמה גדולים קדמוך בזה בהעירותם ואפי׳ למחק איזה דבר שהתלימו לשבוש או לשנות הנוסחא ובמקומות אין מספר כתב רש״י ז״ל הכי גרסינן וכן גרסם על פי ס״ם שלנו והנוסח׳ הישנה הלצה הלכה לה ועל כמה דברים גזרו אמר שהם הוספות מרי אחאי גאון ובדומה. אבל על שני דברים אעירך נא ידידי הגדולים הם אלי. א) אל תשכח מלהעתיק פי׳ רש״י בתלמודך הקצר לפחות מה שנוגע להבנת המלות והענין, אם גם תשמיט את הנוגע אל הפלפול בדברי רש״י (והוא כעט) כי הוא הפרשנדתא וביתו התלמוד כספר החתום לקוראיו.

ב) לא תשכח מלהציב ציונים בכל מקום אשר תשמיט דברים הנוספים לפי דעתך והראות על הגליון אי׳ מקומם בתלמוד ארוך, וכל הרוצה לקרות יבוא ויקרא ויתן לוח קם או לקרבם, ולא על כל מוצא פיך יהיה הקורא, כי מי כל האדם יוכל להדלים על כל דבר המן הישן הוא או מן החדש? *)

עבדך הדורש שלומך ושוהתי מוקירך ומכבדך הצעיר בנימין זאב וואלף (Dr. Landau).
בהרמ״י ז״ל אב״ד בדרעזדען והמדינה.

---

*) המכתב הזה נדפס בהקול 299, עם תשובתי עליו והקורא בו גם כ״מ י תראשי שם דבור היוצה׳ „ואני רק בכוונה מהיקה בו״ לא יספיד רק יורה רוח גדול, כי הוא שייך לעניננו אבל אין כאן מקום להדפיסו שנית.

*) כמו המכתב נדפס בהקול 300 והתשובות מהודית ועוד שני לו נדפס בהקול 309 בבוארש יתר מאד.

מכתב הרב הגדול המפורסם בחבוריו, מדברותיו ומפעלותיו בקהל עדת ישורון הר"ר מרדכי נ"י דר. יאסטראוו. הרב לעדת רודף־שלום בעיר פילאדעלפיא.

Germantown, Oct. 5, 1894.

אדוני היקר!

למלא חפצך הנני לקחת את העונג לגלות דעתי כי התלמוד הקצר (שבחנתי וראיתי את המלאכה) שברצונך להוציאו לאור יהיה לתועלת רבה לתלמידי חכמים, יען כי ע"י לא יצטרכו עוד לפלס להם נתיב בתוך גבכי השקלות והטריות אשר לעתים לא רחוקות אינן שייכות אל עקר הענין שידובר בו. ובנתנך והעתקת ספרי התלמוד הקצר (כפי מלאכתך) לשפה האנגלית, אף אם אמנם עודנה לא מלאכה קלה הוא אבל לא יבצר עוד ממעתיק מבין (מה שאין כן עם התלמוד אשר לפנינו) ובברכי אותך כי חפצך הטוב יצליח בידך, הנני מכבדך מאד

M. Jastrow.

To M. L. Rodkinson.

תעודת הרב הגדול המורה את התלמוד בבית מדרש הרבנים בסינסינאטא הנודע לשם בחבורו הנפלא „מבוא התלמוד" הר"ר משה נ"י דר. מילצינער.

קראתי עלים אחדים מחלק אחד של התלמוד הקצר אשר ה' מיכאל ל' ראדקינסאן אומר להוציא לאור, ואמצא כי למלאכתו נאוה תהלה. ע"י הוצאת התלמוד אשר בזאת תוקל התבונה בדברי התלמוד בכלל ובפרט להמתחילים לפי שממנה נשמטו כל שיח ושיג שאינו שייך אל הענין אשר ידובר בו וכל מאמר מוסגר בדברים זרים אשר יכביד את הבנת הענין, מה גם כי ממני ההפסק השאלות והקריאות כפי המנהג ביתר הספרים יבאו בפנים התלמוד. תקותי חזקה כי אוהבי ספרותנו הישנה יתאמצו בכל עוז להיות לעזר להמחבר הזה בגופם ומאודם למען יהי לאל ידו להשלים את המפעל רב־התועלת הזה.

Cincinnati, Nov., 1894.

Dr. M. Mielziner,

מכתב של הרב הגדול המאיר, שהאיר והעמיד תלמידים רבים אנשי שם, שער מבוא השמים ינה שמו הר"ר יצחק מ. ווייס. (שכתב לאיש אחר שמו לא יזכר).

Cincinnati, Oh., Jan. 14, 1895.

אדון נכבד!

נושא מכתבי זה הוא מ. ל. ראדקינסאן, הנודע אשר חפצתי להיותו לך כי תשים לבך עליו ביותר ולהכיר פעלו.

המפעל אשר האדון ר. עסוק בו, הוצאת תלמוד, מנוה ומתוקן והעתקתו לשפת ענגליש פעל ענק הוא, שאי איש אשר כמותו גם עשה יעשה וגם יכל יוכל. אם יצליח חפצו בידו, או אז תביא פעלו חיים חדשים ליהדות האמעריקני גם פה וגם חוצה לארצנו.

ועתה איפוא יוכל השואל לשאול: היצליח בידו להוציא חפצו אל הפועל? ועל זאת אענה אני, כי בנוגע לחכמתו ודעתו הנני בטוח בו כי יכל יוכל; ובן בנוגע לכח מעשיו אהין להגיד נכון לבי כי חפצו יצליח בידו, כי הוא איש רב עלילה אשר לא ייעף ולא ייגע. ועלינו החובה לעזור לו למען יהי לאל ידו להוציא לאור חלק אחד לדוגמא, למען תוכח דעת הקהל אם הוא הגבר המוכשר למפעל הזה ואם לא.

ועתה מה אני שואל מעמך? כי אם להחזיק ידו בהוצאות הנצרכים לזה למען יוכל להוציא לאור את החלק הראשון. אם החלק הזה יצא מתחת ידו מתקן כהבטחתו, אזי יוכיח כי אמנם ראוי והגון הוא להוציא את הדבר הגדול הזה לפעולות אדם.

Isaac M. Wise.

תעודת הרב הגדול בישראל ובלאומים הנודע בשערים בביאורו הנפלא על ספר „איוב" כש"ת רב בנימין דר. סאלד נ"י.

בשם השם Baltimore, Jan. 16, 1895

אורח נכבד בא לעירנו הוא החכם הרב מיכאל ל. ראדקינסאן הנודע בתלמודו ובקיאותו בספרות העברית הישנה והחדשה, וכי עשר ידות בו בתלמוד ומפרשיו, ובידו מגלת ספר, אשר בשם התלמוד הישן והקצר יכנהו; וישם לפני עלים אחדים נדפסים ממסכתא „ברכות" למבחן, וגם מסכת „שבת" בכתב יד הביא לפני ויחל את פני לשום עליהם עין בקרת חדה, למען, אם אמצא נספרו דברי־חפץ, אוכל להעיד על מלאכתו ועל תכליתה בפני כל קהל עדת ישראל.

לגודל ערך המלאכה ויקרתה בזמן הזה, נעתרתי לו ועברתי על ששה עשר פרקים ממסכת שבת בעיון נמרץ, וכן נתתי עיני את העלים למבחן מדפוס, ששם לפני; והנני עלו מאד להעיד בכתב יושר דברי אמת, כי אמנם מצאתי בם שאהבה נפשי. ויותר לקח לבי הסדור הנאה שנסדרו בו דברי השם בבלי באופן ישר ונאה וכי כל המאמרים צמודים, אחוזים ודבוקים יחד, על פי משפטי ההגיון, והמה קלים להבין עפ"י פירוש רש"י אשר שם בצדם; ונעימים בתפיסתם, כי דבר דבור על אפניו יתנו וכן יסקו במרבותיהם, אם כי המחבר לא הוסיף עליהם מרליה אף מלה אחת, וגם לא שינה את לשונם.

ואם אמנם לא חדשים היו בעיני מאמרי השם ה אשר למדתים לדעת מנעורי הנה מצאתי מצוה דבש הבריר החדש והנאה ותאורנה עיני כי מעתה במוח הנני שהקורא הנבון ירוץ בם בהשכל ודעת, ויהיו בעיניו כאלו כן יקרו מיסי התלמוד ממעיניהם והן יאכו ממקורם. ולכן בעליצת נפשי אמרתי יצליח מבוא יושר חיל.

עד כמה נחוץ כפר כזה בזמננו, שלימודי התלמוד הגדול ורחב ידים עם כל מפרשיו ומבאריו כמו שהוא נדפס עד כה, ולאצור ממנו הפנינים המפוזרות במקומות רבים, עד כי הדרינה לאחרים בתורי שכל, אין באפשרות גם לאנשי מדע העוסקים כל ימיהם אך בחכמה ובמדעים; ואולם בתלמוד הקצר הזה, אשר השקלות וטריות היתרות שאינן מביאין שום תועלת, וכן הדברים מענין אחד אשר נשנו כמה פעמים, יחסרו בו, יוכל כל תורני להשיג בזמן קצר ובלי יגיעה רבה, את כל אשר יחפוץ לבו להבין ולדעת.

הדברים האלה הניעוני לצאת ממקומי ולהיות אני אוהבי הספרות הישנה, נגבורי אומתנו שכבוד

עמנו ותורתו יקר ללבם, בכל מקום שהם, להיות לעזר ולסעד להמחבר המשכיל הזה, לאמץ זרועותיו, לתמכו ולחזקו, למען יוכל להוציא את מחשבתו לפועל ולתת ברכה לבית ישראל בתורתו הישנה אשר כל דברי חפץ טמונים בה.

והיו הדברים האלה אשר דברתי למען האמת והצדק, לאות ולעד לדור אחרון כי גם בבאת תשע־העשרה לא אלמן היה ישראל ממוקירי תורת חז״ל ומתומכי ידי חכמים ובוחרים העוסקים להגדיל תורה ולהאדירה. ומובטחני, שכל תלמיד הגון אשר תצמא נפשו לשאוב מים ממעיני החכמה הקדושה ימצא די „בהתלמוד הקצר" הזה לרות נפשו השוקקה. ויהי נועם ה׳ עליו ועל כל תומכיו ועוזריו בעתירת.

בנימין סאלד.

רב ומורה לעדת אוהב שלום בעיר באלטימארע.

Dr. Benjamin Szold.

מכתב הרה״ג החכם הנודע בשערים לשם ולתהלה הר״ר קויפמאן קאהלער, רב לעדת בית אל בנויארק.

New York, Feb. 12, 1895.

אדון נכבד!

בכל לבבי ובכל נפשי הנני מסכים לדעת הארכיבוד לשערים והרבנים הדוקטורים יאסטראוו ומילצינער בשבח הוצאת התלמוד אשר הוא אומר להדפיס. גם אני אחשב לכשזם, כי בהוציאו לאור את התלמוד הקצר, שממנו נשמטו כל המאמרים המוסגרים אשר יבלבלו דעת הקורא, ואשר יבואו בו כמני ההפסק כדי להקל על המעיין, אז יתענג הקורא גם על המקומות הקשים ולא יהיו לו עוד למשא, ומזה תצא טובה רבת לתלמידי חכמים, בין שהם בני ברית, ובין שאינם בני ברית, אשר על כן חפצי להיות מליץ טוב בעד המשכיל הזה, למען יתמכוהו חובבי ספרות העברית, אשר אך מעטים יחדו מכבם בערת.

דר. ק. קאהלער.

אל מ. ל. ראדקינסאן.

מכתב הרה״ג החכם המפורסם הר״ר ב. דר. פעלזענטהאל.

Chicago, Feb. 14, 1895.

אדון נכבד!

איש לא יכחד כי התלמוד בצורתו הנוכחית כמו שנמסר לנו ע״י מסדריו, גדול הוא מאד בכמותו, ויען זאת כי ע״י עומק הפלפול אשר בו והערבוביא כחומת חומר הסדרים, לא יוכל איש לדעת אותו על בוריו, חוץ מתלמידי חכמים אשר שמו לילות כימים והקדישו את כל חייהם אך לעלות בסבכן זה של הספרות הקדושה. אך בימים האלה ובארצות אשר בהן נפל על כל תלמיד חכם ועל כל מורה צדק לעדתו לקבוע עתים גם לחכמות ומדעים אחרים, דבר שאי אפשר הוא לאדם להקדיש את כל עתותיו אך ללמוד התלמוד לבדו. אשר על כן דבר טוב ויפה תהיה הוצאת התלמוד הקצר ליוב העוסקים בו, ובפרט להתלמידים המתחילים ללמוד אותו, בין שהם לומדים אותו בבתי מדרש ובין שהם לומדים אותו כשהם לעצמם, דבר טוב ויפה יהיה קיצור תלמוד כזה, אשר הדברים היותר נכבדים יתבוננו בו במלין מועטות המחזיקות את המרובה והורם כל מכשול מדרך הלומד, בפרט אם יעשה למוד התלמוד נקל לנבון ע״י כמני ההפסק אשר יבואו בו וע״י הערות ובאורים בשולי העמודים או בכוף הספרים. אשר על כן הנני להליץ בעד התאצת התלמוד הקצר אשר הוא אומר להדפיס לפני כל חובבי ספרות ישרון בכלל ולפני תלמידי בתי מדרש לרת אמונה בפרט, ועל הצעירים בבני עמנו החובה להיות לו לעזר אף אם לא ידעו את התלמוד ואינן נהנין מדברי תורה, והיה להם לתועלת מעשה זבולן „שהיה עוסק בפרקמטיא וממציא מזון לשבט יששכר והם עוסקים בתורה".

עלה והצלח לתת לנו תלמוד קצר אשר יהיה דרוש לחפץ כל מבין עם תלמיד. מכבדך

ב. פעלזענטהאל.

מכתב הרב הגדול המפורסם בתורתו ויראתו וכו׳ וכו׳ רב שבתי מוראיס רב ודרשן בק״ק „מקוה ישראל" בפילאדעלפיא.

אדוני הנודע בשערים והמפורסם!

ביום ש״ק קבלתי הדפים אשר אני מחזיר אתר שעיינתי בם היטב. לא קלה המלאכה אשר העמים מכ״ת עליו ואם יעלה בידו להשלימה באופן שתהיה לישועתה יפה, אומן גדול יקרא ושכר הרבה יטול. הסכמתי לקיצור התלמוד אשר יצא מתחת יד איש נודע בשערים כמהו תהיה למותריו לא לעזר ולא יזיד, כי כה אני שאבוא אחר המלך (מאן מלכי רבנן) כמו רב מרדכי יאסטראו ואחרים המפורסמים. אולם האמת אגיד ולא אכחידנו כי הדפים שקריתי ממסכת ראש השנה ישרו בעיני כאשר כבר הודעתיו.

וה׳ ידריכנו בדרך אמת להגדיל התורה ולהאדירה כאות נפש עבדו, הכו״ח היום זה פילאדעלפיא יע״א בכ״ד לחדש שבט לשנת הכבות בחוזן ת׳ר׳נ׳ה׳ לפ״ק.

הצעיר שבתי מוראיס ס״ט.

ש״ץ בק״ק מקוה ישראל.

To Michael L. Rodkinson, D. T.

מכתב הרה״ג המפורסם כו׳ כו׳ רב שלמה צבי זאננענשיין הרב לעדת „שער השמים" בנוא״ק.

ב׳ ה׳ עש״ק לס׳ שקלים שנת תרנ״ה לפ״ק.

הנה קם הרב המופלג ובופר מהיר כו׳ ה׳ מיכאל לוי ראדקינזאן נ״י והתעורר לישועה גדולה חדשה והוציא לאור „קיצור התלמוד" הזה.

גם אני קראתי בקצת ספרו אשר שם לפני ונוכחתי אני את הדרך הסלולה אשר בחר בה. כל עובר ארחות ים התלמוד אשר ילך בעקבותיו בל יטעה ובל יטה ימין ושמאל, והחוף ימים סים עדם של תורת ישכן לבטח ומשם רואה פרי תלמודו. חכות רבים תלויה בו, ואני תפלה כי משכורתו של המעריך תהיה שלמה! א״ד המדבר לכבוד אבנט׳ של תורה והורגיה.

הק׳ שלמה צבי זאננענשיין.

רב ודרשן לעדת „שער השמים" בעיר נויארק.

מבוא קצר

להתלמוד בכלל, ולמס׳ ראש השנה בפרט.

יען כי עלה הגורל על המסכתא הזאת כי תעלה בדפוס ראשונה, נחשוב לחובה לתת לה מבוא קצר שבו יכנס הקורא המתחיל — הארוך, יבא אי״ה במקומו — והיה אם ימצאו הקוראים, כי דרכנו במבוא הזה אינה דרך כבושה מאשר קדמנו, ידעו כי דרך חדשה היא, אשר תבוטל בהתנגדות רבים, בלא ויכוחים, שאם אמנם יש לנו על מה לסמוך לא נאמר קבלו דעתנו; כי רק דנים אנחנו אבל לא נאמר: „בן יקום" וע״כ חדלנו פה להראות המקורים שמהם שאבנו את דברנו נגד דרכנו בכל אשר חברנו עד כה; ואחרי ההקדמה הקטנה הזאת, נאמר:

א) המשניות שלפנינו ברובן קדומות הנה מאד, כי השומעי לקח בבתי מדרש והחכמה, שהיו נהוגים בישראל עוד מימות יהושפט מלך יהודה, רשמו את דברי החכמים לעצמם, להיות תלמודם רגיל בפיהם, בשפת קצרה וברובם בלשון ששמעום, אך לפעמים הוסיפו עליהם כעין ביאור ופירוש מן הצד, וברבות הימים פרצו המשניות למעלה עד כי עלה מספרם לדעת רבים עד שש מאות סדרים.

ב) תוכן המשניות הקדומות היה המנהג שהיה נוהג בימיהם אצל ראשי העם ומנהיגיו, בין בדברים הנקראים בין אדם למקום כמצות שבת, תפלה וק״ש, טומאות וטהרות ומאכלות אסורות, ובין הדברים שבין אדם לחברו כדיני נשים ועבדים, ודיני ממונות וגם דיני נפשות, שבבתי המדרש היו עסוקים בהם לעשות את המנהג קבע בכל מקום שבני ישראל נמצאים.

ג) ברבות הימים שהחלו להעתיק את המשניות איש מרעהו ובנים ירשום מאבותם והוסיפו עליהם וגרעו מהם, קם רבינו יהודא הנשיא הנקרא עפ״י רוב בשם „רבי" סתם, ויחל לקבץ כל המשניות אל ישיבתו ומהם ברר ובחר וסדר אותם לששה סדרים מיוחדים אשר קרא להם שמות לפי ענינם: זרעים, מועד, נשים, נזקין, קדשים, טהרות; ויקדשם לבית ישראל.

ד) בין המשניות אשר ברר רבי נמצאות אלה שלא שנה את שפתן ותתן לפנינו בלשונן הקדום, אך גם ישנן בהן שהוסיף עליהן וישנן גם אלה שפירש אותן בקצרה ר״ל שהכנים איזה מלות מבארים את הענין בתוך המשנה עצמה כעין מאמר המוסגר, אבל יש בהן גם אלה אשר שנה את לשונן וטעמן מפני שבימיו כבר נשתנה המנהג וקבל צורה אחרת.

ה) הדברים אשר רצה רבי כי יקובלו להלכה באין פוצה פה, שנאן סתם ולא פירש שם האומרם, אך על רבות מהם שלא היה בכחו להכריע את ההלכה, או כי אלה שהיו כבר מפורסמים בעם עם שם האומרם, סדר אותם בשם אומרם ויקרא בשם גם את דעת המנגדים להם, בלא כל הכרעה, אבל ישנן גם אלה אשר אמרם בשם אחרים או יש אומרים, מאשר לא רצה לקרא עליהם שם האומרם כטעמים ידועים.

ו) לא בהסכמת רוב החכמים סדר רבי את משנתו ואדרבה רבים ערערו עליו ויסדרו משניות לעצמן בחשאי שלא היו מתאימות עם משנתו, אבל רבי בכחו הגדול אצל הרשות, בנשיאתו שהנהיג ברמה, ובנכסיו הרבים, כפה את כל מנגדיו שלא ירימו ראש נגדו ותתקבל משנתו לעיני כל ישראל כהתורה הנתנה מסיני; ותלמידיו הגדולים באשר ראו כי כונתו לשם שמים להכעיט המחלוקות בישראל, התרו החזיקו בידו ותורתו נתקבלה.

ז) משניות רבות בער רבי מן העולם אבל לא היה בכחו להשית כלן, ובהתהלכו

לתור ולדרוש אחריהם בבתי מדרשים וישיבות שהיו חוץ למקום ממשלתו, הקיפו עליו כתרנגולי של בית בוקיא והסתירו אותן ממנו ורבות נסדרו גם במקום ממשלתו בחשאי אשר נתפרסמו רק אחרי מותו, אך תלמידי רבי הסירו מהם את השם „משנה" שהוראתה שנית במעלה אחרי תורת משה ויכנון בשם תוספתות שר"ל שנתוספו אח"כ, או כי שהנה רק נוספות ולא מן העקריות וגם ברייתות שר"ל שתחשבנה רק לחיצוניות שנשנו חוץ מן כותלי בית המדרש ולצדדיות ולא לפנימיות ולעקריות, אבל גם בשם הזה נפזרו מיד אחרי מותו בכל העולם וכמעט שהחשיכו זהרה של משנתו של רבי, ולוא לא נתאספו תלמידיו להחזיק ישיבות גדולות להצדיק את משנתו של רבי, כי עתה כמעט לא היתה לה תקומה בין התוספתות וברייתות הרבות שהיו מבליעות אותה ולא נודע כי באה אל קרבנה, שלכן היה כל עסקן של הישיבות במערב ובמזרח, בישיבתן של רב ושמואל בבבל. ור' ינאי ור' יוחנן בפלשתנא, לעסוק ולהגות במשנתו של רבי לתרץ אותה במקום שיש עליה חולקין בתוספתא וברייתות שקראום ע"ש ר' חייא ור' ארשעיא שהיו חביבות בעיני העם; ופעמים רבות קצצו את לשונה והוסיפו עליה בחסורי מחסרא שקבעו בה דעת ולשון הברייתא, או כי אמרו „אימא הכי" ר"ל ההיפוך מן הכתוב במשנה וקראו כאלו כתובה במשנה, למען תתאים או עם התוספתא המתנגדת לה, או עם המנהג שנשתנה וקבל צורה אחרת מאשר היה לו בזמן רבי, ובמקום שלא היה להם ברירה אחרת הוסיפו גם משנה שלימה כצורתה וכלשונה וסדרוה בתוך משנתו.

ח) החכמים שנזכרו בתוך משנתו של רבי או בתוך התוספתות והברייתות נקראו בשם „תנאים", ביחיד „תנא" שהוראתו „מורה", „מלמד" Professor.

ט) לימודיהם של הישיבות במשך שנות מאות שגם אותן רשמו התלמידים לעצמם ונעתקו אח"כ מיד ליד, נקראו בשם גמרא, מן השם גמר וסוף, כי השתדלו לגמור ולהשוות את דברי המשנה והברייתא ועפ"י רוב גם לגמור את ההלכה כזה או כזה, (אם כי לא למעשה כי ע"ז הזהיר רבי יוחנן שלא ינהגו כההלכה הכתובה עד שיאמר בה מפורש כן תעשו), וחכמי הגמרא נקראים בשם אמוראים, ביחיד „אמורא" שהוא „מתורגמן", מפרש ומבאר לעם את הדברים שאינו מבין לבדו. ויען כי הנהו רק מפרש ומבאר, אין לו רשות לחלוק על התנא מן המשנה או הברייתא. אם לא שיש לו תנא אחר הסובר כמותו שאז יוכל להתנצל ולומר, כי דעת התנא ההוא ישרה בעיני יותר מדעת התנא הזה. ורבינא ורב אשי שהיו במאה החמישית, למספר הנהוג, המאה השלישית להאמוראים, החלו לסדר את הגמרא במהדורא קמא ולא עלתה בידם היטב ונצרכו לסדר אותה במהדורא תנינא, אבל בתוך כך נאספו אל עמם והכתבים נתגלגלו מיד ליד עד שקם במאה הששי רבנא יוסי ראש ישיבה האחרונה מהאמוראים בפומבדיתא ויער את לבב חבריו לקבץ את כל הכתבים ולחתום אותם שלא יהיו רשאים להוסיף עליהם, כי ירא היה פן יאבדו הכתבים מן העולם או כי האחרונים יוסיפו עליהם ויעשו בם כרצונם, ובדעתו כי לב המלכות מימות פירוז רשעא לא טוב לבית ישראל וישיבתו היא האחרונה להאמוראים, קבץ בחפזון גדול את כל הכתבים סדרם ויחתמם. והחפזון הזה גרם כי נסדרו מאמרים רבים מאד שלא במקומם הראוי, שנשנו דברים רבים פעמים רבות בלי שינוי לשון ובשינוי ותוספות, וגם מאמרים רבים התגנבו בם מסדרי התלמוד ומנגדיו, מפני שלא היתה להם עת ראויה לבקר את כל המאמרים, (כי אך שבע עשרה שנה מלך רבנא יוסי בישיבתו) ומאמרים רבים הכניסו אויבי התלמוד בזדון למען יאבד התלמוד את ערכו בעיני העמים. שכן התגנב המבטא „הא דרב אשי בדותא היא" כעשר פעמים בתוך התלמוד מה שלא נוכל להאמין כי

מסדרי התלמוד ישתמשו במבטא כזה על אדם גדול וקדוש להם כרב אשי וכיר בנו. וכן בטוים לא נאים על שארי חכמים וגם על האבות והנביאים וכו' וכו' מה גם שאם אמנם לא היו המסדרים האחרונים חכמים כרב אשי וחבריו הלא היו בעלי צורה ובעלי דרך ארץ ולא פיהם יוציא מלין כאלה.—אך התגנבו בתוכו מאנשי דלא מעלי—ואולם חתימת התלמוד לא הועילה וחפצם לא נעשה, כי הרבנן סבוראי שהיו אחריהם וגם הגאונים הכניסו בתלמוד דברים רבים מדעתם והוסיפו עליו בכל דור חמן.

חכמי הגמרא, שלמען תתגדל ותתקדש המשנה ושכל העם יראו שהיא תלויה רק בתורת משה, שמו כל מעינם בה רק להלכה, ולכן דקדקו לא לבד בלשונה, כי גם באותיותיה ודרשו גם מהם מיעוטין וריבוין כבתורת משה והנביאים ובראותם כי אינה מתאמת עם ההלכה בימיהם, דחקו ולחצו אותה בשנוים רבים כאמור למעלה. כאשר כן עשו התנאים עם הכתובים בתנ"ך וכל זה הוכרחו לעשות מפני המנגדים הרבים של הכתות השונות נגד התורה המסורה שלא הודו רק בתורה הכתובה, שמפני זה שאלו חכמי הגמרא על כל דבר שאינו מפורש במקרא, מנלן? וגם התמיה פשיטא! אם דבר זה כתוב מפורש, או כי פשוטו המקרא אינו סובל פירוש אחר מאשר השמיעה המשנה. ועל דברים שבמנהג העבר יסורם ולא יוכלו להועיל להווה ולעתיד, שאלו „למאי הלכתא"?

עד כא' תולדותן בקיצור; ועתה נבאר מטרת ותוכנה של המס' הזאת שאנו עסוקים בה:

חסר הוא בתורת משה, הנביאים והכתובים, עקר גדול שממנו יכולנו לדעת את סדר העולם ודברי הימים, והוא מנין השנים, אשר מבלעדו לא נוכל למצוא ידינו ורגלנו, שלא נאמר מאיזה עת חמן, או באיזה חודש ויום מנו הקדמונים את מנין שנתם. אמנם כתוב מפורש: החודש הזה לכם ראש חדשים. ראשון הוא לכם לחדשי השנה (שמות יב, ד.) שלפי עוסק פשוטו מצוה המחוקק: כי לא לבד שהחודש ניסן יהיה ראשון במעלה, כ"א גם ממנו תתחיל מנין השנה, אבל גם כתוב אחר לפנינו הנראה לכאורה כסותר אותו, והוא „וחג האסיף בצאת השנה" (שם כג, כח) שאם לא נבאר מלות „בצאת השנה" במובן „במשך השנה" יובן עפ"י עוסק הפשט החג של אוסף התבואה בגמר השנה שהיינו חודש אלול. ויען כי קשה היא לפנינו לבא על כונת הכתובים נפן על הסו נשה הידוע לנו מהחיסתוריה ונראה, כי מניסן מנו המלכים את שנתם, לא לבד מלכי המצרים כ"א גם מלכי ישראל משלמה והלאה; ולעומת זה נדע כי כל מלכי המזרח הארמענים והכשדים מנו אז את שנתם מחודש סעפטעמבער שהוא תשרי. ואם אמנם לא נדע איככה התנהגו בני ישראל ברשתם את ארץ כנען אם מנו את שנתם כהעם אשר יצא ממנו, או כי כהעם אשר ירש את מקומו, הנה ברור הוא: כי בזמן המשנה הקדומה, במלות אחרות, בימי הבית השני, מנו את שנתם הכוללת מתשרי; אבל יתבן עם כל זה כי מלכי הבית השני מנו את שנתם מניסן כהמלכים הקודמים (ואולי חשו גם להנכפל במקרא שתי פעמים „לכם ראש חדשים, ראשון הוא לכם" להזהיר שלא תעשו כמעשה הגרם שאתם באים שמה המונים את שנתם מתשרי) ובכל השטרות שגם בני ישראל נקבו בם את שנת מלכיהם כאשר כן היה המנהג אצל כל העמים, היתה איפוא התחלת השנה מניסן. התרומות והמעשרות בזמן הבית השני שברוב שנותיה היתה תחת ממשלת הכהנים ונשמרו בכל תוקף, הפרישו בצאת השנה (למנינה הכללית לא לשנת המלכים) להתרחק מן המחלוקות וערבוביא של התבואות משנה לשנה והוא בחודש אלול. ואך מעשר פירות האילן אחרו עד חודש שבט ר"ל תיכף אחרי החנטה של האילנות ג"כ כדי שלא לערב פירות שנה זו עם שנה הבאה, ולא לתת יד להכהנים הלוים לשלוט במעשי ידם.

²) המשנה הקדומה שכן היתה דרכה לדבר תמיד מן המנהג ולתקן ההלכה

כמוהו ולא לתקן את המנהג מן ההלכה *) בעת שנכנסית משנה זו מצאה ארבעה ראשי שנים, בארבעה חדשים. ותבא היא ותלמד להשות את המנהג הזה בכל מקום יתנבל את היום מהחודש, להראשון בו. וצורת המשנה כאשר היתה טרם שם רבי אותה בסדרה: ארבעה ראשי שנים הן: באחד בניסן, באחד באלול, באחד בתשרי, ובאחד בשבט. שלא היה להם כל צורך לפרש, מפני המנהג שהיה ידוע לכל ישראל, ואף רבי המסדר את המשנה שבימיו לא היו עוד מלכי ישראל וגם כבר נתרופף המעשר והתרומה, מפני שהכהנים הלרם לא שרתו עוד בבהמ"ק וממשלתם הוסרה מידם והזרה לבית דוד, הוסיף בביאור המשנה, למלכים, למעשר בהמה וגם את דעת ר"א ור"ש שאין עוד צורך למקצת החרדים הנוהגים עוד לעשר את בהמתם ואת תבואתם בחודש אלול כי אין חשש אם גם יתערבו בשנה הבאה, ועל כן תעשרנה בשנה הכללית שהיא תשרי, לרמז כי כן היא גם דעתו; (וכן הוסף כדברי ב"ש וב"ה, אולי מפני שבימיו נתאחרה החנטה והוא עצמו היה מבית הלל.)

3) מן המשנה בארבעה פרקים העולם נדון נראה, שכבר בימי המשנה היה יום ראש השנה ביום תשובה, ויען שעקר התשובה היא שעבוד הלב לאבינו שבשמים והתפלה על כליחת החטאים, בא רבי במשנתו (בפרק ראוהו ב"ד) והיה כאשר ירים משה ידו וכו' ללמד כי רק ההסתכלות כלפי מעלה ושעבוד הלב לשמים, ידרש בימי התשובה שהוא מן ר"ה עד יום הסליחה „יוהכ"פ." אך לא ידעה עוד מהספרים הנפתחים בר"ה שהמציאו האחרונים, והמלה „נדון" יש להבינה כמו שאמרו בני בתירא לריב"ז (לקמן בגמרא) נידון ואח"כ נתקע, והראיה מן הכתיב היוצר יחד לבם המבין על כל מעשיהם תתאים לזה, כי ההסתכלות כלפי מעלה גורמת פשפוש המעשים שנעשו למטה.**)

4) אחרי שסדר רבינו את מנין ראשי השנים, את תכלית יום הזכרון, דיני תקיעת ושמיעת שופר בקיצור נמרץ וכן את המנהג שהיה במקדש בשופר שהיה פיו מצופה זהב ושאין שום צורך בהכנה לתקיעת שופר כ"א העובר אחורי בהכנ"ס ושמע קול שופר עשה את חובתו. גם מנהג אמירת הפסוקים של מלכיות זכרונות שופרות לפני התקיעות בקיצור נמרץ, אחרי שכבר הקדים להן את עקר הדבר מהסתכלות כלפי מעלה ושעבוד הלב, האריך מאד בכל המשניות הנוגעות בענין ראיית הלבנה, שאך למנין חדשיה ימנו בנ"י, עדי הראיה, צורת המבלות שהיו לר"ג, והקבלות שהיו לו מאבותיו, כלומר החשבון האמתי, שעל פיהם קבל את העדים, ואת התקנות שהתקין ר' יוחנן בן זכאי שבזה השמיע שיש כח ורשות לגדול הדור להתקין דבר גם אם אינו כתוב בתורה, ואם גם יראה כגורע או מוסיף על דבריה. ושאך ביד הב"ד הגדול הרשות לתקן המועדים והחגים ולא לב"ד אחר ולאנשים פרטים אף שיהיו מגדולי העם, מפני שצריכה היתה אז האריכות הזאת, כי בימיו החלו כבר בני גולה להתאמץ וחפצו להסיר מהם את עול הנשיאות ולתקן המועדים לעצמם עפ"י חשבון חדשי הלבנה. ועל כן האריך לספר מה שקרה לזקנו ר' גמליאל עם ר' דוסא בן הרכינס ועם ר' יהושע שגם תמה החליטו ואמרו שאין לנו אלא מעשה בית דין שבימינו והוא חשוב כמעשה משה רבינו בעצמו אף על פי שנראה לעין כל שמעה או שגה. זו היא כל המסכתא כולה, שממנה תוצאות רבות להיסתוריה ימי קדם. ודל גמור!

*) כל החפץ לדעת את הראיות והנמקות שאין עליהם תשובה לאלו הדברים, יעיין נא במחברתנו ברקאי מצד 20 והלאה בהקדמתנו בשולי הגליון; ובמורה נבוכי הזמן שער י"ג ד"ה: „צורת ההלכה" ויקראנו עד תומו.

**) מאמרו של ר' כרוספדאי בשם ר"י, שג' ספרים נפתחין מקורו מן הברייתא ג' ספרים נפתחים ליום הדין אבל עם חכמת בית הדין התמוהים כפרושו של רש"י (ראה צד 17 בפנים ובאריכות בנוסחאות הישנות במקום הזה) ואשר אמרו משום ר' יוחנן אין לדרוש כי כן דרכם היתה לתלות באילן גדול דבר אשר רצונם היה שיתקבל, ור' יוחנן התיר זאת ולכן תלו בו, ודי למשכיל.

ארבעה ראשי שנים הם: באחד בניסן, ר״ה למלכים ולרגלים. באחד באלול ר״ה למעשר בהמה; ר״א ור״ש אומרים, באחד בתשרי. באחד בתשרי, ר״ה לשנים ולשמיטין וליובלות לנטיעה ולירקות. באחד בשבט, ר״ה לאילן, כדברי ב״ש. ב״ה אומרים, בחמשה עשר בו. גמ׳ למלכים, למאי הילכתא. אמר רב חסדא לשטרות. תנו רבנן מלך שעמד בעשרים ותשעה באדר, כיון שהגיע אחד בניסן עלתה לו שנה; ואם לא עמד אלא באחד בניסן, אין מונין לו שנה, עד שיגיע ניסן אחר. (ב:) וקמ״ל דניסן ר״ה למלכים. ויום אחד בשנה חשוב שנה. ואם לא עמד אלא באחד בניסן, אין מונין לו שנה עד שיגיע ניסן אחר ואע״ג דאימנו עליה מאדר, מהו דתימא נימנו ליה תרתין שנין, קמ״ל. ת״ר, מת באדר ועמד אחר תחתיו באדר, מונין שנה לזה ולזה; מת בניסן ועמד אחר תחתיו בניסן, מונין שנה לזה ולזה; מת באדר ועמד אחר תחתיו בניסן, מונין ראשונה לראשון. ושניה לשני. א״ר יוחנן, מניין למלכים שאין מונין להם אלא מניסן? שנאמר, (מלכים א ו) ,,ויהי בשמונים שנה וארבע מאות שנה לצאת בני ישראל מארץ מצרים בשנה הרביעית בחודש זיו הוא החדש השני למלך שלמה על ישראל'' מקיש מלכות שלמה ליציאת מצרים. מה יציאת מצרים מניסן, אף מלכות שלמה מניסן. ויציאת מצרים גופה מנלן דמניסן מנינן. דילמא מתשרי מנינן? לא סלקא דעתך, דכתיב (במדבר לג) ,,ויעל אהרן הכהן אל הר ההר על פי ה׳ וימת שם בשנת הארבעים לצאת בני ישראל מארץ מצרים בחדש החמישי באחד לחדש'' וכתיב (דברים א) ,,ויהי בארבעים שנה בעשתי עשר חדש באחד לחדש דבר משה ונומר'' מדקאי באב וקרי לה שנת ארבעים, וקאי בשבט וקרי לה שנת ארבעים, מכלל דר״ה לאו תשרי הוא. בשלמא היאך, מפרש דליציאת מצרים, אלא האי, ממאי דליציאת מצרים דילמא להקמת המשכן? שנת ארבעים לנזרה שוה, מה כאן ליציאת מצרים, אף

רש״י

למלכים, רגילים היו לכתוב זמן שטרותיהם לשנות המלך משנה שעמד בה המלך כדאמרי׳ במסכת גיטין משום שלום מלכות, וקבעו חכמים אחד בניסן לתחלת שנתו ואפי׳ עמד בשבט או באדר כלתה שנתו משהגיע ניסן ויתחילו למנות לו שנת שניה. למעשר בהמה, שאין מעשרין מן הנולדים בשנה זו על הנולדים בחבירתה. לשמיטין וליובלות, משנכנס תשרי אסור לחרוש ולזרוע מן התורה. לנטיעה, למנין שני ערלה ואפי׳ נטעה באב כלתה שנתה הראשונה לבוא אלול ובגמ׳ מפרש טעמא בגמ׳. לירקות, למעשר ירק שאין תורמין ומעשרין מן הנלקט לפני ר״ה על של אחר ר״ה. לאילן, לענין מעשר, שאין מעשרין פירות האילן שחנטו קודם שבט על שחנטו לאחר שבט, שבאילן הולך אחר חנטה. גמ׳ למאי הילכתא, כלומר לאיזה הלכה קבעו יום מיוחד למנין המלכים? איזו שייך בו מלך ומלך התחיל שנתו מיום שעמד בו. לשטרות, להבחין איזה שטר חוב מוקדם למלוה ואיזה מאוחר. עלתה לו שנה, כלומר כלתה לו שנתו ומעתה מונין לו שנת שנייה. דאימנו עליה, נמנו חכמיו השרים למנותו. לזה ולזה, הבא לכתוב שטר באדר לאחר שעמד השני, אם רצה לכתוב בשטר בשנת פלוני למלך שמת כותב, ואם רצה כותב בשנת ראשונה למלך פלוני שעמד. מת בניסן ועמד אחר תחתיו בניסן, הוא הדין אם עמד באחד מכל החדשים שעד ניסן הבא, ורצה למנות בכל השטרות שיכתבו משעמד השני למנין שנות הראשון מונה. והרוצה כותב בשנה ראשונה למלך שעמד. ושנייה לשני, הבא לכתוב משעמד זה לא ימנה שנה שנייה למלך שמת, שאין שנה זו שלו ולא ימנה את הראשונה לשני, לקרות שנה שעמד בה שנית, אלא שנייה זו ראשונה לשני. בחדש זיו, הוא אייר כדמפרש קרא הוא החדש השני ואמרינן לקמן ניסן ר״ה לחדשי מנין החדשים. למלך שלמה על ישראל, אשנה הרביעית קאי, ומקרא מסורס הוא: בשנה הרביעית למלך שלמה על ישראל בחדש זיו הוא החדש השני. מקיש מלכות שלמה, לענין מנין השנים ליציאת מצרים שהרי המקרא הזה מנה שנה זו שנת ד׳ מאות ושמונים ליציאת מצרים ובשנת ארבעה למלך שלמה. מה יציאת מצרים, מנין השנים שמונין לה מתחילין בניסן אף מלכות שלמה מניסן. דילמא מתשרי, אע״ג שיצאו בניסן משהגיע תשרי קראו לו שנת שנית, לפי שתשרי ר״ה לשנים ותקופות לבריאת עולם והוא הדין ליציאת מצרים. ויהי בארבעים שנה הואיל משה באר את התורה, מכלל דתשרי

באן ליציאת מצרים. וממאי דמעשה דאב קדים, דילמא מעשה דשבט קדים? לא ס"ד, דכתיב (שם) „אחרי הכותו את סיחון" וכי נח נפשיה דאהרן אכתי הוה סיחון קיים. דכתיב, (ג.) (במדבר כא) „וישמע הכנעני מלך ערד" מה שמועה שמע? שמע שמת אהרן ונסתלקו ענני כבוד וכסבור ניתנה רשות להלחם בישראל. מי דמי. התם כנען הכא סיחון? תנא, הוא סיחון, הוא ערד, הוא כנען. תניא כוותיה דר' יוחנן. מניין שאין מונין להם למלכים אלא מניסן? שנא', (מלכים א ו) „ויהי בשמונים שנה וארבע מאות שנה לצאת בני ישראל מארץ מצרים ונומר" וכתיב, (במדבר לג) „ויעל אהרן הכהן אל הר ההר על פי ה' ונומר" וכתיב „ויהי בארבעים שנה בעשתי עשר חדש" וכתיב (דברים א) „אחרי הכותו את סיחון ונומר" ואומר (במדבר כא) „וישמע הכנעני וגו' ואומר „ויראו כל העדה כי גוע אהרן ונומר", ואומר (שם י) „ויהי בחדש הראשון בשנה השנית ונומר" ואומר (שמות מ) „ויהי בשנה השנית בחדש השני ונומר" ואומר (שם יט) „בחדש השלישי לצאת בני ישראל ונומר" ואומר (ד"ה ב ג) „ויחל לבנות ונומר". א"ר חסדא, לא שנו אלא למלכי ישראל, אבל למלכי אומות העולם מתשרי מנינן, שנאמר, (נחמיה א) „דברי נחמיה בן חכליה ויהי בחדש כסלו שנת עשרים ונומר" וכתיב (שם ב) „ויהי בחדש ניסן שנת עשרים לארתחשסתא ונומר" מדקאי בכסליו וקרי ליה שנת עשרים, וקאי בניסן וקרי ליה שנת עשרים, מכלל דר"ה לאו ניסן הוא. בשלמא היאך מפרש דלארתחשסתא, אלא האי, ממאי דלארתחשסתא? דילמא, (ג:) למנינא אחרינא הוא? אמר רב פפא, שנת עשרים שנת עשרים לגזירה שוה; מה התם לארתחשסתא, אף הכא לארתחשסתא. וממאי דמעשה דכסליו קדים, דילמא מעשה דניסן קדים? לא סלקא דעתך, דתניא, דברים שאמר חנני לנחמיה בכסליו, אמרן נחמיה למלך בניסן, שנאמר, (נחמיה א) „דברי נחמיה בן חכליה ויהי בחדש כסלו שנת עשרים ואני הייתי בשושן הבירה ויבא חנני אחד מאחי ונומר, ושעריה נצתו באש ונומר, ויהי בחדש ניסן שנת עשרים לארתחשסתא המלך יין לפניו ונומר, וייטב לפני המלך וישלחני ואתנה לו זמן". מתיב רב יוסף, (חגי ב) „ביום עשרים וארבעה לחדש בששי בשנת שתים לדריוש" וכתיב, (שם) „בשביעי בעשרים ואחד לחדש" ואם איתא, בשביעי בשנת שלישית מבעי ליה? אמר רבי אבהו כורש מלך כשר היה לפיכך מנו לו במלכי ישראל. מתקיף לה רב יוסף, חדא דא"כ קשו קראי אהדדי! דכתיב (עזרא ו) „ושיציא ביתא דנא עד יום תלתא לירח אדר די היא שנת שית למלכות דריוש מלכא" ותניא, באותו זמן לשנה הבאה עלה עזרא מבבל וגלותו עמו, וכתיב, (שם ז) „ויבא ירושלים בחדש החמישי היא שנת השביעית למלך" ואם איתא, שנת השמינית מיבעי ליה? ועוד, מי דמי, התם כורש הכא דריוש? קשיא. (ד.) ולרגלים, רגלים באחד בניסן הוא, בט"ו בניסן הוא? אמר רב חסדא, רגל, שבו ראש השנה

ר ש"י

לאו ר"ה דאי תשרי ר"ה הוה ליה בשבט שנת מ"א. דילמא לתקמת המשכן, שהיה בשנה השנית. דילמא מעשה דשבט קדים, ובתשרי שלפניו נכנסה שנת ארבעים. אחרי הכותו את סיחון, נאמר במשנה תורה. תניא כוותיה דר' יוחנן, בכולי קראי דאייתי לעיל. ויבא חנני, מירושלים בא שכבר עלו בני הגולה מימות כורש והיו שם בימיו ובימי אחשורוש וארתחשסתא, והוא דריוש שאחר אחשורוש, שנבנה הבית בשנת שתים לדריוש, והרבה נשארו בבבל, ונחמיה בן חכליה היה שר המשקים למלך בשושן הבירה. בששי בשנת שתים, שניהם בנבואות חגי; נבדק במקרא ולא נמצא כתוב בפסוק שני בשנת שתים אך י"ל שלפסוק של מעלה חוזרין קאי שכתוב בו בשנת שתים. ודוא, ואם בניסן מנינן קשו קראי אהדדי. באותו זמן לשנה הבאה, ע"כ שביעית היא לו ממה נפשך. וכתיב בעזרא ויבא ירושלים בחדש החמישי, היא שנת השביעית למלך, ואי מנו לו מניסן שמינית היא, ועוד, אנן בדריוש קיימינן ואת אמרת כורש מלך כשר היה. רגל שבו ר"ה לרגלים, רגל שהוא

לרגלים. נפקא מינה, לנודר. למיקם עליה בבל תאחר, ורבי שמעון היא, דאמר ג׳ רגלים כסדרן וחג המצות תחילה. ת״ר, חייבי הדמין והערכין והחרמין וההקדשות חטאות ואשמות עולות ושלמים, צדקות ומעשרות, בכור ומעשר ופסח, (ד:) לקט שכחה ופאה, כיון שעברו עליהן שלשה רגלים, עובר בבל תאחר; ר״ש אומר שלשה רגלים כסדרן. וחג המצות תחילה. ר״מ אומר, כיון שעבר עליהן רגל אחד עובר בבל תאחר. ר׳ אליעזר בן יעקב אומר, כיון שעברו עליהן שני רגלים, עובר בבל תאחר. ר״א בר״ש אומר. כיון שעבר עליהן חג הסוכות עובר עליהן בבל תאחר. מ״ט דתנא קמא? מכדי מינייהו סליק למה לי למהדר ומיכתב (דברים טז) „בחג המצות ובחג השבועות ובחג הסוכות?״ שמע מינה, לבל תאחר. ור״ש אומר אינו צריך לומר בחג הסוכות, שבו דיבר הכתוב, למה נאמר? לומר שזה אחרון. ור״מ מ״ט? דכתיב (שם יב) „ובאת שמה והבאתם שמה״. ור׳ אליעזר בן יעקב מאי טעמא? דכתיב (במדבר כט) „אלה תעשו לה׳ במועדיכם״ מיעוט מועדים שנים. ור׳ אלעזר בר״ש מ״ט? דתניא ר״א בר״ש אומר: לא יאמר חג הסוכות שבו דיבר הכתוב, למה נאמר? לומר שזה גורם. ור״מ ורבי אליעזר בן יעקב, האי „בחג המצות ובחג השבועות ובחג הסוכות״ מאי דרשו ביה? מיבעי להו לכדרבי אלעזר אמר ר׳ אושעיא, דאמר ר״א א״ר אושעיא: מנין לעצרת שיש לה תשלומין כל שבעה? ת״ל „בחג המצות ובחג השבועות ובחג הסוכות״ מקיש חג השבועות לחג המצות, מה חג המצות יש לו תשלומין כל שבעה, אף חג השבועות יש לו תשלומין כל שבעה. למאי הילכתא כתביה רחמנא לחג הסוכות? לאקושיה לחג המצות, (ה.) מה חג המצות טעון לינה, אף חג הסוכות טעון לינה. והתם מנלן? דכתיב (דברים יז) „ופנית בבקר והלכת לאהליך״. (ה:) כנהני מילי? דתנו רבנן (דברים כג) „כי תדור נדר״. אין לי אלא נדר, נדבה מנין? נאמר כאן נדר ונאמר להלן (ויקרא ז) „אם נדר או נדבה״, מה להלן נדבה עמו, אף כאן נדבה עמו, „לה׳ אלהיך״, אלו הדמין הערכין והחרמין וההקדשות. (דברים כג) „לא תאחר לשלמו״ הוא ולא חילופיו. (שם) „כי דרוש ידרשנו״ אלו חטאות ואשמות עולות ושלמים, (שם)

רש״י

בחדש הנכנס באחד בניסן הוא ר״ה לרגלים. נפקא מינה, להאי ר״ה. לענין נדר שהוא עובר בבל תאחר, ותלה הכתוב אזהרתו בשלשה רגלים ואשמעינן מתני׳ שאינו עובר עד שיהא פסח ראשון לשלשתן, שאם עברו עליו שלא כסדרן אינו עובר. חייבי הדמין, אמר דמי עלי. והחרמין, חרמי גבוה. בכור ומעשר, מעשר בהמה. מכדי מינייהו סליק, כשאמר הכתוב: שלש פעמים בשנה יראה כל זכורך בחג המצות וגו׳ כתוב הוה עולה, כבר כתוב למעלה בענין שמור את חדש האביב: שבעה שבועות תספר לך, חג הסוכות תעשה לך. למה לי למיהדר, ולמכתבינהו בפרש׳ חג הסוכות? ש״מ לבל תאחר. וה״ק היו נראין לפני לשלם נדריכם ולא תבאו ריקם. אין צ״ל חג הסוכות, אף כשחוזרין לבל תאחר לא היה צריך להזכירו שהרי הענין עסוק בו. שבו דיבר הכתוב למה נאמר לומר שזה אחרון, עד שיעבור אותם כסדר הזה. מנין לעצרת, דאילו בחג הסוכות ובח״ג המצות נפקא לן מהתורות איתו חג לה׳ שבעת ימים יכול יהו תחגג כל ז׳? ת״ל אותו, אותו אתה חוגג, ואי אתה חוגג כל ז׳; אם כן למה נאמר ז׳? להשלומין, שאם לא חג חגיגתו בראשון, יקריבנה בשני. טעון לינה. ליל הרשים. ופנית בבקר, ב״ם לא קאמר קרא, שהרי הוא יום שיוצאו לראות בעזרת. מנא הני מילי, דאכל הנך דתניא במתני׳ לעיל איכא בל תאחר? נדר, הרי עלי. נדבה, הרי זו. נאמר להלן נדר, ואם נדר או נדבה וגו׳. אלו הדמין הערכין כו׳, שהן קדשי בדק הבית והולן לה׳ ואין לכהנים בהן כלום. הוא ולא חילופיו, עליו אתה עובר ולא על חילופיו. אלו חטאות ואשמות, שהן נדרשין ממך שהרי חובה הם מוטלין עליך. עולות ושלמים, כגון עולות ראיה ושלמי חגיגה שהן חובה, דאילו דנדר ונדבה ברישא דקרא כתיבי, והיה נמי לבכור ולמעשר ופסח שהן חובה. ה׳ אלהיך אלו צדקות ומעשרות, דהא קרא יתירא הוא, דהוה ליה למכתב כי דרש ידרשנו, ובכר ה׳ כתיב

„ה' אלהיך", אלו צדקות ומעשרות ובכור. (שם) „מעמך", זה לקט שכחה ופאה (שם) „והיה בך חטא" ולא בקרבנך חטא. (ו.) ת"ר. (דברים כג) „מוצא שפתיך" זו מצות עשה. „תשמור" זו מצות לא תעשה. „ועשית" אזהרה לב"ד שיעשוך. „כאשר נדרת", זה נדר. „לה' אלהיך" אלו חטאות ואשמות, עולות ושלמים. „נדבה" כמשמעו. „אשר דברת", אלו קדשי בדק הבית. „בפיך" זו צדקה. אמר רבא, וצדקה מיחייב עלה לאלתר. מ"ט? דהא קיימי עניים. פשיטא! מהו דתימא כיון דבענינא דקרבנות כתיבא, עד דעברי עליה ג' רגלים בקרבנות, קמ"ל, התם הוא דתלנהו רחמנא ברגלים, אבל הכא לא, דהא שכיחי עניים. (ו:) ואמר רבא, כיון שעברו עליו ג' רגלים, בכל יום ויום עובר בבל תאחר. מיתיבי, אחד בכור ואחד כל הקדשים, כיון שעברו עליהם שנה בלא רגלים, רגלים בלא שנה, עובר בבל תאחר! והאי מאי תיובתיה? אמר רב כהנא, מאן דקא מותיב, שפיר קא מותיב: מכדי תנא אלאוי קא מהדר, ליתני בכל יום ויום עובר בבל תאחר? ואידך, תנא למקבעיה בלאו קא מהדר, בלאוי יתירי לא קא מהדר. בשלמא רגלים בלא שנה משכחת לה. אלא שנה בלא רגלים, היכי משכחת לה? הניחא למאן דאית ליה כסדרן, משכחת לה, אלא למאן דלית ליה כסדרן היכי משכחת לה? בשלמא לרבי משכחת לה בשנה מעוברת, דאקדשה בתר חג המצות; דכי מטא שלהי אדר בתראה, שנה מלא, רגלים לא מלו, אלא לרבנן היכי משכחת לה? כדתני רב שמעיה: עצרת, פעמים חמשה פעמים ששה, פעמים שבעה, הא כיצד? שניהן מלאין, חמשה. שניהן חסרין, שבעה. אחד מלא ואחד חסר, ששה. בעי ר' זירא, יורש מהו בבל תאחר? (דברים כג) „כי תדור נדר" אמר רחמנא והא לא נדר, או דילמא (שם יג) „ובאת שמה והבאתם שמה" והא מיחייב! ת"ש, דתני רבי חייא (שם כג) „מעמך", פרט ליורש, והאי „מעמך" מיבעי ליה, זה לקט שכחה ופאה? קרי ביה עמך, וקרי ביה מעמך. בעי רבי זירא, אשה מה היא בבל תאחר? מי אמרינן, הא לא מיחייבה בראיה, או דילמא הא איתה בשמחה?

ר ש"י

לשעיה במקרא, נדרים ביה לאתויי צדקות ומעשרות שכתוב בהן שם זה: ולך תהיה צדקה לפני ה' אלהיך ואכלת לפני ה' אלהיך מעשר דגנך. מעמך זה לקט שכחה ופאה. שהן חלקו של עני דכתיב ביה את העני עמך. ולא בקרבנך חטא, אין הקרבן נפסל בכך. מוצא שפתיך זו מצות עשה, דמשתמע הכי אמר קרא: מוצא שפתיך קיים. תשמור זו מצות לא תעשה, בלא תאחר, כדר' אבין א"ר אילעאי כל מקום שנאמר השמר פן ואל כו'. ועשית, על כרחך, מכאן אזהרה לב"ד לכופו. לה' אלהיך, קרא יתירא הוא לדרשא, לרבות דבר שבחובה. בפיך זו צדקה, קרא יתירא דריש. יקריב אותו, קרא יתירא הוא, דהא כתיב בריישיה יקריבנו. שנה בלא רגלים, לקמיה מפרש. למקבעיה בלאו קא מהדר, להודיעך כל צידי זמן התחלת בל תאחר שבו. בלאוי יתירי לא מהדר, להודיעך לאורך הרבים שבו. הניחא למאן דבעי כסדרן משכחת לה, דעברה שנה ולא עברו רגלים כסדרן, ולמאן דבעין דעברה שנה, אע"פ שלא עברו רגלים כסדרן. רבי, וכבר לית ביה בחדא ודלית עליה בתרא. בשלמא לרבי, דאמר דרש העיבור אינו מן המנין חוץ מי"א יום שבשנת החמה יתירא על הלבנה, משכחת לה בשנה מעוברת. בתר חג המצות, בתוך הרגל, ואית דאמרי לאחר הרגל דהלוי אדר בתרא לאו דוקא, אלא לאחר שיצא אדר קאמר. שנה מלא, ג' מאות וששים וחמשה ימים. פעמי ששה, שהוא שבת בכיון יום החמשים לעומר. שניהם מלאים, ניסן ואייר. הוי מ"ו ימים בניסן ול' דאייר מלא להו חמשים בחמשה בסיון. אחד מלא כו', ומשכחת לה שנה בלא רגלים, כגון שניהם מלאים, ואירע עצרת בה' בסיון, והקדישה למחרת בו' בסיון, ולבנה תבאת הוו שניהן חסרים, ואירע עצרת בז' בסיון, והשנה מלאה ביום ו' בסיון משהקדישו, והרגל לא עבר עצרת עליו. יורש מהו בבל תאחר, על נדרי אביו. קרי ביה עמך ומעמך, הרי"ש בה תרתי: דיעמך משמע ליה חלקו של עני ומ' יתירא למעוטי יורש. מי אמרינן הא לא מיחייבה בראיה, דכתיב כל זכורך, וכיון דלא מחייבה לסיכך

א"ל אביי, ותיפוק ליה, דהא איתה בשכחה! איבעיא להו, בבור, מאימתי מונין לו שנה? אביי אמר משעה שנולד, רב אחא בר יעקב אמר משעה שנראה להרצאה; ולא פליגי, הא בתם, (ז.) הא בבעל מום. בעל מום מי מצי אכיל ליה? דקים ליה ביה שכלו לו חדשיו. ת"ר, באחד בניסן, ר"ה לחדשים, ולעיבורין, ולתרומת שקלים. וי"א אומרים, אף לשכירות בתים. לחדשים מנלן? דכתיב (שמות יב) „החדש הזה לכם ראש חדשים ראשון הוא לכם לחדשי השנה", וכתיב (דברים יז) „שמור את חדש האביב" איזהו חדש שיש בו אביב? הוי אומר זה ניסן, וקרי ליה ראשון. וליכא אדר? בעינא רוב אביב, וליכא. מידי רוב אביב כתיב? אלא אמר רב חסדא מהכא: (ויקרא כג) „אך בחמשה עשר יום לחדש השביעי באספכם את תבואת הארץ" איזהו חדש שיש בו אסיפה? הוי אומר, זה תשרי, וקא קרי ליה שביעי. ואימא אלול? ומאי שביעי, שביעי לאדר? בעינא רוב אסיף, וליכא. מידי רוב אסיף כתיב? אלא אמר רבינא, דבר זה מתורת משה רבינו לא למדנו. מדברי קבלה למדנו, (אסתר ג) „בחדש הראשון הוא חדש ניסן". ולעיבורין. לעיבורין מניסן מנינן? והתניא אין מעברין אלא אדר! אמר רב נחמן בר יצחק, מאי עיבורין? הפסקת עיבורין. ותנא דידה, בהתחלה קמיירי בהפסקה לא קמיירי. ולתרומת שקלים. מנלן? א"ר יאשיה אמר קרא (במדבר כח) „זאת עולת חדש בחדשו לחדשי השנה". אמרה תורה חדש, והבא קרבן מתרומה חדשה; ונכרי שנה שנה מניסן, דכתיב (שמות יב) „ראשון הוא לכם לחדשי השנה". אמר רב יהודה אמר שמואל, קרבנות צבור הבאין באחד בניסן, מצוה להביא מן החדש; ואם הביא מן הישן יצא אלא שחיסר מצוה. ויחיד שהתנדב משלו כשירין, ובלבד שימסרם לצבור. פשיטא! מהו דתימא, ליחוש שמא (ז:) לא ימסרם לציבור יפה יפה, קא משמע לן. ותנא דידן, כיון דקתני אם הביא יצא, לא פסיקא ליה. „וי"א אומרים אף לשכירות בתים". תנו רבנן, המשכיר בית לחבירו לשנה, מונה שנים עשר חודש מיום ליום. ואם אמר לשנה זו, אפילו לא עמד אלא באחד באדר, כיון שהגיע יום אחד בניסן עלתה לו שנה. ואימא תשרי? סתם כי

ר ש"י

לא שייר בה זמן רגלים לכל תאחר. או דילמא מחייבה למיפק משום שמחה, דכתיב ושמחת בחגך. הא בתם, דקאי להרצאה משנראה להרצאה. בעל מום, שנולד במומו וקאי לשחט בדוק, מיום שנולד הוא ראוי לכך ומונין לו משנולד. מי מצי אכיל ליה, ביום שנולד דילמא נפל הוא ואין צריכה שנותיו עד שיהו שמונה ימים? לחדשים, למנין חדשי הלבנה. לעיבורין, קא סלקא דעתיה לישב בית דין ולעיין, אם השנה הבאה צריכה להתעבר. ולתרומת שקלים, להקריב ראשון קרבנות הציבור מתרומת קופות של שקלי שנה זו. אף לשכירות בתים, המשכיר בית לחבירו ואמר לשנה זו, כלתה שנתו באחד בניסן, ואפי' לא דר בו אלא חדש אדר. החדש הזה לכם, ומנין דניסן? דכתיב ויקחו להם שה לפסח, וכתיב בתריה שמור את חדש האביב, שיש בו אביב, שהתבואה בגבעה בו להיות מבושלת כגמר בשולה. בעינא אביב וליכא, שכבר נגמרה בניסן, ואי איכא זרעא אפילה אין זה בכיר, אלא אפיל. ואיכא אדר, דאיכא זרעא דרישא המתבכר מאדר. רוב אביב, שרוב התבואות מתבכרות בו. שיש בו אסיפה, שמכניסין בו פירות לבית מפני הגשמים, וכל הקיץ הן בשדות נדרכין ליבש. אין מעברין, אין מעיינין בצרכי צבור להודיע לגולה שעיברו ב"ד את השנה, שלא ישתכח הדבר עד אדר הבא. אין מעברין אלא אדר, אין מוסיפין חודש על השנה אלא אדר, דכתיב שמור את חדש האביב, חדש הסמוך עבר, שיבוא אביב בזמנו. הפסקת עיבורין, שכיון שקדשו את החדש לשם ניסן פסקה שנה שעברה מלהיות מעוברת עוד שאין רשאין לעשות ניסן אדר, שכבר נכנסת שנה אחרת לענין עיבור. בהפסקה לא קא מיירי, בראשי שנים והפסקה לא קא מיירי. חדש בחדשו לחדשי, חדשי יתירא לדרשא. יפה יפה, בלב שלם. ותנא דידן, דלא תנייה במתני'. כיון דקתני אם הביא יצא לא פסיקא ליה מילתא דלידשבה בראשי שנים. אלא באחד באדר, אבל בבציר מתני לא אמרינן עלתה לו שנה הדי בה שנה שלימה.

אגר איניש ביתא. דכולהו ימות הגשמים אגר; והנא קמא דברייתא, ותנא דידן,
בניסן נמי מישכח שכיח קיטרי: „באחד באלול, ראש השנה למעשר בהמה״. מני?
אמר רב יוסף, רבי היא ונסיב לה אליבא דתנאי: ברגלים סבר לה כרבי שמעון,
ובמעשר בהמה סבר לה כרבי מאיר. אי הכי ארבעה, חמשה הוו? אמר רבא ארבעה
לדברי הכל! לרבי מאיר ארבעה, ד׳ רגלים, לרבי שמעון ארבעה, ד׳ מעשר בהמה.
רב נחמן בר יצחק אמר, ארבעה חדשים. ובהן כמה ראשי שנים. (ה.) „רבי אלעזר
ורבי שמעון אומרים באחד בתשרי״. א״ר יוחנן, ושניהם מקרא אחד דרשו, שנאמר
(תהלים סה) „לבשו כרים הצאן ועמקים יעטפו בר יתרועעו אף ישירו״ ר״מ סבר, אימתי
לבשו כרים הצאן, בזמן שעמקים יעטפו בר; ואימתי עמקים יעטפו בר, מאדר:
מתעברות באדר, ויולדות באב, ר״ה שלהן אלול. רבי אלעזר ור״ש אומרים אימתי
לבשו כרים הצאן? בזמן שיתרועעו אף ישירו. אימתי שבלים אומרות שירה? בניסן;
מתעברות בניסן ויולדות באלול, ר״ה שלהן תשרי. רבא אמר דכ״ע. לבשו כרים הצאן
בזמן שעמקים יעטפו בר באדר, והכא בהאי קרא קמיפלגי (דברים יד) „עשר תעשר״
בשני מעשרות הכתוב מדבר: אחד מעשר בהמה. ואחד מעשר דגן; ר״מ סבר, מקיש
מעשר בהמה למעשר דגן, מה מעשר דגן סמוך לגמרו עישורו. אף מעשר בהמה כמוך
לגמרו עישורו. ור״א ור״ש סברי, מקיש מעשר בהמה למעשר דגן, מה מעשר דגן ר״ה
שלו תשרי, אף מעשר בהמה. ר״ה שלו תשרי. „באחד בתשרי ר״ה לשנים״: למאי
הלכתא? אמר רבי זירא לתקופה. ור״א היא. דאמר בתשרי נברא העולם. רב נחמן
בר יצחק אמר, לדין, דכתיב (דברים יא) „מראשית השנה ועד אחרית שנה״ מראשית
השנה נידון מה יהא בסופה. ממאי דתשרי הוא? דכתיב (תהלים כא) „תקעו בחדש
שופר בכסה ליום חגנו״, אי זהו חג (ח:) שהחודש מתכסה בו? הוי אומר, זה ר״ה.
וכתיב (תהלים כא) „כי חק לישראל הוא. משפט לאלהי יעקב״. ת״ר „כי חק לישראל״
מלמד. שאין ב״ד של מעלה נכנסין לדין, אא״כ קידשו ב״ד של מטה את החדש.

ר ש ״ י

דליכא למימר דארעתא דההיא שתא אגרא דלא שכיר איניש למיגר ביתא לבציר מתלתין יומין, ואיפכא תשרי, ר״ה לשכירות בתים. אם לא עמד אלא בא׳ באלול כיון שהגיע תשרי עליה יו שנתו ומשני כי אגר איניש ביתא בכור יתשרי לבילדו ימי הגשמים אגר. ות״ק דברייתא, דלא אמר לשכירות בתים. קיטרי, עבים מתקשרין תשמים יורדין והוי ימות הגשמים. רבי היא, הוא אמרה למתני׳, ונסיב מילתא הדא כחד תנא. והדא כחד תנא. אי הכי, והד גברא אמרה למתניתין ונסיב מילתיה חדא כחד תנא, חמשה ראשי השנים ניהוו אחד בניסן, וחמשה עשר בניסן, ואחד באלול, ואחד בתשרי, וחמשה עשר בשבט! הא ניחא אי סבירא ליה לרישא כרבי שמעון, שפיר, דלדידה ארבעה ניהוו, דלית ליה אחד באלול, אלא אי הך תנא מברתו קשיא! אמר רבא, לעולם רבי היא, ורבי קאמר: אנא חמשה סבירא לי, ובינהו דבר׳ מודים לי בארבעה. לרבי מאיר, דאית ליה אחד באלול, ד׳ רגלים, ולדידיה בעלי אחד עשר בפל תאו״ה, כדתניא בברייתא דלעיל. ולר״ש ד׳ מעשר בהמה, דליתיה אלא באחד בתשרי, וגיאו מעשר נמי ראש השנה הוא. והן כמה ראשי שנים, הילכך ניכן דאית בית תרי. דר׳ דכתיב ביה. לבשו כרים הצאן, מתלבשות הכבשים שמתעברות. יעטפו בר, שהזריעה צומחת ומכסה ינת. יתרועעו אף ישירו, בניסן באביב זמן הקציר והתבואה בקשי׳ שית והרוח מנשבת והן נוקשים זו על זו, נשמע הקול ונראות כמשוררות. וזמן עיבור בהמה דקה חמשה חדשים. ר״ה שלהן אלול, הסמוך לגמרו זמן דרש והן שלהן לידות השנה. בזמן שיתרועעו, השיבולים. מעשר דגן סמוך לגמרו עשורו, ר״ה למעשרות תשרי והכי תני ליה לקמן, ותשרי סמוך לגמרו הוא, דכל ימות החמה מגדלי לבש בגרנות השדות. לתקופה, למנין שמונין לבריתן ומילוכן של תקופות החמה ומולדות הלבנה מתשרי. לדין, שהקב״ה דן בתשרי את כל באי העולם. שהחודש מתכסה בו, להחוקים כגון שהריות לבני מערב הרינה לבני מזרח לפי שקטנה היא סמוך להודשה. אלא אם כן קדשו החדש כו׳, הה״ד אם קבעו ישראל את חק החדש:

תניא אידך. כי חק לישראל הוא. אין לי אלא לישראל לאוה״ע מנין? ת״ל „משפט לאלהי יעקב״ א״כ מה ת״ל „כי חק לישראל?״ מלמד, שישראל נכנסין תחילה לדין. כדרב חסדא דאמר, מלך וצבור, מלך נכנס תחילה לדין. שנאמר (מלכים א ח) „משפט עבדו ומשפט עמו״ מאי טעמא? אי בעית אימא, לאו אורח ארעא למיקם מלכא אבראי. ואי בעית אימא, מקמי דליפרוש חרון אף. ולשמיטין. מנלן? דכתיב (ויקרא כה) „ובשנה השביעית שבת שבתון יהיה לארץ״ וגמר שנה, שנה מתשרי, דכתיב (דברים יא) „מראשית השנה״. וליובלות. יובלות באחד בתשרי, בי׳ בתשרי הוא? דכתיב (ויקרא כה) „ביה״כ תעבירו שופר״ הא מני, רבי ישמעאל בנו של רבי יוחנן בן ברוקה היא, דתניא (שם) „וקדשתם את שנת החמשים שנה״, מה ת״ל? לפי שנאמר „ביה״כ״ יכול לא תהא מתקדשת אלא מיה״כ ואילך. ת״ל וקדשתם את שנת החמישים מלמד שמתקדשת והולכת מתחילתה, מכאן א״ר ישמעאל בנו של ר׳ יוחנן בן ברוקא: מר״ה עד יה״כ לא היו עבדים נפטרין לבתיהן, ולא משתעבדין לאדוניהם, אלא אוכלין ושותין ושמחין ועטרותיהן בראשיהן; כיון שהגיע יה״כ, תקעו ב״ד בשופר, נפטרו עבדים לבתיהם, ושדות חוזרות לבעליהן. תניא אידך, יובל היא „מה ת״ל?״ לפי שנא׳ „וקדשתם את שנת החמישים״, יכול כשם שמתקדשת והולכת מתחילתה, כך מתקדשת והולכת בסופה; ואל תתמה, שהרי מוסיפין מחול על קודש? ת״ל (שם) „יובל היא שנת החמשים״, שנת החמשים אתה מקדש ואי אתה מקדש שנת החמישים ואחת. (ט.) ורבנן, שנת חמישים אתה מונה, ואי אתה מונה שנת חמישים ואחת. לאפוקי מדר׳ יהודה, דאמר, שנת חמישים עולה לכאן ולכאן, קא משמע לן, דלא. (ט:) תנו רבנן (ויקרא כה) „יובל היא״ אע״פ שלא שמטו אף על פי שלא תקעו. יכול אע״פ שלא שלחו? תלמוד לומר, היא! דברי רבי יהודה; רבי יוסי אומר, „יובל היא״ אע״פ שלא שמטו, אע״פ שלא שלחו, יכול אף על פי שלא תקעו? ת״ל היא! וכי מאחר שמקרא אחד מרבה ומקרא אחד ממעט מפני מה אני אומר יובל הוא אע״פ שלא שלחו ואין יובל אלא א״כ תקעו? לפי שאפשר לעולם בלא שילוח עבדים, ואי אפשר לעולם בלא תקיעת שופר. דבר אחר, זו מסורה לבית דין, וזו אינה מסורה לבית דין. מאי דבר

ר ש״י

והא משפט להקב״ה. מלך וציבור, כשהקב״ה דן אותם מלך נכנס תחילה, משפט עבדו, שלמה קאמר ליה. דליפרוש חרון אף, בשביל עונות ציבור. מנלן, דשנת שמיטה מקודשת מר״ה או ור בעבודת הקרקע? וקדשתם שנת החמשים מה ת״ל, מכיון שאמר שבע שבתות שנים והעברת שופר בחדש השביעי, יודע אני שהיא שנת החמשים, שנים אתה מקדש, כשבשנת יובל נכנסת. מצוה על ב״ד לומר מקודשת השנה. ואי אתה מקדש יום חדש, כר״א בר״ש דאמר לקמן בין שנראה בזמנו בין שלא נראה בזמנו אין מקדשין אותו. לפי שנאמר וקדשתם את שנת החמשים, דילפינן מיניה שמתקדשת מתחילתה. יכול כך מתקדשת בסופה. אחר ר״ה ותמשך עד יה״כ? ואל תתמה, אם מוסיפין אותה בתוך שנה שלאחריה. שהרי מוסיפין מחול על קודש, כדאמרינן לקמן. ת״ל יובל היא, מיעוטא היא. ורבנן, הוא לפי שמקדשתם שתתקדש מתחילתה ולא איצטריך היא למעוטי כוונה דרישי ליה הכי: שנת החמשים אתה מונה ואי אתה מונה שנת היובל שנת חמשים למנין יובל שעבר ואחת למנין יובל הבא, ואי אתה מונה שנת היובל תבא אלא כשי״ת שלאחר היובל. ולאפוקי מדר׳ יהודה, דאמר במסכת נדרים שנת חמשים עולה לכאן ולכאן, שנת היובל ושנה ראשונה לשמיטה הבאה. יובל היא יובל אע״ג ש״א שמטו כו׳, לעיל מיניה כתיב והעברת שופר וקדשתם את שנת החמשים שנה וקראתם דרור והדר כתיב יובל היא תהיה לכם וקרא יתירא הוא לדרשא והכי תדרשנה יובל היא לכם מכל מקום ואפילו לא נעשו בו דברים הללו: העברת שופר ולשוב איש לאחוזתו, אע״פ כן שם היובל עליו להיות אסור בזריעה ובצירה וקצירה. יכול אע״פ שלא שלחו, עבדים, יהא יובל? ת״ל היא, אם עשית דברים הללו היא יובל, ואם לאו אינו יובל. שאפשר לעולם בלא שילוח עבדים, פעמים שאין עבד עברי בישראל שיצטרך שילוח.

אחר? וכי תימא, אי אפשר דליכא חד בסוף העולם דלא משלח, זו מסורה לבית דין וזו אינה מסורה לבית דין. אמר רבי חייא בר אבא א"ר יוחנן זו דברי ר' יהודה ור' יוסי, אבל חכמים אומרים שלשתן מעכבות בו. וקסברי, מקרא נדרש לפניו ולפני פניו ולאחריו. והכתיב „יובל" ההוא דאפילו בחוצה לארץ, והכתיב „בארץ" ההוא, בזמן שנוהג דרור בארץ, נוהג בחוצה לארץ, בזמן שאינו נוהג בארץ, אינו נוהג בחוצה לארץ, ולנטיעה. מנלן דכתיב (ויקרא יט) „שלש שנים ערלים" וכתיב (שם) „ובשנה הרביעית" וילף שנה שנה מתשרי דכתיב (דברים יא) „מראשית השנה". ת"ר, אחד הנוטע ואחד המבריך ואחד המרכיב ערב שביעית, שלשים יום לפני ראש השנה, עלתה לו שנה, ומותר לקיימן בשביעית. פחות מל' יום לפני ראש השנה, לא עלתה לו שנה, ואסור לקיימן בשביעית. (י.) ופירות נטיעה זו, אסורין עד ט"ו בשבט, אם לערלה ערלה, ואם לרבעי רבעי. מה"מ? א"ר חייא בר אבא אמר ר' יוחנן ומטו בה משמיה דר' ינאי, אמר קרא, (ויקרא יט) „ובשנה הרביעית ובשנה החמישית" פעמים שברביעית ועדיין אסורה משום ערלה, ופעמים שבחמישית ועדיין אסורה משום רבעי. (י:) תניא, ר"א אומר, בתשרי נברא העולם, בתשרי נולדו אבות, בתשרי מתו אבות, בפסח נולד יצחק, בר"ה נפקדה שרה רחל וחנה, בראש השנה יצא יוסף מבית האסורין, (יא.) בר"ה בטלה עבודה מאבותינו במצרים, בניסן נגאלו, בתשרי עתידין ליגאל. רבי יהושע אומר בניסן נברא העולם, בניסן נולדו אבות, בניסן מתו אבות, בפסח נולד יצחק, בר"ה נפקדה שרה רחל וחנה, בר"ה יצא יוסף מבית האסורין, בר"ה בטלה עבודה מאבותינו במצרים, בניסן נגאלו, בניסן עתידין ליגאל. תניא רבי אליעזר אומר, מנין שבתשרי נברא העולם? שנ' (בראשית א) „ויאמר אלהים תדשא הארץ דשא עשב מזריע זרע עץ פרי" איזהו חדש שהארץ מוציאה דשאים ואילן מלא פירות, הוי אומר זה תשרי. ואותו הפרק זמן רביעה היתה, וירדו גשמים וצמחו שנאמר (שם ב) „ואד יעלה מן הארץ". ר' יהושע אומר, מנין שבניסן נברא העולם? שנאמר (שם א) „ותוצא הארץ דשא עשב מזריע זרע ועץ עושה פרי" איזהו חדש שהארץ מליאה דשאים ואילן מוציא פירות, הוי אומר זה ניסן; ואותו הפרק זמן בהמה וחיה ועוף שמזדווגין זה אצל זה. שנאמר, (תהלים סה) „לבשו כרים הצאן וגומר", ר"א אומר מנין שבתשרי נולדו אבות? שנאמר (מ"א ח) „ויקהלו אל המלך שלמה

רש"י

ואי אפשר. שלא יהא שופר מצוי בעולם לסייעך יש לנו לומר כשתלה הכתוב לא תלה אלא בדבר המסור לעולם. ר"א תקיעת שופר מסורה לב"ד. לצוות לשלחם לחירות, ושילוח עבדים מסורה ליחידים ואם ימאנו יבטל היובל הלכך לא תלאו הכתוב בו. ולאחריו, שמיטת קרקעות דכתיב בתריה ושבתם איש אל אחוזתו. והכתיב יובל, לרבות בשמטת יובל ח"ל. ולנטיעה מנין, דר"ה שלה תשרי? מבריך, כופף את הזמורה בארץ. מרכיב, אילן בחבירו. עלתה לו שנה. כיון שהגיע יום אחד בתשרי עלתה לו שנה למנין שני ערלה. פחות משלשים יום לא עלתה לו שנה, עד תשרי הבא, אם אינה ערב שביעית, ואם ערב שביעית היא אסור לקיימו משום תוספת שביעית שמוסיפין מחול על קודש. אסורים כו', ואע"פ שאמרנו עלתה לו שנה אם חנטו בה פירות לאחר ר"ה של שנה שלישית עד עדיין אסורין הן ערלה משום ערלה, שאע"פ שראש השנה תשרי לנטיעה, ט"ו בשבט ר"ה לאילן: וזו כבר נעשית אילן, לציבור אין שנתה מתחדשת לצאת מידי ערלה עד ט"ו בשבט. כגא הני מילי, ששנות ערלה ורבעי נמשכין לאחר פירות החנוטים קודם ט"ו בשבט לאחר שכלו שלשת שני ערלה? ומטו בה, יש מבין ומבררין בשמועה זו לאומרה משמיה דר' ינאי. פעמים שברביעית, כגון אם מיהר פירותיו לחנוט ברביעית לפני שבט. פעמים שבחמישית, כגון פירות שחנטו בה קודם שבט משנת חלול. נולדו אבות, אברהם ויעקב. נפקדה שרה, בא זכרונה לפניו ונגזר עליה הריון. בטלה עבודה מאבותינו, ששה חדשים לפני גאולתם פסק השיעבוד. עץ פרי, שנגמר פריו. ועץ עושה פרי ולא עץ פרי גמור. לבשו כרים, בזמן שמתעברות שטלים בניסן.

כל איתן ישראל בירח האיתנים בחג" ירח שנולדו בו איתני עולם. מאי משמע דהאי איתן לישנא דתקיפי הוא? כדכתיב (במדבר כד) „איתן מושבך", ואומר (מיכה ו) „שמעו הרים את ריב ה׳ והאיתנים מוסדי ארץ". רבי יהושע אומר „מנין שבניסן נולדו אבות? שנאמר (מלכים א ו) „ויהי בשמונים שנה וארבע מאות שנה לצאת בני ישראל מארץ מצרים בשנה הרביעית בחדש זיו" בירח שנולדו בו זיותני עולם. מ״ד בניסן נולדו, בניסן מתו; מ״ד בתשרי נולדו, בתשרי מתו. שנאמר (דברים לא) „ויאמר אליהם בן מאה ועשרים שנה אנכי היום" שאין ת״ל היום, ומה ת״ל היום? היום מלאו ימי ושנותי, ללמדך שהקב״ה יושב וממלא שנותיהם של צדיקים מיום ליום ומחדש לחדש, שנאמר (שמות כג) „את מספר ימיך אמלא". בפסח נולד יצחק, מנלן? כדכתיב (בראשית יח) „למועד אשוב אליך" אימת קאי? אילימא בפסח, וקאמר ליה בעצרת, בחמשין יומין מי קא ילדה? אלא דקאי בעצרת וקאמר ליה בתשרי, אכתי בחמשה ירחי מי קא ילדה? א״א דקאי בחג וקאמר ליה בניסן, אכתי בשיתא ירחי מי קא ילדה? תנא אותה שנה מעוברת היתה, ואמר מר זוטרא, אפי׳ למ״ד יולדת לתשעה אינה יולדת למקוטעין, יולדת לשבעה יולדת למקוטעין שנאמר (שמואל א א) „ויהי להקופת הימים" מיעוט תקופות שתים ומיעוט ימים שנים. בר״ה נפקדה שרה, רחל וחנה, מנלן? א״ר אלעזר, אתיא פקידה פקידה, אתיא זכירה זכירה, כתיב ברחל (בראשית ל) „ויזכור אלהים את רחל", וכתיב בחנה (שמואל א א) „ויזכרה ה׳" ואתיא זכירה זכירה מר״ה, דכתיב (ויקרא כג) „שבתון זכרון תרועה"; פקידה פקידה, כתיב בחנה (שמואל א ב) „כי פקד ה׳ את חנה" וכתיב בשרה (בראשית כא) „וה׳ פקד את שרה". בר״ה יצא יוסף מבית האסורין, מנלן? דכתיב (תהלים פא) „תקעו בחדש שופר בכסה ליום חגנו כי חק לישראל הוא ונומר" (יא:) „עדות ביהוסף שמו בצאתו ונומר". בראש השנה בטלה עבודה מאבותינו במצרים, כתיב הכא (שמות ו) „והוצאתי אתכם מתחת סבלות מצרים" וכתיב התם (תהלים פא) „הסירותי מסבל שכמו". בניסן נגאלו, כדאיתא. בתשרי עתידין ליגאל: אתיא שופר שופר, כתיב הכא „תקעו בחודש שופר" וכתיב התם (ישעי׳ כז) „ביום ההוא יתקע בשופר גדול". רבי יהושע אומר בניסן נגאלו, בניסן עתידין ליגאל, מנלן? אמר קרא (שמות יב) „ליל שמורים" ליל המשומר ובא מששת ימי בראשית. (יב.) ת״ר, חכמי ישראל מונין למבול כר׳ אליעזר, ולתקופה כרבי יהושע; חכמי אומות העולם מונין אף למבול כר׳ יהושע. ולירקות. תנא לירקות ולמעשרות ולנדרים, לירקות מאי ניהו, מעשר ירק? היינו מעשרות! הנא דרבנן,

---

ר ש״י

בחודש זיו, אייר הוא, שנולדו בו זיותני עולם. כשנתחדש אייר נולדו כבר בניסן, א״נ דמנין דניסן ותקופה נמשך בתוך אייר של לבנה. לתתנאות, להגות. למועד אשוב אליך, ליום הבא ראשון ולפרי בן. אפילו למ״ד, במסכת נדה, אינה יולדת למקוטעין, אלא לחדשים שלמים של שלשים יום. עדות ביהוסף שמו, בתרית דהדוא קרא כתיב דכי חק לישראל. הסירותי מסבל שכמו, ביוסף כתיב בתר עדות ביהוסף. המשומר ובא, לגאולה. חכמי ישראל מונין למבול כרבי אליעזר, מונין שנות נח ובריאת עולם ושנות הדורות מתשרי תחלת השנים, ולא משום דסבירי להו בתשרי נברא העולם, אלא דתשרי ראש השנה לשנים; ולתקופה כרבי יהושע, כשמונין תקופת החמה והלבנה מונין מניסן, לומר שבניסן נבראו, ובתחילת ליל רביעי שמשה חמה בניסן, לפיכך אין תקופת ניסן נופלת אלא בד׳ רביעי היום. אף למבול, כלומר למנין שנות הדורות מתחילין בניסן למנות, ומבול בא׳ ירח, ע״כ משתאמר באחת ושש מאות בראשון שחרבו המים, ניסן הוא שהרי משפט דור המבול שנים עשר חדש. הלירקות, מעשר ירק לענין חדש וישן, שאין תורמין מירק הנלקט ערב ר״ה על הנלקט אחר ראש השנה. ולנדרים, לקמן מפרש. הנא דרבנן, דמעשר ירק קבוע ר״ה לענין חדש וישן כמעשר ירק דרבנן, ותרי תנאי מעשר דגן דאמא לו יום קבוע לחדש וישן שלו. ותנא וידן,

וקתני דאורייתא. וליתני דאורייתא ברישא? איידי דחביבא ליה אקדמיה. ותנא דידן תנא דרבנן וכ"ש דאורייתא. ת"ר ליקט ירק ערב ר"ה עד שלא תבא השמש וחזר וליקט (יב:) משתבא השמש, אין תורמין ומעשרין מזה על זה, לפי שאין תורמין ומעשרין לא מן החדש על הישן ולא מן הישן על החדש. אם היתה שנייה נכנסת לשלישית, שנייה מעשר ראשון ומעשר שני, שלישית מעשר ראשון ומעשר עני. מנה"מ? אמר ריב"ל (דברים כו) „כי תכלה לעשר את כל מעשר תבואתך בשנה השלישית שנת המעשר", שנה שאין בה אלא מעשר אחד, הא כיצד? מעשר ראשון ומעשר עני. ומעשר שני יבטל; או אינו אלא אף מעשר ראשון נמי יבטל? ת"ל (במדבר יח) ואל הלוים תדבר ואמרת אליהם כי תקחו מאת בני ישראל את המעשר אשר נתתי לכם מאתם בנחלתכם" הקישו הכתוב לנחלה, מה נחלה אין לה הפסק, אף מעשר ראשון אין לו הפסק. ולנדרים וכו'. ת"ר, המודר הנאה מחבירו לשנה, מונה שנים עשר חודש מיום ליום, ואם אמר לשנה זו, אפילו לא עמד אלא בעשרים ותשעה באלול, כיון שהגיע יום אחד בתשרי, עלתה לו שנה, לצעורי נפשיה קביל עליה והא אצטער ליה. ואימא ניסן? בנדרים הלך אחר לשון בני אדם. תנן התם, התלתן משתצמח, התבואה והזיתים משיביאו שליש, מאי משתצמח? משתצמח לזרעים. התבואה והזיתים משיביאו שליש, מנה"מ? אמר רב אסי א"ר יוחנן ומטו בה משמיה דרבי יוסי הגלילי, אמר קרא (דברים לא) „מקץ שבע שנים במועד שנת השמטה בחג הסוכות" שנת השמטה מאי עבידתיה בחג הסוכות, שמינית היא? אלא לומר לך כל תבואה שהביאה שליש בשביעית לפני ר"ה אתה נוהג בו מנהג שביעית בשמינית. אמר ליה רבי זירא לרב אסי. (יג.) ודילמא לא עייל כלל וקאמר רחמנא השמט והזיל עד חג הסוכות? לא ס"ד, דכתיב (שמות כג) „וחג האסיף בצאת השנה" מאי אסיף? אילימא חג הבא בזמן אסיפה, הכתיב „באספך". אלא מאי אסיף, קציר. וקים להו לרבנן,

---

רש"י

דתנא לירקות ולא תנא למעשרות. תנא דרבנן, ואשמעינן דיום קבוע לו כ"ש דאורייתא. ליקט ירק, אשמועינן דירק בתר לקיטה אזיל לענין מעשר, ואע"פ שגדל בשנה א', אם נלקט בשתי שנים הוי חדש וישן, שאין תורמין מן החדש על הישן, דכתיב שנה שנה. שנייה, מה שנלקט בשנת שנייה של שמיטה מעשר ראשון ללוי ומעשר שני בירושלים, ומה שנלקט בשנה שלישית מעשר ראשון ומעשר עני. מנא הני מילי, דבשלישית אינו נוהג בה מעשר שני. שנה שאין נוהג בה אלא אחד, מן המעשרות שנהגו בשתי שנים שלפניה. הא כיצד מעשר ראשון, יתן כדרך שנתן עד הנה. ומעשר עני, יוכיח במקום מעשר שני כדכתיב לגר ליתום ולאלמנה, והוא מעשר עני. או אף מעשר ראשון יבטל, ושנת המעשר חד קאמר, הדיא דמפרש ואזיל ללוי לגר ליתום ולאלמנה, והוא מעשר עני שאף לוי בכלל עני שאין לו חלק בארץ. ובא הלוי, ומעשר ראשון כל זמן שנא' ובא הלוי וגו' והא בשנה שלישית כתיב: מקצה שלש שנים תוציא ובא הלוי וגו'. לשון בני אדם, שאין אדם נודר אלא על לשון שהוא רגיל לדבר, ודרך בני אדם לקרות תשרי ר"ה. התילתן, מין קטנית. כשתצמח, יותר שנת צמיחתו הוא מתעשר ולא אחר שנת לקיטתו. כשתצמח לזרעים, שהזרע צומח בתוכו. התבואה, דגן ותירוש קרויין תבואה, דכתיב כתבואת גורן וכתבואת יקב. והזיתים, יצהר משיביאו שליש מתעשרין אחר שנת שהגיעו בו לשליש בין שנייה אם שלישית. מנא הני מילי, אתבואה ואזיתים קאי דמעשר דידהו דאורייתא, ומנלן דבתר שליש אזלי? מאי עבידתיה, לקרות חג הסוכות בסוף שבע שנים שנת השמטה, הרי כבר יצאה השביעית מר"ה וכבר נכנסה שמינית. אלא לומר לך כו', והכי קרא יש לך דבר שהוא של שביעית והוא אסור כשביעית ואיזו זו תבואה שהגיעה שליש. ודילמא לא עייל כלל, ואפילו לא התחילו לתבשל בשביעית קאמר רחמנא כנוהו שביעית לימשך איסורה עד חג הסוכות מלדרוש ולקצור. לא ס"ד, ולא תיקרי קרא אלא כשתביאו שליש וסוכה קרא אחרינא. מאי חג האסיף, אילימא דהוא יום סוכות ומשום דבא בזמן אסיפה למה לי דכתיב בתר קרא תרי זימני? הא כתיב בהדיא קרא נמי באספך את מעשיך. אלא מאי

דכל תבואה שנקצרה בחג, בידוע שהביאה שליש לפני ר"ה, וקא קרי לה בצאת השנה. מתקיף לה רבי חנינא, ומי מצית אמרת דהאי אסיף קציר הוא, והכתיב (דברים טז) "באספך מגרנך ומיקבך", ואמר מר בפסולת גורן ויקב הכתוב מדבר? א"ר זירא הא מילתא הואי בידן, ואתא ר' חנינא ושדא ביה נרגא, אלא, מנלן? כדתניא, רבי יונתן בן יוסף אומר (ויקרא כה) "ועשת את התבואה לשלש השנים", (יג.) אל תקרא לשלש, אלא לשליש. והא מיבעי ליה לגופיה? כתיב קרא אחרינא (ויקרא כה) "וזרעתם את השנה השמינית ואכלתם מן התבואה ישן עד השנה התשיעית". תנן התם, האורז והדוחן והפרגין והשומשמין שהשרישו לפני ר"ה, מתעשרין לשעבר ומותרין בשביעית, ואם לאו אסורין בשביעית ומתעשרין לשנה הבאה. אמר רבה, אמור רבנן: אילן בתר חנטה, תבואה וזיתים בתר שליש, ירק בתר לקיטה, הני כמאן שוינהו רבנן? הדר אמר רבה, מתוך שעושין פרכין פרכין אזלי רבנן בתר השרשה. (יד.) תניא רבי יוסי הגלילי אומר (דברים טז) "באספך מגרנך ומיקבך" מה גורן ויקב מיוחדין שגדילין על מי שנה שעברה ומתעשרין לשנה שעברה, אף כל שגדילין על מי שנה שעברה, מתעשרין לשנה שעברה, יצאו ירקות שגדילין על מי שנה הבאה, ומתעשרין לשנה הבאה. רבי עקיבא אומר "באספך מגרנך ומיקבך" מה גורן ויקב מיוחדין שגדילין על רוב מים ומתעשרין לשנה שעברה, אף כל שגדילין על רוב מים, מתעשרין לשנה שעברה, יצאו ירקות שגדילין

ר ש"י

אסיף קציר, וחה"ק וחג אשר הוא באספך את מעשיך מן השדה, אסיף אשר אתה קוצר בו אינו משנה הנכנסת, אלא משנה היוצאת, ולסוף כאן שקציר החג הולך אחר שנה שעברה, וקים להו לרבנן שאמרו התבואה אחר שליש, דכל תבואה שנקצרת ברגל בידוע שהביאה שליש לפני ר"ה, וקא קרי לה בצאת השנה, שהיא משנה היוצאת, אלמא תבואה אחר שליש. דהאי אסיף קציר, דקאמרת דהאי אסיף יתירא למידרשיה לשון קציר הוא, והא כתיב, בעלמא באספך מגרנך ומיקבך. ואמר מר, שלמדך הכתוב לעשות סכך של סוכה בפסולת גורן ויקב כגון קשין וזמורות, דבר שאין מקבל טומאה וגידולו מן הארץ. הא מילתא הוה בידן, היינו סבורין שנלמוד מכאן שתבואה אחר שליש. ואתא רבי חנינא שדא ביה נרגא, לומר דהאי אסיף שפיר משתמע בלישנא דקרא ולאו יתירא הוא. ועשת את התבואה לשלש השנים אל תקרי לשלש אלא לשליש, שעשיתה כשהיא בשליש בישולה. לגופיה, תשובה על מה נאכל בשנה השביעית. האורז והדוחן כו', מיני קטניות הן. מתעשרין לשעבר, במעשרות שנה שעברה, אם שניה מעשר שני ואם שלישית מעשר עני. ומותרין בשביעית, אם השרישו ערב שביעית לפני ר"ה, ומתעשרים לשנה הבאה, בשנת לקיטתן אם מעשר עני שנה היא, שאינה שביעית. בתר חנטה, לקמן תנא לה באילן שחנטו פירותיו קודם חמשה עשר בשבט, שהוא ר"ה לאילנות, מתעשר לשנה שעברה. ירק בתר לקיטה, כדאמרן לעיל ליקט ירק ערב ר"ה כו'. הני, קטניות כמאן שוינהו, שהלכו בהן אחר השרשה. מתוך שעושין פרכין פרכין, מתוך שגדלין קשר קשר, שאין נלקטין כאחד, אלא היום לוקטין ומפרכין מעט, ולמחר מעט, ונמצאו חדש וישן מעורבין יחד, הנפרכין לפני ר"ה עם הנפרכין לאחר ר"ה, אם הולכין בהן אחר לקיטה כשאר ירק כשהוא בפרכים מעשרותיו, הו"ל כמעשר מן החדש על הישן ומן הישן על החדש, אזלי בהו בתר השרשה, שבשנה אחת משרשת כל השדה, שהרי בבת אחת זורעין אותה ומעשר פירות האילן וקטניות וירק מדרבנן הן, ומסורה ביד חכמים לקבוע זמן לפי דעתם לכל אחד ואחד. באספך מגרנך ומיקבך, מכאן סמכו חכמים לקבוע זמן מעשר ירק דרבנן אחר לקיטה לאסמכתא בעלמא, כל אסיף שלך יהא כתרומת גורן ויקב, שהלכה בהן תורה אחר שנה שתביאות שליש, הרי שהלכה בהן אחר שנה שגדלו בשנה, שתבואת שליש שלהן היא גדילתן, שבאותה שנה ראויה ליקצר בדוחק. אף כל בו', לכך הלכו באילן אחר חנטה, שכל גדילת פירותיו ע"י שהלכלות שרף האילן לפני חנטה הוא. יצאו ירקות שגדילין על שנה הבאה, והיינו שנת לקיטתן, שהרי נגזזין אותה והיא תחלת גדילת. רוב מים, הם מי גשמים, שרוב ארצם גדלים על ידם. על כל מים, אף על שאובין שגדלין ומשקין אותן תמיד, כענין שנאמר והשקית ברגלך כגן הירק, סתם גן הירק דרכו בהשקאה. בצלים חכריסים, שאין נקשין גדולין כשאר בצלים. ומל

על כל מים ומתעשרין לשנה הבאה. מאי בינייהו? א"ר אבהו בצלים הסריקין ופול המצרי איכא בינייהו: דתנן, בצלים הסריסין ופול המצרי שמנע מהן מים שלשים יום לפני ראש השנה, מתעשרין לשעבר ומותרין בשביעית, ואם לאו אסורין בשביעית ומתעשרין לשנה הבאה. באחד בשבט ר"ה לאילן. מ"ט? א"ר אלעזר א"ר אושעיא הואיל ויצאו רוב גשמי שנה. אע"פ שרוב תקופה מבחוץ. ת"ר, מעשה ברבי עקיבא שליקט אתרוג באחד בשבט, ונהג בו שני עישורין: (יד:) אחד כדברי בית שמאי, ואחד כדברי בית הלל. רבי יוסי בר יהודה אומר לא מנהג בית שמאי ובית הלל נהג בה, אלא מנהג רבן גמליאל ור' אליעזר נהג בה. באחד בשבט כבית שמאי נהג בה? אמר ר' חנינא ואיתימא רבי הנניא הכא באתרוג שחנטו פירותיה קודם חמשה עשר ראידך שבט עסקינן, ובדין הוא אפילו קודם לכן, ומעשה שהיה כך היה. רבינא אמר כרוך ותני: לא אחד בשבט היה, אלא ט"ו בשבט היה, ולא מנהג בית שמאי ובית הלל נהג בה אלא מנהג רבן גמליאל ורבי אליעזר נהג בה. (טו.) אמר רבה בר הונא: אף על גב דאמר רבן גמליאל אתרוג אחר לקיטה כירק, ראש השנה שלו שבט. מאי שנא התם דקתני: אם היתה שנייה נכנסת לשלישית, ומאי שנא הכא דקתני: אם היתה שלישית נכנסת לרביעית? מילתא אגב אורחיה קמ"ל, דאתרוג קשיא ליה ידא, ואיידי דממשמשי בה כולי עלמא בשביעית, לא טענה פירי עד תלת שנין. בעא מיניה רבי יוחנן מרבי ינאי: אתרוג ראש השנה שלו אימתי? אמר ליה: שבט. שבט דחדשים, או שבט דתקופה? א"ל: דחדשים. בעא מיניה רבא מרב נחמן, ואמרי לה רבי יוחנן מרבי ינאי: היתה שנה מעוברת מהו? א"ל, הלך אחר רוב שנים. (טו:) איתמר, רבי יוחנן ור"ש לקיש אמרי תרוייהו: אתרוג בת ששית שנכנסה לשביעית, לעולם ששית. כי אתא רבין א"ר יוחנן: אתרוג בת ששית שנכנסה לשביעית אפי' כזית ונעשית ככר, חייבין עליה משום טבל. ת"ר, אילן שחנטו פירותיו קודם ט"ו בשבט, מתעשר לשנה שעברה, אחר חמשה עשר בשבט

ר ש " י

המצרי. שורשו לירק, ראי זרעו לזרע קטנית הוא ולא הזכירו בו אלא אחר השרשה. איכא בינייהו. כגון שמנע מהם מים ולא השקן ל' יום לפני ר"ה ולקטן אחר ר"ה, דתנן, כו' ר' יוסי הגלילי אית ליה הא מתני', דכיון דמנע מים שלשים יום לפני ר"ה נמצאו גדלין על מי שנה שעברה, ולר"ע הרי גדלים על כל מים ומתעשרין להבא. באחד בשבט ר"ה לאילן, ואין תורמין מפירות אילן שחנטו פירותיו קודם לכן על פירות דאילן שחנטו לאחר מכאן. הואיל ויצאו רוב גשמי שנה, שכבר עבר רוב ימות הגשמים שהוא זמן רביעה ועלה השרף באילנות ונמצאו הפירות חונטין מעתה. שליקט אתרוג, פירות אילן אתרוג. שני עישורים, מעשר שני בשנה שניה ומעשר עני בשנת שלישית, שהיתה שניה נכנסת לשלישית. אחד כדברי ב"ש, שאמרו נתחדש שנה כבר נכנסת שלישית מכשחשכה. ואחד כדברי ב"ה, דאמרין לא נתחדשה שנה עד חמשה עשר בו. לא מנהג ב"ש כו', שני עישורין שנהג בה לאו משום כספק כב"ש כספק כב"ה, אלא משום כספק הלכה כר"ג, דאומר אתרוג אחר לקיטה כירק, או שמא כר"א דאמר אחרי חנטה הלכו בו כשאר אילנות. דאידך שבט, דאשתקד, ובט"ו בשבט דאשתקד נכנסה שנה שלישית ועדיין לא יצאת שלישית, נמצאת שחנטה בשנייה ונלקטה בשלישית. ובדין הוא, דאם לקטה קודם לכן נמי הוה נוהג בה שני עישורין, משום מנהג דר"ג ור"א. אלא מעשה שהיה, באחד בשבט היה. כרוך ותני, כגזל את דברי רבי יוסי שנה בה שתי מחלוקות. אתרוג קשיא ליה ידא, קשה לקין האתרוג ידים ממשמשות בו. שבט דחדשים, של לבנה. או שבט דתקופות, לסוף שלשים של תקופת טבת נכנס שבט של חמה. היתה שנה מעוברת מהו, איזהו ר"ה? שבט הסמוך לטבת, או אדר הראשון שהוא במקום שבט? אחר רוב שנים, מי ששמו שבט. לעולם ששית, חייבת במעשר ופטורה מן הביעור. אפילו כזית, אפילו לא גדלה בששית אלא מעט ורובה גדלה בשביעית עד שנעשית ככר, חייבת משום טבל דבתר חנטה אזלינן. שתי בריכות סיר, אין לשון זה נופל אלא בעופות, כדתנן: חלוקת פירות שובך

מתעשר לשנה הבאה. אמר ר' נחמיה: במה דברים אמורים באילן שעושה שתי בריכות בשנה; שתי בריכות ס"ד? אלא אימא כעין שתי בריכות, אבל אילן העושה בריכה אחת, כגון דקלים וזיתים וחרובין, אף על פי שחנטו פירותיהן קודם ט"ו בשבט, מתעשרין לשנה הבאה. א"ר יוחנן, נהגו העם בחרובין כרבי נחמיה. איתיביה ר"ש לקיש לרבי יוחנן: בנות שוח שביעית שלהן שנייה, מפני שעושות לשלש השנים? אישתיק. (טז.) **מתני'** בארבעה פרקים העולם נידון: בפסח על התבואה, בעצרת על פירות האילן, בר"ה כל באי עולם עוברין לפניו כבני מרון, שנאמר (תלים לג) „היוצר יחד לבם המבין אל כל מעשיהם", ובחג נידונין על המים. **גמ'** הי תבואה. אילימא הא תבואה דקיימא? כל הני הרפתקי דעדו עלה אימת איתדון? אלא תבואה דמזדרעה, למימרא דחד דינא מתדנא? והתני': תבואה שאירע בה קרי או אונס קודם הפסח, נידונית לשעבר, לאחר הפסח נידונית להבא, אדם שאירע בו קרי או אונס, קודם יה"כ נידון לשעבר, לאחר יה"כ נידון להבא! אמר רבא, ש"מ תרי דיני מתדנא. אמר אביי, הלכך כי חזי איניש דמצלח זרעא אפלא, ליקדים וליזרע הרפא, דעד דממטי למדייניה, קדים סליק. מני מתני'? לא ר"מ, ולא ר' יהודה, ולא ר' יוסי, ולא רבי נתן! דתניא: הכל נידונים בר"ה, וגזר דין שלהם נחתם ביה"כ, דברי ר"מ; רבי יהודה אומר, הכל נידונין בר"ה, וגזר דין שלהם נחתם כל אחד ואחד בזמנו: בפסח על התבואה, בעצרת על פירות האילן, בחג נידונין על המים, ואדם נידון בר"ה, וגזר דין שלו נחתם ביה"כ; רבי יוסי אומר, אדם נידון בכל יום, שנאמר (איוב ז) „ותפקדנו לבקרים" רבי נתן אומר, אדם נידון בכל שעה, שנאמר (שם) „לרגעים תבחננו" וכי תימא לעולם רבי יהודה היא, וכי קתני מתני' אגזר דין, אי הכי, קשיא אדם? אמר רבא, האי תנא דבי ר' ישמעאל היא, דתנא דבי רבי ישמעאל: בארבעה פרקים העולם נידון; בפסח על התבואה, בעצרת על פירות האילן, בחג נידונין על המים, ואדם נידון בר"ה, וגזר דין שלו נחתם ביה"כ, וכי קתני מתני', אתחילת דין. אמר רב חסדא: ורבי יוסי מ"ט לא אמר כרבי נתן? בחינה עיוני בעלמא היא. פקידה נמי עיונא בעלמא היא? אלא אמר רב חסדא טעמיה דרבי יוסי מהכא (מלכים א ח) „לעשות משפט עבדו ומשפט עמו ישראל דבר יום ביומו". א"ר יוסף כמאן מצלינן האידנא אקצירי ואמריעי? כרבי יוסי. תניא א"ר יהודה משום ר"ע, מפני מה אמרה תורה הביאו עומר בפסח? מפני שהפסח זמן תבואה הוא: אמר הקב"ה, הביאו לפני עומר בפסח, כדי שתתברך לכם תבואה שבשדות; ומפני מה אמרה

ר ש"י

מפריח הברכה ראשונה. כעין שתי בריכות, שאין פירותיו נגמרין בא' כגון תאנים כדאמרן גבי קבניות מתוך שעושין פרכין. אבל אילן, שפירותיו נלקטין באחד, בתר לקיטה אזלינן בהו. בנות שוח, מפרש במסכת ע"ז תאיני חיורתא. שביעית שלהן שנייה, שביעית שלהן נוהגת בשנה שנייה של שמטה. מפני שעושות לשלש שנים, פירות החונטים בה בשביעית אין נגמרין עד שנה שנייה של שמטה. מתני' בארבעה פרקים, בשנה. גמ' תבואה דקיימא, השתא במחובר. הרפתקי, מקראות. דעדו עלה, שעברו עליה. דמזדרעה, שעתיד לזרוע במרחשון הבא. דחד דינא, פעם אחת. קרי, כגון ברד או שדפון. נידונית לשעבר, קודם שנזרעת דהיינו פסח של אשתקד. נידונית להבא, בפסח שאחר זריעתה. נידון לשעבר, וביה"כ של אשתקד נגזר עליו. להבא, ביה"כ שעבר עכשיו בקרוב. תרי דיני מיתדנא, קודם זריעתה וכסוף לקציר. כי חזי איניש דמצלח זרעא אפלא, רפות וכוסמת שנזרעין במרחשון שאין ממהרין להתבשל. ליקדים וליזרע הרפא, השעורה ממהרת להתבשל וזורעים אותה בשבט ואדר, דכיון דאפלא מצלח שמע מינה לטובה נידון בפסח שעבר, לפיכך ימהר לזרוע בזריעה שנית. דעד דממטי למדיניה, בפסח הבא. קדים סליק, ותרי קמת ואינו ממהר שוב להתקלקל. וכי קתני מתני', ארבעה פרקים אגזר דין. קשיא אדם, דתני

תורה הביאו שתי הלחם בעצרת? מפני שעצרת זמן פירות האילן הוא, אמר הקב"ה: הביאו לפני שתי הלחם בעצרת, כדי שיתברכו לכם פירות האילן. ומפני מה אמרה תורה, נסכו מים בחג? אמר הקב"ה: נסכו לפני מים בחג, כדי שיתברכו לכם גשמי שנה, ואמרו לפני בר"ה: מלכיות, זכרונות ושופרות; מלכיות, כדי שתמליכוני עליכם; זכרונות, כדי שיעלה זכרוניכם לפני לטובה, ובמה? בשופר. א"ר אבהו, למה תוקעין בשופר של איל? אמר הקב"ה: תקעו לפני בשופר של איל, כדי שאזכור לכם עקידת יצחק בן אברהם, ומעלה אני עליכם כאילו עקדתם עצמכם לפני. (טז:) א"ר יצחק, אין דנין את האדם אלא לפי מעשיו של אותה שעה שנאמר (ראשית כא) "כי שמע אלהים אל קול הנער באשר הוא שם"; וא"ר יצחק, ג' דברים מזכירין עונותיו של אדם, אלו הן. קיר נטוי, ועיון תפלה, ומוסר דין על חבירו, דא"ר אבין כל המוסר דין על חבירו הוא נענש תחילה, שנאמר (שם יו) "ותאמר שרי אל אברם חמסי עליך", וכתיב (שם כג) "ויבא אברהם לספד לשרה ולבכתה [וה"מ דאית ליה דינא בארעא (בב"ק צג)]; וא"ר יצחק, ד' דברים מקרעין גזר דינו של אדם, אלו הן: צדקה, צעקה, שינוי השם, שינוי מעשה; צדקה, דכתיב (משלי י) "וצדקה תציל ממות", צעקה, דכתיב (תהלים קז) "ויצעקו אל ה' בצר להם וממצוקותיהם יוציאם", שינוי השם, דכתיב (ראשית יז) "שרי אשתך לא תקרא את שמה שרי כי שרה שמה", וכתיב, "וברכתי אותה וגם נתתי ממנה לך בן", שינוי מעשה, דכתיב (יונה ג) "וירא האלהים את מעשיהם", וכתיב, (שם) "וינחם האלהים על הרעה אשר דבר לעשות להם ולא עשה", וי"א אף שינוי מקום, דכתיב (בראשית יב) "ויאמר ה' אל אברם לך לך מארצך" והדר, "ואעשך לגוי גדול". א"ר כרוספדאי א"ר יוחנן, ג' ספרים נפתחין בר"ה: אחד של רשעים גמורין, ואחד של צדיקים גמורין, ואחד של בינוניים; צדיקים גמורין נכתבין ונחתמין לאלתר לחיים, רשעים גמורין נכתבין ונחתמין לאלתר למיתה. בינוניים תלויין ועומדין מר"ה ועד יוה"כ, זכו, נכתבין לחיים, לא זכו, נכתבין למיתה. א"ר אבין, מאי קרא? (תהלים סט) "ימחו מספר חיים ועם צדיקים אל יכתבו". תניא ב"ש אומרים ג' כתות הן ליום הדין: אחת של צדיקים גמורין, ואחת של רשעים גמורין, ואחת של בינוניים; צדיקים גמורין נכתבין ונחתמין לאלתר לחיי עולם. רשעים גמורין נכתבין ונחתמין לאלתר לגיהנם, שנאמר (דניאל יב) "ורבים מישני אדמת עפר יקיצו אלה לחיי עולם ואלה לחרפות לדראון עולם", בינוניים יורדין לגיהנם (יז.) ומצפצפים ועולין, שנאמר (זכריה יג) "והבאתי את השלישית באש וצרפתים כצרוף את הכסף ובחנתים כבחון את הזהב הוא יקרא בשמי ואני אענה אותו", ועליהם אמרה חנה (שמואל א ב) "ה' ממית ומחיה מוריד שאול ויעל". בה"א "ורב חסד", מטה כלפי חסד, ועליהם אמר דוד (תהלים קי)

ר ש "י

מתני' בר"ה ורבי יהודה בחג אמר. ובי קתני מתניתין, ארבעה פרקים. אתחלת דין, אבל גזר דין דאדם ביוה"כ. קציר, תולים. פי"ע, ת"ח יהן השותי כח. כרבי יוסי, דאמר אדם נידון בכל יום ויתפלל שידונו אותו לזכות. שתבואת זמן תבואה היא, זמן שהתבואה נידונת בו. שתי הלחם, יוצאו על פירות האילן שדן בתירין להביא בכורים. של אותה שעה, ואפילו הוא עתיד להרשיע לאחר זמן. שנאמר באשר הוא שם, אינו דן את הקולם אלא במעשו. קיר נטוי, ועובר תחתיו ומזכיר עונותיו, שאומרים כולם ראוי זה ליעשות לו נס? ומתוך כך הוא נבדק. עיון תפלה, בוטח על תפלתו שתהא נשמעת ומתאמץ לכוין לבו. מוסר דין, כמו ישפוט ה' ביני וביניך, אומרים כולם ראוי הוא שיענש חבירו על ידו? דבא אברהם וגו', הוא קבר אותה. שינוי מעשה, שב מרעתו. שלשת ספרים נפתחין, ספרי זכרון של מעשה הבריות. ליום הדין, כשיחיו המתים, רשעים גמורים, רובם עונות. בינוניים, מחצה על מחצה. מצפצפים, צועקים ובוכים מתוך יסורין שבה אתת ועולין. מטה כלפי חסד, תשיל ומחצה על מחצה הם מטה את ההכרע לצד זכות.

„אהבתי כי ישמע ה׳ את קולי", ועליהם אמר דוד כל הפרשה כולה „דלותי ולי יהושיע". פושעי ישראל בגופן, ופושעי עכו"ם בגופן יורדין לגיהנם ונידונין בה י"ב חדש, לאחר י"ב חדש גופן כלה ונשרף ורוח מפזרתן תחת כפות רגלי צדיקים, שנא׳ (מלאכי ג) „ועסותם רשעים כי יהיו אפר תחת כפות רגליכם". אבל המינין והמסורות והאפיקורסים שכפרו בתורה, ושכפרו בתחיית המתים, ושפירשו מדרכי צבור, ושנתנו חיתיתם בארץ חיים, ושחטאו והחטיאו את הרבים, כגון ירבעם בן נבט וחביריו, יורדין לגיהנם ונידונין בה לדורי דורות, שנאמר (ישעיה כו) „ויצאו וראו בפגרי האנשים הפושעים בי" וגומר, גיהנם כלה והן אינן כלין, שנאמר (תהלים כב) „וצורם לבלות שאול", וכל כך למה? מפני שפשטו ידיהם בזבול, שנאמר „מזבול לו". ועליהם אמרה חנה (שמואל א ב) „ה׳ יחתו מריביו". א"ר יצחק בר אבין, ופניהם דומין לשולי קדירה. ואמר רבא ואינהו משפירי שפירי בני מחוזא, ומקריין בני גיהנם. פושעי ישראל בגופן מאי ניהו? אמר רב קרקפתא *) דלא מנח תפילין. פושעי עכו"ם בגופן, בעבירה. ושנתנו חיתיתם בארץ חיים, אמר רב חסדא, „זה פרנס המטיל אימה יתירה על הציבור שלא לשם שמים. א"ר יהודא אמר רב, כל פרנס המטיל אימה יתירה על הצבור שלא לשם שמים, אינו רואה בן תלמיד חכם, שנאמר (איוב לז) „לכן יראוהו אנשים לא יראה כל חכמי לב". בה"א ורב חסד מטה כלפי חסד, היכי עביד? רבי אליעזר אמר, כובשו, שנאמר (מיכה ז) „ישוב ירחמנו יכבוש עונותינו". ר׳ יוסי בר חנינא אמר נושא, שנאמר (שם) „נושא עון ועובר על פשע". תנא דבי רבי ישמעאל. מעביר ראשון ראשון, וכן היא המדה. אמר רבא, ועון עצמו אינו נמחק, דאי איכא רובא עונות מחשיב בהדייהו. ואמר רבא, כל המעביר על מדותיו, מעבירין לו על כל פשעיו, שנאמר „נושא עון ועובר על פשע", למי נושא עון? למי שעובר על פשע. רב הונא בריה דרב יהושע חלש, על רב פפא לשיולי ביה, חזייה דחליש ליה עלמא, אמר להו: צביתו ליה זוודתא. לסוף איתפח, הוה מיכסיף רב פפא למיחזייה, א"ל מאי חזית? אמר להו אין הכי הוה, ואמר להו הקב"ה הואיל ולא מוקים במיליה, לא תקומו בהדיה, שנאמר „נושא עון ועובר על פשע" למי נושא עון? לעובר פשע; (שם) „לשארית נחלתו" אמר רבי אחא בר חנינא, אליה וקוץ בה: לשארית נחלתו, ולא לכל נחלתו, (יל:) למי שמשים עצמו כשירים. רב הונא רמי: כתיב (תהלים קמה) „צדיק ה׳ בכל דרכיו", וכתיב, „וחסיד בכל מעשיו"? בתחלה צדיק, ולבסוף חסיד.

רש"י

המינין, האנשים אשר הפכו דברי אלהים חיים לרעה. והמסורות, מלשינים. אפיקורוס, מבזה תלמידי חכמים. שכפרו בתורה, האומרין אין תורה מן השמים. תורם, כמו תורתם. שפשטו ידיהם בזבול, שהחריבו בית המקדש. בני מחוזא, מעונגים ומעדנים היו. ומקרין בני גיהנם, כך יקראו להם. [בעבירה, בעריות שבין נח מוזהר עליו כדאיתא בד׳ ארבע מיתות (תוספות)]. כובש, את כף המאזנים של זכות ומכריעין את העונות. נושא, מגביה כף מאזנים של עון. מעביר ראשון ראשון, עון שבראשונים הבאים להם לכף מעבירו ומוכחו וכך היא המדה. ועון עצמו אינו נמחק, דאי איכא רובא עונות בתרי ההוא עון מתחשב בהדייהו. המעביר על מדותיו, שאינו מדקדק למדוד מדה למצערים אותו. מעבירין לו על כל פשעיו, אין מדת הדין מדקדקת אחריהן. צביתו ליה זוודתא, הכינו לו צדה לדרך, מת הוא צידת המתים? תכריכין. איתפח, נתרפא. דכי הוה, מיתה נגזרה עלי. לא מוקי׳ במיליה, אינו מעמיד על מדותיו. לא תקומו בהדיה, לא תדקדקו אחריו. אליה, שמינה יש כאן. וקוץ בה, כלומר דבר תגרובן יש כאן, אבל יש בתוכה דבר קשה שאינו שוה לכל. צדיק, במשפט אמת. חסיד, נכנס לפנים מן השורה. ולבסוף, יכולין

*) עיין הערה על פירושו של המאמר הזה בסוף המסכתא.

רבי אלעזר רמי, כתיב (שם סב) „ולך ה׳ חסד״, וכתיב „כי אתה תשלם לאיש כמעשהו״? בתחילה כי אתה תשלם כמעשהו, ולבסוף ולך ה׳ חסד. אילפי ואמרי לה אילפא רמי, כתיב (שמות לד) „ורב חסד״, וכתיב „ואמת״? בתחילה ואמת, ולבסוף ורב חסד. „ויעבור ה׳ על פניו ויקרא״, א״ר יוחנן אלמלא מקרא כתוב אי אפשר לאומרו, מלמד שנתעטף הקב״ה כשליח צבור והראה לו למשה סדר תפלה, אמר לו כ״ז שישראל חוטאין, יעשו לפני כסדר הזה, ואני מוחל להם. „ה׳ ה׳״ אני הוא קודם שיחטא האדם, ואני הוא לאחר שיחטא האדם ויעשה תשובה; „אל רחום וחנון״ אמר רב יהודה ברית כרותה לי״ג מדות שאינן חוזרות ריקם, שנאמר (שם) „הנה אנכי כורת ברית״. א״ר יוחנן, גדולה תשובה שמקרעת גזר דינו של אדם, שנאמר (ישעיה ו) „השמן לב העם הזה וגו׳ ובאזניו ישמע ולבבו יבין ושב ורפא לו״. א״ל רב פפא לאביי, ודלמא לפני גזר דין? א״ל „ורפא לו״, כתיב, איזהו דבר שצריך רפואה? הוי אומר זה גזר דין! מיתיבי השב בינתים, מוחלין לו, לא שב בינתים, אפילו הביא כל אילי נביות שבעולם אין מוחלין לו? לא קשיא, הא ביחיד, הא בצבור. ת״ש, (תהלים קז) „יורדי הים באניות עושי מלאכה במים רבים המה ראו מעשי ה׳ וגו׳ ויאמר ויעמד רוח סערה ותרומם גליו יחוגו וינועו כשכור וגו׳ ויצעקו אל ה׳ בצר להם וגו׳ יודו לה׳ חסדו ונומר״, עשה להן סימניות, כאכן ורקן שבתורה, לומר לך צעקו קודם גזר דין, נענין, צעקו לאחר גזר דין, אינן נענין? הני נמי כיחידין דמו. ת״ש, שאלה בלוריא הגיורת את רבן גמליאל: כתיב בתורתכם (דברים י) „אשר לא ישא פנים״, וכתיב (במדבר ו) „ישא ה׳ פניו אליך״, נטפל לה רבי יוסי הכהן, אמר לה אמשול לך משל, למה הדבר דומה? לאדם שנושה בחבירו מנה, וקבע לו זמן בפני המלך, ונשבע לו בחיי המלך, הגיע זמן ולא פרעו, בא לפייס את המלך, ואמר לו עלבוני מחול לך, לך פייס את חבירך; הכא נמי, כאן בעבירות שבין אדם למקום, כאן בעבירות שבין אדם לחבירו. (עד.) וגזר דין דיחיד תנאי היא, דתניא, היה ר״מ אומר: שנים שעלו לגרדום לידון ודינן שוה, זה ירד וזה לא ירד, זה ניצל, וזה לא ניצל; מפני מה זה ירד, וזה לא ירד, זה ניצל וזה לא ניצל? זה התפלל ונענה, וזה התפלל ולא נענה. מפני מה זה נענה, וזה לא נענה? זה התפלל תפילה שלימה, נענה, וזה לא התפלל תפילה שלימה, לא נענה. רבי אלעזר אמר, כאן קודם גזר דין, כאן לאחר גזר דין. רבי יצחק אמר, יפה צעקה לאדם בין קודם גזר דין בין לאחר גזר דין. וגזר דין דציבור מי מיקרע? והא כתוב אחד אומר (ירמיה ד) „כבסי מרעה לבך״, וכתיב (שם ב) „כי אם תכבסי בנתר ותרבי לך בורית נכתם עונך לפני״, מאי לאו כאן קודם גז״ד, כאן לאחר גז״ד? לא, אידי ואידי לאחר גזר דין, ולא קשיא, כאן בגזר דין שיש עמו שבועה, כאן בגזר דין שאין עמו שבועה, כדרב שמואל בר אמי, דאמר רב שמואל בר אמי, ואמרי לה א״ר שמואל בר נחמני א״ר יונתן, מנין לגזר דין שיש עמו שבועה שאינו נקרע? שנאמר

רש״י

כשיראה שאין העולם מתקיים בדין. ה׳ ה׳, מדת רחמים, אני מרחם קודם וגם אחר שיחטא אם ישוב. ברית כרותה לשלש עשרה מדות הללו שאם יזכירום ישראל בתפלות תעניתם אינן חוזרות ריקם. הנה אנכי כורת ברית, על האמור למעלה. בינתים, בין ראש השנה ליום הכפורים. סימניות, בין פסוק לפסוק יש סימנין המוכן כזה ?. אכן ורקן, באין לדרשה לסתם את הדבור כאכן ורקן שהן מיעוטין לומר לא בכל שעה שיצעקו אל ה׳ בצר להם יוציאם ממצוקותיהם, אלא אם כן צעקו קודם גזר דין. לגרדום, בית ועד שדנים בו נפשות להריגה. ודינם שוה, שניהם נתפשו על דבר אחד. זה ירד, מן המטה. וזה ניצל, מן הדונג. תפילה שלימה, נתכוון. ויחיד איכא, מצוי לו דכתיב בהמצאו. כבני אמרנא, כבבשים שמונין אותן לעשרן ויוצאין זה אחר זה בפתח קטן שאין

(שמואל א ג) „ולכן נשבעתי לבית עלי אם יתכפר עון בית עלי בזבח ובמנחה”. אמר רבא, בזבח ובמנחה אינו מתכפר, אבל מתכפר בתורה. אביי אמר, בזבח ובמנחה אינו מתכפר, אבל מתכפר בתורה ובגמילות חסדים. רבה ואביי מדבית עלי קאתו; רבה דעסק בתורה, חיה ארבעין שנין; אביי דעסק בתורה ובגמילות חסדים חיה שיתין שנין. ת״ר, משפחה אחת היתה בירושלים שהיו מתים מהן בני י״ח שנה, באו והודיעו את רבן יוחנן בן זכאי, אמר להם, שמא ממשפחת עלי אתם? דכתיב ביה (שם ב) „וכל מרבית ביתך ימותו אנשים”, לכו ועסקו בתורה וחיו. הלכו ועסקו בתורה וחיו. והיו קורין אותה משפחת רבן יוחנן על שמו. אמר רב שמואל בר איניא משמיה דרב, מניין לגזר דין של צבור, שאע״פ שנחתם, נקרע? שנאמר (דברים ד) „כה׳ אלהינו בכל קראנו אליו”, והכתיב (ישעיה נה) „דרשו ה׳ בהמצאו” התם ביחיד, הכא בציבור. ביחיד אימת? אמר רבה בר אבוה, אלו עשרה ימים שבין ר״ה ליה״כ. בר״ה כל באי העולם עוברין לפניו כבני מרון. מאי כבני מרון? הכא תרגימו כבני אימרנא; ר״ש לקיש אמר כמעלות בית מרון. ורב יהודה אמר שמואל כחיילות של בית דוד. אמר רבה בר בר חנה א״ר יוחנן, וכולן נסקרין בסקירה אחת. אמר רב נחמן בר יצחק אף אנן נמי תנינא (תהלים לג) „היוצר יחד לבם” היוצר רואה יחד לבם ומבין אל כל מעשיהם. **מתני׳** על ששה חדשים השלוחין יוצאין: על ניסן מפני הפסח. על אב מפני התענית. על אלול מפני ר״ה. על תשרי מפני תקנת המועדות, על כסליו מפני חנוכה, ועל אדר מפני הפורים. וכשהיה ב״ה קיים יוצאין אף על אייר, מפני פסח קטן. **גמ׳** וליפקו נמי אתמוז וטבת? (יח:) דאמר רב חנא בר ביזנא אמר ר״ש חסידא, מאי דכתיב (זכריה ח) „כה אמר ה׳ צבאות צום הרביעי וצום החמישי וצום השביעי וצום העשירי יהיה לבית יהודה לששון ולשמחה”. קרי להו צום, וקרי להו ששון ושמחה? בזמן שיש שלום, יהיה לששון ולשמחה, אין שלום, צום? אמר רב פפא הכי קאמר: בזמן שיש שלום יהיו לששון ולשמחה, יש גזרת המלכות, צום, אין גזרת המלכות ואין שלום, רצו מתענין, רצו אין מתענין. אי הכי, ט״ב נמי? אמר רב פפא, שאני ט׳ באב הואיל והוכפלו בו צרות. דאמר מר בט׳ באב חרב הבית בראשונה ובשנייה ונלכדה ביתר ונחרשה העיר. תניא אמר ר״ש, ד׳ דברים היה ר״ע דורש ואני אין דורש כמותו: צום הרביעי, זה תשעה בתמוז, שבו הובקעה העיר, שנאמר (ירמיה נב) „בחדש הרביעי בתשעה לחדש וגו׳ ותבקע העיר”, ואמאי קרי ליה רביעי? רביעי לחדשים. צום החמישי, זה ט׳ באב, שבו נשרף בית אלהינו ואמאי קרי ליה חמישי? חמישי לחדשים. צום השביעי, זה ג׳ בתשרי, שבו נהרג גדליה בן אחיקם ששקולה מיתתן של צדיקים כשריפה בית אלקינו. ואמאי קרי

ר ש״י

לצאת כאחד. כמעלות בית מרון, הדרך קצר ואין שנים יכולין לילך זה בצד זה. כחיילות של בית דוד, מרון, לשון מרות ואדנות, וכך היו מונין אותם: יוצאים זה אחר זה בצאתם למלחמה. אף אנן נמי תנינא, דכולן נסקרים בסקירה אחת. מתני׳ על ששה חדשים השלוחים יוצאים, שקדשו ב״ד החדש ע״פ עדים כשראו את החדש ומודיעים השלוחים לגולה יום שקדשוהו, אם ביום שלשים, והחדש שעבר חסר, או ביום ל״א, החדש שעבר מלא. ועל אלול מפני ר״ה, מודיעים מתי התחיל אלול ועושין ר״ה ביום שלשים לאלול כהלכה, דרוב שנים אין אלול מעובר. ועל תשרי מפני תקנת המועדות, לאחר שקדשוהו ב״ד לתשרי השלוחין יוצאין ליום המחרת והולכין עד מקום שיכולין להגיע עד החג ומודיעין אם עיברו בית דין את אלול ואם לאו. פסח קטן, פסח שני. גמ׳ דאמר רב חנא בר ביזנא כו׳, דכולהו ימי תענית נינהו בזמן הזה שאין ב״ה קיים. שיש שלום, שאין יד אומות העולם תקיפה על ישראל. יהיו לששון ולשמחה, לאסור בהספד ובתענית. יש גזרת המלכות צום, חובה להתענות בהן. רצו אין מתענין, וכיון דרשות הוא לא מטרחינן שלוחים עלייהו. ד׳ דברים

ליה שביעי? שביעי לחדשים. צום העשירי, זה עשרה בטבת, שבו סמך מלך בבל על ירושלים, שנאמר (יחזקאל כד) „ויהי דבר ה׳ אלי בשנה התשיעית בחדש העשירי בעשור לחדש לאמר בן אדם כתב לך את שם היום את עצם היום הזה סמך מלך בבל אל ירושלים", ואמאי קרי ליה עשירי? עשירי לחדשים, והלא היה ראוי זה ליכתב ראשון, ולמה נכתב כאן? כדי להסדיר חדשים כתיקנן; ואני איני אומר כן, אלא צום העשירי. זה חמשה בטבת, שבו באת שמועה לגולה שהוכתה העיר, שנאמר (שם לג) „ויהי בשתי עשרה שנה בעשירי בחמשה לחדש לגלותנו בא אלי הפלים מירושלים לאמר הוכתה העיר", ועשו יום שמועה כיום שריפה, ונראין דברי מדבריו, שאני אומר על ראשון, ראשון ועל אחרון, אחרון, והוא אומר על ראשון, אחרון, ועל אחרון, ראשון, א״א שהוא מונה לסדר חדשים, ואני מונה לסדר פורעניות. איתמר, רב ורבי חנינא אמרי, בטלה מגילת תענית; ר׳ יוחנן וריב״ל אמרי, לא בטלה מגילת תענית; רב ור׳ חנינא אמרי בטלה מגילת תענית, הכי קאמר: בזמן שיש שלום, יהיו לששון ולשמחה, אין שלום, צום; והנך נמי כי הני. ר׳ יוחנן ור׳ יהושע בן לוי אמרי לא בטלה מגילת תענית, והני הוא דתלינהו רחמנא בבנין ב״ה, אבל הנך כדקייכו קיימי. (יט.) מתיב רב טובי בר מתנה: בעשרים ותמניא ביה אתת בשורתא טבתא ליהודאי דלא יעידון מאורייתא. שגזרה המלכות גזירה, שלא יעסקו בתורה, ושלא ימולו את בניהם, ושיחללו שבתות. מה עשה יהודה בן שמוע וחביריו? הלכו ונטלו עצה ממטרונית אחת, שכל גדולי העיר מצוין אצלה, אמרה להם: בואו והפגינו בלילה. הלכו והפגינו בלילה; אמרו: אי שמים! לא אחיכם אנחנו? ולא בני אב אחד אנחנו? ולא בני אם אחת אנחנו? מה נשתנינו מכל אומה ולשון, שאתם גוזרין עלינו גזירות קשות? וביטלום ואותו היום עשאוהו יום טוב. ואי ס״ד, בטלה מגילת תענית, קמייתא בטיל. אחרנייתא מוסיפין? (יט:) תנאי היא, דתניא: הימים האלו הכתובין במגילת תענית בין בזמן שבית המקדש קיים, בין בזמן שאין בה״מ קיים, אסורין; דברי ר״מ. רבי יוסי אומר: בזמן שבה״מ קיים, אסורין, מפני ששמחה היא להם, אין בית המקדש קיים, מותרין, מפני שאבל הוא להם והילכתא בטלו, והילכתא לא בטלו קשיא הילכתא אהילכתא? לא קשיא, כאן בחנוכה ופורים, כאן בשאר יומי. על אלול מפני ר״ה ועל תשרי מפני תקנת המועדות. כיון דנפקי להו אאלול, אתשרי לכה להו? וכי תימא, דילמא עברוה לאלול? והאמר רבי חיננא בר כהנא אמר רב מימות עזרא ואילך לא מצינו אלול מעובר; לא מצינו, דלא איצטריך; הא איצטריך מעברינן ליה? הא מקלקל ר״ה! מוטב תיקלקל ראש השנה, ולא יתקלקלו כולהו מועדות. דיקא נמי,

---

ר ש״י

דילו בו, זו אחת מהן והני שנוין בתוספתא דסוטה. סמך מלך בבל, התחיל לצור עליה. שמועה לגולה, שגלות יכניה. שאני אומר על ראשון, שבסדר מקרא. ראשון, לפורענות בתחילה הובקעה העיר ואחר כך נשרף הבית בתשעה באב ובתשרי שלאחריו נהרג גדליה ובטבת שלאחריו באתה [illegible] על אחרון, [illegible] ראשון לפורענות שהרי התחילת כבר [illegible] הובקעה, נמצא [illegible] שהוא ראשון במקרא אחרון לשמיעת בבל, שהוא מאוחר במקרא. א״א שהוא מונה לסדר חדשים, ואמר שלא הקפיד המקרא אלא על סדר החדשים, לכך מנה תמוז קודם לטבת, ואני מונה אף לסדר פורענות. בטלה מגילת תענית, ימים טובים שקבעו חכמים על נסים שאירעו בהם ואסרום בתענית. אין שלום צום, ואף ג׳ דבזמן הבית קריהו מועדים טובים. והנך נמי. דמגילת תענית, כי תני משרית להו, כי היכי דתני בטלי, תני נמי בטלי. דתלינהו בבנין, דעל ידי החורבן הוקבעו לצום ועל ידי הבנין הוקבעו ליו״ט. בעשרין ותמניא בית. באדר. דלא יעידון מן אורייתא, שלא יעבירו לנתק עצמן מן התורה. הפגינו, צעקו בשוקים וברחובות. תנאי היא, אי בטלה מגילת תענית, הא איצטריך, אי משום ירקא, אי מפום

דקתני על תשרי מפני תקנת המועדות, יו"ט. ועל כסליו מפני חנוכה ועל אדר מפני הפורים. ואילו נתעברה השנה, יוצאין אף על אדר שני מפני הפורים לא קתני? מתניתין דלא כרבי, דתניא רבי אומר אם נתעברה השנה, יוצאין אף על אדר השני מפני הפורים. (כ.) כי אתא עולא אמר, עברוה לאלול. אמר עולא, ידעי חברין בבלאי מאי טיבותא עבדינן בהדייהו. מאי טיבותא? עולא אמר משום ירקא, ורבי אחא בר חנינא אמר משום מתיא. מאי בינייהו? איכא בינייהו יו"ט הסמוך לשבת בין מלפניה בין מלאחריה: מאן דאמר משום ירקא, מעברינן, ומ"ד משום מתיא, אפשר בעממי. אי הכי, מאי שנא לדידן אפילו לדידהו נמי? לדידן חביל לן עלמא, לדידהו לא חביל להו עלמא. איני, והתני רבה בר שמואל, יכול כשם שמעברין את השנה לצורך, כך מעברין את החדש לצורך? ת"ל, (שמות יב) „החדש הזה לכם ראש חדשים". כזה ראה וקדש? אמר רבא, ל"ק, כאן לעבורו, כאן לקידושו. והכי קאמר: יכול כשם שמעברין את השנה ואת החדש לצורך, כך מקדשין את החדש לצורך? ת"ל „החדש הזה לכם" כזה ראה וקדש. (כ:) אמר שמואל יכילנא לתקוני לכולה גולה. אמר ליה אבא אבוה דרבי שמלאי לשמואל ידע מר האי מילתא דתניא בסוד העיבור: נולד קודם חצות או נולד אחר חצות? א"ל, לא; אמר ליה, מדהא לא ידע מר, איכא מילי אחרנייתא דלא ידע מר. כי סליק רבי זירא שלח להו: צריך שיהא לילה ויום מן החודש, וזו שאמר אבא אבוה דר' שמלאי: מחשבין את תולדתו, נולד קודם חצות בידוע שנראה סמוך לשקיעת החמה, לא נולד קודם חצות בידוע שלא נראה סמוך לשקיעת החמה. למאי נפקא מינה? אמר רב אשי, לאכחושי סהדי. אמר

ר ש"י

מתיא. והא קמיקלקלא ראש השנה, דנמצא שלא עשאום בני הגולה בתחלתה אם מעברין אלול. ידעי חברין בבלאי, כלומר נותנין לב להכיר טובה שעושין עמהן בני ארץ ישראל שעיברו את אלול. משום ירקא, להפריד שבת ויו"ט זה מזה, כדי שלא יכמושו ירקות הנאכלות כשהן חיים בשבת שאחר יו"ט או ביו"ט שאחר שבת. משום מתיא, להפריד שבת ויו"ט זה מזה, שלא יסריח מת שימות באחד מהן שהוא ראשון, ולא יקבר לא היום ולא למחר. מאי בינייהו, תרוייהו איתנהו. אפשר בעממי, דאפי' מת ביו"ט ראשון יתעסקו בו עממין. לדידן חביל לן עלמא, אנו בני בבל הם לנו העולם ויש לנו הבל, לפי שבבל עמוקה היא ואינה ארץ הרים וגבעות כא"י, ואין השרב בא אליה, ואין בני ארץ ישראל צריכין לעבר משום מתיא ומשום ירקא, אלא בשבילנו. איני, ומי מעברינן חודש לצורך. כשם שמעברין את השנה לצורך, מפני האביב והתקופה ופירות האילן כדאיתא בפ' קמא דסנהדרין. כזה ראה וקדש, כיון שנראית קדש בו ביום. לעבורו, לעשות את החדש מלא לצורך מותר. לקדשו, ביום שלשים והלבנה לא נראית, ואם ימתינו עד יום מחר יהא שבת ויום הכפורים נכונין, אין מקדשין לצורך. כזה ראה וקדש, ראה תחלה ואח"כ קדש, אבל כשאינה מעברו ראה וקדש הוא. יכילנא לתקוני, בלא ראיית עדים כי בקי אני בתולדות הלבנה והילוכה וסדר המזלות. סוד העיבור, ברייתא שנויה ברמזים. או לאחר חצות, בך שנוי בה ורמז בעלמא הוא לומר קודם חצות חילוק בנולד לאחר חצות. ידע מר, מה חילוק יש? שלח להו, לחביריו שבבבל שני דברים שלמד כאן. מן החדש, היום הולך אחר הלילה להיות היום מן החדש שהיה בו ליל שלפניו, לומר שאם נראית הלבנה הישנה במזרח יום עשרים ותשעה שהוא ליל שלשים אין מקדשין אותו ביום שלשים. אבוה דר' שמלאי, לפני שמואל. ולא ידע לפרש מה חילוק בין נולד קודם חצות לנולד לאחר חצות, אני מפרשה לכם. מחשבין, את מולד הלבנה. נולד קודם חצות, היום בידוע שנראה היום קודם שתשקע החמה שאין הלבנה מתכסה מבני א"י שהם במערב אלא שש שעות אחר חידושה מתוך קוטנה שהלבנה לערים בשש שעות לאחר חידושה בקרן מערבית דרומית ונראית להם. אחר חצות, בידוע שלא יראה היום שהוא קטנה כל שש שעות ונעלמת מעין כל. למאי נפקא מינה, למישרא? הרי על פי עדים אנו מקדשין! לאכחושי סהדי, אם נולד אחר חצות, ואמרו ראינו החדשה לפני שקיעת החמה, כדי לקדשו היום, עדי שקר הם. כל ספקא לקמיה שרינן, אין אנו צריכין להקדים פסח או סוכות בי"ד ליום שלשים

רבי זירא אמר רב נחמן כל ספיקא לקמיה שדינן, למיטרא דחמיסר ושיתסר עבדינן ארביסר לא עבדינן. ול עבד נמי ארביסר, דילמא חסרוה לאב וחסרוה לאלול? (כא) תרי ירחי חסירי קלא אית להו. לוי איקלע לבבל בחדסר בתשרי, אמר בסים תבשילא דבבלאי ביומא רבא דמערבא. אמרי ליה, אסהיד! אמר להו, לא שמעתי מפי ב"ד: מקודש. מכריז רבי יוחנן, כל היכא דמטו שלוחי ניסן ולא מטו שלוחי תשרי ליעבדו תרי יומי: גזירה ניסן אטו תשרי. רבא הוה רגיל דהוה יתיב בתעניתא תרי יומי; זימנא חדא אשתכח כוותיה. ר"נ יתיב בתעניתא כוליה יומי דכיפורי. לאורתא אתא ההוא גברא, א"ל למחר יומא רבה במערבא. קרי עליה (איכה ד) קלים היו רודפינו. אמר להו רב נחמן להנהו נחותי ימא: אתון דלא ידעיתו בקביעא דירחא, כי חזיתו סיהרא דמשלים ליומא, בעירו חמירא. (כא:) מתני' על שני חדשים מחללין את השבת על ניסן ועל תשרי, שבהן שלוחין יוצאין לסוריא, ובהן מתקנין את המועדות. וכשהיה בית המקדש קיים מחללין אף על כולן מפני תקנת הקרבן. גמ' על ב' חדשים ותו לא? ורמינהו, על ו' חדשים השלוחין יוצאין! אמר אביי ה"ק: על כולן שלוחין יוצאין מבערב, על ניסן ועל תשרי עד שישמעו מפי ב"ד: מקודש! ת"ר, מנין שמחללין עליהן את השבת ת"ל (ויקרא כג) „אלה מועדי ה' אשר תקראו אותם במועדם". יכול כשם שמחללין עד שיתקדשו כך מחללין עד שיתקיימו? ת"ל „אשר תקראו אותם", על קריאתם אתה מחלל, ואי אתה מחלל על קיומן. וכשהיה ב"ה קיים מחללין אף על כולן מפני תקנת הקרבן. ת"ר, בראשונה היו מחללין אף על כולן, משחרב בית המקדש אמר להן רבן יוחנן בן זכאי: וכי יש קרבן? התקינו שלא יהו מחללין אלא על ניסן ועל תשרי בלבד. מתני' בין שנראה בעליל בין שלא נראה בעליל מחללין עליו את השבת. רבי יוסי אומר, אם נראה בעליל אין מחללין עליו את השבת. מעשה שעברו יותר מארבעים זוג ועיכבם ר"ע בלוד, שלח לו ר"ג אם מעכב אתה את הרבים נמצאת מכשילן לעתיד לבא. גמ' ת"ר, (קהלת יב) „ביקש קהלת למצוא דברי חפץ" ביקש קהלת לדון דינין שבלב שלא בעדים ושלא בהתראה, יצתה ב"ק ואמרה לו „וכתוב יושר דברי אמת", (שם יז) ע"פ שנים עדים וגומר" (כב.) מעשה שעברו יותר

ר ש"י

של אדר ושל אלול מחמת ספק. שמא קדשו ב"ד את החדש ביום עשרים ותשעה, אבל צריכין אנו לעשות יום טוב שני ביום כ"ז מספק שמא עיברו ב"ד את האדר וקבעו ניסן ביום שלשים ואחד וכן באלול. למיטרא דחמיסר ושיתסר כו', בניהותא. כלומר אפשעינן רב נחמן הכי, דילמא חסרו לאב. והשתא יום עשרים ותשעה באלול שלנו שעיברנו את אב היה יום שלשים שלהן וקבעו בו ראש השנה, וכן לענין ניסן דילמא חסרו לשבט. בסים תבשילא דבבלאי, אכלו להם שמקדים בית ב"ב שבא"י, שהרי ב"ד עיברו את החדש והיו מתענים. אסהיד, ונקבל עלינו ולא נאכל. לא שמעתי מפי ב"ד מקודש. שלא הייתי במקום שישבו סנהדרין שם. דמטו שלוחי ניסן. מגיעין למקום שאין שלוחי תשרי מגיעין, שהרי אין ימים טובים בנתיים לעכבם ובתשרי יש ר"ה ויה"כ שאין השלוחין הולכין בו. ליעבדו תרי יומי, כמי ואע"פ שהגידו להם השלוחים יום קביעתו. גזירה ניסן אטו תשרי, שאם תנהגם לעשות בניסן יום אחד ינהגו כן בתשרי שלא ע"פ שלוחים ופעמים שטעו. יתיב בתעניתא תרי יומי, עם לילותיהם, שמא עיברו ב"ד את החדש ויום אחד עשר שלנו הוא עשירי שלהן. כיהרא דמשלים ליומא, שהירח משלים באורו עם הנץ החמה שאינו מישיר עד שעת זריחה. מתני' מחללין את השבת, עדים שראו את החדש. שבהם שלוחים, ב"ד שולחין לסוריא להודיע יציאת יום קביעתם. תקנת קרבן. של ר"ח שיקרב בזמנו. גמ' יוצאין מבערב, ואין ממתינין עד למחר שישמעו מקודש מפי ב"ד. על ניסן ועל תשרי, אין שלוחין יוצאין עד שישמעו מפי ב"ד מקודש. במועדם שלא יעבור המועד של זמן קריאתן. יכול כשם שמחללין, העדים כדי שיתקדשו בזמן. כך מחללין, השלוחים עד שיתקיימו המועדות בזמנן. מתני' (נראה בעליל, מפרש בגמרא לשון גלוי כמו בעליל לארץ). אין מחללין, לפי שאין צורך. ארבעים זוג, שני

מארבעים זוג ועיכבן ר"ע כו׳. תניא א"ר יהודה, ח"ו שר"ע עיכבן, אלא שזפר ראש גדר של גדר עיכבן, ושלח רבן גמליאל והורידוהו מגדולתו. **מתני׳** אב ובנו שראו את החדש ילכו, לא שמצטרפין זה עם זה, אלא שאם יפסל אחד מהן, יצטרף השני עם אחר. ר"ש אומר, אב ובנו וכל הקרובין כשרין לעדות החדש. א"ר יוסי, מעשה בטוביה הרופא, שראה את החדש בירושלים הוא ובנו ועבדו משוחרר, וקבלו הכהנים אותו ואת בנו, ופסלו את עבדו. וכשבאו לפני ב"ד קבלו אותו ואת עבדו, ופסלו את בנו. **גמ׳** א"ר לוי, מאי טעמא דר"ש? דכתיב (שמות יב) „ויאמר ה׳ אל משה ואל אהרן בארץ מצרים לאמר החדש הזה לכם" עדות זו תהא כשרה בכם. ורבנן, עדות זו תהא מסורה לכם. אמר מר עוקבא אמר שמואל הלכתא כר"ש. **מתני׳** אלו הן הפסולין: המשחק בקוביא, ומלוי ברבית ומפריחי יונים, וסוחרי שביעית, ועבדים. זה הכלל: כל עדות שאין האשה כשרה לה, אף הן אינן כשירין לה. מי שראה את החדש, ואינו יכול להלך, מוליכים אותו על החמור, אפילו במטה, ואם צודה להם, לוקחין בידן מקלות, ואם היתה דרך רחוקה. לוקחין בידם מזונות, שעל מהלך לילה ויום מחללין את השבת, ויוצאין לעדות החדש, שנאמר (ויקרא כג) „אלה מועדי ה׳ אשר תקראו אותם במועדם".

הדרן עלך ארבעה ראשי שנים

אם אינן מכירין אותו, משלחין עמו אחר להעידו. בראשונה היו מקבלין עדות החדש מכל אדם, משקלקלו הבייתוסים, התקינו, שלא יהו מקבלין אלא מן המכירין. **גמ׳** מאי אחר? (כב:) זוג אחר. ה"נ מסתברא, דאי לא תימא הכי? אם אינן מכירין אותו. מאי אותו? אילימא אותו חד, וחד מי מהימן? (ת"ים צא) „מ״שפט" כתיב ביה, אלא מאי אותו, אותו הזוג, ה"נ מאי אחר, זוג אחר. וחד לא מהימן? והתניא, מעשה ברבי נהוראי שהלך אצל העד להעיד עליו בשבת באושא? סהדא אחרינא הוה באושא, ואזל רבי נהוראי לאצטרופי בהדיה. אי הכי, מאי למימרא? מהו דתימא מספיקא לא מחללינן שבתא, קמ"ל! כי אתא עולא אמר: קדשוה לירחא במערבא. אמר רב כהנא לא מיבעיא עולא דגברא רבה הוא דמהימן, אלא אפילו איניש דעלמא נמי מהימן, מ"ט? כל מילתא דעבידא לאגלויי לא משקרי בה אינשי. בראשונה היו מקבלין עדות החדש מכל אדם וכו׳. תנו רבנן: מה קילקול קילקלו הבייתוסין? פעם אחת בקשו להטעות את חכמים, שכרו שני בני אדם בד׳ מאות זוז, אחד משלנו ואחד משלהם,

---

רש"י

עדים זוג אחר זוג. שוזר, כך שמו. מתני׳ שאם יפסל, יפסל בציו כשיבדקוהו. גמ׳ תהא כשרה בכם, ואע"פ שהם אחים. תהא מסורה לכם, לחשובי הדור אני כותב שיקבלו העדות ויקדשו החדש ולא להכשיר קרובים בא. מתני׳ המשחק בקוביא, חתיכות של עצם שמשחקין בערבון. ומלוי ברבית, לאו גזלנין דאורייתא נינהו ושפסלם משום אל תשת ע"ד חמס. מפריחי יונים, היינו נמי כעין קוביא. וסוחרי שביעית, עוסקין בסחורה בפירות שביעית, ולפי שנחשדו כל אלו לעבור על דת מחמת ממון חשדום להיות מעידים שקר ע"י ממון ושוחד. מי שראה את החדש כו׳, מרכיבין אותו אף בשבת. ואם צודה להם, אם יש אורבים בדרך, הבייתוסים והבותים הם היו אורבים להם לעכבם כדי להטעות את חכמים.

הדרן עלך ארבעה ראשי שנים

אם אינן מכירין, ב"ד את העד אם נאמן וכשר הוא. משלחין, ב"ד שבעירו. אחר עמו, להעיד עליו לפני ב"ד הגדול. גמ׳ חד מי מהימן, לעדות החדש. באושא, כשישבה סנהדרין שם ושם היו מקדשין את החדש. סהדא אחרינא הוה באושא, המכיר את העד הזה. מספיקא, שמא אין אותו העד בביתו. להטעות את החכמים, שאירע יום ל׳ של אדר בשבת ולא נראה חדש בזמנו, והבייתוסין מתאוין שיהא יום ראשון של פסח בשבת כדי שתהא הנפת העומר באחד בשבת, ועצרת

שלהם העיד עדותו ויצא, שלנו אמרו לו: אמור, כיצד ראית את הלבנה? אמר להם עולה הייתי במעלה אדומים, וראיתיו שהוא רבוץ בין ב׳ סלעים, ראשו דומה לעגל, אזניו דומין לגדי, קרניו דומות לצבי, חנבו מונחת לו בין ירכותיו, והצצתי בו ונרתעתי ונפלתי לאחורי, ואם אין אתם מאמינים לי, הרי מאתים זוז צרורין לי בסדיני. אמרו לו מי הזקיקך לכך? אמר להם, שמעתי שבקשו ביתוסים להטעות את חכמים, אמרתי אלך אני ואודיע להם, שמא יבואו בני אדם שאינם מהוגנין ויטעו את החכמים. אמרו לו מאתים זוז נתונין לך במתנה, והשוכרך ימתח על העמוד. באותה שנה התקינו שלא יהו מקבלין אלא מן המכירין. **מתני׳** בראשונה היו משיאין משואות, משקלקלו הכותים התקינו שיהו שלוחין יוצאין. כיצד היו משיאין משואות? מביאין כלונסאות של ארז ארוכין, וקנים ועצי שמן ונעורת של פשתן, וכורך במשיחה ועולה לראש ההר, והצית בהן את האור, ומוליך ומביא ומעלה ומוריד עד שהוא רואה את חבירו שהוא עושה כן בראש ההר השני, וכן בראש ההר השלישי. ומאין היו משיאין משואות? מהר המשחה לסרטבא, ומסרטבא לגרופינא, ומגרופינא לחוורן, ומחוורן לבית בלתין, ומבית בלתין לא זזו משם, אלא מוליך ומביא, ומעלה ומוריד, עד שהיה רואה כל הגולה לפניו כמדורת האש. **גמ׳** ת״ר, אין משיאין משואות אלא על החדש שנראה בזמנו לקדשו; ואימתי משיאין? לאור עיבורו. למימרא דאחסר עבדינן אמלא לא עבדינן? (כג.) וליעביד אמלא ולא ליעביד אחסר כלל? א״ר אביי משום ביטול מלאכה לעם שני ימים. כיצד היו משיאין משואות מביאין כלונסות וכו׳. אמר ר׳ יהודה, ד׳ מיני ארזים הן: ארז, קתרום, עץ שמן, וברוש; קתרום, אמר רב, אדרא. א״ר יוחנן, כל שיטה ושיטה שנטלו אומות מירושלים עתיד הקב״ה להחזירה לה, שנאמר (ישעיה מה) „אתן במדבר ארז שיטה״, ואין במדבר אלא ירושלים, שנאמר (שם סד) „ציון מדבר היתה״ וגו. ואמר רבי יוחנן, כל הלומד תורה ומלמדה במקום שאין תלמיד חכם, דומה להדס במדבר, דחביב; וא״ר יוחנן, אוי להם לרומאים שאין להם תקנה, שנאמר (שם ס) „תחת הנחשת אביא זהב ותחת הברזל אביא כסף ותחת העצים נחשת ותחת האבנים ברזל״. תחת רבי עקיבא וחביריו מאי מביאין? ועליהם הוא אומר (יואל ד) „ונקיתי דמם לא נקיתי״. ומאין היו משיאין משואות כו׳ ומבית

ר ש״י

„אחד בשבת, לפי שהן דורשין ממחרת השבת שנאמר, ממחרת שבת בראשית במשמע. אחד משלנו, ולא הכירוהו. מאתים זוז נתונים לך במתנה, ותהא רשאי ליקחן ואעפ״י שלא השלמת תנאי שלך. והשוכרך ויש רשות לב״ד לקנוס ממון, ולעשותו הפקר. ימתח על העמוד, ילקה. בראשונה היו משיאין משואות, לאחר שקדשו החדש ולא היו צריכין לשגר שלוחים לשלוח לגולה להודיע, כי המשואות מודיעים אותן. משקלקלו הכותים, והשיאו גם הם משואות שלא בזמן החדש להטעות ישראל וג׳ ד׳ לא היו משיאין משואות אלא בחדש שנתקדש ביום ל׳ כדאמרי׳ בגמרין, וכשלא היו משיאין לערב של יום ל׳ הכל יודעין שהחדש מעובר, ופעם אחת עיברו ב״ד את החדש ולא השיאו משואות לערב ל׳, והכותים השיאום בהרים שלהם והטעו את בני הגולה לעשותו חסר. ארוכים, כדי שיראו למרחוק. וקנים ועצי שמן ונעורת של פשתן כל אלו מרבים שלהבת. וכורך במשיחה, קושרם בחוט של משיחה בראשי הכלונסות. ומאין היו משיאין משואות, כלומר מה שם ההרים? מהר המשחה, מתחילין, הוא הר הזיתים שלפני ירושלים עד שרואין כן בהר סרטבא. להודיע לבני הגולה, בני בבל אנשי פומבדיתא, והמה מודיעין לכל בני מדינת בבל. גמ׳ לקדשו, להודיע שנתקדש. לאור עיבורו, לערב יום שלשים נגהי ל״א. יום שלשים קרוי יום עיבורו. וליעביד אמלא, ולא אחסר, וכי מקלע ר״ח חסר בערב שבת ולא עבדינן מידע ידעי דחסר הוא, דכל דרשים חסרין לא עבדינן והאי נמי לא עבור. אמר אביי משום ביטול מלאכה כו׳, אין לך ר״ח שאין מתבטלין בני הגולה ממלאכה שני ימים: יום ל׳ שמא היום ר״ח, ויום ל״א שמא עיברו את החדש והיום

בלתיך. מאי בית בלתין? אמר רב (כג:) זו בירם. מאי גולה? אמר רב יוסף, זו פומבדיתא. מאי כמדורת האש? תנא כל אחד ואחד נוטל אבוקה בידו ועולה לראש גגו. מתני' חצר גדולה היתה בירושלים ובית יעזק היתה נקראת, ולשם כל העדים מתכנסין. וב"ד בודקין אותם שם וסעודות גדולות עושין להם, בשביל שיהו רגילין לבא. בראשונה לא היו זזין משם כל היום. התקין רבן גמליאל הזקן, שיהו מהלכין אלפים אמה לכל רוח; ולא אלו בלבד, אלא אף חכמה הבאה ליילד, והבא להציל מן הדליקה, מן הגייס, ומן הנהר, ומן המפולת, הרי אלו כאנשי העיר, ויש להם אלפים לכל רוח. כיצד בודקין את העדים? זוג שבא ראשון, בודקין אותן ראשון, ומכניסין את הגדול שבהן ואומרין. לו: אמור, כיצד ראית את הלבנה, לפני החמה, או לאחר החמה? לצפונה, או לדרומה? כמה היה גבוה? ולאין היה נוטה? וכמה היה רחב? אם אמר לפני החמה, לא אמר כלום. ואח"כ היו מכניסין את השני ובודקין אותו, אם נמצאו דבריהם מכוונים, עדותן קיימת, ושאר כל הזוגות שואלין אותן ראשי דברים, לא שהיו צריכים להם, אלא כדי שלא יצאו בפחי נפש, בשביל שיהו רגילים לבוא: גמ' היינו לפני החמה, היינו לצפונה? היינו לאחר החמה, היינו דרומה? אמר אביי, פגימתה לפני החמה, או לאחר החמה, אם אמר לפני החמה, לא אמר כלום, דא"ר יוחנן, מאי דכתיב (איוב כה) „המשל ופחד עמו עושה שלום במרומיו". מעולם לא ראתה חמה פגימתה של לבנה, ולא פגימתה של קשת. (כד.) כמה היה גבוה ולאין היה נוטה כו'. תנא חדא: לצפונה דבריו קיימין, לדרומה לא אמר כלום, והתניא איפכא: לדרומה דבריו קיימין, לצפונה לא אמר כלום? לא קשיא. כאן בימות החמה, כאן בימות הגשמים. ת"ר, אחד אומר גבוה ב' מרדעות, ואחד אומר ג', עדותן בטילה, אבל מצטרפין לעדות אחרת. ת"ר, ראינוהו במים, ראינוהו בעששית, ראינוהו בעבים, אין מעידין עליו; חציו במים חציו ברקיע, חציו בעבים, אין מעידין עליו, כל הכי חזו יה ואזלי? אמר אביי ה"ק: ראינוהו מאלינו ושבנו לראותו מדעתינו ולא ראינוהו, אין מעידין עליו, מ"ט? אומר כוביתא דעיבא בעלמא הוא דחזי. מתני' ראש ב"ד אומר מקודש. וכל העם עונין אחריו מקודש מקודש. בין שנראה בזמנו, בין שלא נראה בזמנו מקדשין אותו. ר"א בר צדוק אומר, אם לא נראה בזמנו אין מקדשין אותו, שכבר קידשוהו שמים. גמ' מנהני מילי? א"ר חייא בר גמדא א"ר יוסי בן שאול

רש"י

ר"ה אבל כי עברינן משואות אמ"ר לאחר יום ל' ידעי שבום ל' נקבע ועשו מלאכה למחר. אדרא, בר שם האילן. לא נקיתי, לא אנקם כדמם של ישראל. מתני' כל העדים מתכנסין, ביום השבת שחללו לבא ולהעיד. לא היו זזין משם, לפי שיצאו חוץ לתחום אין לו אלא ד' אמות. ומן הנהר, שהוא גדל פתאום ושוטף את בני העיר ואת הילדים. לפני החמה, החמה הולכת לעולם ממזרח לדרום ומדרום למערב וממערב לצפון, והלבנה אינה נראית ביום שלשים לעולם אלא סמוך לשקיעת החמה, שמתוך שהיא דקה והלבנה אינה נראית בעוד שהחמה בגבורתה: מדלא קתני למזרחה או למערבה שמע מינה אין נראית להם בדרום וקא ב"ד שהיו שואלין את העדים: אם ראית כשהלכת לפני החמה, אי לאחריה, לצפונה של חמה ראיתם אותה, או לדרומה של חמה? כמה היה גבוה, מן הארץ, לפי ראיית עיניכם. ולאין היה נוטה, ראשי הפגימה לאיזה צד נוטין; לצד צפון, או לצד דרום? גמ' היינו לפני החמה היינו לצפונה. הא דהא מילתא היא כדפריש לעיל. פגימתה לפני החמה, פונה לצד החמה או לצד אחר, והכי קתני מתני' אם אמר לפני החמה לא אמר כלום, דמעולם לא ראתה חמה פגימתה של לבנה. בימות הגשמים נמצאת לבנה בצפון, ובימות החמה נמצאת בדרום. אבל מצטרפין לעדות אחרת, אחד מהן מצטרף עם עד אחר שיאמר כמותו. ראינוהו במים, תוך נהר או מעין ראינו דמותה של לבנה. בעבים, יום המעונן היה, וראינוה מאירה דרך עוביו של עב. כל הכי חזו ואזלי, וכי לעולם הם צריכים לראות?

אמר רבי, אמר קרא (ויקרא כג) „וידבר משה את מועדי ה'" מכאן שראש ב"ד אומר מקודש. וכל העם עונין אחריו מקודש מקודש. מנלן? אמר רב פפא, אמר קרא (שם) „אשר תקראו אותם", קרי ביה אתם. ר"נ בר יצחק אמר (שם) „אלה הם מועדי" הם יאמרו מועדי. מקודש מקודש תרי זימני למה לי? דכתיב „מקרא קודש". ר"א בר צדוק אומר אם לא נראה בזמנו אין מקדשין אותו. תניא לימו א מר, בזמנו אין מקדשין אותו, שלא בזמנו מקדשין אותו: רבי אלעזר אומר, בין כך ובין כך אין מקדשין אותו, שנאמר (שם כה) „וקדשתם את שנת החמשים" שנים אתה מקדש ואי אתה מקדש חדשים. א"ר יהודה אמר שמואל, הלכה כרבי אלעזר בר צדוק. אמר אביי, אף אנן נמי תנינא: ראוהו ב"ד וכל ישראל, נחקרו העדים ולא הספיקו לומר מקודש עד שחשיכה, הרי זה מעובר; מעובר אין, מקודש לא? מעובר אצטריכא ליה, ס"ד אמינא הואיל וראוהו ב"ד וכל ישראל, איפרסמא ולא ליעברוה, קמ"ל. מתני' דמות צורות לבנה היו לו לר"ג בטבלא ובכותל בעלייתו, שבהן מראה את ההדיוטות ואומר: הכזה ראית, או כזה? גמ' ומי שרי? (כד:) והתניא „לא תעשון אתי" לא תעשון כדמות שמשי המשמשין לפני, כגון חמה ולבנה, כוכבים ומזלות? שאני ר"ג, דאחרים עשו לו. והא ר"י האחרים עשו לו וא"ל שמואל לר"י: שיננא, כמי עיניה דדין? התם חותמו בולט הוה ומשום חשדא. ומי חיישינן לחשדא? והא ההוא בי כנישתא דשף ויתיב בנהרדעא דהוה ביה אנדרטא, והוה עיילי רב ושמואל ואבוה דשמואל ולוי ומצלו התם ולא חיישי לחשדא? רבים שאני. והא ר"ג יחיד הוה? כיון דנשיא הוא שכיחי רבים גביה. ואבע"א להתלמד עבד, וכתיב (דברים יח) „לא תלמד לעשות", אבל אתה למד להבין ולהורות. מתני' מעשה שבאו שנים ואמרו: ראינוהו שחרית במזרח (כה.) וערבית במערב, א"ר יוחנן בן נורי. עדי שקר הם, כשבאו ליבנה קיבלן רבן גמליאל; ועוד באו שנים ואמרו: ראינוהו בזמנו ובליל עבורו לא נראה, וקיבלן ר"ג. א"ר דוסא בן הורכינס עדי שקר הם; היאך מעידין על האשה שילדה, ולמחר כריסה בין שיניה? אמר לו ר' יהושע: רואה אני את דבריך. שלח לו ר' גמליאל: גוזרני עליך שתבא אצלי במקלך ובמעותיך ביה"כ שחל להיות בחשבונך. הלך ומצאו רבי עקיבא מיצר. אמר לו, יש לי ללמוד שכל מה שעשה ר"ג עשוי, שנאמר (ויקרא כג) „אלה מועדי ה' מקראי קודש אשר תקראו אתם" בין בזמנן בין שלא בזמנן, אין לי מועדות אלא אלו. בא לו אצל ר' דוסא בן הורכינס, אמר לו: אם באין אנו לדון אחר בית דינו של רבן גמליאל, צריכין אנו לדון אחר כל בית דין ובית דין שעמד מימות משה ועד עכשיו, שנאמר (שמות כד) „ויעל משה ואהרן נדב ואביהוא ושבעים מזקני ישראל" ולמה לא נתפרשו שמותן של זקנים? אלא ללמד שכל שלשה ושלשה שעמדו בית דין על ישראל הרי הוא כבית דינו של משה. נטל מקלו ומעותיו בידו והלך ליבנה אצל ר"ג ביום

ר ש"י

מעידינן, כדי להעיד עליו. בגביתא עיבא, עגול של עב לבן. מקראי קדש, תרי זימני משמע. בזמנו אין מקדשין אותו, שאינו צריך חיזוק. מעובר אין, דמשמע כשחשיכה נתעבר. ומקודש לא, קתני הרי זה מתקדש למחר. אצטריכא ליה, כלומר לעולם למחר בעי קידוש, והא דלא תניה משום דאצטריכא לאשמועינן מעובר, דבזמנו ראוהו, סד"א לא ליעברוה, ואי תנא הרי זה מתקדש למחר הוה אמינא לעולם מיהא קמא מתקנינן מועדות. דשף ויתיב בנהרדעא, מקום הוא, ויש פותרין שחרב וחזר ונבנה. אנדרטא, צלם דמות המלך. והא ר"ג יחיד הוה, תיחוש נמי לחשדא. מתני' ראינוהו שחרית במזרח, את הישנה. וערבית במערב, את החדשה. עדי שקר הם, דקימא לן עשרים וארבעה שעי מכסי סיהרא. ראינוהו בזמנו, ביום שלשים. וליל שלשים, שהיו מצפין ב"ד והעם שתהא נגלה ויראוה מאחר שהקדים ראות ביום, לא נראה להם.

שחל יוה"כ להיות בחשבונו. עמד רבן גמליאל ונשקו על ראשו, אמר לו: בוא בשלום רבי ותלמידי, רבי בחכמה, ותלמידי שקבלת את דברי. גמ' תניא אמר להם רבן גמליאל לחכמים: כך מקובלני מבית אבי אבא, פעמים שבא בארוכה ופעמים שבא בקצרה. רבי חייא חזייא לסיהרא דהוה קאי בצפרא דעשרים ותשעה. שקל קלא פתק ביה. אמר, לאורתא בעינן לקדושי בך, ואת קיימת הכא? זיל איכסי! אמר ליה רבי לרבי חייא, זיל לעין טב וקדשיה לירחא, ושלח לי סימנא: דוד מלך ישראל חי וקים.
תנו רבנן, פעם אחת נתקשרו שמים בעבים ונראית דמות לבנה בעשרים ותשעה לחדש, כסבורים העם לומר ר"ה, ובקשו בית דין לקדשו, אמר להם ר"ג: כך מקובלני מבית אבי אבא: אין חדושה של לבנה פחותה מעשרים ותשעה יום ומחצה ושני שלישי שעה וע"ג חלקים, ואותו היום מתה אמו של בן זזא והספידה ר"ג הספד גדול, לא מפני שראויה לכך, אלא כדי שידעו העם שלא קידשו בית דין את החדש. בא לו אצל ר' דוסא בן הורכינס כו'. ת"ר, למה לא נתפרשו שמותם של זקנים הללו? שלא יאמר אדם: פלוני כמשה ואהרן? פלוני כנדב ואביהוא? פלוני כאלדד ומידד? ואומר (שמואל א יב) "ויאמר שמואל אל העם ה' אשר עשה את משה ואת אהרן", ואומר (שם) "וישלח ה' את ירובעל ואת בדן ואת יפתח ואת שמואל" ירובעל, זה גדעון, ולמה נקרא שמו ירובעל? שעשה מריבה עם הבעל, בדן זה שמשון, ולמה נקרא שמו בדן? דאתי מדן, יפתח כמשמעו, (כה:) ואומר (תה"ל צט) "משה ואהרן בכהניו ושמואל בקוראי שמו", שקל הכתוב שלשה קלי עולם כשלשה חמורי עולם לומר לך, ירובעל בדורו כמשה בדורו, בדן בדורו כאהרן בדורו, יפתח בדורו כשמואל בדורו; ללמדך שאפילו קל שבקלין ונתמנה פרנס על הצבור הרי הוא כאביר שבאבירים, ואומר (דברים יז) "ובאת אל הכהנים הלוים ואל השופט אשר יהיה בימים ההם", וכי תעלה על דעתך שאדם הולך אצל הדיין שלא היה בימיו? הא אין לך לילך אלא אצל שופט שבימיו, ואומר (קהלת ז) "אל תאמר מה היה שהימים הראשונים היו טובים מאלה". נטל מקלו ומעותיו בידו. ת"ר, אמר לו: אשרי הדור שהגדולים נשמעים לקטנים ומתוך זה נושאים הקטנים ק"ו בעצמן.

הדרן עלך אם אינן מכירין

ראוהו בית דין וכל ישראל, נחקרו העדים ולא הספיקו לומר מקודש, עד שחשיכה, הרי זה מעובר. ראוהו ב"ד בלבד, יעמדו שנים ויעידו בפניהם ויאמרו:

רש"י

רואה אני את דבריך, לעבר את החדש. הלך ומצאו, הלך ומצאו ר"ע לרבי יהושע מיצר על שהנשיא גזר עליו לחלל יוה"כ. אשר תקראו, בקריאת בית דין תלאו הכתוב. בא לו, רבי יהושע אצל רבי דוסא. גמ' חזייא לסיהרא, ללבנה. שקל קלא, חתיכת רגבים. לאורתא בעינן לקדושיה, צריכין אלו לעשות הלילה יו"ט של ר"ח לעבר את אלול. ואת קיימת הכא, ואם תהא נראית ערבית שוב לא יקדשו את החדש למחר. זיל לעין טב וקדשיה. מורי פירש שגזרו שמד במקומו שלא יקדשו את החדש. דוד מלך ישראל, נמשל כלבנה שנאמר בו כסאו כשמש נגדי כירח יכון לעולם. שידעו שלא קדשו ב"ד את החדש, שאין מספידין בר"ח. שלא יאמר אדם, על ב"ד שבימיו וכי פלוני ופלוני כמשה ואהרן שאשמע להן עכשיו שלא נתפרשו אומר לו אם אינו כמשה ואהרן, הרי הוא כאחד משאר זקנים שאינך יודע מי הם. אשר עשה את משה ואת אהרן, שמואל הנביא אמר לישראל הקב"ה עשה לכם נסים ע"י ששה זקנים הללו: משה ואהרן ירובעל ובדן ויפתח ושמואל. ושמואל בקוראי שמו. הרי ששקל הכתוב שמואל עם משה ואהרן, ובכתובים הראשונים כתוב ירובעל בדן ויפתח עם משה ואהרן ושמואל שלשה קלים עם שלשה חמורים. הא אין לך לילך כו', הרי למדך הכתוב כאן, שאין לך לבקש אלא שופט שהיה בימיך.

הדרן עלך אם אינן מכירין

מקודש מקודש. ראוהו שלשה והן ב"ד, יעמדו השנים וישיבו מחביריהם אצל היחיד ויעידו בפניהם ויאמרו מקודש מקודש, שאין היחיד נאמן ע"י עצמו. **גמ'** ראוהו ב"ד יעמדו שנים ויעידו בפניהם: ואמאי, לא תהא שמיעה גדולה מראייה? א"ר זירא, כגון שראוהו בלילה. ראוהו שלשה והן בית דין יעמדו שנים וישיבו מחביריהם אצל היחיד. אמאי הכא נמי נימא לא תהא שמיעה גדולה מראייה? וכי תימא ה"נ כגון שראוהו בלילה, היינו הך? סיפא איצטריכא ליה, דאין היחיד נאמן על ידי עצמו, דסלקא דעתך אמינא הואיל ותנן דיני ממונות בשלשה, ואם היה מומחה לרבים דן אפילו ביחיד, הכא נמי ניקדשיה ביחידי? קא משמע לן! ואימא הכי נמי? אין לך מומחה לרבים בישראל יותר ממשה רבינו, וקאמר ליה הקב"ה עד דאיכא אהרן בהדך, דכתיב (שמות יב) „ויאמר ה' אל משה ואל אהרן בארץ מצרים לאמר החדש הזה לכם". למימרא דעד נעשה דיין? לימא מתני' דלא כר"ע, דתניא, סנהדרין שראו אחד שהרג את הנפש (כו.) מקצתן נעשו עדים, ומקצתן נעשו דיינין, דברי רבי טרפון; רבי עקיבא אומר, כולן נעשין עדים, ואין עד נעשה דיין? אפילו תימא רבי עקיבא, עד כאן לא קאמר רבי עקיבא התם, אלא בדיני נפשות, דרחמנא אמר (במדבר לה) „ושפטו העדה והצילו העדה" וכיון דחזיוה דקטל נפשא, לא מצי חזו ליה זכותא, אבל הכא, אפילו רבי עקיבא מודה. **מתני'** כל השופרות כשרים חוץ משל פרה, מפני שהוא קרן. אמר רבי יוסי, והלא כל השופרות נקראו קרן! שנאמר (יהושע ו) „במשוך בקרן היובל". מאי משמע דהאי יובלא לישנא דדכרא הוא? דתניא, אמר ר' עקיבא, כשהלכתי לערביא היו קורין לדכרא, יובלא. (כו:) לא הוו ידעי רבנן מאי (משלי ד) „סלסלה ותרוממך" יומא חד שמעוה לאמתא דבי רבי, דהוות אמרה להההוא גברא, דהוה קא מהפך בשעריה. „אמרה ליה עד מתי אתה מסלסל בשערך? לא הוו ידעו רבנן מאי (תהלים נה) „השלך על ה' יהבך". אמר רבה בר בר חנה, יומא חד הוה אזילנא בהדי ההוא טייעא, הוה דרינא טונא, ואמר לי שקול יהביך ושדי אגמלאי. **מתני'** שופר של ראש השנה של יעל פשוט. ופיו מצופה זהב, ושתי חצוצרות מן הצדדין, שופר מאריך וחצוצרות מקצרות, שמצות היום בשופר: ובתעניות בשל זכרים כפופין, ופיהן מצופה כסף. ושתי חצוצרות באמצע, שופר מקצר וחצוצרות מאריכות. שוה היובל לר"ה לתקיעה ולברכות, ר"י אומר בר"ה תוקעין בשל זכרים. וביובלות בשל יעלים. **גמ'** אמר ר' לוי מצוה של ר"ה ושל יה"כ בכפופין, ושל כל השנה בפשוטין.

ר ש"י

ונחקרו העדים, אי נמי נחקרו העדים. ראוהו ב"ד בלבד, שאין מי שיעיד אלא הם, ולאו אריפא קאי בבמוך לחשיבה, אלא שהיה שהות לקדש. יעמדו שנים ויעידו בפניהם, ואע"פ שכולן ראוהו. ויעידו בפניהם. השנים. שאין היחיד נאמן, לומר מקודש בפני עצמו, לכך צריך להושיב מחביריהן אצלו. גמ' ואמאי, יעמדו שנים ויעידו הא ראוהו כולן יקדשוהו בראייתם. שראוהו בלילה, הילכך למחר אי לאו שמיעה על כח יקדשו. למימרא דעד נעשה דיין, כי שראוי להיות עד בדבר נעשה דיין, ואלו כולן ראוים להיות עדים שהרי כולם ראוהו. מקצתן נעשין עדים, ויעידו בפני חבריהם. ומקצתן נעשין דיינים, אבל המעידים לא ישבו וידונו עמהם, הכי עדות החדש נמי לא אכשרנא במתני' להיות העדים נעשים דיינים, דא"כ למה לי יושיבו מחביריהם? יעידו בפני יחיד ואחר כך ישבו הם עמו ויקדשו. כולן עדים הם, ראוים להעיד. והצילו העדה, יחפשו בזכותו. מתני' שהוא קרן, אינו קרוי שופר תני יה"כ שופר כתיב. בקרן היובל, ויובל דיכרא הוא. ופיו מצופה זהב, בשל מקדש קאמר. שופר מאריך, לאחר שחצוצרות פוסקין תקיעתן, נשמע קול השופר. ובתעניות, דאמרינן בתעניות תקעו הכהנים תקעו. בשל זכרים, אילים שנתכן כפופין. ושתי חצוצרות באמצע, שני שופרות לזה אלו מכאן ואחד מכאן והן באמצע. שמצות היום בחצוצרות, דלכנופיא בעלמא ניתנו וכל כנופיא בחצוצרות דכתיב והיה לך למקרא העדה. להקיעת

והתנן שופר של ר"ה של יעל פשוט? הוא דאמר כי האי תנא; דתניא ר' יהודה אומר, בר"ה היו תוקעין בשל זכרים כפופין, וביובלות בשל יעלים. במאי קמיפלגי? מר סבר בר"ה כמה דכייף איניש דעתיה טפי מעלי, וביה"כ כמה דפשיט איניש דעתיה טפי מעלי, ומר סבר בראש השנה כמה דפשיט איניש דעתיה טפי מעלי, ובתעניות כמה דכייף איניש דעתיה טפי מעלי. (כז.) ופיו מצופה זהב. והתניא ציפהו זהב במקום הנחת פיו פסול, שלא במקום הנחת פיו כשר? אמר אביי, כי תנן נמי כתניתין שלא במקום הנחת פה תנן. ושתי חצוצרות מן הצדדים. ותרי קלי מי משתמעי? לכך מאריך בשופר, לידע שמצות היום בשופר. ובתעניות של זכרים כפופין ופיו מצופה כסף. מאי שנא התם דזהב, ומ"ש הכא דכסף? כל כינופיא דכסף הוא, דכתיב (במדבר י) „עשה לך שתי חצוצרות כסף". רב פפא בר שמואל סבר למיעבד עובדא כמתניתך, אמר ליה רבא: לא אמרו אלא במקדש. תניא נמי הכי. במה דברים אמורים במקדש, אבל בגבולין, מקום שיש חצוצרות אין שופר, מקום שיש שופר אין חצוצרות. וכן הנהיג רבי חלפתא בציפורי, ורבי חנניא בן תרדיון בסכני; וכשבא דבר אצל חכמים אמרו: לא היו נוהגין כן אלא בשערי מזרח ובהר הבית בלבד. אמר רבא ואיתימא ריב"ל מאי קרא? דכתיב (תהלים צח) „בחצוצרות וקול שופר הריעו לפני המלך ה'", לפני המלך ה' הוא דבעינן חצוצרות וקול שופר, אבל בעלמא לא. שוה היובל לר"ה לתקיעה ולברכות כו'. א"ר שמואל בר יצחק כמאן מצלינן האידנא: זה היום תחילת מעשיך זכרון ליום ראשון? כר' אליעזר, דאמר בתשרי נברא העולם. מתיב רב עינא: שוה יובל לר"ה לתקיעה ולברכות. והא איכא זה היום תחילת מעשיך זכרון ליום ראשון, דבר"ה איתא וביובל ליתא? כי קתני אשארא. **מתני'** שופר שנסדק ודבקו פסול, דיבק שברי שופרות פסול; (כז:) ניקב וסתמו אם מעכב את התקיעה פסול, ואם לאו כשר. התוקע לתוך הדות, או לתוך הפיטס, אם קול שופר שמע יצא, ואם קול הברה שמע לא יצא; וכן מי שהיה עובר אחורי בית הכנסת, או שהיה ביתו סמוך לבית הכנסת, ושמע קול שופר, או קול מגילה אם כיון לבו יצא, ואם לאו לא יצא, אע"פ שזה שמע וזה שמע: זה כיון לבו, וזה לא כיון לבו. **גמ'** ת"ר, ארוך וקצרו כשר. גרדו והעמידו על גלדו כשר; ציפהו זהב מבפנים פסול, מבחוץ, אם נשתנה קולו מכמות שהיה פסול, וא"ל כשר; ניקב וכתמו אם מעכב את התקיעה פסול, וא"ל כשר; נתן שופר בתוך שופר, אם קול פנימי שמע יצא, ואם קול חיצון שמע לא יצא. דיבק שברי שופרות פסול. ת"ר. הוסיף עליו כ"ש, בין במינו בין שלא במינו פסול; ניקב וסתמו בין במינו ובין שלא במינו פסול: רבי נתן אומר, במינו כשר שלא במינו פסול. אר"י, והוא שנפחת רובו. מכלל דבמינו אע"פ שנפחת רובו כשר; ציפהו זהב מבפנים פסול,

---

ר ש"י

בפשוטין, ולברכות, דבעי למימר תשע ברכות ביום הכיפורים של יובל. נמי דשל כל השנה, של תעניות. במאי קא מיפלגי, תנא קמא ור' יהודה. כמה דכייף איניש, בתפלתו פניו כבושין לארץ טפי עדיף. כמה דפשיט טפי עדיף, הילכך בראש השנה בפשוטין דתפלה היא ויום הכפורים נמי מקום דהוה בגזירה שוה ובתענית דלכינופיא לא איכפת לן ועבדינן כפופין להכירא. במקום הנחת פה פסול, שהתקיעה בזהב ולא בשופר. לכך מאריך בשופר. תירוצא הוא. למיעבד עובדא, בחצוצרות ושופר. מקום שיש שופר, כגון ר"ה ויובל. מקום שיש חצוצרות, כגון תעניות. הנהיג, כשמנהגינו שופר וחצוצרות. ובהר הבית, הוא מילתא היא בשערי מזרח בהר הבית, וי"א בשערי מזרח בעזרת נשים. מתני' ודבקו, בדבק. מכל דהוה ליה כשני שופרות. על גלדו, גלד דק. פסול, שהתקיעה בזהב. לא יצא, דאיכא מחיצות, הפנימי מפסקת התקיעה. במינו כשר, אם אינו מעכב את התקיעה. נסדק, כולו, וכן נסדק לרחבו, כל רחבו לתקיעה. אם נשתייר בו, כן מקום

מבחוץ אם ניתנה קולו מכמות שהיה פסול, ואם לאו כשר; נכדק לארכו פסול, לרוחבו אם נשתייר בו שיעור תקיעה כשר, ואם לאו פסול; וכמה שיעור תקיעה? פירש רשב"ג, כדי שיאחזנו בידו ויראה לכאן ולכאן; היה קולו דק או עבה או צרור כשר, שכל הקולות כשירין בשופר. שלחו ליה לאבוה דשמואל: קדחו ותקע בו יצא. פשיטא! כולהו נמי מיקדח קדחו להו! אמר רב אשי שקדחו בזכרותו, כהו דתימא מין במינו חוצץ? קמ"ל! התוקע לתוך הבור או לתוך הדות. אמר רב הונא, לא שנו אלא לאותן העומדים על שפת הבור, אבל אותן העומדין בבור יצאו. (כח.) שמע מקצת תקיעה בבור, ומקצת תקיעה על שפת הבור, יצא; מקצת תקיעה קודם שיעלה עמוד השחר, ומקצת תקיעה לאחר שעלה עמוד השחר, לא יצא. אמר ליה אביי, מאי שנא התם, דבעינא כולה תקיעה בחיובא וליכא? הכא נמי בעינא כולה תקיעה בחיובא וליכא? הכי השתא! התם לילה לאו זמן חיובא הוא כלל, הכא בור מקום חיובא הוא לאותן העומדין בבור. למימר דכבר רבה: שמע סוף תקיעה בלא תחילת תקיעה יצא, ומכ"ש תחילת תקיעה בלא סוף תקיעה יצא? ת"ש! תקע בראשונה ומשך בשנייה כשתים, אין בידו אלא אחת, ואמאי תסלק לה בתרתי? פסוקי תקיעתא מהדדי לא פסקינן. אמר רבא, המודר הנאה מחבירו, מותר לתקוע לו תקיעה של מצוה; המודר הנאה משופר, מותר לתקוע בו תקיעה של מצוה. ואמר רבא, המודר הנאה מחבירו, מזה עליו מי חטאת ביאות הגשמים, אבל לא ביאות החמה. המודר הנאה ממעיין, טובל בו טבילה של מצוה. ביאות הגשמים, אבל לא ביאות החמה. שלחו ליה לאבוה דשמואל: כפאו ואכל מצה יצא. כפאו מאן? א"ר אשי, שכפאוהו פרסיים. אמר רבא, זאת אומרת התוקע לשיר יצא. פשיטא, היינו הך! מהו דתימא, התם אכול מצה אמר רחמנא, והא אכל. (כח:) אבל הכא (ויקרא כג) „זכרון תרועה" כתיב והאי מתעסק בעלמא הוא, קמ"ל! איתיביה, נתכוון שומע, ולא נתכוון משמיע, משמיע ולא נתכוון שומע לא יצא, עד שיתכוון שומע ומשמיע. בשלמא נתכוון משמיע ולא נתכוון שומע, כסבור חמור בעלמא הוא. אלא נתכוין שומע ולא נתכוון משמיע. היכי משכחת לה, לאו בתוקע לשיר? דילמא דקא מנבח נבוחי. א"ל אביי, אלא מעתה, הישן בשמיני בסוכה ילקה? א"ל, שאני אומר מצות אינו עובר עליהן אלא בזמנן. מתיב רב שמן בר אבא, מנין לכהן שעולה לדוכן, שלא יאמר הואיל ונתנה לי תורה רשות לברך את ישראל אוסיף ברכה אחת משלי, כגון (דברים א)

ר ש" י

נבדק עד מקום הנקב אם שיעור תקיעה כשר. צרור, לשון יבש. קדחו, נקבו וקדח נקב הנקב את קאמר. שקדחו בזכרותו, כשהוא כתוב בבהמה עצם בולט מן הראש שנכנס לתוכו ומוציא; אותו מתוכו, וזה לא הוציאו, אלא נקב את הזכרות. אותן העומדין בבור יצאו שהן קול השופר לעולם שמעו. שמע מקצת התקיעה בבור כו', קא סלקא דעתך והכי קאמר: היה עומד הוא בשפת הבור וחבירו תוקע בבור ויצא לדרון בחצי התקיעה, ואשמעינן הכא דמקצת נמי יוצא. קודם עמוד השחר, לאו זמניה הוא כדאמרינן במסכת מגילה: כל היום כשר לתקיעת שופר וילפינן מקרא יום תרועה יהיה לכם, יום ולא לילה. תקע בראשונה, בפשוטה שלפני תרועת המלכיות. ומשך בשנייה, בפשוטה של אחריה כשתים ונתכוון לצאת בה אף ידי פשוטה שלפני תרועת הזכרונות שעתיד עליו לתקוע תיבה זו. מותר לתקוע לו, מצוה דבוריהו בשום דמצות לאו ליהנות ניתנו. חבירו מזה עליו ביאות הגשמים, שאין כאן אלא הנאת קיום המצות. אבל לא ביאות החמה, דאיכא הנאת הגוף. שכפאוהו פרסיים, ואע"ג שלא נתכוון לצאת ידי חובת מצה בליל ראשון של פסח יצא. התוקע לשיר, לשורר וזומר כך שמעתי מפי מורי הזקן. פשיטא, וזאת אומרת כן. מהו דתימא התם אכול מצה קאמר רחמנא והא אכל, ותהנה באכילתו הלכך לאו מתעסק הוא. קא משמע לן, דאע"ג דמתעסק הוא יצא. אלא מעתה, דאין מתכוון למצוה כמתכוון דמי. הישן

„ה' אלהי אבותיכם יוסף עליכם?" ת"ל (שם ד) „לא תוסיפו על הדבר" והא הכא, כיון דבריך ליה עברה ליה זמניה, וקתני דעבר? אמר רבא, לצאת לא בעי כוונה, לעבור בזמנו לא בעי כוונה, שלא בזמנו בעי כוונה. אמר ליה רבי זירא לשמעיה, (כט.) איכוון ותקע לי, אלמא קסבר משמיע בעי כוונה? תנאי היא, דתניא שומע שומע לעצמו, ומשמיע משמיע לפי דרכו; א"ר יוסי, בד"א בשליח צבור, אבל ביחיד לא יצא עד שיתכוין שומע ומשמיע. מתני' (שמות יז) „והיה כאשר ירים משה ידו וגבר ישראל" וגו' וכי ידיו של משה עושות מלחמה או שוברות מלחמה? אלא לומר לך: כל זמן שהיו ישראל מסתכלין כלפי מעלה ומשעבדין את לבם לאביהם שבשמים, היו מתגברים. ואם לאו היו נופלים; כיוצא בדבר אתה אומר (במדבר כא) „עשה לך שרף ושים אותו על נס והיה כל הנשוך וראה אותו וחי" וכי נחש ממית או נחש מחיה? אלא בזמן שישראל מסתכלין כלפי מעלה ומשעבדין את לבם לאביהם שבשמים, היו מתרפאין, ואם לאו, היו נמוקים. חרש, שוטה וקטן אין מוציאין את הרבים ידי חובתן. זה הכלל: כל שאינו מחוייב בדבר, אינו מוציא את הרבים ידי חובתן: גמ' ת"ר, הכל חייבין בתקיעת שופר. כהנים ולוים וישראלים, גרים ועבדים משוחררים וטומטום ואנדרוגינוס. מי שחציו עבד וחציו בן חורין, טומטום אינו מוציא לא את מינו ולא את שאינו מינו. אנדרוגינוס מוציא את מינו, אבל לא את שאינו מינו. אמר מר, הכל חייבין בתקיעת שופר: כהנים לוים וישראלים. פשיטא! אי הני לא מיחייבי, מאן מיחייבי? כהנים איצטריכא ליה, ס"ד אמינא הואיל ותנן, שוה היובל לר"ה לתקיעה ולברכות, מאן דאיתיה במצות היובל, איתיה במצות דראש השנה, והני כהנים הואיל וליתנהו במצות דיובל. איכא במצוה דראש השנה לא ליחייבו? קמ"ל! תני אהבה בריה דרבי זירא: כל הברכות כולן, אע"פ שיצא מוציא, חוץ מברכת הלחם וברכת היין, שאם לא יצא מוציא, ואם יצא אינו מוציא. בעי רבא, (כט:) ברכת הלחם של מצה וברכת היין של קידוש היום מהו? כיון דחובה היא, מפיק, או דילמא, ברכה לאו חובה היא? תא שמע, דאמר רב אשי, כי הוינן בי רב פפי הוה מקדש לן, וכי הוה אתי אריסיה מדברא הוה מקדש להו. תנו רבנן, לא יפרוס אדם פרוסה לאורחין, אלא אם כן אוכל עמהם, אבל פורס הוא לבניו ולבני ביתו, כדי לחנכן במצות, ובהלל ובמגילה אף על פי שיצא מוציא.

הדרן עלך ראוהו בית דין

רש"י

בשמיני בכוונה, שלא לשום מצוה. ילקה, שהרי עובר משום בל תוסיף? מצוה אין עובר עליו, בבל תוסיף אלא בזמנו כגון חמשה מינין בלולב אבל תוספת יום על ימים או שעה על שעה אין זה מוסיף. איכוון ותקע לי, תתכוין לתקוע בשמי להוציאני ידי חובתי. משמיע בעי כוונה, להוציא השומע. גמ' ועבדים משוחררין, אבל שאינן משוחררין לא. וטומטום ואנדרוגינוס, שמא זכר הוא. מי שחציו עבד, משום צד חירות שבו. את מינו, טומטום כמותו, שמא תוקע זה נקבה וחבירו זכר. מוציא מינו, אנדרוגינוס כמותו. מי שחציו עבד כו', דלא אתי צד עבדות דמשמיע ומפיק לצד חירות דשומע. אף על פי שיצא מוציא, שהרי כל ישראל ערבין זה בזה למצות. חוץ מברכת הלחם והיין, שאינן חובה אלא שאסור ליהנות מן העולם הזה בלא ברכה. ברכת הלחם, של אכילת מצה שמברכין לפניה המוציא. וברכת היין, שמברכין לפני קידוש. מהו, על אכילת מצה ומקדש ישראל לא תיבעי לך דחובה נינהו ומפיק, אלא ברכת המוציא וברכת היין. ואי אפשר דלא יתיב ליה לחד מינייהו לסעוד הכי ברכה מאי? כיון דחובה היא, אכילת מצה חובה עליו וכן קידוש היום חובה עליו. או דלמא, ברכת הנאה לאו חובה למצוה אתיא שאף בכל המצוות היא נוהגת. לא יפרוס, ברכת המוציא שאינה חובה עליהם.

הדרן עלך ראוהו בית דין.

יום טוב של ראש השנה שחל להיות בשבת, במקדש היו תוקעין, אבל לא במדינה; משחרב בית המקדש התקין רבן יוחנן בן זכאי, שיהו תוקעין בכל מקום שיש בו בית דין. אמר רבי אלעזר, לא התקין רבן יוחנן בן זכאי, אלא ביבנה בלבד; אמרו לו אחד יבנה ואחד כל מקום שיש בו בית דין. ועוד זאת היתה ירושלים יתירה על יבנה, שכל עיר שהיא רואה ושומעת וקרובה ויכולה לבוא תוקעין, וביבנה לא היו תוקעין, אלא בבית דין בלבד. גמ' מנה"מ? אמר רבא רבנן הוא דגזור ביה, כדרבה, דאמר רבה הכל חייבין בתקיעת שופר, ואין הכל בקיאין בתקיעת שופר, גזירה שמא יטלנו בידו, וילך אצל הבקי ללמוד, ויעבירנו ד' אמות בר"ה. והיינו טעמא דלולב, והיינו טעמא דמגילה. משחרב בית המקדש התקין רבן יוחנן בן זכאי כו'. תנו רבנן, פעם אחת חל ר"ה להיות בשבת, והיו כל הערים מתכנסין, אמר להם רבן יוחנן בן זכאי לבני בתירה: נתקע; אמרו לו: נדון; אמר להם: נתקע ואח"כ נדון; לאחר שתקעו אמרו לו: נדון. אמר להם: כבר נשמעת קרן ביבנה, ואין משיבין לאחר מעשה. אמרו לו אחד יבנה ואחד כל מקום שיש בו ב"ד. אמר רב הונא, (ל.) בפני בית דין, לאפוקי שלא בפני בית דין דלא? והא, כי אתא רב יצחק בר יוסף אמר, כי הוה מסיים שליחא דציבורא תקיעה ביבנה, לא שמע איניש קל אוניה מתקיעתא דיחידאי? בפני ב"ד היו תוקעין. איתמר נמי, אמר רבי אין תוקעין אלא כל זמן שב"ד יושבין. יתירה על יבנה וכו'. רואה פרט ליושבת בנחל, שומעת פרט ליושבת בראש ההר, קרובה פרט ליושבת חוץ לתחום, ויכולה לבוא פרט למפסיק לה נהרא. מתני' בראשונה היה הלולב ניטל במקדש שבעה, ובמדינה יום אחד, משחרב בית המקדש התקין רבן יוחנן בן זכאי שיהא לולב ניטל במדינה שבעה זכר למקדש, ושיהא יום הנף כולו אסור. גמ' ומנלן דעבדינן זכר למקדש? דאמר קרא (ירמיה ל) „כי אעלה ארוכה לך וממכותיך ארפאך נאם ה' כי נדחה קראו לך ציון היא דורש אין לה" מכלל דבעיא דרישה. ושיהא יום הנף כולו אסור. אמר רב נחמן בר יצחק רבן יוחנן בן זכאי (ל:) בשיטת רבי יהודה אמרה, דאמר (ויקרא כג) „עד עצם היום הזה" עד עצמו של יום, וקסבר עד ועד בכלל. ומי סבר לה כותיה והא מפליג פליג עליה? דתנן, משחרב בית המקדש התקין רבן יוחנן בן זכאי שיהא יום הנף כולו אסור; א"ר יהודה. והלא מן התורה הוא אסור, דכתיב עד עצם היום הזה? התם ר' יהודה הוא דקא טעי: איהו סבר רבן יוחנן בן זכאי מדרבנן קאמר, ולא היא. מדאורייתא קאמר. והא התקין קתני? מאי התקין, דרש והתקין. מתני' בראשונה היו מקבלין עדות החדש כל היום. פעם אחת נשתהו העדים מלבוא ונתקלקלו הלוים בשיר. התקינו שלא יהו מקבלין אלא עד המנחה. ואם באו

ר ש"י

אבל לא במדינה, לא בירושלים ולא בגבולין. אלא ביבנה, שהיתה שם סנהדרין גדולה בימיו, וכן בכל מקום שגלתה סנהדרין. ועוד זאת היתה ירושלים, בעודה בבנינה יתירה בתקיעת שבת על יבנה. גמ' גזירה שמא יטלנו וכו', ובמקדש לא גזור דאין איסור שבות דרבנן במקדש. והיו כל הערים, שסביבות יבנה, מתכנסים, לשם לשמוע תקיעה משלוחי בית דין לפי שהיו תלוין בן בירושלים. בני בתירה, גדולי הדור היו. נדון, אם יש לגזור אף במקום בית דין שמא יעבירנו. ואין משיבין לאחר מעשה, כבר תקעו שנעשה לנו מעשה על עצמנו. איתמר נמי, כרב הונא. אין תוקעין, יחידים ביום הכפורים ביובל, אלא בזמן שב"ד יושבין במקומן והתוקעין תוקעין בכל העיר. מתני' ושיהא יום הנפת עומר כולו אסור לאכול מן החדש, ומדאורייתא משהאיר מזרח מותר. בשיטת ר' יהודה אמרה, דאמר מן התורה אסור כל היום בזמן הזה דקסבר עד ועד בכלל. מדרבנן קאמר, כלומר הוא בא לגזור עליו משום ההוא טעמא דלעיל דשמא יבנה. דרש והתקין, דרש להם המקרא ותקן שינהגו איסור, לפי שעד עכשיו היה היתר בדבר משקרב העומר שהעומר מתיר. מתני' נוהגים אותו היום

עדים מן המנחה ולמעלה, נוהגין אותו היום קודש ולמחר קודש. משחרב בהמ״ק התקין רבן יוחנן בן זכאי שיהו מקבלין עדות החדש כל היום. **גמ׳** מה קילקול קילקלו הלוים בשיר? א״ל ר׳ זירא לאהבה בריה פוק תני להו: התקינו שלא יהו מקבלין עדות החדש, אלא כדי שיהא שהות ביום להקריב תמידין ומוספין ונסכיהם, ולומר שירה שלא בשיבוש. (לא.) תניא רבי יהודה אומר משום ר״ע: בראשון מה היו אומרים? (תהלים כד) „לה׳ הארץ ומלואה״ על שם שקנה והקנה ושליט בעולמו; בשני מה היו אומרים? (שם מח) „גדול ה׳ ומהולל מאד״ על שם שחילק מעשיו ומלך עליהן; בשלישי היו אומרים: (שם פב) „אלהים נצב בעדת אל״ על שם שגילה ארץ בחכמתו והכין תבל לעדתו; ברביעי היו אומרים: (שם צד) „אל נקמות ה׳״ ע״ש שברא חמה ולבנה ועתיד ליפרע מעובדיהן; בחמישי היו אומרים: (שם פא) „הרנינו לאלהים עוזנו״ על שם שברא עופות ודגים לשבח לשמו; בששי היו אומרים: (שם צג) „ה׳ מלך גאות לבש״ על שם שגמר מלאכתו ומלך עליהן: בשביעי היו אומרים: (שם צב) „מזמור שיר ליום השבת״, ליום שכלו שבת. אמר ר׳ נחמיה, מה ראו חכמים לחלק בין הפרקים הללו? אלא בשביעי על שם ששבת; וקמיפלגי בדרב קטינא, דאמר רב קטינא שיתא אלפי שני הוי עלמי וחד חריב, שנאמר (ישעיה ב) „ונשגב יי׳ לבדו ביום ההוא״, אביי אמר תרי חרוב שנאמר (הושע ו) „יחיינו מיומים״. במוספי דשבתא מה היו אומרים? אמר רב ענן בר רבא אמר רב, הזי״ו ל״ך. ואמר רב חנן בר רבא אמר רב, כדרך שחלוקים כאן כך חלוקין בבית הכנסת. במנחתא דשבתא מה היו אומרים? אמר ר׳ יוחנן, אז ישיר. ומי כמוך, ואז ישיר. איבעיא להו, הני כולהו בחד שבתא אמר להו. או דילמא כל שבתא ושבתא אמרי חד? תא שמע, דתניא א״ר יוסי. עד שהראשונה אומרת אחת שנייה חוזרת שתים, שמע מינה כל שבתא ושבתא אמרי חד. שמע מינה. אמר רב יהודה בר אידי א״ר יוחנן, עשר מסעות נסעה שכינה, מקראי ובנגדן גלתה סנהדרין, מגמרא. מלשכת הגזית, לחנות, ומחנויות לירושלים, ומירושלים

ר ש ״ י

קודש, בראש השנה קאי דמשתחשכה לילי עשרים והשלה נהגו בו קודש שמא יבואו עדים מחר ויקדשוהו ב״ד ונמצא שהלילה הזה ליל י״ט הוא וכן למחר כל היום עד המנחה, ואם באו עדים קודם המנחה בית דין מקדשים את החדש ונודע שיפה נהגו בו קודש, ואם מן המנחה ולמעלה באו אע״פ שאין ב״ד מקבלין אותן לקדשו היום ויעברו את אלול ויקדשוהו למחר אעפ״כ גומרים אותו בקדושה ואסור במלאכה דילמא אתי לזלזולי ביה לשנה הבאה ויעשו בו מלאכה כל היום דאמרו אשתקד נהגנו בו קודש הגם מן המנחה ולמעלה חזרנו ונהגנו בו חול. גמ׳ פוק תני להו, שנה להם ברייתא זו שבמשנה ילמדו שאמרו שיר של חול. לה׳ הארץ, כל המזמור. שקנה, שמים וארץ. והקנה, תבל ליושבי בה כלומר קונה כדי להקנות. שחילק מעשיו, הבדיל רקיע בין עליונים לתחתונים ונתעלה וישב במרום. מה ראה ר״ע לחלק בין הפרשיות הללו, שכל שבעת ימים נאמרין הפרקים הללו על שם שבעה ימי שבת על שם לחנא. וקא מיפלגי בדרב קטינא, ר׳ נחמיה לית ליה דרב קטינא, אלא דאביי. במוספי דשבתא, מאי שיר אמרי. הזי״ו ל״ך, פרשת שירת האזינו דחלקים אותה לששה פרקים: האזינו, זכור ימות עולם, ירכיבהו על במותי ארץ, וירא ה׳ וינאץ, לולי כעס אויב אגור, כי ידין ה׳ עמו. כדרך שחולקין, פירקי דשירה הזאת כאן. כך חולקין בבית הכנסת, כך קורין אותם ששה הקורין בספר תורה והוי׳ קורא מן השירה הלזו. אז ישיר, שירת הים עד מי כמוכה. ומי כמוכה, עד סוף השירה. ואז ישיר, ישראל עלי באר. בחד שבתא אמרו להו, הללים. או דילמא, כל פרק ופרק לשבת אחת פרק אחד. עד שהראשונה, שירת המוספין חוזרת דלילה פעם אחת. שניה, שירת המנחה של תמיד הערבים. חוזרת שתים, דהתם שית פירקי והכא תלתא: האזינו בשבת אחת, זכור בשבת שניה וכן כולם. עשר מסעות כו׳ בשום דאיירי מתני׳ בתקנות של יבנה נקט לה הכא. נסעה שכינה, להסתלק מעל ישראל מעט מעט כשחטאו. (מקראי, כלומר דיש להו הסמכי אקראי). מלשכת הגזית לחנות, חנויות עשו להם בהר הבית

ליבנה, (לא:) ומיבנה לאושא, ומאושא ליבנה, ומיבנה לאושא, ומאושא לשפרעם, ומשפרעם לבית שערים, ומבית שערים לצפורי, ומצפורי לטבריא, וטברי' עמוקה מכולן, שנאמר (ישעיה כט) „ושפלת מארץ תדברי". רבי אלעזר אומר שש גלות, שנאמר (שם כו) „כי השח יושבי מרום קריה נשגבה ישפילנה ישפילה עד ארץ יגיענה עד עפר" אמר ר' יוחנן, ומשם עתידין ליגאל שנאמר (שם לב) „התנערי מעפר קומי שבי". מתני' אמר ר' יהושע בן קרחה, ועוד זאת התקין רבן יוחנן בן זכאי, שאפילו ראש בית דין בכל מקום, שלא יהו העדים הולכין אלא למקום הועד. גמ' ההיא איתתא דאזמנוה לדינא קמיה דאמימר בנהרדעי, אזל אמימר למחוזא ולא אזלה בתריה, כתב פתיחא עילווה. אמר ליה רב אשי לאמימר: והא אנן תנן אפילו ראש בית דין בכל מקום, שלא יהו העדים הולכין אלא למקום הועד? א"ל, הני מילי לענין עדות החודש אבל הכא (משלי כב) „עבד לוה לאיש מלוה". ת"ר, אין כהנים רשאין לעלות בסנדליהם לדוכן, וזו אחד מתשע תקנות שהתקין ריב"ז: שית דהאי פירקא וחדא דפרקא קמא, ואידך דתניא: גר שנתגייר בזמן הזה צריך שיפריש רובע לקינו. אמר רשב"א, כבר נמנה עליה רבן יוחנן וביטלה, מפני התקלה. ואידך? פלוגתא דרב פפא ורנב"י: רב פפא אמר כרם רבעי, רב נחמן בר יצחק אמר לשון של זהורית. (לב.) מתני' סדר ברכות: אומר אבות וגבורות וקדושת השם, וכולל מלכיות עמהן ואינו תוקע. קדושת היום ותוקע, זכרונות ותוקע, שופרות ותוקע, ואומר עבודה והודאה וברכת כהנים. דברי ר' יוחנן בן נורי; אמר לו ר"ע: אם אינו תוקע למלכיות, למה הוא מזכיר? אלא אומר אבות וגבורות וקדושת השם, וכולל מלכיות עם קדושת היום ותוקע, זכרונות ותוקע, שופרות ותוקע, ואומר עבודה והודאה וברכת כהנים. גמ' ת"ר, מנין שאומרים מלכיות זכרונות ושופרות? ר"א אומר, דכתיב, (ויקרא כג) „שבתון זכרון תרועה מקרא קודש" שבתון זה קדושת היום, זכרון אלו זכרונות, תרועה אלו שופרות, מקרא קודש קדשהו בעשיית מלאכה. אמר לו רבי עקיבא: מפני מה לא נאמר שבתון שבות שבו פתח הכתוב תחילה? אלא שבהן קדשהו בעשיית מלאכה. זכרון אלו זכרונות, תרועה אלו שופרות, מקרא קודש זו קדושת היום. מנין שאומרים מלכיות? תניא רבי אומר (שם) „אני ה' אלהיכם ובחדש השביעי" זו מלכות; ר' יוסי בר יהודה אומר אינו צריך, הרי הוא אומר (במדבר י) „והיו לכם לזכרון לפני אלהיכם" שאין ת"ל אני ה' אלהיכם, ומה ת"ל? זה בנה אב לכל מקום שנאמר בו זכרונות, יהיו מלכיות עמהן. מתני' אין פוחתין מעשרה מלכיות, מעשרה זכרונות, מעשרה שופרות; רבי יוחנן בן נורי אומר, אם אמר ג' ג' מכולן יצא גמ' הני עשרה מלכיות כנגד מי? אמר רבי כנגד עשרה הילולים שאמר דוד בספר תלים. הילולים טובא

ר ש"י

וישבו שם. ומיבנה לאושא, יבנה בימי רבן יוחנן, אושא בימי רבן גמליאל, וחזרו מאושא ליבנה. ובימי רבן שמעון בנו חזרו. בית שערים וציפורי וטבריא כולן בימי רבי היו, וטבריא עמוקה מכולן, שכולם היו אז מכל המקומות שגלו. שש גלות, השתא הוא דשפילנה תרי דשפילה תלת עד ארץ ארבע יגיענה חמשה עד עפר שש ודסמי למימר דשפילנה עד ארץ ולעפר. מתני' אלא למקום הועד, והסנהדרין יקבשוהו בלא ראש ב"ד. גמ' נחיתא, שכר שבתא. דאי"כ, אם אתה מפריחן. שית דהאי פירקא, חדא האי וחמש דמתני' התקין שיהו תוקעין ושיהא לולב ניטל שבעה ושיהא יום הנף כולו אסור ושיהו מקבלין כל היום ושלא יהו עדים הולכין אלא למקום הועד. וחדא דפרקא קמא, שלא יהו מחללין אלא על ניסן ותשרי בלבד. רובע, שקל ושהיינו חצי דינר והן הן דמי קן, והלכך יפריש רובע לקינו שמא יבנה בית המקדש במהרה ויקריבנו. מתני' אבות וגבורות כו' וקדושת היום ותוקע כו'. דמצות בשלש תקיעות של שלש שלש. גמ' שהרי פתח בו הכתוב תחילה, והוא בא להזהיר על המלאכה שהוא עיקר. אני ה' אלהיכם, דלעני ולגר תעזוב וסמיך ליה

הוו? הנך דכתיב בהו (תהלים קנ) „הללוהו בתקע שופר". רב יוסף אמר כנגד עשרת הדברות שנאמרו לו למשה בסיני. רבי יוחנן אמר, כנגד עשרה מאמרות שבהן נברא העולם. אם אמר שלש שלש מכולן יצא. איבעיא להו, היכי קתני: שלש מן התורה, שלש מן הנביאים, ושלש מן הכתובים, דהוו תשע, ואיכא בינייהו חדא? או דילמא, אחד מן התורה, ואחד מן הנביאים, ואחד מן הכתובים, דהוין להו שלש, ואיכא בינייהו טובא? ת"ש, דתניא: אין פוחתין מעשרה מלכיות, מעשרה זכרונות, מעשרה שופרות, ואם אמר שבע מכולן, יצא, כנגד שבעה רקיעים. רבי יוחנן בן נורי אומר, הפוחת לא יפחות משבע, ואם אמר שלש מכולן יצא, כנגד תורה נביאים וכתובים, ואמרי לה כנגד כהנים לוים וישראלים. אמר רב הונא אמר שמואל הלכה כרבי יוחנן בן נורי. מתני' אין מזכירין מלכיות, זכרונות ושופרות של פורענות, מתחיל בתורה ומשלים בנביא; רבי יוסי אומר, אם השלים בתורה יצא. (לב:) גמ' מלכיות כגון (יחזקאל כ) „חי אני נאם ה' אם לא ביד חזקה, ובזרוע נטויה ובחמה שפוכה אמלוך עליכם" ואע"ג דא"ר נחמן: כל כי האי ריתחא לירתח קב"ה עלן וליפרוקינן, כיון דבריתחא אמור אדכורי רתחא בריש שתא לא מדכרינן; זכרון כגון (תהלים עח) „ויזכור כי בשר המה" וגו' שופר, כגון (הושע ה) „תקעו שופר בגבעה" וגו'. אין מזכירין זכרון של יחיד ואפילו לטובה, כגון (תהלים קו) „זכרני ה' ברצון עמך", פקדונות הרי הן כזכרונות כגון (בראשי' כא) „וה' פקד את שרה". וכגון (שמות ג) „פקוד פקדתי אתכם" ד"ר יוסי, ר' יהודה אומר, אינן כזכרונות. ולרבי יוסי נהי נמי דפקדונות הרי הן כזכרונות, וה' פקד את שרה פקדון דיחיד הוא? כיון דאתו רבים מינה כרבים דמיא. (תהלים כד) „שאו שערים ראשיכם וגו'. עד מלך הכבוד סלה" ראשונה שתים, שנייה שלש, דברי ר' יוסי, ר' יהודה אומר, ראשונה אחת, שנייה שתים (שם מז) „זמרו אלהים זמרו זמרו למלכנו זמרו כי מלך כל הארץ אלהים" שתים, דברי ר' יוסי: ר' יהודה אומר, אחת; ושוין (שם) „במלך אלהים על גוים אלהים ישב על כסא קדשו" שהיא אחת. זכרון שיש בו תרועה, כגון (ויקרא כג) „שבתון; זכרון תרועה מקרא קודש", אומרה עם הזכרונות, ואומרה עם השופרות, דברי ר' יוסי; ר' יהודה אומר, אינו אומרה אלא עם הזכרונות בלבד; מלכות שיש עמו תרועה, כגון (במדבר כג) „ה' אלהיו עמו ותרועת מלך בו", אומרה עם המלכיות ואומרה עם השופרות, דברי ר' יוסי; ר' יהודה אומר, אינו אומרה אלא עם המלכיות בלבד. תרועה שאין עמה לא כלום, כגון (במדבר כט) „יום תרועה יהיה לכם" אומרה עם השופרות, דברי רבי יוסי; רבי יהודה אומר, אינו אומרה כל עיקר. מתחיל בתורה ומשלים בנביא. ר' יוסי אומר משלים בתורה, ואם השלים בנביא יצא. תניא נמי הכי א"ר אלעזר ברבי יוסי, ותיקין היו משלימין אותה בתורה. בשלמא זכרונות ושופרות איכא טובא אלא מלכיות תלת הוא דהוין (שם כג): „ה' אלהיו עמו ותרועת מלך בו" (דברים לג), „ויהי בישורון מלך" (שמות טו), „ה' ימלוך לעולם ועד" ואנן בעינן עשר וליכא? אמר רב הונא תנא (דברים ו) „שמע ישראל

רש"י

בחדש השביעי זכרון תרועה. אני ה' אלהיכם, הוא לשון אני אחן לכם. גמ' או דילמא, האי ג' ג' אמלכיות וזכרונות ושופרות קאי. שלש למלכיות, ושלש לזכרונות, ושלש לשופרות, דהוו להו אחת מן התורה ואחת מן הנביאים ואחת מן הכתובים. גמ' ורבים אתו מינה, בההיא פקידה. שנייה שתים, מי הוא זה מלך הכבוד לאו כמנינא. זמרו למלכנו, לא קא חשיב רבי יהודה דלא אמלכותיה אלא על אומה אחת. ושוין כו' דלא מנינן ישב על כסא קדשו בלשון מלכות. עם הזכרונות, תרועה לאו לשון שופרות הוא עד המזכיר שופר בתורה. ומשלים בנביאים, והכתובים בנתיים. בתורה, דהוה להו ארבע מן התורה שלש בתחילה ואחד בסוף.

ה׳ אלהינו ה׳ אחד" מלכות, דברי ר׳ יוסי, ר׳ יהודה אומר אינה מלכות, (דברים ד) „וידעת היום והשבות אל לבבך כי ה׳ הוא האלהים אין עוד", מלכות, דברי ר׳ יוסי; ר׳ יהודה אומר, אינה מלכות (שם) „אתה הראית לדעת כי ה׳ הוא האלהים אין עוד מלבדו". מלכות, דברי ר׳ יוסי; רבי יהודה אומר אינה מלכות. מתני׳ העובר לפני התיבה בי״ט של ר״ה השני מתקיע, ובשעת ההלל הראשון מקרא את ההלל. גמ׳ מאי שנא שני מתקיע? א״ר יוחנן בשעת גזירת המלכות שנו. מתני׳ שופר של ר״ה אין מעבירין עליו את התחום, ואין מפקחין עליו את הגל, לא עולין באילן, ולא רוכבין ע״ג בהמה, ולא שטין על פני המים, ואין חותכין אותו בין בדבר שהוא משום שבות, בין בדבר שהוא משום לא תעשה; אבל אם רצה ליתן לתוכו מים או יין, יתן. אין מעכבין את התנוקות מלתקוע, אבל מתעסקין עמהן עד שילמדו, והמתעסק לא יצא, והשומע מן המתעסק לא יצא. גמ׳ מ״ט? שופר עשה הוא, וי״ט עשה ולא תעשה, ואין עשה דוחה את לא תעשה ועשה. (לג.) אין מעכבין את התינוקות מלתקוע. הא נשים מעכבין? והתניא: אין מעכבין לא את הנשים ולא את התינוקות מלתקוע בי״ט? אמר אביי, ל״ק, הא ר׳ יהודה, הא רבי יוסי ורבי שמעון, דאמרי נשים סומכות רשות. „עד שילמדו". אמר רבי אלעזר אפילו בשבת. תנ״ה, מתעסקין בהן עד שילמדו אפילו בשבת, ואין מעכבין התינוקות מלתקוע בשבת, ואין צריך לומר ביום טוב. עכובא הוא דלא מעכבין, הא לכתחילה לא אמרינן תקעו? לא קשיא כאן (לג:) בקטן שהגיע לחינוך, כאן בקטן שלא הגיע לחינוך. מתני׳ סדר תקיעות שלש של שלש שלש. שיעור תקיעה כשלש תרועות, שיעור תרועה כג׳ יבבות. תקע בראשונה ומשך בשנייה כשתים אין בידו אלא אחת. מי שבירך ואחר כך נתמנה לו שופר, תוקע ומריע ותוקע ג׳ פעמים. כשם ששליח ציבור חייב, כך כל יחיד ויחיד חייב. רבן גמליאל אומר: שליח ציבור מוציא את הרבים ידי חובתן. גמ׳ והתניא שיעור תקיעה כתרועה? אמר אביי, תנא דידן קא חשיב תקיעות דכולהו בבי ותרועות דכולהו בבי; תנא ברא קא חשיב חד בבא, ותו לא. שיעור תרועה כג׳ יבבות. והתניא שיעור תרועה כשלשה שברים? אמר אביי, בהא ודאי פליגי, דכתיב (במדבר כט) „יום תרועה יהיה לכם" ומתרגמינן יום יבבא יהא לכון, וכתיב באמיה דסיסרא (שופטים ה) „בעד החלון נשקפה ותיבב אם סיסרא". מר סבר גנוחי גנח, ומר סבר ילולי יליל. תנו רבנן, מנין שבשופר?

ר ש״ י

בעינן כשר, וארבע מהן הורה דקאמר ר׳ משלים בתורה. מתני׳ מתקיע, המתפלל תפלת מוספין מתקיע, התהלל, דבר״ה ליכא הלל כדאמרינן בערכין ד ב. גמ׳ בשעת גזירת המלכות שנו, אויבים גזרו שלא יתקעו והיו אורבין להם כל שש שעות לקץ תפלת שחרית לפי העבודה לתקוע במוספין. מתני׳ את התחום, לילך חוץ לתחום לשמוע תקיעה. מים בה, ולא אמרינן קא מתקן מנא. גמ׳ תינוקות הוא דלא מעכבין, דבעי לחנוכינהו. הא נשים מעכבין, דפטורות לגמרי דמ״ע שהזמן גרמא הוא, וכי תקען איכא בל תוסיף. סומכות רשות אלמא אע״ג דפטירתו קרא ליכא איסורא הו״ה למצות עשה שהזמן גרמא. קטן שהגיע לחנוך, מתעסקין בהן שילמדו וכ״ש דאין מעכבין. מתני׳ שלש כו׳, אחת למלכיות ואחת לזכרונות ואחת לשופרות. שלש של שלש, תקיעה ותרועה ותקיעה לכל אחת ואחת. שלש יבבות, ג׳ קולות בעלמא כל שהוא. בראשונה, פשוטה שלפני התרועה. ומשך בשניה, תקיעה של אחר התרועה משך כשתים לצאת בה ידי שתים שהיה צריך לתקוע זו פשוטה שלאחריה דמלכיות ופשוטה שלפניה דזכרונות. אין בידו אלא אחת, דפסוקי תקיעה אחת לשתים לא מפסקינן. מי שבירך, התפלל תפלת מוספין ובירך תשעה ברכות. ג׳ פעמים, בשביל מלכיות וכן בשביל זכרונות וכן בשביל שופרות. גמ׳ בכולהו בבי, והכי קאמר שיעור ג׳ תקיעות כג׳ תרועות, דהדרא בבא, שיעור התקיעה כשיעור התרועה ותרוייהו חדא מילתא אמרי. שברים, ארוכים מיבבות. אמר אביי בהא ודאי פליגי, אע״ג דאוקימנא דרישא לא פליגי על כרחך בהא מיהא פליגי. דמתרגמינן, תרועה יבבא ובאימיה דסיסרא כתיב נמי האי לישנא ותיבב.

ת״ל (ויקרא כה) „והעברת שופר תרועה״ ומנין שפשוטה לאחריה? תלמוד לומר „תעבירו שופר״, ואין לי אלא ביובל, בראש השנה מנין? תלמוד לומר „בחדש השביעי״. (לד.) שאין ת״ל „בחדש השביעי״, ומה ת״ל בחדש השביעי? שיהו כל תרועות החדש השביעי זה כזה. מנין לשלש של שלש שלש? ת״ל „והעברת שופר תרועה, שבתון זכרון תרועה, יום תרועה יהיה לכם״. והאי תנא מייתי לה בג״ש ממדבר, דתניא (במדבר י) „ותקעתם תרועה״ תקיעה בפני עצמה ותרועה בפני עצמה; אתה אומר תקיעה בפני עצמה ותרועה בפני עצמה, או אינו אלא תקיעה ותרועה אחת היא? כשהוא אומר (שם) „ובהקהיל את הקהל תתקעו ולא תריעו״ הוי אומר תקיעה בפני עצמה ותרועה בפני עצמה; ומניין שפשוטה לפניה? תלמוד לומר (שם) „ותקעתם תרועה״. ומניין שפשוטה לאחריה? תלמוד לומר (שם) „תרועה יתקעו״. רבי ישמעאל בנו של רבי יוחנן בן ברוקא אומר, אינו צריך: הרי הוא אומר „ותקעתם תרועה שנית״, שאין ת״ל שנית, ומה ת״ל שנית? זה בנה אב, שכל מקום שנאמר תרועה תהא תקיעה שנייה לה; אין לי אלא במדבר, בר״ה מניין? ת״ל תרועה תרועה לג״ש; ושלש תרועות נאמרו בר״ה (ויקרא כג) „שבתון זכרון תרועה״, (במדבר כט) „יום תרועה״, (ויקרא כה) „והעברת שופר תרועה״, שתי תקיעות לכל אחת ואחת, מצינו למדין ג׳ תרועות וששה תקיעות נאמרו בר״ה. איתקין רבי אבהו בקסרי: תקיעה, שלש שברים, תרועה, תקיעה. מה נפשך! אי ילולי יליל לעביד תקיעה תרועה ותקיעה, ואי גנוחי גנח לעביד תקיעה שלשה שברים ותקיעה? מספקא ליה: אי גנוחי גנח, אי ילולי יליל. תקע בראשונה ומשך בשניה כשתים· א״ר יוחנן שמע (לד:) תשע תקיעות בתשע שעות ביום יצא. תניא נמי הכי, שמע תשע תקיעות בתשע שעות ביום יצא, מט׳ בני אדם כאחד תקיעה מזה ותרועה מזה יצא ואפילו בסירוגין. ואפילו כל היום כולו. ת״ר, תקיעות אין מעכבות זו את זו, ברכות אין מעכבות זו את זו, תקיעות וברכות של ר״ה ושל יה״כ מעכבות. מי שבירך ואח״כ נתמנה לו שופר תוקע ומריע ותוקע· טעמא דלא הוה ליה שופר מעיקרא, הא הוה ליה שופר מעיקרא, כי שמע להו אסדר ברכות שמע להו· רב פפא בר שמואל קם לצלויי, אמר ליה לשמעיה כי נהירנא לך, תקע לי. אמר ליה רבא, לא אמרו אלא בחבר עיר. תניא נמי הכי כשהוא שומען, שומען על הסדר ועל סדר ברכות: במה דברים אמורים בחבר עיר. אבל שלא בחבר עיר שומען על סדר ברכות; ויחיד שלא תקע, חבירו תוקע לו; ויחיד שלא בירך, אין חבירו מברך עליו; ומצוה בתוקעין יותר מן המברכין; כיצד? שתי עיירות באחת תוקעין ובאחת מברכין, הולכין למקום שתוקעין, ואין הולך למקום שמברכין פשיטא! הא דאורייתא הא דרבנן? לא צריכא, דאע״ג דהא ודאי והא ספק. כשם ששליח צבור

רש״י

גנוחי גנח, כאדם הגונח מלבו כדרך החולים שמאריכין בגניחותיהן. ילולי יליל, כאדם הבוכה ומקונן קולות קצרים כסמוכין זה לזה. שאין תלמוד לומר, דהא כתב לן בהדיא מקודשות דיום הכפורים בחדש השביעי הוא והכא יום הכפורים כתיב. והעברת, פשוטה משמע העברת קול אחד. תעבירו, הרי העברת תחלה וסוף ותרועה כתיבא בנתיים. שלש שלש, מנין דהנך פשוטה לפניה ולאחריה ותרועה באמצע עבדינן תלתא זימני: למלכיות חדא ולזכרונות חדא ולשופרות חדא? ת״ל תרועה, תלתא זימני, לכל אחד פשוטה לפניה ופשוטה לאחריה. ממדבר, שתהא פשוטה לפניה ופשוטה לאחריה. בפני עצמה כו׳, דלא תימא חדא היא וה״ק היו תוקעין תרועה. או אינו, אלא אחת היא וה״ק היו תוקעין תרועה. כשהוא אומר תתקעו ולא תריעו מכלל דבמסעות תתקעו ותריעו קאמר ותרועה לא קרי לה תקיעה. והקעתם, חדא תרועה. שאין ת״ל שנית, שכבר אמר ותקעתם תרועה תנינא מוכחת שלוני כי הדר אמר ותקעתם פשיטא דשנית הוא. תהא תקיעה שנית לה. והכי קאמר ותקעתם תקיעה שנית לתרועה. מספקא ליה, היכי תרועתו. תשע תקיעות, תרועות

חייב כך כל יחיד ויחיד כו׳. תניא, אמרו לו לרבן גמליאל · לדבריך למה צבור מתפללין? אמר להם כדי להסדיר שליח צבור תפילתו. אמר להם ר״ג: לדבריכם למה ש״צ יורד לפני התיבה? אמרו לו, כדי להוציא את שאינו בקי, אמר להם: כשם שמוציא את שאינו בקי, כך מוציא את הבקי. ארבב״ח אר״י, מודים חכמים לר״ג. ורב אמר עדיין היא מחלוקת. ומי אמר רבי יוחנן הכי והאמר ר׳ חנה ציפוראה א״ר יוחנן הלכתא כרבן גמליאל, הילכתא מכלל דפליגי? (לה.) אמר רב נחמן בר יצחק מאן מודים, רבי מאיר; והלכה מכלל דפליגי, רבנן. דתניא, ברכות של ר״ה ושל יה״כ שליח ציבור מוציא הרבים ידי חובתן, דברי ר״מ; וחכ״א, כשם ששליח צבור חייב, כך כל יחיד ויחיד חייב. מאי שנא הני? אילימא משום דנפישי קראי? והאמר רב חננאל אמר רב, כיון שאמר ובתורתך כתוב לאמר שוב אינו צריך? אלא משום דאוושי ברכות. איתמר, אמר רבי יהושע בן לוי: אחד יחיד ואחד ציבור כיון שאמר ובתורתך כתוב לאמר שוב אינו צריך. א״ר אלעזר, לעולם יסדיר אדם תפילתו ואח״כ יתפלל. א״ר אבא, מסתברא מילתיה דר׳ אלעזר בברכות של ר״ה ושל יה״כ ושל פרקים, אבל דכל השנה לא. איני, והא רב יהודה מסדר צלותיה ומצלי? שאני רב יהודה, כיון דמתלתין יומין לתלתין יומין הוא מצלי, כפרקים דמי. כי אתא רבין א״ר יעקב בר אידי א״ר שמעון חסידא, לא פטר רבן גמליאל אלא עם שבשדות, מ״ט? משום דאניסי במלאכה, אבל בעיר לא.

הדרן עלך יום טוב וסליקא לה מסכת ראש השנה.

ר ש״ י

נמי קאמר. תקיעות וברכות, דעלמא כגון תעניות אין מעכבין זו את זו אם בירך ולא תקע. כי נהירנא לה, לכיון שבירכתי הברכות. אלא בחבר עיר, חבורת צבור, אבל יחיד מברך את כולו ואח״כ תוקע תשע תקיעות. הזא ודאי והא בספק, ודאי הוא ין שאם ילך אצל המברכין ימצא שם עשרה ואם ילך אצל התוקעין שמא כבר עמדו והלכו לביתם. למה צבור מתפללים, בלחש. מודים חכמים, אחר שנחלקו חזרו והודו. מאן מודים, לו בברכות של ראש השנה ויה״כ ר״מ. והלכה מכלל דפליגי, דקאמר ר׳ יוחנן הלכה כרבן גמליאל בהך ומשמע מכלל דעמדו במחלוקתן. רבנן, שאר החכמים חוץ מר״מ. דנפישי קראי, דאיכא דמוספי ראש השנה וריה ומלכיות וזכרונות ושופרות. כיון שאמר ובתורתך כתוב, כלומר כיון שאמר נעשה ונקריב לפניך כמצות רצונך כמו שכתבת עלינו בתורתך. אין צריך, לזכור מקראות המוספין. אלא משום דאוושי, שהרי כאן תשע ואריכות וטעמות דאין דכל בקיאין בהן. ושל פרקים, מועדות. מתלתין לתלתין, שהיה מחזר תלמודו כל שלשים יום. פוטר היה כו׳, ששייך מוציאם. אבל דעיר לא, משום דלא אניסי ויכולין להסדיר תפלתן.

הדרן עלך יום טוב וסליקא לה מסכת ראש השנה.

נגמרה מבית הדפוס יום ב׳ ר״ח אדר תרנ״ה לפ״ק, בעזר החונן לאדם דעת. וכשם שזכינו לסדר ולגמור את הראשונה, כן יזכנו לסדר ולגמור את המסכתא האחרונה. אמן.

CPSIA information can be obtained
at www.ICGtesting.com
Printed in the USA
LVOW03*0142160216
475272LV00015B/136/P

9 781297 531958